W9-BZS-192

FORE WARNING

WILLIAM T. JAMES General Editor

HARVEST HOUSE PUBLISHERS
Eugene, Oregon 97402

Verses in the introduction and chapters 1, 3, 6, 7, 8, 9, 12, and 13 are taken from the King James Version of the Bible.

Verses in chapters 2, 4, 5, 10, and 11 are taken from the New American Standard Bible, © 1960, 1962, 1963, 1968, 1971, 1972, 1973, 1975, 1977 by The Lockman Foundation. Used by permission.

Verses in chapters 10 and 14 are taken from the Holy Bible, New International Version®, Copyright © 1973, 1978, 1984 by the International Bible Society. Used by permission of Zondervan Publishing House. The "NIV" and "New International Version" trademarks are registered in the United States Patent and Trademark Office by International Bible Society.

Cover by Paz Design Group, Salem, Oregon

Observations by individual authors in this book do not necessarily represent the views of the other authors or the publisher. All authors, however, are in agreement that Christ alone is the way to salvation through His shed blood on Calvary for the remission of sin. Likewise, all are in agreement that Christ's return for all believers is imminent.

FOREWARNING
Copyright © 1998 by Harvest House Publishers
Eugene, Oregon 97402

Library of Congress Cataloging-in-Publication Data

James, William T., 1942–
      Forewarning / William T. James, general editor
             p. cm.
     Includes bibliographical references.
     ISBN 1-56507-774-1
     1. End of the world—Prophecies. I. Title.
BT876.J36 1998
236—dc21

97-44714
CIP

Printed in the United States of America.

98 99 00 01 02 03 /BP/ 10 9 8 7 6 5 4 3 2

Contents

Part 3
History's Deadliest Storm/God's Eternal Grace

INTRODUCTION

Earth's Stormy Horizon

William T. James

Prophetic thunder sounded in the distance Monday, June 9, 1997, when two ancient biblical predictions collided somewhere over Jerusalem. Daniel 12:4 bumped against Zechariah 12:2,3 and the resultant rumble circled the globe instantaneously.

Cable News Network (CNN) conveyed the message. Not a late-breaking report or new revelation—observers of biblical prophecy had known about the story for weeks—but astounding proof that heavenly promises are being fulfilled. When *real-time* satellite broadcast technology informed an already deeply troubled world that a singular red-colored cow threatens world peace and stability, Revelation lightning surely must have flashed above the Plain of Esdraelon where Armageddon awaits.

Perhaps it is good to note here that the Jewish law of sacrifice requires a heifer whose coat was made of pure, that is, total, red hue. The commingling of any other colors made the animal unacceptable for the purification ritual of sprinkling the ashes over the sacrificial utensils. The slightest blemish would disqualify the beast for use in any future temple sacrifice. Thus, the intense interest in this contemporary heifer of apparently pure red color.

The CNN newsman, Walter Rogers, talked about the all-red heifer which appeared on the television screen. He told of elaborate security arrangements being made by the Israeli government for the animal. One man interviewed said, "I'm saying, kill the cow."

Rogers explained, "David Landau is an Israeli newspaper editor. He warns that in the hands of fanatic Jews, this cow could trigger a religious war between Jews and Muslims."

The Israeli newspaper editor spoke again in a British accent: "Let's say to Israel, which, after all, is still a secular state, '[You have] got to put a stop to this.'" The newspaper man indicated that he believed Israel must put an end to the red heifer controversy or risk Israel being likened to radical Iranian fundamentalists.

The CNN reporter then explained further, "In the Bible, in Numbers, there are instructions to slaughter and burn a red heifer and cover one's self with the ashes, an ancient purification ritual that enables the biblical Jewish priest to go atop the Temple Mount. Today, the Temple Mount is a Muslim shrine, a mosque, so Jews worship at the wailing wall adjoining the ruins of the foundation of their ancient temple. Religious Jews believe man's impurity forbids them from returning to the Temple Mount to worship, theology providing a kind of buffer zone that separates Jews from Muslims. But spiritual purification with ashes of that rare red heifer could take away the buffer zone."

Landau, the newspaper editor, related his recurring nightmare. "In my nightmare, I see people killing the cow, masses of them climbing up to the Temple Mount which, after all, is a holy Muslim site at this time and has been for 1300–1400 years. And then we'll be up against a war of religion."

CNN's reporter offered conjecture while the cameras panned the scene. "Far-fetched? Perhaps. But note the bulletin board [at the school] where the red heifer is being raised. Below it is an etching of the revered first-century Jewish temple which was destroyed by the Romans. In the dreams of some, the miracle of the red heifer could mark the time to rebuild a third Jewish temple where a Muslim mosque now stands."

An interviewed priest said, "They say that if it's really a red cow, then Messiah must be coming."

CNN's Rogers analyzed: "Israel's senior rabbis hesitate to pronounce this *the* biblical cow and nobody's marching yet. Still, below the surface, there is a streak of mysticism and fanaticism here. And in a worst-case scenario, some fear that religious extremists might just use that cow to try to force God's hand to bring about a Jewish return to the Temple Mount, thereby enraging hundreds of millions of the world's Muslims. And there is a vagueness about the rabbis' plans for the cow."

The rabbi then said, "None of these people would seriously consider taking this red cow to the Temple Mount unless the time was right for it."

Rogers concluded, "Her name is Melody and anywhere else, she'd be just a cow. But this is the Middle East and here there's a fine line between heifers, hamburgers and holy wars."[1]

While there is considerable debate among prophecy scholars concerning whether or not this red heifer portends significance within the end-time scenario, the story itself portrays in astounding fashion that God's Word is truth from beginning to end. Technology today disseminates staggering amounts of knowledge through broadcasts beamed from satellites to points around the world. Transmissions run like lightning through time and space to illuminate the minds of men, even while their hearts grow darker with sin.

Daniel 12:4, "...many shall run to and fro, and knowledge shall be increased..." links Zechariah 12:2,3, "...Behold, I will make Jerusalem a cup of trembling.... And in that day will I make Jerusalem a burdensome stone..." to 2 Thessalonians 2:4 "...so that he, as God, sitteth in the temple of God, showing himself that he is God." Scriptures prophesy that the third temple will be built. Perhaps the most fascinating aspect of the red heifer intrigue is that Jewish rabbis are thinking in terms of temple worship again, one more strong indicator that a growing number within Israel desire to rebuild a temple.

But their plans face formidable obstacles. Seeds of war in the Middle East are germinating while Israel yearns for peace and safety. Fear of Armageddon runs rampant throughout the region and infects the world at large.

We are witnessing the fulfillment of prophecy today at a pace unparalleled in human history. Could perhaps the sealed book of Daniel 12:4 now be opened? Are the forbidden seven thunders of the angel with the little book in Revelation 10 beginning to sound in our time?

Prophetic State of the Nations

Thunderous developments of prophetic significance build ominously on the twenty-first century horizon. Nations continue to configure into what looks to be the precise arrangement predicted in God's Word.

Israel, the centerpiece of prophecy so far as national entities are concerned, comes ever closer to resembling the cup of trembling and the burdensome stone Zechariah 12 prophesies it will become. A growingly hostile diplomatic world community continues to bully the tiny state with high-pressure tactics ever closer to the table of pseudo peace where the prophet Daniel foretold Israel will sign the covenant made with death and hell. Israel sits at the center of the nerve jangling calm before the storm. From her vantage, jagged flickers of satanic lightning threaten from every direction. Each peace negotiation promising to dissipate the gathering clouds of hatred serves only to exacerbate the peace effort.

While Palestinian Arabs in general stand on the sidelines haplessly, militants and terrorists among their number ignite, then fan the fires of anti-Semitism, fires which seem to be bursting forth in every region of the world.

Islamic fanatics continue to dominate the region's geopolitical agenda. Those elements now possess weapons of frightening potential. And, in a twisted bit of end time irony, Israel is playing a part in arming those enemies.

A *National Review* article reports,

> new Chinese weapons based in part on Israeli technology may already be going to Iran. At Zhuhai, China revealed that it is now the fourth country, after Russia, Israel, and South Africa, to produce a helmet-sighted air-to-air missile. The helmet sight is a copy of the Russian model, but the missile it will guide is derived from the Israeli Python-3. This system will equip China's new F-8II M fighters, which reportedly will be part of a new $4.5 billion purchase of Chinese weapons. Iranian pilots could become competent with helmet-sighted missiles well before U.S. pilots get theirs in 2003 or 2004—if they're lucky. This will only better prepare Iran's pilots for the day they receive their…J-10 fighters.

All this should alarm responsible officials in Moscow, Jerusalem, and capitals across Europe, but there is no evidence that this is happening. Even more astounding is the lack of audible concern from the Clinton Administration...[2]

Hostile Islamic forces want to drive the tiny state from the Middle East. Nothing less than complete eradication of the Jews will do, according to their leaders such as Syria's Hafez Il-Assad, Iraq's Saddam Hussein, and Iran's Mohammed Khatami.

Egypt continues to stir restlessly to Israel's south. Hosni Mubarek comes increasingly under pressures exerted by Zionist-hating Islamic influences. He must acquiesce to their designs or ultimately suffer a fate like that of Anwar Sadat.

Africa to the southwest is in constant intramural turmoil, agitated by, among other things, Islamic factions led by such diabolical and unpredictable characters as Libya's Khadafi.

Where might the United States fit in this era prior to the end times? Since this nation presently quakes under tremendous pressure exerted by anti-God influences, what can we expect but an even more turbulent future?

Because America is not mentioned by name as having a role to play along with those nations specifically mentioned in God's prophetic word, the question must be raised, *What will happen to this, probably the most materially blessed nation ever?* The God of heaven says that from those to whom much is given, much is required. Certainly history proves that every great nation and empire of the past which chose to chart its own course apart from God has fallen to outside enemies or else has degenerated and faded into oblivion.

America, who under the current administration plays the potentially deadly game of false peacemaking, is possibly writing her own ticket to the graveyard of nations where those who have cursed rather than blessed Abraham, Isaac, and Jacob lie. Even a casual observer of history and the current political scene can see how America has slipped from its once great heights as a world leader.

Barring nuclear attack or complete civil breakdown due to racial strife and moral decadence, America seems destined to be no

more than a part of the now developing Roman empire as prophesied by Daniel the prophet and John the apostle.

This is not to say that there is no hope for America. 2 Chronicles 7:14 says: "If my people…will humble themselves and pray
and seek my face and turn from their wicked ways, then will I…
heal their land." This is true for all nations just as John 3:16 is true
for all individuals. But the time for action is now, before God's final
judgment arrives.

Russia writhes in turmoil created by ultra-hardline military
leaders who crave a return to absolute power. The Magog scenario
as outlined in Ezekiel seems to be taking shape rapidly with
Turkey's movement into the Islamic camp (even though that
nation's leadership has temporarily returned to a mildly democratic
form).

The entire region north of Israel has formed into a loose confederation through agreements and treaties and looks like a precursor of the force prophesied to storm toward Palestine.

Unfolding history continues to show Russia being forced into
uniting with the swiftly developing pan-Islamic coalition. Pressing
needs tug Mother Russia toward the center of what doubtless will
become the Magog Ezekiel 38 and 39 tell us will thrust southward
over the mountains of Israel to "take great spoil." Whoever emerges
as Russia's dominant leader must come to grips with the fact that
he exists in a power sphere boiling with fanatical Islamic anti-
Jewish zeal. Oil rich Arabic power brokers comprise a collective
economic marketplace any future Russian leader will need in order
to revitalize the nation's desperately depressed economy. Russia's
military, reportedly on the brink of rebellion because the troops, in
many cases, have not been paid for months, stands ready as an
unstoppable juggernaut to invade regions to the south in order to
obtain the spoils of war. Leaders like Alexander Lebed and Vladimir
Zhirinovsky appear to have full support of hardline generals who,
for all practical purposes, can and will supersede Kremlin orders if
circumstances warrant. With Boris Yeltsin's serious health problems and growing political problems within government, anything
can happen in Russia.

How long will it be until Gog thinks the *evil thought* of Ezekiel
38, when it decides to invade Israel for its resources? How close are
we to the time when the Magog forces turn their attention from
trying to improve their social, cultural, and fiscal problems through

diplomatic overtures to the western powers and suddenly realize that they can solve everything by one massive assault on the vast riches of the Middle East—the oil reserves, the tremendous mineral wealth in the Dead Sea, warm water ports for military purposes and for import and export?

China continues to solidify its position in the Asian Orient, bullying its neighbors with awesome military might. Sino economic power will doubtless dominate the whole region, influence which is already spilling over into the world economic sphere. For example, China is alleged to have peddled influence and made under-the-table deals with some U.S. officials who work in government at the highest levels.

Given China's tendency toward controversial and often hostile demeanor, e.g. as when they recently lobbed missiles into the waters just off Taiwan, her takeover of Hong Kong will doubtless present the international scene with a bleak picture.

China baffles the sensibilities of those who yearn for a return to sane thinking in matters of America's foreign policy. That nation is perhaps the most genocidal state on the planet. Remember when the Chinese soldiers, in front of the TV-camera-aided eyes of the entire world, massacred more than 4000 defenseless people in Tiananmen Square?

Chinese Communist officials smiled tightly into the cameras and forced the networks to withdraw coverage. Still, we do business with the government of China even though that government continues to enslave its people, murder female babies, force abortion, euthanasia, and sterilization on them, and threatens its neighbors with aggression if western technology and wealth are denied them.

The following portion of a *National Review* article expands on the threat China poses:

> Asia's most dangerous arms race is the race to arm China. In fact, as the Clinton Administration looks the other way, the world is witnessing perhaps the most geo-strategically dangerous transfer of power since Germany and other states helped create the early Soviet Union's military-technical base. The Administration's lack of concern might be acceptable if the country in question were not firing nuclear-capable missiles to scare its neighbors, not enforcing claims to territory hundreds of

miles from its shores, and not selling both nuclear and missile technologies to rogue states.

China, however, is doing all these things and is none too subtle about its intention of eventually displacing American power in Asia. The day when China will be able to do so is drawing nearer as its People's Liberation Army gains access to cutting-edge foreign military technology...[3]

Surely present-day China, symbolized like ancient China by the dragon serpent, will be a major player, if not the chief player, in the *kings of the east* force prophesied to march 200 million soldiers across the dried-up Euphrates River at the time of Armageddon.

That nation, supposedly joining the civilized nations of the world by adopting western economic practices, does nothing to assuage our apprehensions while she absorbs Hong Kong and presents that acquisition as a façade for her willingness to westernize her leaders who drool at the prospect of wrapping their hands around the throats of the free Chinese on Taiwan.

Uniting Europe is perhaps just months away from gelling into the last empire of Nebuchadnezzar's dream. A single currency under the Maastricht Treaty scheduled for January 1, 1999, will bring the Europeans together in monetary union as the world's most powerful economic bloc. With all of the players in line with what the prophetic word predicts for the end time alignment of nations, it is realistic to believe that the man called Antichrist is poised to come forward with satanically inspired answers to the great world chaos that will take place when the church is removed from planet Earth.

The Accelerating Apostasy

The third member of the unholy trinity (Satan, Antichrist, and the False Prophet) must surely be standing somewhere in the shadows very near to the end-time spotlight. His presence can be sensed in the outcry for a broad-minded tolerance that will bring everyone together in peace, harmony, and equality.

Warnings of impending judgment flash across the darkening humanistic horizon. The *falling away* prophesied by the apostle Paul manifests itself in growing, God-rejecting, man-centered doctrines that move humanity ever farther down a broadway toward apocalypse. Ecumenism, in the religious sense, forms the nucleus of the apostasy we see developing. Many sparks initiated by Satan fire from that nucleus. This generation continues to create and worship idols of many sorts.

Violation of the commandment, *"Thou shalt have no other gods before me,"* has never in human history been more observable than in our time. Idolatry is the core of the boil which God must lance. Idolatry of every spiritualistic and materialistic sort marks ours as a generation almost totally turned from the Creator.

From self-centered pleasures we are free to pursue to hedonistic activities promised through virtual reality technology, evidence builds an indefensible case indicting ours as the generation of the *falling away* prophesied for the time when the *man of sin* appears on the world scene.

Sadly, if we are honest, we see even evangelical Christians falling into the ecumenical idolatrous trap. As unpleasant and as unpopular as it is to point a finger of condemnation, it must be done, although from a position of Christ-centered discernment, concern, and love.

Discernment must begin with absolute fidelity to the gospel message. There must be no compromise with any one, any organization, or any teaching that proposes any other gospel than the blood atonement paid by Jesus Christ for the remission of sin. The Son of God's sacrifice upon the cross of Calvary, His burial and resurrection constitute the one and only plan God has ever offered for reconciling lost mankind to himself.

Paul the apostle wrote, "But though we, or an angel from heaven, preach any other gospel unto you than that which we have preached unto you, let him be accursed" (Galatians 1:8).

The Heathen Rage

Jesus said that one sign leading to apocalypse would be the seas and waves roaring. The seas and the waves are to be viewed, I believe, as both literal and symbolic.

America's and the world's many sins congeal to form the dark clouds of godlessness over a planet that must surely soon face God's wrath.

These sins include:

- homosexuality
- abortion
- euthanasia
- serial killings
- abuse and misuse of women and children
- breakdown of families
- pornography
- gambling
- white collar crime
- fornication
- adultery
- entertainment madness and addictions

And from the political sphere:

- a presidential administration immersed in daily crises because of alleged illegal and/or illicit activities
- governmental usurpation of the God-ordained role families should have in the rearing and nurturing of children
- a convoluted court system more geared to protecting criminals than protecting victims of crime
- genocidal atrocities around the world
- wars and rumors of wars

And in the spiritual realm:

- the Pope linking God's perfect creation account to the godless lie, evolution
- turning to psychics, astrologers, and purveyors of black magic rather than to God.

A storm of monumental proportion, spawned by man's foolish attempts to become his own god, moves ever closer. Already, squalls dump satanically driven deluges of filth into our lives. Political correctness is the rage of the day. Governments must mandate equality and redistribution of wealth based upon the ruling elite's god-like noblesse oblige. They alone have the right to decide what is best for the rest of us because they alone know what is best for us.

Through social engineering they construct for themselves power bases that keep them in positions of authority, thus in control of humanism's machinery.

America's entertainment industry in particular incessantly barrages our senses with what it considers proper in today's "enlightened" age. Anything goes. If it feels good, do it. There are no absolutes except the absolute that there are no absolutes. Thus the Judeo-Christian God is not only irrelevant, but non-existent.

A blatant example that God has been relegated to second-class status or worse is the recent case in which a federal judge ordered a lower court judge to remove a copy of the Ten Commandments from his courtroom wall. The lower court judge refused and the governor of his state backed him up in his refusal to take the document down. Kennedy family representatives then bestowed the "Profiles in Courage" award to the judge for his bravery, not to the one who refused to remove the copy of the Ten Commandments, but rather to the judge who ordered the document taken off the wall!

In our society, it seems that every religious view provides a pathway to godhood, that is, to salvation, except the bigoted, narrow-minded way of the cross upon which Jesus Christ died.

Ted Turner of network television fame summarized the entertainment industry's humanistic worldview several years ago when he said that he needs no one to die for him in order to attain salvation. He added that Christianity, in his view, is a religion of losers.

This generation is in the midst of an immense humanistic storm. Its ramifications are potentially deadly. Consider the UN conferences on globalization which have taken place over the past several years in Rio de Janeiro, Venice, Cairo, Beijing, Istanbul, Rome, and New York. Those conferences consistently spew out socio-economic, geopolitical, and religious restructuring agendas. They are blatant attempts by socialist architects to install themselves as gods of this world, which is humanism in its essence.

Man's incessant drive to be his own savior was evident at the *Rio Plus Five Earth Summit* in New York City last year. A CNN news story reported May 23, 1997, that delegates from 170 countries were meeting to formulate specific goals to cut carbon dioxide emissions, which had increased since the 1992 Earth Summit in Brazil.

CNN reported, "Vice President Al Gore told the UN General Assembly, 'Our task must be to chart the course for years to come....'"

An activist spoke before the CNN camera with irritation in her voice: "The world really needs to wake up to the fact that the trends are running in the wrong direction, that we cannot measure success by the number of treaties, the number of conferences...."

The agitated woman was right, of course. The world should wake up to the fact that mankind is headed in the wrong direction, a direction opposite to that prescribed by God. Unfortunately, she, like one of the conference leaders whose statement was then aired in the report, proposed the same answer they always propose. "There can be no redress of the imbalances in ecologies, in educational profit, without UN additional resources...."[4]

They proposed such things as a global tax that would hit hardest the nations who produce and consume energy at the greatest levels. The implication is that those nations damage *Mother Earth* and must be made to pay reparations to the rest of earth's inhabitants who live in closer harmony with their environment.

While Christians who seek to obey God's will should be among the first to do all that is reasonable to keep the planet clean and beautiful, we assert that man is to have dominion. We are to serve God, not our planet, which has been given "motherhood" status by environmentalists. Certainly, we are not to surrender national sovereignty and autonomy to a select group of would-be gods whose globalist agenda requires our tithe.

Indeed, this generation seems to be living in a time identical to the time biblical prophets foretold will mark the generation alive at the very end of the Church Age.

End-Time Technologies

These and other achievements marking mankind's progress combine to generate a tempest that harbors incalculable tragedy as the twentieth century closes and the twenty-first begins:

- Biochips implanted beneath the skin
- Smart cards containing virtually all data since birth on the individuals who carry them
- Electronic funds seriously considered to replace easily stolen and/or counterfeited currencies
- Satellites linked to transponders for tracking individuals while they move upon the earth

- Knowledge exploding with exponential growth in every discipline
- Computerized artificial intelligence which is progressing geometrically
- Superweaponry at least seven years advanced beyond what the public at large knows about
- Virtual reality devices soon to be available for home use promising sensual pleasures to satisfy every lust of the flesh.

So many developments are occurring simultaneously that it is impossible to stay abreast of technology breakthroughs. Computer systems we install for home or business use today are well on the way to obsolescence by the time we learn to use them proficiently.

Lest anyone say that our individual liberty is in no danger from *Big Brother*-type intrusion, please consider the following notice I received with my June 1997 bank statement:

> Regulatory alert. Federal government to require direct deposit. On July 26, 1996, the federal government launched a program to virtually eliminate the check as a federal payment instrument. Beginning immediately in some cases, Uncle Sam will issue regular payments only through electronic funds transfer (direct deposit). If you began receiving regular payment from Uncle Sam after July 25, 1996, you are affected now. These payments will be made without checks, only through direct deposit. The only exception involves a complex waiver process. This includes payment for Social Security, veteran's benefits, federal government and military salaries, government and military pensions, and similar payments made on a regular basis. If you began receiving regular payment from the federal government prior to July 26, 1996, the payments will be converted to direct deposit no later than January 1, 1999.

Interestingly enough, that is the same date European Monetary Union (EMU) is to go into effect, according to the Maastricht Treaty. (Read Chapter 7, "New Europe's Eye of the Tornado," to get insights into the powerful economic dynamo that will generate Antichrist's rise to power.)

Daniel 12 and Revelation 13 prophetically warn about these last-days control technologies. Thankfully, God's thoughts and ways are far beyond mortal man's ability to surprise Him.

Biogenetic research, e.g., gene-splicing, DNA experimentation, cloning and other forms of genetic engineering all have the potential to unleash monstrous mutations into the world. Even well-intentioned forays into preventative and curative medicines have already wrought bacteriological and viral mutants resistant to most antibiotics and other treatments. Technology contributes to much of the end-time thunder for the coming Tribulation storm.

Terry Cook presents a fascinating and engrossing look into the latest technologies as they might relate to prophecy and what they portend while we look toward the year 2000 and beyond. (Read "Today's Technology Churns Toward the Mark of the Beast," Chapter 4.)

Control Technologies to Implement Elite Agenda

Why are such technologies of control being developed? Certainly, one does not have to be a "conspiracy nut" to see the dehumanizing potential, the possibility of using such technology for evil purposes. Many secular news programs and documentaries have put forward Orwellian "Big Brother" scenarios since 1984. Again, the elitists among our number claim to know what is best.

Fallen man is, in these last days, boring full steam ahead under the satanic delusion that man will, through ingenuity, enterprise, and humanistic altruism, ultimately harness three major influences upon human activity. Thus they will bring under control the chaotic state in which man currently struggles. Energy, ecology, and economy reined in by an elite class who knows what is best for the rest of us will, in the final analysis, prove to be key parts of the formula for man building a heaven on earth of peace, prosperity, and something akin to immortality.

While most of humanity goes its own way apart from God down the broadway that leads to oblivion, the would be ruling elite work to save the world. To those elite, the rest of mankind, whether existing in darkest Africa or whether engaged in nine-to-five workdays in suburban America, is the savage element which must be subdued and reeducated for the world order to come. Once the factors that impact the behavior of the savages are harnessed, life will improve to the point that the savages will submit to the reeducation process more readily.

They think that when energy is produced through environmentally safe means and equally distributed, the ecology of *Mother Earth* will improve dramatically. The savages, too, will improve dramatically as their environment changes their lot in life for the better. Thus, their hostility for one another will cease.

The resultant changes in attitudes and behavior will spark increased productivity and an ever-increasing economic prosperity. Finally, man will have restored or, if you will, achieved, ideal habitat for maintaining social and cultural equilibrium.

Those of the radical environmentalist movement, the antinuclear groups like Greenpeace, fanatic animal rights activists, the champions of all the ultra-liberal causes within U.S. governmental agencies and even UN agencies who operate from power bases funded by U.S. tax dollars, are determined to create heaven on earth. These and all other *save-the-earth* factions pursue their agendas for prideful, personal aggrandizement by and large. It is their chosen method of working their way to salvation.

This assessment is not being judgmental. Their causes are scripturally untenable because the true God of the creation they claim they want to save is left totally out of their thinking while they go about their self-righteous endeavors.

That God will judge man's feeble attempts to produce heaven on earth through humanistic effort is the subject matter of much of Revelation. God himself casts *wormwood* into the waters. He causes much of the green grass and all other vegetation to be scorched by fire. He causes the seas and the rivers to be turned to blood and all life in the sea to die. His *bowls of wrath* judgments seem to mock mankind's efforts today to create a pristine environment such as that which surrounded the Garden of Eden.

Sin caused all of God's pristine creation to decay. Sin must be judged and so it will be. Jesus Christ himself will restore the earth and make all things new again.

Mother Earth worshipers do not have solutions to the problems mankind faces. Rather, they are a major part of the reasons God has issued a foreboding forecast for the end-of-time period Jesus called the *Tribulation*.

The Tribulation Storm

When Jesus Christ's voice calls believers of the Church Age to himself in the Rapture, the Tribulation will break upon mankind with fury unprecedented in earth's history.

Pre-rapture depravity and geophysical upheavals will, at the time of the Apocalypse, seem to have been mere thundershowers. The time for warning will then be passed. Humankind will reap the whirlwind crop it spent millennia sowing. When the four horsemen of Revelation 6 thunder upon the world scene, they will bring horrific tribulation unparalleled in human history, according to Jesus in Matthew 24:21: "For then shall be great tribulation, such as was not since the beginning of the world."

But There Is Good News

Jesus Christ is that Good News. The gospel message overcomes all the frightening, depressing news of history. This same Jesus who issued the Tribulation storm warning also said, "…I am the way, the truth, and the life…" (John 14:6).

Jesus said through John the apostle's writing in scripture: "For God so loved the world, that he gave his only begotten Son, that whosoever believeth in him [Jesus Christ] should not perish, but have everlasting life" (John 3:16).

Jesus promised each and every person who trusts Him and Him alone for salvation of his or her soul a thrilling future that will wipe every tear from every eye forever. Jesus said, "In my Father's house are many mansions; if it were not so, I would have told you. I go to prepare a place for you" (John 14:2).

All prophetic indicators point to the coming of the one called Antichrist. Humanism has paved a smooth road for his ascension. But before the beast arrives at that pinnacle, Jesus Christ will disrupt this world system in an astonishing millisecond. Paul the apostle announced that thrilling event almost 2000 years ago.

"In a moment, in the twinkling of an eye, at the last trump; for the trumpet shall sound, and the dead shall be raised incorruptible, and we shall be changed" (1 Corinthians 15:52).

All of us involved in the production of this volume pray that you will come to know our Lord in the personal, intimate way Jesus prayed of the heavenly Father in John 17, "That they all may be one; as thou, Father, art in me, and I in thee, that they may be one in us...."

The Christian walk in today's world is all-important. We are to be salt and light for a decaying, sin-darkening world, working diligently to put forward the only hope for humanity, Jesus Christ. At the same time, we are commanded to be looking for His imminent return. "And what I say unto you I say unto all, Watch" (Mark 13:37).

If you do not know Jesus in that personal, intimate way, listen to the lovingly whispered urging within your thoughts. It is the voice of the Holy Spirit calling you to accept the Savior right this moment. Pray this prayer:

"Lord Jesus, be merciful to me, a sinner. I turn from my sins and, with your help, will follow you wherever you lead. I trust in you with all my heart."

With Jesus Christ as the captain of your salvation, you need never fear the storms of life or the transition between life in this world and eternity that is called death. Jesus is the Way, the Truth, and the Life.

▼　▼　▼

Part I

DISTANT PROPHETIC RUMBLINGS

Flashes of Falling Away

Dave Hunt

The subject of the last days inevitably raises the question of the signs which mark this climactic period of history—a period which includes the Rapture of the church to heaven, the Second Coming of Christ with His saints in power and glory to rescue Israel and to destroy Antichrist, followed by His thousand-year millennial reign from Jerusalem on the throne of His father David. One immediately recalls the "signs" given by Christ in His Olivet Discourse, which have been widely publicized in sermons, books, and videos:

"...wars and rumours of wars...nation shall rise against nation, and kingdom against kingdom: and there shall be famines, and pestilences, and earthquakes...these are the beginning of sorrows" (Matthew 24:6-8).

There is no denying that these specific "sorrows" have been both prominent and accelerating since Israel, in 1948, became a nation in possession of the land of her fathers again, in fulfillment of the specific promises God made to His ancient people through His prophets more than 2000 years ago. Since that remarkable rebirth of Israel, the intensity and frequency of these signs has increased like the birthpangs of a woman approaching her time of delivery, exactly as Christ foretold. There has, however, been such emphasis upon these oft-mentioned signs of the nearness of Christ's return that the first words of Christ's response have been largely overlooked and His solemn warning neglected:

> And Jesus answered and said…Take heed that no man *deceive* you. For many shall come in my name, saying, I am Christ, and shall *deceive* many….(Matthew 24:4,5).

> And many *false* prophets shall rise, and shall *deceive* many….(verse 11).

> For there shall arise *false* Christs, and *false* prophets, and shall shew great signs and wonders; insomuch that, if it were possible, they shall *deceive* the very elect (verse 24). [Emphasis added.]

It is essential to note that the very *first* sign (and thus the most important one) Jesus gave in response to His disciples' query was *religious deception*: "take heed that no man *deceive* you." It is significant, too, that His revelation of this primary sign was phrased as a warning: "take heed," or *beware*. He repeated this sign two more times for emphasis and explained the nature of the coming deception: it would involve *false Christs*, *false prophets*, and *false signs and wonders*. Moreover, His repetition of the word "many" four times indicates that this deception will not be hidden in a corner but will be a worldwide delusion deceiving multitudes.

A Solemn Warning for the Last Days

Paul uses similar language and issues a similar warning in referring to the last days: "Let no man deceive you by any means…." A time of deception is coming, says Paul, so take care. But in echoing Christ's warning about apostasy, Paul provides an added insight. He reveals that the spiritual deception to which Christ referred, though it will of course involve rank unbelievers following false Christs and false prophets, will infect the professing church; it will involve a "falling away," or apostasy:

"for that day [of the Lord] shall not come except there come a falling away first, and that man of sin [Antichrist] be revealed, the son of perdition" (2 Thessalonians 2:3).

While a true Christian cannot fall away, a false Christian can. Fall away from what? From the faith in Christ which he or she has outwardly professed but without inward reality. These apostates, however, will not leave the church and announce themselves as atheists. They will not convert to Buddhism or Hinduism. While there are always some exceptions, it is important to understand that the apostasy doesn't represent a massive defection from Christianity but a turning away from the truth within the professing church.

Christ warns us in Matthew 24 not to be deceived by false Christs and false prophets and lying signs and wonders. Paul repeats the warning, but with an added dimension: to beware of being deceived into thinking that the apostasy won't come. It will. *It must*. Surely Paul would not speak in this manner unless in the last days the popular view would be to reject the idea of apostasy within the church. The grave danger will be that of following false prophets who, with their signs and wonders, will seem to back up their false teaching that revival, not apostasy, is the order of the day. Paul therefore says, "Don't let anyone deceive you with sweet talk about revival: the apostasy *must* come or the day of the Lord cannot begin."

A False "Signs and Wonders" Movement

That fact becomes clearer when we refer to other passages of Scripture. Christ's statement about false signs and wonders is clarified as we are given further insights into the nature of the apostasy. False signs and wonders will be an integral part of the apostasy. The departure from the truth will be spearheaded by apparent miracle workers and the delusion will be made possible by a prevailing emphasis upon experience over doctrine. Paul says, "For the time will come when they will not endure sound doctrine" (2 Timothy 4:3). And Christ declares:

"Many will say to me in that day, Lord, Lord, have we not prophesied in thy name? and in thy name have cast out devils? and in thy name done many wonderful works?

And then will I profess unto them, I never knew you: depart from me, ye that work iniquity" (Matthew 7:22, 23).

These apostates of whom Christ speaks did not lose their salvation; they were *never saved* ("I *never* knew you"). Yet they outwardly appeared to be high-profile Christian leaders apparently performing signs and wonders *in the name of Christ*. They didn't leave the church to become atheists or to join some non-Christian religion. They remained in the church. They even called Jesus Lord—but without really knowing Him. Tragically, they seemed to think that their ability to prophesy and to perform wonders proved that they belonged to Him. Clearly, doctrine is out and experience is in; and the signs and wonders are so impressive that doctrine no longer matters.

Surely these of whom Christ speaks in Matthew 7 must be the same "false Christs and false prophets" to whom He refers in Matthew 24. It is certainly sobering that the signs and wonders these false professors are able to perform are apparently so impressive that even the very elect might be deceived by them were they not given discernment by the Holy Spirit. We can only conclude that something more than mere trickery is involved. These wonder-workers are backed by the power of Satan, whom they unwittingly serve in the name of the Lord.

Paul indicates as much when he gives us further insight into this great sign of the last days. After a solemn warning that in the last days "perilous [extremely dangerous] times shall come," Paul makes this remarkable statement:

"Now as Jannes and Jambres withstood Moses, so do these [apostates] also resist the truth: men of corrupt minds, reprobate concerning the faith" (2 Timothy 3:8).

Jannes and Jambres weren't skeptics or atheists, they were the magicians in Pharaoh's court who, through the power of Satan, duplicated (up to a point) the miracles God did through Moses and Aaron. Paul is telling us clearly that the last days opposition to the truth will not come so much from atheists on the outside of the church (though they are always there) but from those within who are *reprobate* concerning the faith, depraved men who corrupt the truth. And they do so by performing apparent miracles in Christ's name which (when more than mere trickery) are actually by the power of Satan. In that way they deceive and lead many astray—not out of the church, but into false doctrine and thus a false hope within the church. Satan has no more effective tactic to damn souls!

An Inside Job!

Other Scriptures confirm those above. Jude, for instance, said that we must "earnestly contend for the faith once delivered to the saints" (Jude 3). Contend against whom? Not primarily against god-less enemies outside the church but against those within: "For there are certain men crept in unawares" (verse 4). *Crept in* where? Obviously, inside the church. That is where the problem lies in the last days.

Paul confirms Jude. Addressing the Ephesian elders, Paul said, "For I know this, that after my departing shall grievous wolves enter in among you, not sparing the flock. Also of your own selves shall men arise, speaking perverse things to draw away disciples after them" (Acts 20:29,30). The spiritual deception of which Christ warned would be rampant *within* the church. Some of those very Ephesian elders whom Paul had hand-picked, trained, and ordained would turn out to be apostates and hear Christ's damning words, "Depart from me!"

In confirmation of all of the above, Christ warned His disciples that "the time cometh, that whosoever killeth you will think that he doeth God service" (John 16:2). This is a most remarkable prophecy. Obviously Christ is not referring to persecution by athe-ists. He did not have in mind the slaughter of Christians by the Cae-sars or by Mao or Stalin or Hitler, for they did not believe they were serving God thereby. Of course, when the Jews killed the early Christians, they thought they were serving God; and so did the Roman Catholics when they slaughtered the true Christians before and after the Reformation; and so did the Muslims when they killed Christians. But none of these killings was the complete fulfillment of Christ's prophecy.

That word "whosoever" is the key. Neither the pharisees nor the popes were alone in killing Christians. Others were pursuing them to the death at the same time. But Christ is saying that a time is coming when *whosoever*, in other words, *everyone* who kills Christians will think he is serving God. That can only mean that a world religion to which *everyone* must belong is coming, a religion that will seek to exterminate true Christians in the name of God. John saw the same scene in the future:

> And it was given unto him [Antichrist] to make war with the saints, and to overcome them....
>
> And I beheld another beast...he exerciseth all the power of the first beast...and causeth the earth and them which dwell therein to worship the first beast....

And he had power to...cause that as many as would not worship the image of the beast should be killed (Revelation 13:7-15).

Not Revival, But Apostasy

Even more solemn is an added dimension to Paul's declaration concerning the coming apostasy. Whereas Christ warned of deception, Paul said it is *essential:* "for that day [of the Lord] shall not come except there come a falling away [apostasy] *first*." This statement, as we have noted, is preceded by the strange warning, "Let no man deceive you...."

Clearly Paul, by the leading of the Holy Spirit, anticipated the very delusion we find in our day: the rejection of the biblical teaching concerning apostasy and the insistence that we are in the midst of or at least are building up to the "greatest revival in the history of the church." Such is the prevailing teaching today among charismatics and even noncharismatics. The promise of revival will be a deception, he warns, so beware. Instead of a great revival in the last days directly preceding the Rapture, there will be a great apostasy—a falling away from the faith.

Christ refers again to this falling away more subtly when He raises the question, "When the Son of man cometh, shall he find [the] faith on the earth" (Luke 18:8)? While the definite article is not included in most translations, it is obviously implied here and is found in other exhortations, such as in Jude. Christ is not referring to just any "faith" but to *"the faith* which was once [for all] delivered unto the saints" (Jude 3) and for which we are to "earnestly contend." This is the faith from which great numbers (seemingly even the vast majority) will fall away.

One of the greatest contributors to the falling away we are seeing today is the false view of faith promoted by the so-called "faith teachers" of the "faith movement," also known as the "positive confession movement." They promote a "faith" largely devoid of moral and doctrinal content and which promises that whatever one truly believes and confesses with one's lips will come to pass. This self-centered heresy is deadly.

Today's False "Faith"

That we must earnestly contend for the faith against those who have crept into the church implies that the battle is not so much *faith* against *no faith*, but rather *true* faith against *false* faith. And that is precisely what we see today. Even the world is into "faith" and "spirituality." Articles in leading medical journals cite studies showing that those who have *any* "religious faith" are more likely to recover from illness. *Christianity Today* recently ran a major article naïvely promoting these studies as though they were supportive of the truth.[1]

Multitudes of Christians imagine that faith is believing that what they are praying for will occur, and that if they truly believe, they will have whatever they ask. Obviously, if things happen because one believes they will happen, then one does not need God. This is mind power, not "faith in God" as Christ taught. It is faith in faith, which Kenneth Hagin teaches, calling it "the law of faith."[2]

This delusion comes from Eastern mysticism and is found not only in all the Mind Science cults (Science of Mind, Christian Science, Unity, et al.) but in the Positive Thinking of Norman Vincent Peale, the Possibility Thinking of Robert Schuller, and in the Positive Confession teaching of Kenneth Hagin, Kenneth Copeland, Frederick Price, David Yonggi Cho, and others. No one expressed it more clearly than Ernest Holmes, founder of the Church of Religious Science:

> Man, by thinking, can bring into his experience whatsoever he desires...[i.e., as little gods we each create our own world].[3]

> We are co-partners with the Infinite...a Universal Creative Mind which receives the impress of our thought and acts upon it.[4]

Norman Vincent Peale borrowed the phrase "Positive Thinking" from Charles Fillmore (founder of Unity)[5] and credited Ernest Holmes with making him into a positive thinker.[6] Said Peale, "Positive thinking is just another term for faith."[7] On the contrary, atheists can be positive thinkers. Peale claimed that man's empowerment could be realized by visualizing God as "energy" ("God is energy," said Peale) and inhaling this energy and visualizing it permeate one's being.[8]

If faith in faith or in some "higher power" is all one needs, as Alcoholics Anonymous and the various Twelve-Step Programs in churches teach (there are over 500 participants a week in Bill Hybel's Willow Creek Community Church[9]) then there is no true faith. "God" is no more than a placebo that triggers some inner power to heal. Indeed, Peale declared that in prayer we commune not with the God who created us but with "the great factor within [one]self, the deep subconscious mind."[10]

The Major Sign is Here Today

Differing insights into last days apostasy are given throughout the Bible. A major factor accompanying the departure from the faith will be "giving heed to seducing spirits and doctrines of devils" (1 Timothy 4:1). Through the occult teaching that one can visualize Jesus and carry on a conversation with Him, a legion of seducing spirits has been loosed in the church. Richard Foster tells us that through visualization "Jesus Christ will actually come to you."[11] Calvin Miller, in an InterVarsity book, teaches the same,[12] as do the inner healers and many Christian psychologists. Of course, it is not Jesus they see and converse with, but a demon masquerading as "Jesus." Yet even when the deception ought to be obvious, leading Christians embrace and promote it.

In her eighteenth book, *Lonely No More*, best-selling Christian author and leader Karen Mains provides a clear example of a seducing spirit and its doctrines of devils. A popular speaker at women's conferences, Karen, at the time that book was published, was a "chairperson of the trustee board for InterVarsity Christian Fellowship/USA."[13] She tells how at Cenacle, a Catholic contemplative center, using visualization for contact, her alleged "male-self" from her dreams turns into an "idiot-child sitting at a table." Fully awake, she sees its "totally bald" head "lolled to one side... drooling...emaciated and malnourished...a little skeleton of a ragamuffin...[with] sad, huge eyes...." Under the guidance of her "spiritual director" (a Jungian Catholic nun), Karen is convinced that this visualized "idiot child" which has now come alive to her is, in fact, the "Christ child" within, that part of herself "that is Christ" and has been attempting to woo her![14]

Paul presents yet another characteristic of the apostasy: "For men shall be lovers of their own selves" (2 Timothy 3:2). This false teaching is rampant in the church today through Christian psychology. It came from a godless psychologist named Erich Fromm who called "belief in God...a childish illusion."[15] He claimed that when Christ said, "Love your neighbor as yourself," He meant that we must learn to love ourselves before we can love our neighbors or God. In fact, the church had always interpreted that verse to mean that we love ourselves too much and need to give some of that love to our neighbors, not that we don't love ourselves enough.

Robert Schuller promoted that false view in his book, *Self-Love, the Dynamic Force of Success*. From there the lie spread throughout the church. The exploding new men's movement, Promise Keepers, has been foremost in promoting this and other delusions of Christian psychology. A newsletter stated:

> Many Christian single men have fought the battle to build their own self-worth, self-esteem, and self-love. They have learned that it is impossible to have a healthy relationship with others while having an unhealthy relationship with one's self. Jesus recognized this when He challenged us to love our neighbor as we would love ourself (Mark 12:31).[16]

Yes, some people say, "I hate myself!" How do we reconcile that statement, earnestly uttered, with the biblical declaration, "No man ever yet hated his own flesh" (Ephesians 5:29)? What that person actually hates may be his appearance, clothes, job, salary, the way people look down upon or mistreat him, etc. But he doesn't hate *himself*. If he did, he would be *glad* he was homely, had poor clothes, low income, and was abused by others. The fact that he complains about these things proves that he loves himself, exactly as the Bible says. He needs to give some of that love to his neighbor, not learn to love himself more.

It was surely not a "negative self-image" that was Lucifer's downfall but a very "positive" one. More than 200 years ago, William Law expressed what Christians had always understood:

> Self-love, self-esteem, and self-seeking are the essence and the life of pride; and the Devil, the father of pride, is never absent from these passions, nor without an influence in them....[17]

The last-days apostasy will also be characterized by a rejection of the church's Rapture to heaven: "There shall come in the last days scoffers...saying, Where is the promise of his coming?"

(2 Peter 3:3,4). The apostasy involves claiming that revival rather than the Rapture is imminent and denying that apostasy must come. Again, these days are upon us, and we need not quote the many Christian leaders who ridicule belief in the Rapture, calling it an escape theory. Their books and tapes are readily available.

How is such a departure from the faith possible, and how can it gather momentum in the name of the Lord Jesus Christ under the umbrella of revival and a great prayer and fasting movement? Simply because, at the heart of the apostasy is a rejection of the primacy of sound doctrine: "For the time will come when they will not endure sound doctrine" (2 Timothy 4:3). And here again this day is upon us with a vengeance, as we will now document.

A False "Church Growth/Signs and Wonders" Movement

Yes, the Bible definitely predicts a last-days signs and wonders movement. That is clear from the verses to which we have referred. However, Scripture tells us that this signs and wonders movement will not be of God but of Satan. It will be a delusion that will deceive many. The topic on everyone's lips and mind today is *revival*. It comes as a shock to many to learn that the word revival does not occur even once in the entire King James Bible. The hope of revival that excites so many today is not even a biblical concept. Unfortunately, lack of space prevents us from elaborating.

In his new book, *Confronting the Powers*, Fuller Theological Seminary professor C. Peter Wagner seeks to explain and biblically justify the false revival now being promoted. Wagner calls John Wimber "my mentor."[18] He introduces to readers terms that were unknown only a few years ago: territorial spirits, spiritual mapping, Spiritual Warfare Network, A.D. 2000 Movement, ground-level spiritual warfare, occult-level spiritual warfare, strategic-level spiritual warfare, cosmic-level spiritual warfare, praise marches, prayer-walking, prayer journeys, prayer expeditions, praying through windows, etc. Wagner says that these new concepts and practices (of which Jesus, Paul, and the early church knew nothing) hold the key to spiritual breakthrough and worldwide revival.[19]

Similarly, and in agreement with Wagner and Wimber, Christian TV and radio and best-selling books persuasively argue that we are in the midst of the greatest revival of Christianity in the history of the world. This revival is claimed to be characterized by *power*: power to prophesy, to speak in tongues, to heal the sick, to confront evil spirits, and even to raise the dead. Enthusiasts point to plenty of apparent evidence of the vaunted "revival" spreading rapidly throughout the world from such places as the former Toronto Vineyard, the Brownsville Assembly of God in Pensacola, Florida, Benny Hinn's church in Orlando, Florida, and his huge televised crusades, to mention a few centers of this delusion.

To justify the unbiblical physical manifestations accompanying this movement (hysterical laughing, weird twitchings and contortions, animal noises and mannerisms, etc.) John Wimber says that God is greater than His Word. He waves the Bible and declares that when the Holy Spirit moves, He doesn't go by this book. There is a mad thirst for *power* and its supposed manifestations. One can view numerous videos from the Brownsville Assembly of God in Pensacola where hundreds surge forward at an altar call—*without the gospel having been preached*. People come from all over the world to "get it," meaning the physical manifestations of supposed Holy Spirit power.

Nicky Gumbel, the curate of Holy Trinity Brompton (HTB) Anglican Church in England, tells how he was swept into this new "move of the Spirit." Gumbel testifies that he felt "something like 10,000 volts" of electricity going through his body when Wimber prayed for him. Prayed for what? For *power*. (The Brownsville revival began when evangelist Steve Hill, having just come from HTB, related his experiences there.) Said Gumbel approvingly on a teaching tape:

> The American [Wimber]…just said, 'More power….' It was the only thing he ever prayed. I can't remember him ever praying anything else….[20]

But Isn't Apostasy Old News?

Someone will say that apostasy had already begun in Paul's day or at least shortly after his death. That is true. Jude testified that when he wrote his short epistle the apostates had already entered into the church. The Roman Catholic Church, certainly, has been in apostasy for 1500 years. There is, however, something new about the apostasy we are now seeing which points to the final fulfillment of biblical prophecies in our day.

It is generally believed that the Roman Catholic Church was the only representation of Christianity on earth prior to the Reformation. Even today's evangelical leaders echo the lie of Roman Catholic apologists that, since the Roman Catholic Church was the only church prior to the sixteenth century, then if it was in apostasy, Christ's promise that the gates of hell would not prevail against His church failed. The truth, however, is that an evangelical church comprised of millions of true believers always existed and was always persecuted by Rome. Martin Luther himself said:

> We are not the first to declare the papacy to be the kingdom of Antichrist, since for many years before us so many and such great men (whose number is large and whose memory is eternal) have undertaken to express the same thing so clearly and plainly.[21]

Who were these to whom Luther referred? We have a letter dated 1429 (100 years before the Reformation) from Pope Martin V commanding the King of Poland to *exterminate* the Hussites. Jan Hus had been martyred in 1415. But for 1000 years before that there were the Vaudois, Albigenses, Waldenses, and other similar groups of evangelical Christians. These simple believers were the object of repeated crusades (larger and more numerous than those fought for the "Holy Land") in which the popes offered "the remission of all sins to everyone who should slay a heretic."[22]

Tragically, the false accusations made by the inquisitors to justify their slaughter of the "heretics" are still found in encyclopedias to deceive the unwary today. For the truth, one must look to other sources, such as John Fox's *Book of Martyrs*, *The Martyr's Mirror* (published in 1631), Samuel Morland's *The History of the Evangelical Churches of Piedmont* (published in 1648), or to other books written nearer to the time. Even *Halley's Pocket Bible Handbook* tells the truth.

And here we confront a disturbing example of the new ecumenical characteristic of the last days apostasy. The Billy Graham Evangelistic Association (BGEA) acquired the printing rights to *Halley's Pocket Bible Handbook* and printed a special Billy Graham Crusade edition of it in 1962, 1964, and 1969. In so doing, they deleted dozens of pages of vital historical facts concerning the evil of some of the popes and of Rome's persecution and slaughter of Christians. Truth was sacrificed on the altar of ecumenism in order not to offend Rome, and readers were robbed of indispensable information. The following is a sample of facts carefully presented by Halley, which the Graham organization eliminated from its special edition:

> [The Albigenses] preached against the immoralities of the [Catholic] priesthood, pilgrimages, worship of saints and images...opposed the claims of the Church of Rome; made great use of the Scriptures....By 1167 they embraced possibly a majority of the population of South France....In 1208 a crusade was ordered by Pope Innocent III; a bloody war of extermination followed, scarcely paralleled in history; town after town was put to the sword and the inhabitants murdered without distinction of age or sex...within 100 years the Albigenses were utterly rooted out.

> [Two centuries later] between 1540 and 1570 no fewer than 900,000 Protestants were put to death in the Pope's war for the extermination of the Waldenses. Think of monks and priests directing, with heartless cruelty and inhuman brutality, the work of torturing and burning alive innocent men and women, and doing it in the name of Christ, by the direct order of the "Vicar of Christ"!

> ...on the night of August 24, 1572, 70,000 Huguenots, including most of their leaders, were massacred [St. Bartholemew's massacre]. Some 200,000 [more] perished as martyrs...[and] 500,000 fled to Protestant countries.[23]

To carefully suppress such essential information not only robbed readers but dishonored the martyrs and the Lord for whom they died. The courage of the martyrs, who gave their lives for Christ rather than to deny His Word, puts to shame those who hid that truth from a generation which desperately needs to know it!

Down through the centuries, though the major visible church with its headquarters in Rome was deep in apostasy, there were millions who gave no allegiance to Rome. They sought to follow the New Testament and remain pure. Then came the Reformation. As a result, most of these groups were gradually absorbed into and disappeared among the so-called Protestants. And now the Protestants are turning back to Rome, and the apostasy, for the first time in history, is becoming worldwide!

Trashing the Reformation

One of the most significant events in the history of Christianity in nearly 500 years took place March 29, 1994. Leading evangelicals and Catholics signed a joint declaration, *Evangelicals & Catholics Together: The Christian Mission in the Third Millennium* (ECT). The document says, "...we [Evangelicals and Catholics] thank God for the discovery of one another as brothers and sisters in Christ."[24]

That statement overturns the Reformation! Evangelicals have endorsed and joined Rome's longstanding apostasy! The March 30 *New York Times* news release said in part:

> They toiled together in the movements against abortion and pornography, and now leading Catholics and evangelicals are asking their flocks for a remarkable leap of faith: to finally accept each other as Christians. In what's being called a historic declaration, evangelicals including Pat Robertson and Charles Colson joined with conservative Roman Catholic leaders today in...urging Catholics and evangelicals...to stop aggressive proselytization of each other's flocks.

> John White, president of Geneva College and former president of the National Association of Evangelicals, said the statement represents a "triumphalistic moment" in American religious life after centuries of distrust....

> Other evangelical endorsers include the heads of the Home Mission Board and Christian Life Commission of the Southern Baptist Convention, the nation's largest Protestant denomination, and Bill Bright, founder of Campus Crusade for Christ...Mark Noll of Wheaton University...Os Guinness, Jesse Miranda (Assemblies of God), Richard Mouw (President, Fuller Seminary), J.I. Packer and Herbert Schlossberg.

Robert Simonds, Southern California chairman of the National Association of Evangelicals, "applauded the declaration" and said he hoped it would bring "increased cooperation between evangelicals and Catholics...." Amazingly, the document claims that all Catholics hold the same faith as evangelicals. That idea would be a shock both to the martyrs and those who burned them at the stake for what were recognized at that time as such vast differences in belief that the faithful were willing to die for them!

Rome has neither changed its beliefs nor rescinded its more than 100 anathemas damning those who accept the biblical gospel. Nevertheless, Billy Graham has said, "I've found that my beliefs are essentially the same as those of orthodox Roman Catholics."[25] Upon receiving an honorary doctorate at Belmont Abbey (a Jesuit college), Graham said, "The gospel that built this school and the gospel that brings me here tonight is still the way of salvation"[26]— an unthinkable statement in light of Rome's undeniably false gospel of works, ritual, purgatory, indulgences, prayers to the saints, and the perpetual *sacrifice* of Christ in the mass. In justification of burning the martyrs, the highest Roman Catholic authority states:

> If anyone says that the sacraments of the New Law [Roman Catholic rituals] are not necessary for salvation but...that without them...men obtain from God through faith alone the grace of justification...let him be anathema.

> If anyone says that in the mass a true and real sacrifice is not offered to God...let him be anathema.

> If anyone says that the sacrifice of the mass is...a mere commemoration of the sacrifice consummated on the cross but not a propitiatory one...and not to be offered for...the dead, for sins...let him be anathema.[27]

The last words of Hugh Latimer, martyred for rejecting the mass, ring in our consciences. Bound back-to-back to the stake with Nicholas Ridley, Latimer, England's most effective gospel preacher at that time, was heard to exclaim as the flames engulfed them: "Be of good comfort, Master Ridley, and play the man. We shall this day, by God's grace, light such a candle in England as I pray shall never be put out." Today's apostasy is determined to extinguish that "candle," though the evangelical leaders doing so would not have known the gospel but for the faithfulness of such martyrs!

Such is the heritage of today's evangelicals, which this document (ECT) now rejects. We are asked to believe that the Reformers were deluded, that like all active Catholics today they were saved but didn't know it. The tens of millions of Catholics who since then have received Christ by faith alone and left the Catholic Church have also been deceived. The whole evangelical church of today is equally deluded about what it means to be a Christian. Colson, Robertson, Bright et al., have revised both history and the gospel of our salvation!

The Return to Rome

Pope Paul VI said to Sri Chinmoy, a Hindu leader, "Your gospel and my gospel are the same." And now evangelical leaders are saying to Rome, "Your gospel and our gospel are the same." Billy Graham has recommended a biography of Pope Paul VI which encouraged "devotion to Mary, the Saints, worship of the wafer at the Mass, and trust in the sacraments for salvation." He called the book "a classic in devotion."[28] Having visited Pope John Paul II several times, Graham calls him "the world's greatest evangelist"[29] and says that any differences in their theology "are not important as far as personal salvation is concerned."[30] Tell that to the millions who died at the hands of Rome because of very real differences that Graham now denies!

On the Phil Donahue Show, Billy Graham praised the Pope as "a moral and spiritual leader" that the American people could look up to and said, "Thank God, I've got somebody to quote now with some real authority."[31]

The move back to Rome has been underway for many years under the leadership of Billy Graham and his magazine, *Christianity Today*. Senior editor, Kenneth Kantzer, in a *CT* editorial, honored Pope John Paul II as "the successor of Saint Peter" whom "God has called…to forge a united church…[whose] priority to the Christian message…endear[s] him to the hearts of evangelicals."[32] Apparently the martyrs died for a semantic misunderstanding which has lately been clarified!

In his 1977 crusade on the campus of Notre Dame University, Graham's invitation certainly confused the gospel: "Many of you want to come tonight and reconfirm your confirmation. You want to reconfirm the decision that you made when you joined the church." He made a similar appeal for people to "reconfirm their confirmation" at his Milwaukee crusade in August 1978. In Milwaukee, 3500 names of those who went forward were turned over to the Roman Catholic Archdiocese.[33] At Billy Graham's Vancouver,

British Columbia crusade in October 1984, David Cline, vice-chairman of the organizing committee, had this to say: "If Catholics step forward there will be *no attempt to convert them and their names will be given to the Catholic church nearest them.*" (Emphasis added.)[34]

Says Graham, "We're delighted that the Roman Catholic Church now cooperates with us wherever we go."[35] That cooperation involved about 400 Catholic "counselors" in Graham's mid-September, 1990, crusade at Nassau Coliseum, Long Island. The local Catholic Charismatic Renewal Office exulted that the crusade would "provide opportunities for Catholics who attend to be reconnected to their parishes via Catholic Bible study."[36] England's Cardinal Hume wrote a letter thanking Billy for sending him 2100 converts from his 1989 London crusade and for helping them renew their Roman Catholic faith.[37] As long ago as his 1952 Pittsburgh crusade, Graham told newspaper reporter William McElwain:

"Many of the people who have reached a decision for Christ at our meetings have joined the Catholic church and we have received commendations from Catholic publications for the revived interest in their church following one of our campaigns."[38]

We thank God that Billy Graham has preached the gospel and souls have been saved. Unfortunately, however, he has also done much to undermine that gospel. Of course, Graham, the BGEA, and *Christianity Today* have not been alone in bringing evangelicals back to Rome. Paul and Jan Crouch and TBN are at the forefront of this move. Crouch believes in the apparitions of Mary and even that Mary has appeared to him and Jan. He recently said:

"In the 1980s, David Duplessis, father of modern Pentecostalism, visited Medjugorie...and concluded what *he* experienced was...a revival, the likes of which he had given up seeing in his lifetime, and he spotted no 'bad fruit.' The heavenly apparitions, concluded the great Charismatic leader, were 'of God'" (emphasis in original).[39]

Also leading the march back to Rome are Pat Robertson's Christian Coalition, *Charisma* magazine, Promise Keepers (which has a Roman Catholic on its board, uses a Catholic evangelist at its meetings, just revised its statement of faith to satisfy Catholics, and cooperates closely with Rome), and others. John Wimber, head of the Vineyard Movement, from which Promise Keepers came, has called the Pope "a born-again evangelical...[who] is preaching the gospel as clearly as anybody is preaching it in the world today."[40]

Bill Bright and Campus Crusade for Christ have worked closely with Catholics for years and have welcomed a number of them on staff. So have John Wimber and the Vineyard churches he founded.

Former Vineyard pastor John Goodwin tells of being present when Wimber addressed about 5000 people. Says Goodwin:

> John Wimber actively promotes the reunification of the Protestants and the Catholics. I was there at a seminar, a pastors' conference in Anaheim. The archbishop of the archdiocese was attending, sitting up in front with his robes on....John asked him to stand up and said to him, "I want to apologize to you on behalf of all Protestants for leaving the Catholic Church and for the things we've said about you and the Church."

> When Pope John Paul II designated the last decade of this century for "world evangelization," John Wimber, head of the Vineyard churches, exclaimed, "This is one of the greatest things that has ever happened in the history of the Church...I am thrilled with the Pope and glad that he is calling the Church to this goal, to this work."[41]

An article titled "YWAM Builds Bridges to Catholics" makes it clear that YWAM (Youth With A Mission) works with Catholics as well as Christians here in the U.S. and overseas. It shows a picture of Billy Graham meeting with the Pope and states that "Beginning in 1978, YWAM workers in Austria began to cooperate with Catholics....In 1984, YWAM adopted a policy allowing staff to work with Catholics....YWAM has installed a Catholic, Rob Clarke, as director of its discipleship training school in Dublin....YWAM's missionaries are not aiming to lure Catholics out of their churches...[but] helping to establish Christ-centered evangelistic Catholic communities."[42]

The Leaders of Apostasy

The Scriptures to which we have referred clearly indicate that the last-days apostasy will come from within the church and will be led by false Christs and false prophets who will compromise the gospel and God's Word and rely upon outward manifestations and apparent miracles. Again, this is precisely what we see today.

Examples of those who have preached a false gospel and crept into the church unawares in our day are legion. Space limits us to a few. At the top of the list one finds Norman Vincent Peale. His books have sold many millions of copies. The most shocking thing about Peale is his acceptance by the evangelical church. Millions of those who call themselves born-again Christians and attend evangelical churches read his books and find nothing wrong with them. He has been praised by Billy Graham and other evangelical leaders. Though he died recently, his books, magazines, and tapes continue to infect the church.

In 1984, on the Phil Donahue program, Peale said: "It's not necessary to be born again. You have your way to God; I have mine. I found eternal peace in a Shinto shrine...I've been to Shinto shrines, and God is everywhere." Shocked, Phil Donahue responded, "But you're a Christian minister; you're supposed to tell me that Christ is the way and the truth and the life, aren't you?" Peale replied, "Christ is one of the ways. God is everywhere."[43]

Peale was the keynote speaker at Mormon President Spencer W. Kimball's 85th birthday celebration in 1980. He called the Mormon leaders "men of God...[who] are doing God's work...by their fruits ye shall know them...." Because Kimball was "so deeply spiritual," Peale asked him, "Will you bless me?"[44]

Perhaps Peale, who was a 33° Mason (more than 1 million Southern Baptists and many of their clergy are Masons), favored Mormonism because it is so much like Masonry. Each state in the U.S. has a Supreme Grand Lodge of Freemasonry and most Grand Lodges publish a *Monitor* for the guidance of members in the official doctrines and practices. Consider the following from the *Kentucky Monitor*:

> The three really great rituals of the human race are the Prajapati ritual of ancient Hinduism, the Mass of the Christian [Roman Catholic] Church, and the Third Degree of Masonry.
>
> [T]ogether they testify to the profoundest insight of the human soul: that God becomes man that man may become God![45]

Next on the list of leaders of today's apostasy comes Robert Schuller, to whom President Clinton, in his January 1997 Inaugural address, referred as "one of America's best-known pastors." Schuller calls Peale "the man who has impacted and influenced my thinking and my theology and my life more than any other living person...."[46] Schuller, through his *Hour of Power*, has the largest television audience of any Christian program, reportedly going into 20 million homes.[47] As pastor of the Crystal Cathedral in Garden Grove, California, Schuller has said, "It was Dr. [Norman Vincent] Peale who got me to go to Los Angeles...and it was [Billy] Graham who first got me to go on TV."[48]

Schuller preaches what he unashamedly calls a "man-centered theology," though theology is the study of God. He perverts "Thou shalt have no other gods before me," to mean, "Believe in the God who believes in you!"—though the Bible warns, "Cursed be the man that trusteth in man" (Jeremiah 17:5). He says it's destructive of the gospel to call anyone a sinner, and declares:

> That's what sets me apart from fundamentalists, who are trying to convert everybody to believe how they believe....We know the things the major faiths can agree on. We try to focus on those without offending those with different viewpoints, or without compromising the integrity of my own Christian commitment.[49]

Of course, the major faiths don't even agree on God, and certainly not on the gospel that saves—so Schuller can have little to say of any substance. He has said, "When we built this church [the Crystal Cathedral], our aim was to construct such a building that it would stand for centuries."[50] Obviously he does not entertain the hope of the imminent Rapture of the church as did the early Christians. Schuller went to Rome to get the Pope's approval of a drawing of the Crystal Cathedral, saying he wouldn't have dared to build it without first getting the "Holy Father's apostolic blessings."

John Wimber, of course, is another key figure in the apostasy. He gave us numerous false prophets in Kansas City and elsewhere and the "praise and worship" movement with its rock beat, shallow words, and hypnotic repetition. The Toronto laughing revival has spread mainly through the Vineyards. Promise Keepers is also a Vineyard movement and was begun largely to fulfill Vineyard prophecies about stadiums being filled to overflowing with people excited about Jesus, and accompanying miracles.

The Toronto Vineyard church, which became the center of the laughing revival, has been removed by John Wimber from the Fellowship of Vineyard Churches. This action has been mistakenly taken as a sign that Wimber is maturing and rejecting some of the excesses that he once embraced. In fact, Wimber wrote the foreword to the book on "Holy Laughter" by Jon Arnott, head pastor of the now disfellowshipped Toronto Vineyard. Toronto was disfellowshipped not for "holy laughter," but for trying to find specific verses in the Bible to explain the animal noises.

Many other Vineyard churches, such as the St. Louis Vineyard Christian Fellowship, continue their involvement in "holy laughter." Its pastor, Randy Clark, brought the laughing revival to Toronto. Clark "got it" from Rodney Howard-Browne at Kenneth Hagin Jr.'s Rhema Bible Church in Tulsa and continues to promote this movement worldwide. Moreover, Clark was attracted to Howard-Browne because "people shaking, falling, laughing" reminded him of what he had seen "years earlier in the Vineyard revivals."[51]

Apostasy and "Progress in Religion"

One of the more notable leaders in the apostasy is John Marks Templeton, a wealthy Wall Street money manager. His beliefs are so contrary to biblical teaching that it is astonishing how he could have "crept in *unawares*." Templeton's beliefs are expressed clearly in his many writings. He is an evolutionist and a pantheist ("God is billions of stars in the Milky Way....Time and space and energy are all part of God...God is five billion people on Earth...God is untold billions of beings on planets of millions of other stars"[52] He is a universalist and occultist who rejects Christ as the only Savior, claims that heaven and hell are states of mind we create here on earth, that truth is relative, and that Christianity is no longer relevant. Yet this man is highly acclaimed in evangelical circles. He was on the Board of Princeton Theological Seminary[53] and for fifteen years was on the Board of Managers of the American Bible Society,[54] in spite of his rejection of the Bible as God's Word. Norman Vincent Peale called Templeton "the greatest layman of the Christian Church in our time,"[55] an amazing tribute to an anti-Christian!

Templeton's 1994 book, *Discovering The Laws of Life*, is pure occultism. Instead of warning against it, *Christianity Today* devoted the entire back cover of its April 24, 1994 issue to an ad promoting it. Headlined "WILL INSPIRE MILLIONS OF READERS," the ad contained the endorsements of Norman Vincent Peale (who also wrote the foreword), Robert Schuller, Billy Graham, and two prominent Catholic New Age leaders, Theodore M. Hesburgh (former president of Notre Dame University) and J. Peter Grace (head of the Knights of Malta, sworn to defend the pope). Here are sample quotes from the book:

> [T]he basic principles for leading a "sublime life"…may be derived from any religious tradition—Jewish, Muslim, Hindu, Buddhist and others as well as Christian.…

> [A]stronauts travel[ed] into outer space…[and] did not bring back any evidence of heaven. And whereas drills had penetrated the earth, they'd found oil, not hell, in the depths…spiritual theorists are inclined to conceive of [heaven and hell] as states of mind.…

> Through our choices and attitudes we create our own heaven or hell right here on earth…the only place we can find heaven is in our own hearts.…

> Our innate goodness is an essential fact of our existence…of God within us.

> Be honest. Be true. Love all parts of yourself…the god-hood within you…is in a state of becoming perfect.[56]

Templeton and his neo-pagan views were first introduced to the church in 1986 by Robert Schuller. Schuller's *Possibilities* magazine put Templeton's picture on its front cover, and its major article was an interview with Templeton. In it he expressed his Unity/Religious Science/New Age beliefs: "Your spiritual principles attract prosperity to you…material success…comes…from being in tune with the infinite.…The Christ spirit dwells in every human being whether the person knows it or not…nothing exists except God."[57] These heresies were enthusiastically promoted by Schuller to his vast audience of readers.

Templeton's writings are readily available in any bookstore, thus any Christian leader can know his beliefs. Nevertheless, this man is accepted in the church and is embraced and praised by Billy Graham, Charles Colson, and Bill Bright, among others. Each of them has been the recipient of the annual Templeton Prize for Progress in Religion. It is larger than the Nobel Prize. What Templeton means by "progress in religion" and what he intended by establishing the prize should prevent any evangelical from accepting it. The "progress in religion" he envisions is clearly toward Antichrist's world religion:

> [T]he doctrinal formulations of Christianity have changed and will change from age to age....Christians think God appeared in Jesus of Nazareth two thousand years ago for our salvation and education. But we should not take it to mean that...progress stopped...that Jesus was the end of change....To say that God cannot reveal Himself again in a decisive way [through other Messiahs]...seems sacrilegious....[58]

> As the religious forms of traditional Judaism and Christianity are losing their powers to inform the contemporary mind, the West desperately needs religious geniuses who can create new imaginal forms....

> "Theologians...must begin to explore the vast unseen dimensions of our evolving universe...."[59]

> I am hoping we can develop a body of knowledge about God that doesn't rely on ancient revelations or scripture [such as the Bible!]...that is scientific...and is not disputed because of divisions between religions or churches or ancient scripture or liturgy....[60]

> The next stage of human divine progress on the evolutionary scale needs...geniuses of the spirit, blazing trails for the rest of us to follow. To encourage progress of this kind, we have established the Templeton Foundation Prizes for Progress in Religion.[61]

In keeping with his idea of "progress" in religion, Templeton suggests, "Maybe one of the attributes of God is change."[62] That is indeed true of his "god," but the God of the Bible declares, "for I am the Lord, I change not" (Malachi 3:6). The very idea of "progress in religion" denies the gospel of Jesus Christ. Christianity is not a religion, nor is it subject to progressive development. Nor does Christianity maintain a friendly, ecumenical relationship with the world's religions, but opposes all of them as devices of Satan. Every true Christian, by the very tenets of his faith, must be uncompromisingly opposed to Templeton's neo-pagan beliefs and the prize he offers.

It would be clearly dishonest for anyone to accept the Templeton Prize for Progress in Religion who was not in complete sympathy with its purpose and the beliefs behind it. The very reception of the prize by any individual constitutes an endorsement of all that the prize represents in the mind of its founder. Try to imagine Elijah accepting an ecumenical prize from the prophets of Baal, or Paul from the pagan leaders of his day!

Yet Billy Graham, Charles Colson, and Campus Crusade for Christ founder Bill Bright not only accepted the prize but praised the prize and the man behind it. Upon accepting it at the first news conference, Colson said, "I salute Sir John for establishing this award and doing it in such a generous way...." His acceptance speech was made at the 1993 Parliament of the World's Religions in Chicago. The meeting was opened with a Muslim prayer and closed with a Buddhist prayer. Tragically, Colson never gave the gospel to the robed religious leaders on the platform behind him and their followers filling the large auditorium. Bill Bright was even more effusive in his acceptance speech at a Catholic Church in Rome:

> The prestigious Templeton Prize, to me, because of the nature of its objective, is greater than any other prize that could be given for any purpose. So I am deeply humbled and greatly honored to be the recipient of this 1996 magnificent Templeton Prize. I would like to thank and commend Sir John Templeton for establishing this prize....[63]

More examples could be given to prove that the prophecies of Christ, of Paul, of Peter, and of Jude concerning the last days apostasy are coming to pass in our day. We have not named names in order to denigrate anyone, but to show the extent of the delusion. It would hardly do to say in general terms that ecumenism and apostasy are being promoted by Christian leaders without concrete evidence identifying them.

Furthermore, we have avoided naming the leaders of the more obvious heresies within the charismatic movement such as Kenneth Hagin, Kenneth Copeland, Frederick Price (who say we are little gods and create reality with our minds), Morris Cerullo (who says that when you look at Morris Cerullo you look at God), Yonggi Cho (who says we must visualize to have faith), and so many others. Several authors have pointed out their errors and the fact that they are playing a large part in the apostasy and false revival.

We have taken our examples from among those who are more highly regarded in evangelical circles in general and whose influence is the greatest among mainstream evangelicals. That will be the last bastion of true faith to fall. We have not had space to show from the Scriptures *why* the apostasy must come, but it should be clear that its coming is essential in preparing the world for the Antichrist.

Neither do we desire to engender discouragement. Our Lord's desire is that we should not be ignorant of Satan's devices and should arm ourselves well against them. Then we can face the end times, of which we are assuredly a part, with confidence and with hope.

▼　▼　▼

CHAPTER 2

Gathering Clouds of Global Godlessness

Bill Perkins

As the world gently rotates on its pre-ordained axis, the majestic calm of each new morning gives all God's creatures new hope. The past is over and all things are new. Yet looming in the not-too-distant future is a fast-approaching horror that will forever change the morning calm. This horror is not confined to one area of the world, not restrained to one country, and not restricted to non-believers. It is the dawning of the scripturally prophesied era of total global godlessness, the time when God allows the world to be led by Satan himself—right to the point of annihilation.

> For this reason, rejoice, O heavens and you who dwell in them. Woe to the earth and the sea, because the devil has come down to you, having great wrath, knowing that he has [only] a short time (Revelation 12:12).

But before the clock strikes midnight on God's prophetic clock, the world is a stage being set for the final dramatic act. Satan won't jump out of the sky and demand that the world worship him. He knows better. He's had 6000 years of practice using the same old lies. In fact, the two most common lies today are the two lies recorded in the book of Genesis some 6000 years ago: 1) You will not die (reincarnation) and 2) you can be God (New Age principle). There's a lot of truth to the adage that says if you repeat something long enough, eventually people will believe it.

Satan's Quest

Satan also knows better than to move too quickly. The master of deception, he is slowly, meticulously, fitting together a global noose that will eventually allow him total control of the world. With that control, he can compel people to worship him. From the beginning, that's what he's always wanted.

> But you (Satan) said in your heart,
> I will ascend to heaven;
> I will raise my throne above the stars of God,
> And I will sit on the mount of assembly
> In the recesses of the north
> I will ascend above the heights of the clouds;
> I will make myself like the Most High (Isaiah 14:13,14).

He even had the audacity to try to persuade Jesus to worship him.

> Again, the devil took Him to a very high mountain, and showed Him all the kingdoms of the world, and their glory; and he said to Him, All these things will I give You, if You fall down and worship me (Matthew 4:8,9).

But what he couldn't get Jesus to do, he will succeed in forcing the whole world to do.

> The man of lawlessness is revealed, the son of destruction, who opposes and exalts himself above every so-called god or object of worship, so that he takes his seat in the temple of God, displaying himself as being God (2 Thessalonians 2:3).

> And he causes all, the small and the great, and the rich and the poor, and the free men and the slaves, to be given a mark on their right hand, or on their forehead, and [he provides] that no one should be able to buy or to sell, except the one who has the mark, [either] the name

of the beast or the number of his name (Revelation 13:16,17).

That's total global control. But how is this possible? How could the world, with its vast size and diversity, be moved to the point of total control by one force? Can the British and the Chinese bank together? Can the Jews and the Muslims worship together? Can the Africans and the Japanese agree to be governed under the same authority? Not unless God's permissive will allows it. And He will.

The Balance of Good and Evil

God currently allows a delicate balance of good and evil in the universe. We live in a period defined by most scholars as the "Church Age," during which the Holy Spirit is present on earth and offsets Satan's every move. Even with the rapid growth of seemingly unrestrained evil, Christianity nevertheless continues to grow in numbers and maturity. For every depraved act, there is a righteous deed. As evil builds upon evil, Christianity builds on the Rock. Both evil and good are increasing proportionately on the scales until the day when God removes the counterweight, leaving evil no restraint.

> For the mystery of lawlessness is already at work; only he who now restrains [will do so] until he is taken out of the way (2 Thessalonians 2:7).

This balance will come to a screeching halt when God removes the Holy Spirit, containing the true Body of Christian Believers, from the earth, formally ending the Church Age. Then and only then will Satan have his prophesied day of unrestricted godlessness—if only for a time.

> Woe to the earth and the sea, because the devil has come down to you, having great wrath, knowing that he has [only] a short time (Revelation 12:12b).

Satan's Latter-Day Tactics

Until that time, and as evil grows, Satan desires to influence ungodly deeds to his advantage. After all, he is the "god" of this earth.

> The god of this world has blinded the minds of the unbelieving, that they might not see the light of the gospel of

the glory of Christ, who is the image of God (2 Corinthians 4:4).

Whether it's in the political, economic, or religious arena, Satan
continues to gain more and more control. His followers, knowingly
or unknowingly, are getting the earth ready for his takeover. As for
the last 2000 years, the true Church—and specifically the American Christians with their world-wide influence—is still his nemesis
and therefore his target. Satan has worked hard to compromise the
testimony of these Western saints. And it really hasn't been that difficult. His chief weapon? Appealing to mankind's sin nature, something God warned Christians to guard against.

> For all that is in the world, the lust of the flesh and the
> lust of the eyes and the boastful pride of life, is not from
> the Father, but is *from the world* (1 John 2:16, emphasis
> added).

The lust of the flesh, the lust of the eyes, and the pride of life
can all be enticed with one thing: money. Through the lure of
money, Satan has achieved in one generation almost everything he
needs for total control. Christians and non-Christians alike are
embroiled daily in the evils of misplaced priorities.

It's not too difficult to understand how non-believers are led
astray. Satan is their father. Not surprisingly, they trust their father
and their father has lied to them.

> *You are of [your] father* the devil, and you want to do the
> desires of your father. He was a murderer from the begin-
> ning, and does not stand in the truth, because there is no
> truth in him. Whenever he speaks a lie, he speaks from
> his own [nature;] for he is a liar, and the father of lies
> (John 8:44, emphasis added).

What Happened to Christians in America?

It may be easy to see how non-Christians are suckered in by
Satan, but it's downright embarrassing that Christians are so easily
deceived. We should know better. Yet we often fall for the same lies
as the non-Christians: "Have it all" and "have it now." And nowhere
in the world is this more obvious than in the United States, the
home of the most economically viable body of believers in the world.
Satan has to compromise the nation that was built on Christian

principles and, in its early years, led by godly men who openly trusted God.

Because of the Christian foundation laid by the founding fathers, the 1800s in the United States saw great revivals. Men like Jonathan Edwards and D.L. Moody led tens of thousands to a saving knowledge of Jesus Christ. By the middle of the nineteenth century, Christian ideals, principles, and influence permeated every corner of the U.S. The nation had come through a long depression that helped build strong families which depended on God. Even the vast majority of non-Christians were aware of God and acted on biblical morals. America was great because America was good. And America was good because she was founded on the Judeo/Christian principles found in the Bible.

> Do not be anxious then, saying, "What shall we eat?" or "What shall we drink?" or "With what shall we clothe ourselves?" For all these things the Gentiles eagerly seek; for your heavenly Father knows that you need all these things. *But seek first His kingdom and His righteousness; and all these things shall be added to you* (Matthew 6:31-33, emphasis added).

Yet, within just 50 short years, Satan has managed to spiritually derail the most solidly Christian nation in the world. Today, in the 1990s, a majority of believers totally misses the Christ-centeredness taught in the Bible. Instead, they have allowed Satan to slowly and gently steer them away from biblical principles and entice them to center their lives around what they want and what they think they should have. Few American Christians diligently seek out what God would desire in their lives.

Satan knows better than to try to trim the top of the tree in order to ensure lasting changes. Rather, he works from the bottom up and he began deep within Christendom. In the 1950s, seminaries began turning out liberal pastors who openly defied the Doctrine of Inerrancy of Scripture. By the 1960s, this watered-down doctrine began to take its toll. With cracks in its biblical foundation, the church began to have less and less influence. More and more people looked to the government, not God, for meeting housing needs, training their children, regulating their lives, and settling disagreements. And, there to fill the gap, was Satan, disguised as "bank credit" to provide the "good things" in life. Christians fell for the ruse hook, line, and sinker, seeking every material possession available as if they were managing their own money instead of acting as stewards of God's assets. Today in America, it seems that Christians and non-Christians differ little in their emphasis on material possessions.

Debt: The Spiritual Barometer

Larry Burkett, who teaches Christians how to manage their money according to scriptural principles, has often said that he can tell a great deal about one's spiritual condition and priorities by analyzing his or her cancelled checks. It's easy to see the order of our priorities by looking at where we spend our money.

"Number one" of God's Ten Commandments warns us: "You shall have no other gods before me" (Exodus 20:3).

Satan has done a masterful job of turning money—and what it can buy—into our god of choice and he has used it to preoccupy Christians while he systematically dismantles our foundations. American Christians choose to forget biblical principles and, as a result, spend money on misplaced priorities, which can be translated "ungodly purchases."

Optional debt, that debt which we create by borrowing in order to have something sooner rather than later, is one good example of misplaced priorities by American Christians. For instance, a car loan represents optional debt. If we desire a car so badly that we can't wait to save the money to purchase it, then we take on optional debt. If we charge a vacation, a washing machine, or a television, and don't pay the entire bill when it comes due, we add to our optional debt. It would be easy to argue that acquiring optional debt is pure and simple sin because it circumvents, rather than waits on, God's timing for provision.

Of course, not all debt is optional debt. And borrowing is not an across-the-board evil. But God does warn us about the realities of borrowing money unnecessarily: "The rich rules over the poor, And the borrower [becomes] the lender's slave" (Proverbs 22:7).

There are times when, because of unforeseen circumstances, a person may need to borrow money just to feed his family. Or a medical cost may come out of nowhere. But that's not why most people borrow. Christians, just like non-Christians, borrow to have it now rather than later. They elect to circumvent God's provision and to operate on their own timetable rather than God's.

This is not a gray area. Having tons of debt is not of God; therefore, it is of Satan. And it has cost the Christian community dearly: billions of dollars annually in interest alone. Billions of God's assets wasted because of undisciplined lifestyles.

> Let your character be free from the love of money, *being content with what you have;* for He Himself has said, "I will never desert you, nor will I ever forsake you" (Hebrews 13:5, emphasis added).

Subtly using the lust of the eyes, Satan has tied the fiscal hands of Christians in the most economically influential nation in the world. Many American Christians are knee-deep in the world's system. Because of this, they have to walk to the world's beat, making it that much easier for Satan to orchestrate his evil plans.

Satan Attacks the Family

Combining both the lust of the eyes and the pride of life, Satan has used money to achieve his goal of splitting apart the foundation of the family unit in America. God charges men with three primary jobs: provision, teaching, and protection. Satan knows Scripture; he quoted it out of context to Jesus in the desert. His evil scheming has worked so well that today, the average Christian man in America has failed in all three areas. And because of that, America has lost its godly direction.

The Husband As a Provider

The most basic duty of the husband is to provide for his family. The Bible puts it in rather harsh terms:

> But *if anyone does not provide for his own,* and especially for those of his household, he has denied the faith, and *is worse than an unbeliever* (1 Timothy 5:8, emphasis added).

Worse than an unbeliever! But God tells us He will reward the hard-working, Christ-centered husband:

> When you shall eat of the fruit of your hands,
> You will be happy and *it will be well with you* (Psalm 128:2, emphasis added).

Even more interesting is the following verse, which is also part of the reward for the hard-working husband:

> *Your wife* shall be like a fruitful vine,
> *Within your house,*
> Your children like olive plants
> Around your table (Psalm 128:3, emphasis added).

God promises that if a man is diligent, works hard, and trusts Him, he will be rewarded by his wife being at home. In fact, in his letter to Titus, Paul specifically said women should work at home.

> Older women likewise are to be reverent in their behavior, not malicious gossips, nor enslaved to much wine, teaching what is good, that they may encourage the young women to love their husbands, to love their children, [to be] sensible, pure, *workers at home,* kind, being subject to their own husbands, that the word of God may not be dishonored (Titus 2:3-5, emphasis added).

In the Old Testament, the husband is commanded to stay home with his new bride.

> When a man takes a new wife, he shall not go out with the army, nor be charged with any duty; he shall be free at home one year and shall give happiness to his wife whom he has taken (Deuteronomy 24:5).

That gave the husband a full year at home to not only get to know his wife, but also to teach her spiritual things—which is his God-ordained responsibility.

> And if they desire to learn anything, let them ask their own husbands at home; for it is improper for a woman to speak in church (1 Corinthians 14:35).

The husband providing for the family, with home as the foundation, used to be as American as the stars and stripes. And this was a major deterrent to Satan's grand plan until he used, again, money and easy credit as a vehicle to break up the family. Impatient, and wanting to have more, there are husbands have sent their wives to work outside the home, and there are wives who have entered the work force of their own accord. And once outside the home, and outside the husband's protective covering, Satan has pounded away on wives with lies from the feminist movement.

Too many Christians see nothing wrong with women working outside the home—merely for more money. The most precious asset God gave man, a loving help mate, seems to be worth more in purchasing power than for that purpose God intended—becoming a supporting wife. Satan has simply made it a priority to get mom out of the house, and with her has gone the family. The sensitive and supportive side of the marriage has poured the best part of her day into pursuing the material things for which husband and wife can't wait. And by so distracting the guard of the home-front, Satan has been able to take easy shots at other areas of the family: it has been open season.

Satan knows Scripture charges men with the responsibility of elevating their wives to the highest degree.

> Husbands, love your wives, *just as Christ also loved the church* and gave Himself up for her (Ephesians 5:25, emphasis added).

Satan has worked hard to get husbands to equate love with the value of material presents given to their wives. But God equates love with patience.

> Love is *patient*... (1 Corinthians 13:4a).

Impatience to have material things has in America today given Satan a wedge with which to begin dismantling the family unit. Many wives, when working outside the home, often must expend their best energy and attention on the job, leaving little for husband and family. Rather than her day peaking at home, she crashes. Emotionally and physically drained, she becomes far less the wife and mother she wants to be or God intended her to be.

The toll has, of course, been devastating. Satan has been able, in many cases, to enter the home through drugs, ungodly music, unsafe friends, advertising propaganda, and hundreds of other ways. The love and pursuit of money in our nation and the consequences thereof bear out the truth of God's Word:

> For the *love* of money is a root of all sorts of evil, and some by longing for it have wandered away from the faith, and pierced themselves with many a pang (1 Timothy 6:10, emphasis added).

Divorce is as commonplace among Christians in America as it is among non-Christians. Incredibly, one of every two "Christian" marriages ends in divorce. And, despite the extra income provided by working wives, the number one reason cited for divorce is money problems. But, in truth, money has not been the problem.

The children of Christian homes, the building blocks of future Christian strongholds with value far exceeding rubies, have been severely neglected. These children have paid a great price for moms who are gone during the day and whose sensitivity is dulled at night. Women, who have been equipped with a special, God-given love for their children, often don't have the sensitivity to pick up on the little signals after shouldering the responsibilities and priorities demanded by their jobs. And when they do pick up on such subtleties, they're often too tired and exhausted to exert more than a token effort at resolving the problem. And deep down, women know this, so guilt reigns. All because husbands want "things" more than they want to serve God.

The Husband as a Teacher

The man of the family—not the woman, not the church—is also charged with teaching his family. And the most important thing he is to teach his children is spiritual truth. Yet many Christian men allow their kids to be shuttled to and from schools that forbid the mention of Jesus' name while actively promoting the godless principles of Satan.

Many schools themselves are in a free-fall downward toward total depravity, teaching everything and anything but Jesus Christ. Public schools more and more emphasize social engineering and less and less emphasize the basics such as science, math, and history. Today, schools don't "educate," they "train." The new Outcome-Based Education and Goals 2000 programs teach children not to think for themselves, but to react. And they teach that the correct reactions are based on an atheistic worldview; God can't be mentioned.

Perverted so-called lifestyles and activities are given equal credibility with the traditional family. This redefining of family structure contributes to rampant drug abuse and crime. Rapes devastate lives daily. Negative, non-Christian peer pressure is strong. The instruction offered at many public schools advocates New Age and occultic thinking, which are satanic in origin. Tragically, many

Christian parents continue to send their kids to these kinds of schools. And that's exactly what Satan wants, because Christian schools, and especially home schools, can be a major deterrent to his plan.

The problem, however, is not with the schools, but with the Christian fathers. God is clear in his instruction to fathers:

> And you shall love the LORD your God with all your heart and with all your soul and with all your might. And *these words,* which I am commanding you today, shall be on your heart; and *you shall teach them diligently to your sons* and shall talk of them *when you sit* in your house and *when you walk* by the way and *when you lie down* and *when you rise up.* And you shall bind them as a sign on your hand and *they shall be as frontals on your forehead.* And you shall *write them on the doorposts of your house* and on your gates (Deuteronomy 6:5-9, emphasis added).

Teaching children is supposed to be an all-day affair, with the entire process overseen by the husband. A typical child's day should be oriented around God, Scripture, and praise. But by using tools such as debt, working wives, and the ever-present enticement to buy more things, Satan has kept most husbands' eyes off of the Lord and away from the truth.

The Husband As a Protector

The third and the most important accomplishment of Satan as he readies the world for his control has been the demise of the husband's role as a protector of his family. God warns that our biggest battles are against spiritual forces.

> Put on the full armor of God, that you may be able to stand firm against the schemes of the devil. For *our struggle is not against flesh and blood, but against the rulers, against the powers, against the world forces of this darkness,* against the spiritual [forces] of wickedness in the heavenly [places] (Ephesians 6:11-12, emphasis added).

Today, it is difficult to locate a man in America who teaches the Bible to his family the way God intended; prays *with* his family morning, noon, and night; or is a living testament of faith by trusting God in every facet of life. How few men really understand, biblically, where they have been, where they now are, and where they are going.

Satan has succeeded in neutralizing America, a once-great Christian nation. In the past, this great country has been used by God in so many wonderful ways. But now, the United States is no longer a hindrance to Satan's grand plan. Instead, America has become a tool of evil conquest. Worldwide, she actively promotes an environment for Satan to control the world. America's leaders are corrupt, her finances on borrowed time. Satan has, sadly, won this battle by compromising Christian men with misplaced priorities.

Worldwide, Satan is still being checked by the Holy Spirit as thousands of new believers come to a saving knowledge of Jesus, mainly in Third World countries. But to Satan's credit, his world-wide noose is ever-tightening. And when that day comes, when the restraint is lifted, the big lie will unfold, and a new era will begin: the prophesied era of total global godlessness.

> And then that lawless one will be revealed whom the Lord will slay with the breath of His mouth and bring to an end by the appearance of His coming; [that is,] the one whose coming is in accord with the activity of Satan, with all power and signs and false wonders, and with all the deception of wickedness for those who perish, because they did not receive the love of the truth so as to be saved. And for this reason God will send upon them a deluding influence so that they might believe what is false, in order that they all may be judged who did not believe the truth, but took pleasure in wickedness (2 Thessalonians 2:8-12).

And America, which seems to be growing into the daughter of the Babylonian system, will come to its end. Some have even suggested that the following verses may actually be written about her demise:

> After these things I saw another angel coming down from heaven, having great authority, and the earth was illumined with his glory. And he cried out with a mighty voice, saying, Fallen, fallen is Babylon the great! And she has become a dwelling place of demons and a prison of every unclean spirit, and a prison of every unclean and hateful bird. For all the nations have drunk of the wine of the passion of her immorality,

and the kings of the earth have committed [acts of] immorality with her, and the merchants of the earth have become rich by the wealth of her sensuality. And I heard another voice from heaven, saying, Come out of her, my people, that you may not participate in her sins and that you may not receive of her plagues; for her sins have piled up as high as heaven, and God has remembered her iniquities. Pay her back even as she has paid, and give back [to her] double according to her deeds; in the cup which she has mixed, mix twice as much for her. To the degree that she glorified herself and lived sensuously, to the same degree give her torment and mourning; for she says in her heart, *I sit [as] a queen and I am not a widow,* and will never see mourning. For this reason in one day her plagues will come, pestilence and mourning and famine, and she will be burned up with fire; for the Lord God who judges her is strong. And the kings of the earth, who committed [acts of] immorality and lived sensuously with her, will weep and lament over her when they see the smoke of her burning, standing at a distance because of the fear of her torment, saying, Woe, woe, the great city, Babylon, the strong city! For in one hour your judgment has come. And the merchants of the earth weep and mourn over her, because no one buys their cargoes any more; cargoes of gold and silver and precious stones and pearls and fine linen and purple and silk and scarlet, and every [kind of] citron wood and every article of ivory and every article [made] from very costly wood and bronze and iron and marble, and cinnamon and spice and incense and perfume and frankincense and wine and olive oil and fine flour and wheat and cattle and sheep, and [cargoes] of horses and chariots and slaves and human lives. And the fruit you long for has gone from you, and all things that were luxurious and splendid have passed away from you and [men] will no longer find them. The merchants of these things, who became rich from her, will stand at a distance because of the fear of her torment, weeping and mourning, saying, Woe, woe, the great city, she who was clothed in fine linen and purple and scarlet, and adorned with gold and precious stones and pearls; for in one hour such great wealth has been laid waste! And every shipmaster and every passenger and sailor, and as many as make their living by the sea, stood at a distance, and were crying out as they saw the smoke of her burning, saying, What [city] is like the great city? And they threw dust on their heads and were crying out, weeping and mourning, saying, Woe, woe, the great city, in which all who had ships at sea became rich by her wealth, for in one hour she has been laid waste! Rejoice over her, O heaven, and you saints and apostles and prophets, because God has pronounced judgment for you against her. And a strong angel took up a stone like a great millstone and threw it into the sea, saying, Thus will Babylon, the great city, be thrown down with violence, and will not be found any longer. And the sound of harpists and musicians and flute-players and trumpeters will not be heard in you any longer; and no craftsman of any craft will be found in you any longer; and the sound of a mill will not be heard in you any longer; and the light of a lamp will not shine in you any longer; and the voice of the bridegroom and bride will not be heard in you any longer; for your merchants were the great men of the earth, because all the nations were deceived by your sorcery. And in her was found the blood of prophets and of saints and of all who have been slain on the earth (Revelation 18, emphasis added).

▼   ▼   ▼

CHAPTER 3

Harbingers of Humanism's Hurricane

Daymond R. Duck

Harbingers are people, signs or things that announce or foretell something before it happens. John the Baptist was a harbinger of the first coming of Jesus when he cried, "Prepare ye the way of the Lord, make his paths straight" (Matthew 3:3). He was a harbinger of the death of Jesus when he said, "Behold the Lamb of God, which taketh away the sin of the world" (John 1:29). Jonah was a harbinger of the death, burial, and resurrection of Jesus when he spent three days and three nights in the belly of a whale (Matthew 12:38-40). Budding trees are a harbinger of spring. Falling leaves are a harbinger of winter. Harbingers are forerunners of things to come.

Humanism is the philosophy and vain deceit of worldly men who have accepted the false and dark teachings of a godless society while rejecting the true and clear teachings of the Bible (Colossians 2:8). Humanists do not believe our God is the Creator of all things. They say, "No deity will save us; we must save ourselves." They say, "Promises of immortal salvation or fear of eternal damnation are both illusory and harmful." They say, "We strive for the good life, here and now"—their "good life" including abortion, homosexuality,

lesbianism, euthanasia, assisted suicide, etc. They say, "our commitment to all mankind is the highest commitment of which we are
capable." In short, humanists have rejected the Christian's God,
the Christian's Savior, and the Christian's Bible (see Humanist Manifesto I and II).

Hurricanes begin as pleasing gentle breezes. When they blow
stronger, they are called trade winds. In some cases, the helpful trade
winds turn into tropical depressions. Some tropical depressions turn
into tropical storms. And some tropical storms turn into hurricanes.
The hurricanes begin as minimal damage or Category I hurricanes.
Some become moderate damage or Category II hurricanes, some
extensive damage or Category III hurricanes, some extreme damage
or Category IV hurricanes, and a few become catastrophic damage or
Category V hurricanes. These are among the costliest, deadliest, and
most destructive of all disasters. Overwhelming winds, torrential
rains, flooding, and the resulting tornadoes can cut a trail of chaos
and devastation hundreds of miles long. Some hurricanes affect
whole continents. Some last for weeks.

Harbingers of humanism's hurricane are signs that a very
influential group of Christ-rejecting humanists are on the brink of
initiating a worldwide storm of apocalyptic proportions, a storm
more devastating than the combined destruction of all Category V
hurricanes ever to ravage the earth. These humanists are usually
intellectuals or high achievers, or both, in the fields of law, religion,
government, industry, science, and business. Many sincerely believe
they are going to eliminate bigotry, poverty, racism, war, and the
like. They truly believe they are laying the foundation for an
improved world—a new and better world. They believe their form
of knowledge is higher than ours and that they know what is best
for every human being on earth. They even believe, in their vanity,
that they have the right to make those decisions. But some have no
religion. Some are involved in the occult. Some worship pagan gods
and goddesses. And because they have rejected the true God of the
Bible, they lack real spiritual wisdom and have darkened minds. So,
step-by-step, they are ignorantly and unwittingly fulfilling the bleak
visions of Bible prophets who forecast a coming day of world government accompanied by a storm from the heart of hell (Zephaniah
1:15; Revelation 13). Here in America, where we are supposed to
have a government "of the people, by the people and for the

people," what these humanists are doing should be called "tyranny."

A UN World Government

Batten down the hatches! Ominous black clouds are swirling all around us and the entire world is showing signs of a major storm. Satan's age-old blueprint for world domination is finally being transformed into a world government in the form of the United Nations. Around the world, decisions are being made behind closed doors to usurp the sovereignty of nations by absorbing them into an all-powerful United Nations world regime. In New York, Rio de Janeiro, Vienna, Cairo, Copenhagen, Beijing, Istanbul, Washington, and a host of other major cities far and near, decisions have already been made and implemented to give the United Nations power and authority over the entire world. Every individual on earth is being affected. It is now easy to see the dark days of a United Nations-created world government on the turbulent horizon. The entire world will soon come under the domination of a popular, peace-preaching politician who will later shed his peace-maker image and be revealed as the Serpent-inspired Antichrist.

UN Treaties

In less time than many think, a one-world government will be in place. The United Nations is gaining this awesome status through treaties, most of which are coming into effect because they are being willingly signed by supportive and gullible national leaders. But in some developing countries, they are coming into effect as the direct result of extortion and threats from two of the major orchestrators of world government: the World Bank and the U.S. State Department.

The United States is one example. The Constitution of the United States sets forth the fundamental laws of our country. Those laws establish the nature of our national government. Article VI of our Constitution contains a clause called the supremacy clause. In part, it says,

> All treaties made, or which shall be made, under the authority of the United States, shall be the supreme law of the land; and the judges in every state shall be bound

thereby, anything in the constitution or laws of any state
to the contrary notwithstanding.

Most authorities agree that this means when our state laws conflict with our national laws, the national laws are superior. They
even say that it means when our national laws conflict with our
treaties, the treaties are superior. That puts a powerful punch into
our treaties. They override our federal, state, and local laws. They
cede some of our national sovereignty to other powers. Thus, every
treaty bears the potential of turning partial control of our lives over
to a global body.

Iraq is a second example. When Saddam Hussein started the
Persian Gulf War by sending troops into Kuwait, the United States
was recognized as the most powerful nation on earth. We did not
need anyone's approval to throw the Iraqis out. But President
George Bush turned to the United Nations for permission to act.
After his overwhelming force proved successful, the United Nations
used its position of power to extract treaties from Saddam Hussein.
Those treaties eroded some of Iraq's national sovereignty. Saddam
was forced to receive United Nations inspectors. He was required to
reveal certain military secrets. And he had to stop selling valuable
oil until he complied. He is currently receiving approval to sell
small quantities of oil, but all sales must comply with United
Nations-dictated guidelines.

In Somalia, United Nations troops were deployed ostensibly to
feed the poor. They did. But the United Nations also used the occasion to establish the government it wanted. In Haiti, the United
Nations authorized the United States to deploy warships under the
guise of bringing down a renegade general. They did. But they also
used that force to set up the regime of a United Nations-approved
political leader.

In some countries, the force has been economic pressure
instead of planes, ships, bombs, and troops. Nations turning to the
International Monetary Fund and the World Bank for financial
assistance have had to wait on approval until they signed certain
agreements. This has been an effective way of forcing renegade
nations into signing treaties they might not otherwise sign. Busi-
nesswoman and free-lance journalist Joan M. Veon has spoken to
many African delegations about the economic threats they receive
from the World Bank, but their response was they dare not pull

their membership out of the World Bank for fear of grave economic sanctions. Soon small and great, rich and poor, free and bond from every kindred, tongue, people, and nation on earth will be forced to bow down to the commands of this wicked world government and its one-world leader.

Going, Going, Gone

In her *Briefing Book: UN Conferences and Goals and How They Will Affect the Family, the Church, and Society,* Joan M. Veon writes,

> When most states have agreed to a treaty, it may be considered to represent "customary" international law—law that is binding on all states, even those who *have not* indicated their agreement to the treaty[1] [emphasis added].

How about that! Under international law, nations may be considered bound by treaties they never ratified. Even worse, in cases where a head of state signs a treaty that has not been approved by the proper body, that nation can still be considered bound by the treaty.

That is exactly what is happening in the United States. For a treaty to be ratified in this country, it must pass with at least two-thirds of the vote in the Senate. Then it must be signed by the President. Even though a 1989 treaty called "The United Nations Convention on the Rights of the Child" has not passed in the Senate, President Clinton still signed it. That puts it into effect under international law. And to top that, First Lady Hillary Rodham Clinton is using the White House Women's Commission to implement it through action and mandate.

Consider what that does:

- The Bible teaches Christians to discipline their children (Proverbs 22:15; 23:13). But under international law, children now have the right to freedom from all forms of physical and mental violence. The parental right to spank children is now gone.

- The Bible teaches Christians to attend church (Hebrews 10:25). But under international law, children now have the right to freedom of religion. The parental right to require children to attend church is now gone.

- The Bible teaches Christians the lust of the eyes is not of God (1 John 2:16). But under international law, children now have the right to obtain information on sexual matters. The parental right to deny children access to pornography is now gone.

- The Bible teaches Christians to put God before all other gods (Exodus 20:3). But under international law, children now have the right to freedom of assembly. So the parental right to pull children out of cults, drug gangs, and the like is now gone.

We do not have to fly around in a hurricane-hunter airplane to see what is happening. Under the banner of protecting children, a humanist world government is putting Christians in the position of having to choose between obeying God's Word or obeying international law. Violators are not currently being punished, but when the courts are empowered they will be. Then an evil world government can easily throw down the gauntlet and turn this into a Christian holocaust.

Persecution

Jesus was talking about the Tribulation Period when He said, "children shall rise up against their parents, and shall cause them to be put to death" (Mark 13:12). The apostle Paul identified one of the signs of the last days as children who are "disobedient to parents" (2 Timothy 3:2). That violent conflict between children and parents could be one of the things Jesus was referring to when He said, "Then shall they deliver you up to be afflicted, and shall kill you: and ye shall be hated of all nations for my name's sake" (Matthew 24:9). That is hard to imagine. But we need to keep something in mind: It is easier for heaven and earth to pass away than it is for one jot or tittle of Bible prophecy to go unfulfilled.

Too many people are thinking, "This hurricane won't hit me." But the weather patterns are shifting, the climate is changing, and there won't be any safe havens. The Biblical weather vane says this hurricane will strike the whole earth. What will happen when a Christian father's desire for his child to attend church conflicts with the child's international right to freedom of assembly? What will happen when a Christian mother's desire to control what her child observes conflicts with the child's international right to view pornography on the Internet? We need to stop pulling the ostrich routine. It will be difficult for any parent to fight child abuse charges under international law.

The UN Conference on Environment and Development (a.k.a. The Earth Summit)

In 1992, bureaucrats and environmental extremists from 178 nations answered the call to meet in Rio de Janeiro to develop, strengthen, and finalize plans for tackling global environmental concerns. The stated purpose of that meeting was to find ways to protect the earth's ozone layer, to control global warming, to limit greenhouse gas emissions, to protect the world's plants and animals, etc. That was not the first meeting for many of these people. Some had been part of a 1988 meeting that successfully developed plans to phase out the use of CFCs in aerosol cans, air conditioners, refrigerators, insulation products, and industrial cleansers.

Most Christians are not against that. In fact, most quickly agree that there is nothing wrong with protecting the environment, developing cleaner-burning fuels, stopping the destruction of natural resources, eliminating wasteful practices, and preventing the deforestation of our planet. Some Christians are actively involved in environmental clean-up programs, some are organizing and participating in recycling programs, and some are using their hard-earned assets to help out. Some are giving their time to educate people on the importance of these things. Some are even changing their lifestyles to accomplish these things. They rightly believe that all these things fall under God's instructions for us to take care of His creation.

But more than a few Christians are against the godless humanists with a hidden agenda for world control who are pushing through treaties that wipe out our national sovereignty, treaties that give foreigners say-so over large areas of our country, treaties that elevate the status of trees and animals above the status of human beings, treaties that allow international bureaucrats to use "junk science" to create, exaggerate, and perpetuate false crises to justify the seizing of power, and treaties that turn control of large areas of our lives over to an antichrist world government. Many Christians question the compassion and morality of people who scream at the death of one baby seal while applauding the death of millions of unborn children, who chain themselves to trees to protect one spotted owl while refusing to lift a finger to help the multitudes who lost their jobs in the process, who ruin a man for plowing in his own field and jail a man for selling a can of Freon to go in an automobile air conditioner. Many Christians question the motives and sanity of those who want to require a couple to get a license to have children, who want to put sterilants in public drinking water to destroy the ability of people to have children, and who think the eradication of the sick and elderly is a proper solution to food shortages, the high cost of health care, etc. Many Christians believe the Word of God has been turned upside down and discarded by those who obviously value bugs, fish, owls, rats, rocks, seals, snails, trees, whales, creeks, rivers, and lakes more than they value precious God-given human life.

The Convention of Biological Diversity

One treaty coming out of the Earth Summit is popularly called the "Bio-Diversity Treaty." That treaty requires companies that create and sell products derived from plants and animals to share their profits with the countries from which those plants and animals originated. It also calls for designating large areas of the United States as "biosphere reserves." An estimated 51 million acres of land have already been gobbled up and classified as "World Heritage Sites." They include such highly cherished areas as the Grand Canyon, the Smoky Mountains, the Everglades, Yosemite, and Yellowstone. In the not-too-distant future, most United States citizens will be unable to do anything with, or in, these areas without United Nations approval. Obtaining that will be next to impossible and violators will be severely punished under international law.

But it does not end there. Plans have already been made to set aside several million more acres around these parks by having them classified as "buffer zones." Development, mining, and other activities in these areas will not be controlled as tightly as in the biosphere reserves, but it will still be greatly restricted. That is why people living in these areas are already losing their jobs and property. That is why World Heritage Committee members from Europe and Asia traveled to Wyoming in 1995 to seize and shutdown the privately owned Crown Butte's New World gold mine.[2] That is why many of our best citizens will have to relocate to other parts of the country in not too many years.

And there is more. Those dedicated to this cause hope to eventually set restrictions on how approximately one-half of the United States can be used. To protect plants and animals, efforts will be made to restore large areas of the nation back to the conditions that existed before Columbus discovered America. Do not think this is far-fetched. Much of the world already thinks Americans consume, own, and pollute too much. They want a share of what we have and something done to slow us down. When they out-vote us in the United Nations, our citizens will vacate the biosphere reserves, some of our jobs might be moved to other countries, and we might park our automobiles, melt our plows, get out our hoes, turn off our machines, work with our hands, and leap back into the horse-and-buggy days.

Former United States President George Bush refused to sign this treaty for two reasons. He said it would be very expensive to enforce, and it would cost American corporations too much to comply. Senator Jesse Helms blocked it in the Senate Foreign Relations Committee. He and several other faithful senators said major revisions were needed to protect America's interests. But President Clinton comes from a different mold. He signed it in 1993.

Bio-Diversity in Maryland

Hurricane warning flags are popping in the gusty wind all along the beautiful coasts of Maryland. Efforts are now being made to turn the Old Line State into a biodiversity testing ground. Two bills, known as "Rural Legacy" and "Smart Growth," are already pending in the state House and Senate to create and empower a new form of government. If ratified, the new government will then dictate and control all development so that large areas of the state can be sealed off. People living in those areas will receive no state funding for things like hospitals, job programs, libraries, schools, welfare, and the like. Highways, water lines, gas lines, and power lines will be built around those areas, but not to, through, or in them. Unemployment will rise, forcing job seekers to relocate. The loss of government money will force people needing assistance to move to approved areas. Private property rights will be wiped out, causing property values to plunge and forcing people to sell their land and buildings to the new government. Critics say the net effect will be to force people into government-approved "human islands" or "human habitat" zones. Wake up America! The weather is changing. Many foreigners and intellectuals do not understand how radical they are. They believe all property belongs to the world. A humanist hurricane is building and some of the best things that ever happened to us are already being blown away.

The UN Convention on Human Rights
(a.k.a. The World Conference on Human Rights)

In 1993, delegates and activists from nearly 180 nations traveled to Vienna, Austria, to establish a long list of international human rights. Their list included international economic rights, international cultural rights, and international social rights.

International economic rights clearly transfer the wealth of prosperous nations to impoverished nations. It is a slick way of saying that delegates want to turn the bounties of developed nations over to poorly developed nations and is nothing more than a redistribution of the world's wealth. More than a few call this socialism.

International cultural and social rights modify the conduct of men and women to conform to the politically correct wishes of a humanist, anti-Christ United Nations society. It eliminates all cultural and social practices based on the inferiority or superiority of either sex. Men and women can no longer be stereotyped into specific categories of employment or service. There can be no distinction among people as to race, sex, language, religion, or political opinion. The Bible's instructions regarding these issues mean nothing to these people, who have delegated to themselves the absolute right to define proper conduct. They want to micromanage our lives, standardize the cultures of the world, and minimize or eliminate all nationalism.

The UN International Conference on
Population and Development

In 1994, the United Nations delegates and extremists in the feminist movement met in Cairo, Egypt, to deal with women and their reproductive needs. Family planning and population control were high on the agenda. According to the Bible, abortion is wrong. Innocent blood is not something to be shed (Proverbs 6:16-19).

Children are not something to be killed (Exodus 20:13). But the United States delegation pushed hard to make this abomination an internationally recognized "right." That would force nations to legalize this shameful practice and require taxpayers to pay for it. The sordid attempt failed. But the radical feminists who dominated the United States delegation picked up valuable support. They resurrected the issue in later conferences and plan to keep raising it until they get it passed. When they do, Planned Parenthood will receive the funds to place abortion clinics and condom distribution centers in every town on earth. Mandatory population control, compulsory sterilization, and coerced abortions will roll across the globe like a giant, hurricane-induced tidal wave. Then all the legislative victories conservative Christians have won in recent years will immediately drown in the whipped-up sea of international laws.

The UN World Summit for Social Development (a.k.a. The Social Summit)

In March 1995, the moral climate continued to worsen as delegates and groups from 117 nations met in Copenhagen, Denmark, supposedly to deal with social issues. But it seems that a second and higher priority loomed underneath the wavy surface. Several world leaders attended, including United States Vice President Albert Gore, Jr., and First Lady Hillary Rodham Clinton. Mrs. Clinton announced that the United States would contribute an additional $118 million to worldwide social development causes. Included among these "causes" is funding to support abortion. Her generous gift of taxpayer dollars is enough to exterminate a large number of the world's unborn children.

Among the social issues discussed were things like poverty, unemployment, and social equality. Diversity was a favorite topic. The Biblical family begins with marriage between a man and a woman. But the word "family" was redefined to include homosexual marriages. The group is seeking to define the world's values with a World Social Charter and a World Constitution of Rights.

Education was a big issue—not education in reading, writing, and arithmetic, but rather, education on abortion, condoms, homosexual rights, euthanasia, and things like that. Outcome Based Education (OBE), Goals 2000, and groups like the Homosexual and Bi-sexual

Youth Clubs took root in United Nations conferences. They were built into treaties, fashioned into international law, and passed on to national leaders who pushed them down to the state and local level. Every level of America's once outstanding education system has been corrupted. That is why we now have these loathsome things polluting our local schools.

Architects of this summit called for a world tax to finance their global ambitions. They also pushed revising the United Nations Charter, giving themselves more power, allowing themselves more meetings, and expanding the powers of the International Court. They even took steps to turn the United Nations into a global cop with power to oversee the world's militaries.

The UN World Conference on Women
(a.k.a. The Women's Conference)

In September 1995, the growing hurricane strengthened again as the delegates and activists gathered in Beijing, China. First Lady Hillary Rodham Clinton headed up the United States group.

This group claimed it was meeting to deal with obstacles to the advancement of women. But it was obvious they wanted nothing to do with the important role of women as outlined in the Bible. Rather, the conference turned into a forum for an attack on traditional marriages. Delegates and activists described the family as a major cause of women's problems. They ignored the birth, nurture, and care of children, and they redefined the word "family" to include same-sex marriages. They expanded the word "gender" from two groups, male and female, to five groups: homosexual, bisexual, transsexual, male, and female. They praised homosexuality and lesbianism, despised traditional family relationships, and called men oppressors of women. They called women the objects of male domination and abuse, and they made another attempt to make abortion a human right and another attempt to end all discrimination against women.

The conference discussed economic equilibrium for women. Many delegates want women to hold half of all jobs, own half of all land, hold half of all offices, and control half of everything. If they get what they want, half of all military personnel, half of all business people, half of all construction workers, half of all preachers, half of all farmers, and half of every other occupation on earth will be female. Large companies will be hog-tied. And lawsuits will skyrocket.

What our precious and easily deceived children are being taught in school was a big issue again. Notice some of the things in the Draft Platform For Action:

> Article 74 reads, "Action should focus on elimination of social stereotypes from curricula, text books and teacher training…"

> Article 92 encourages the revision of "school curricula and teaching materials."

> Article 108 encourages the "dissemination of gender-sensitive programs."[3]

These people apparently believe that they are intellectually superior to everyone else. Their elitist mentality frames their opinion that they are the ones most qualified to decide what our children need to learn in school. They want complete control of our children so they can indoctrinate them with their pagan beliefs. They want to make the good and great God of the Bible irrelevant. They want to legislate an un-Christian worldview. And they want to push their social evils on the whole world.

This is a hurricane warning. We must recognize the intensity and gravity of this wicked storm, keeping in mind that these things are being presented in the form of treaties so they will be binding upon the United States and supersede all we do on the federal, state, and local level.

The UN Conference on Human Settlements (a.k.a. Habitat II)

In 1996, the political climate worsened when bureaucrats and activists traveled to Istanbul, Turkey, to set up what some are calling a "global dictatorship."[4] The main goal of that conference was to lay the foundation for achieving "sustainable development." According to Joan Veon:

> Sustainable development basically says that today's generation must ensure that future generations have the access to the same amount of resources which we have today. When you analyze this concept, you readily see

that it means that all phases of life and production must
be monitored as well as how much people consume. It
also means that the world must be equal with regard to
distribution or resources. What it does not mean is that a
person will continue to live life as we have known up
until this point for everything we do and eat must be
monitored so that the future generations will have some
resources too.[5]

Think about that! No individual on earth will be allowed to consume more than is needed for basic physical survival. In order to
reduce world consumption of food and raw materials, people will be
forced to reduce the size of their automobiles, houses, families, and
almost everything else. In order to ensure they are complying, all
buying and selling will have to be monitored. In order to be fair to
others in the world, wages will have to be standardized and consumption in wealthy nations will have to be drastically reduced.
Those who refuse to comply may well become statistics in what is
considered by some to be a badly needed and desirable population
reduction.

This program to control all buying and selling sounds a lot like
the dreaded Mark of the Beast of Revelation 13:16-18. The United
States is even selling super-computers to other nations to keep
track of such things. The prophetic implications are horrible.

There is more. The United Nations even wants to tell us what
kind of government we can have. The UN, no longer the paper tiger
that came on the scene as a gentle trade wind in 1945, is now a
blustering bureaucratic monster that thinks it has enough huff and
puff to dictate our laws. According to Trisha Katson,

The conference wants the UN to play global manager by
overseeing national, regional, state and local governments and by restructuring national governments and
cities. Unelected city administrators worldwide will be
asked to redesign regulations, political systems and judicial and legislative procedures to accomplish UN goals.

The UN has asked the lawmakers of sovereign nations to
restructure their political and legal systems to reach sustainable development goals.

> If U.S. lawmakers refuse to restructure the Constitution to fit this radical proposal, it appears the Habitat agenda will be dictatorially imposed upon the American people.
>
> A clue as to how Habitat II will be enforced and implemented is provided by a report from the 28-member UN-funded Commission on Global Governance. It was published after a three-year study. The 410-page *Our Global Neighborhood* calls for world government by the year 1998.[6]

The United Nations also wants to create a civil society with input from approved non-governmental organizations (NGOs). Approved NGOs are those sympathetic to these radical United Nations causes. They include such groups as Planned Parenthood, National Abortion Rights League, and the National Black Women's Health Project. Unapproved NGOs the United Nations is unwilling to hear from include such groups as Eagle Forum, Concerned Women of America, and National Right to Life. Notice that they do not want to hear from the Christian groups. They prefer to ignore God's answers to the world's problems. What kind of world government will we have if Christians are excluded from writing the laws? What kind of world religion will we have if Christians are not allowed to provide moral input? They certainly will not honor the Lord Jesus.

The World Food Summit

This 1996 summit in Rome, Italy, was a project of radicals in the UN Food and Agriculture Organization that dealt mainly with food and population control. To control hunger, this group wants to control population growth. To control population growth, it wants to control the size of the family. Sustainable development received a big boost at this summit. Commenting on sustainable development, David Rothbard of the Washington-based Committee For A Constructive Tomorrow said,

> It really is a very nebulous term. It can mean anything you want it to mean. What do they [UN delegates] say it means? They say that it means having a sustainable level of people, just a limited number of people, using a limited number of resources so that it would be able to sustain

our population and the earth's bounty for future generations. That's what they claim. In reality, sustainable development really means no development at all. What they
want to do is lower the standard of living in the United
States down to that of, say, Bangladesh. They believe, and
they have even had in their documents, many of the UN
documents, that they think that about one to two billion
people is a good carrying capacity. And that's why we need
to have measures to encourage, or some would even say,
control population so that we can really reduce the numbers down from about five and one-half or six billion right
now down to that one billion level.[7]

A Future World Conference

Plans are being made for a United Nations World Conference on
Global Governance to be held in 1998. Those working on this con-
tend that national sovereignty is outmoded, that the rights of
nations must give way to the interests of the global neighborhood.
They are trying to empower the United Nations in four areas:
Global Values, Global Security, Global Development, and Global
Governance. Let's look at these separately.

Global Values—The United Nations is trying to establish a long
list of universal values to guide nations and individuals. These
values will "transcend economic, national, religious and social division." They will not be Christian values. They will be the values of
the politically correct humanists, witches, mystics, goddess worshipers, peaceniks, environmentalists, and a wide assortment of
other ungodly activists who deem the blood of Jesus a repulsive
thought and bow down before the altars of Satan. These are people
who say nature is holy; people who have created a religion out of
the environment, people who perceive Judeo-Christian values a primary cause of the world's problems. They contend that the idea
that human beings are higher creatures than a plant or an animal is
wrong. They call people "the pollution of the earth," "the AIDS of
the earth," "a viral epidemic of the earth," etc.[8]

What we are seeing here is the rise of a would-be world religion,
a religion that is trying to establish a list of acceptable doctrines
and practices. Such a religion is what we might expect from
MYSTERY BABYLON THE GREAT, THE MOTHER OF HARLOTS

AND ABOMINATIONS OF THE EARTH (See Revelation 13:6; 17:1-18). Those who wonder about this need to look no further than Vice President Al Gore's book, *Earth in the Balance*. There the man who could be the next president of the United States expresses the belief that Christianity and the other religions that believe in one God cannot meet the needs of modern society. He believes we need a "pan-religious perspective" for our future one world religion. The coming False Prophet would love this un-Christian doctrine.

Global Security—The world government industry wants to establish a permanent United Nations army funded by international fees and taxes on such things as weapons sales, petroleum products, ocean fishing, ocean mining, international air travel, international sea travel, international mail, the buying and selling of national currencies, and more. With its own source of revenue, it would no longer be forced to rely on sovereign nations for money. It would not have to heed the demands of "rich nations" such as the United States. And it would be in a stronger position to force "rich nations" such as the United States to comply with its own sovereign will. Its world army would be authorized to cross borders. Its troops could intervene in the internal affairs of nations. They could disarm nations, restrict trade, confiscate privately owned firearms, and punish people in a wide variety of ways. This could be the beginning of the military superpower that dominates the world during the Tribulation Period (Revelation 13:4).

Beware of those who want to reduce military spending in the United States. Not all have pure motives. Some want the savings to go to the United Nations. They want the money spent on a global army with sole loyalty to a global government. They want American citizens to finance the world military and foreign citizens to control it. Because American troops might refuse to take on rebellious American citizens, they want foreign troops with powerful weapons stationed on United States soil. They want large military bases for those foreign troops and large detention centers run by foreigners inside our own borders. This Trojan horse will stir up more than the climatologists. And it will most surely energize those in the militia movement.

Global Development—The United Nations wants to give more power to the International Monetary Fund and the World Bank. It wants these institutions to manage the world's economy. It wants them to monitor and control financial investment and development around the world. Hopefully, they can alleviate poverty, immigration problems, pollution, land deterioration, and more. This amounts to nothing more than global control of the world's wealth. It will involve taxation to finance projects in poorly developed countries. It will include a way to monitor who is buying and selling. Authorities will need to know who is building, what they are building, where they are building, what they are tearing down, and more. Before that runs its course, many will have to take Satan's Mark (Revelation 13:16,17).

Global Governance—The United Nations wants to create an International Criminal Court, an International Citizens Court, and to expand the powers of the International Court of Justice. It also wants to increase the enforcement powers of the international legal system to finance and support a worldwide rule of law. Without these, how can a world government make war on individual citizens? How can it gain power over all kindreds, and tongues, and nations (Revelation 13:7)? It cannot. But with these it can use the bluster and thunder of scare tactics, large fines, and stiff jail sentences to bludgeon the citizens of the world into submission (Revelation 20:4).

Now think with me just a minute. Americans have learned the hard way that unelected judges consider constitutions to be their enemy. Some seem to love to declare things unconstitutional. What if these international judges do what some current American judges are doing? What if they start legislating from the bench? What if they start making law instead of interpreting law? What if they allow one person, the Antichrist or the False Prophet, to tell them how to rule on violations of international law?

The State of the World Forum

In September 1995, strong and threatening political winds blew at a very important conference in San Francisco. It was not a United Nations conference. But it was billed as "the birth of the first global civilization." And it was designed to increase the role of the United Nations in world government. So we can accurately call it a "United Nations-related conference."

Something dramatic happened on the third day of that event. The cherished flags of the many nations present were taken down and replaced with a golden image of the world's undivided land masses. Replacing all those once revered symbols with one new symbol was meant to signify the birth of a new world government.

Nearly 500 of the world's most powerful people attended, criticizing nationalism, democracy, and resistance to a United Nations world government and issuing calls to turn control of all nuclear weapons over to the United Nations. The "Final Report" recommended placing conventional military forces under the direction of United Nations commanders. These forces would be divided into regional forces given the authority to ignore borders, and they could attack deep within the heart of any nation, including the United States. This group plans to hold several more conferences by the year 2000.

Arms reduction sounds good. But with so many people hating America, it seems like a poor time to give control of our nuclear weapons to radicals and extremists from other countries, a poor time to put our troops under the command of foreigners, a poor time to send our loyal troops out of the country, and a poor time to beat our swords into plowshares. Is it wise to create an army more powerful than ours? Should we give anyone the authority to ignore our borders? Should we give some of our most powerful weapons to foreign troops and station them on our own soil? If we are not careful, our nation will be surrendered to the very kind of ugly tyranny America's founding fathers fled.

Taking Shape

When United Nations Secretary-General Boutros Boutros-Ghali spoke to world leaders in New York on October 24, 1996, he said this about the United Nations Charter:

> Chapter Eight of the charter refrains from defining very precisely what it means by "regional arrangements and agencies." But it clearly sees regionalism and internationalism working not at odds, but together.

He was talking about dividing the world government into regions. Depending upon who we listen to, anywhere from three to ten regions are envisioned. Each region will have a regional overlord with its own army.

In the thirteenth chapter of Revelation, we read about the rise of Antichrist. John says, "And I stood upon the sand of the sea, and saw a beast rise up out of the sea, having seven heads and ten horns, and upon his horns ten crowns, and upon his heads the name of blasphemy" (Revelation 13:1). According to the Bible, these ten horns with ten crowns represent ten kings or ten regional governments that will support, and reign with, the Antichrist during the turbulent Tribulation Period (Daniel 7:24; Revelation 17:12). The Antichrist will be a man who is so full of evil the Bible calls him a beast (Revelation 13:18). He will rise to power in Europe. From there he will move to the throne of world government. Then the hurricane will really start rolling.

Closing Remarks

All the prophetic indicators say the hurricane season has arrived. All the signs are pointing to one-world government. With the ability to enact taxes, and control of institutions like the World Bank and the IMF, this world government will soon be an economic superpower. With a military in control of all nuclear weapons, and regional armies to oversee the world, it will soon be a military superpower. With a worldwide set of social values that transcend all religious rights, it will soon be a religious superpower. With a system of courts, lawyers, and police to back it up, it will soon be a legal superpower. These are the traits of the satanic kingdom of Antichrist. And that is not something we should expect in the distant future. It is a building hurricane, gaining power, swirling just offshore, waiting to strike a darkened and unsuspecting world on a moment's notice. Most Christians are unaware of this. But those who are believe the only thing holding it back is the Restrainer mentioned in the Bible (2 Thessalonians 2:5,6). The persecution and death of Christians is a very real danger.

The ultimate source of this darkness is not flesh and blood. "We wrestle not against flesh and blood, but against principalities, against powers, against the rulers of darkness of this world, against spiritual wickedness in high places" (Ephesians 6:12). Satan is the prince of this world. He has always intended to set up a world government and it looks like he has succeeded. Conservative Christians call his reign the Tribulation Period.

Anyone who tries to stop this is doomed to fail. But there is a chance we can delay it. The United Nations cannot seize our sovereignty, but some of our blind leaders seem to be stupid enough to sign it away. The United Nations cannot take our nuclear weapons, but some of our gullible leaders seem to be stupid enough to turn them over. The United Nations cannot tell us how much electricity to use, how much food to eat, how many children to have, where to live, what to drive, how to wash our clothes, how to mow our yard, etc., but many of our voters seem uninformed enough to elect leaders who will relinquish this power.

Let me suggest that we learn what the Bible says on these important issues, that we keep a wary eye on the United Nations, that we learn to counter the glowing reports we hear about that organization, that we do more than call or write our congressmen and senators—that we get involved, that we make our salvation sure, that we tell others about Christ, and that we earnestly pray for our nation. The progressive deterioration of America is directly linked to our involvement with the United Nations. We will not survive this hurricane unless we shore up our nation with true revival.

Above all, this is just a light and momentary affliction. God is still in control. Hurricanes are just a lot of hot air. And they always blow themselves out. The same book that forecasts many of these bad things closes with good news: *we win!*

▼ ▼ ▼

CHAPTER 4

Today's Technology Churns Toward the Mark of the Beast

Terry L. Cook

If there is one statement that no one questions, it is that technology is burgeoning forward at a staggering record pace. What seemed to be advanced technology about 18 months ago is now considered obsolete. And no matter how you view the designers of these "techno-monsters" (who, generally speaking, are fine people just trying to make the world run more efficiently) the result of all this information and the ability to access it in one location inevitably will lead to abuse by the controller of the data, whether political, commercial, medical, taxes, personal, *et al.* Surveillance and control is the future name of the game—we are much further down the road toward a cashless society than most people know, and positive biometric identification (eye scan, fingerprints, palm prints, voice matching, thermal facial scans, and something that ties an identifying biological feature to digitized data stored in the master computer) is the next logical step in the progression of the technology.

The first topic I'd like to discuss deals with RFID transponders (biochip implants) and the more recent of this technology, as it pertains to worldwide identification, LUCID 2000.™ After an extensive personal interview with Dr. Jean-Paul Creusat, designer of the LUCID 2000™ System, it is abundantly clear that the goal of his company is to put an identification mark of some kind on every person on the globe, and he is convinced that this is *a good thing!*

Biochip Implants...Ready or Not!

Mr. Donald G. Small of Hughes Identification Devices made the following profound statement (excerpted from the video *Mark of the New World Order):*

> We are not part of a military program to implant tags in humans. In fact, we are not part of any plan to implant tags in humans. But a glass encapsulated animal tag only begs the question of the definition of what type of animal, and if that definition is a mammal, certainly it would include man. Are humans running around somewhere on the globe with RFID tags implanted in them? Yes! Absolutely, conclusively so.[1]

In recent years, a lot of progress has been made in the area of implantable biochip technology. The above comment suggests that we are crossing the line between animal and human applications, and Hughes Identification Devices has been at the forefront of this development. Effective August 29, 1993, the Safe Medical Devices Act required all medical implants to be accompanied with a biochip which contains vital information. Hughes Identification Devices is the main supplier of these medical biochips. A recent article in *Popular Science* entitled "Future Watch: The Body Binary" (October 1994) predicts, "Within the next ten years, we'll have miniature computers inside us to monitor and perhaps even control our blood pressure, heart rate, and cholesterol. Within 20 years, such computers will correct visual and hearing signals, making glasses and hearing aids obsolete."

As technology advances, the various uses for microchips and biochips seems to be limited only by our imagination, a truly frightening thought considering the humanistic/futuristic society in which we live. Today, the most popular application of the implantable biochip transponder is for the purpose of animal or pet identification.

Surely the day is drawing near when "He causes all, the small and the great, and the rich and the poor, and the free men and the slaves, to be given a mark in their right hand or in their forehead" (Revelation 13:16).

Animal Implants: Lost and Found Technology

During the late 1970s, pet owners and animal shelters around the country became increasingly aware of the need to identify or track animals in order to return lost pets to their owners. This seemingly harmless and beneficial idea gave rise to an entire industry now devoted to this very purpose; however, this technology has ominous overtones for anyone concerned about the potential for human application.

The basic prototype for the microchip used in the biochip transponder was introduced in 1979 by California inventor Mike Beigel. AVID, Inc. (American Veterinary Identification Devices) was incorporated in Norco, California in 1985 and spent the next six years in research and development. Implantable microchips were tested first in 1987 when International InfoPet Systems, based in Agoura Hills, California, started marketing a microchip made by Destron IDI. By 1991, the market began to heat up and Destron IDI sold its identification technology to Hughes Aircraft, and converted its Boulder, Colorado location to a research facility, and merged with a Minnesota-based firm. Destron-Fearing Corporation now offers a wide selection of implantable biochips. Also in 1991, Infopet changed hands and became Infopet Identification Systems, which markets a microchip developed by Trovan. Trovan is a German-based subsidiary of AEG/Telefunken, which is the major supplier of this technology in Europe. Countries using this technology include Austria, France, Germany, Holland, Ireland, Spain, Italy, Switzerland, and the Scandinavian countries, as well as Australia, the United Kingdom, and the United States. At this same time, AVID, Inc. introduced a third type of microchip, and Texas Instruments has gotten into this growing market. By 1993, one industry observer described the implantable ID market as a "mosaic of technology."

Various animal shelters, clinics, and humane societies have begun calling for a unified ID system. "Last spring, the National Animal Control Association, members of which include animal shelters and humane societies, suggested a boycott of microchips until the companies agree to share enough information so any chip could be read by any scanner."[2] AVID and Destron agreed on the need to develop a standard system, while InfoPet was not so willing.

Lindy Harton, an Infopet Senior Account Executive, says her chips and scanners are better because they work from a farther distance and don't have to be used as closely. In the end, she argues, "The best technology will win." Currently, AVID has the most popular technology because its scanner can read at least four microchips used in the United States. In 1992, Destron entered negotiations with Texas Instruments Corporation to develop jointly a worldwide operating standard for animal ID. Daryl Yurek, Chairman of Destron, says, "Developing and implementing a worldwide standard paves the way for governments and government agencies to adopt electronic identification without worrying about being locked into a single proprietary technology." Doesn't a worldwide operating standard for electronic identification sound like a great idea? Just think of all the happy pets and pet owners who will benefit from this wonderful technology! Try to imagine a future world dictator getting hold of this technology and you will have some idea what the New World Order is all about.

Regardless of manufacturers' claims, even the best of existing low-frequency passive transponder technology is limited in its read-range capability. In other words, existing technology generally is limited in its transmission range to within less than two feet from the animals into which transponders have been injected. In fact, the majority are limited to a 2"-12" read-range. However, although little information is currently available, in Europe fish are being tracked with some type of new long-range radio frequency transponder technology. Transponders are being inserted into the stomachs of these fish, which apparently are being tracked by some means of long-range satellite or Global Positioning System (GPS).

So how does this implantable biochip technology actually work? The basic system consists of an implantable biochip transponder and an external scanning device. The transponders come in various sizes, the smallest of which is about the size of an uncooked grain of rice, or 11 mm (see illustration below).

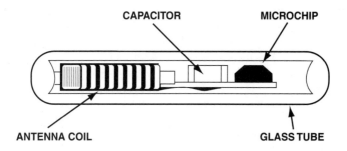

CAPACITOR   MICROCHIP

ANTENNA COIL   GLASS TUBE

**INJECTABLE
TRANSPONDER
CONFIGURATION**

The transponder is a glass tube made of soda lime glass which is known for biocompatibility. During manufacture, this glass tube is hermetically sealed so it is not possible for any body fluids to reach the internal electronics. There are only three components inside. The first is a computer microchip (a custom integrated circuit) which contains the unique ID number which has been laser etched onto the surface of the microchip. Once the microchip has been encoded or encrypted by the manufacturer, it is impossible to alter. The second component is a coil of copper wire wound around a ferrite (iron) core. This coil functions as a tiny radio antenna to pick up the radio signal from the external scanner and to send back the encoded ID number. The third component is a capacitor which tunes or facilitates the signal to and from the microchip.

The transponder is a passive device, meaning it has no batteries and never can wear out. It is energized by a low-frequency radio wave from the scanner. Most scanners use a frequency of 125 kHz, the signal used in AM medium-wave broadcasting. These low-frequency radio waves can penetrate all solid objects except those made of metal. Electronic ID based on these radio signals is referred to as Radio Frequency Identification (RFID). Once the scanner is activated, it digitally displays the decoded ID number on a liquid crystal screen. Destron can encode up to ten digits on their smallest biochip. Texas Instruments has a brand new chip which will allow the encoding of up to 19 digits. The smallest biochips can be programmed with up to 34 billion code numbers. A spokesman from Trovan says that with the latest technology "the number of possible code combinations is close to one trillion." Folks, that is a lot of identification capability.

One of the more interesting features of the implant technology is the injection system. The trademark name for Destron's injection system is called "Life Chip." It would be hard to imagine a more deceptive title than this, especially as this technology moves closer and closer to human applications. "There is a way which seems right to a man, but its end is the way of death" (Proverbs 14:12). Each transponder comes pre-packed inside a sterilized needle, which is discarded after use. Because of the sharpness of the needle, "there is minimum discomfort." Special injectors are necessary because most transponders come with an antimigration tip. In order to prevent the biochip from moving around, one end is sheathed in a polypropylene shell. This coating offers a surface with which fibrous connective tissue begins to bond within 24 hours after the injection. In other words, once the biochip is implanted, it becomes part of you with an "unlimited lifespan" (Trovan). "Once implanted, the identity tag (RFID) is virtually impossible to retrieve. Surgical removal, using the most advanced radiograph techniques available is extremely difficult."[3]

The final stage in the biochip technology is the ability of the scanner to transfer ID codes to a variety of external computers and printers. Government animal regulation and control agencies, shelters, and clinics participate in this network. Infopet can identify any of its registrants through the microchip number—pet's name, owner's name, social security number, zip code, or telephone number. AVID is participating with the PETtrac, which is a national computer network. The average cost for pet identification is $30.00. It should be noted that this technology is not limited to pets, livestock, or fisheries. The developers at Trovan envision a day when transponders will replace the bar code system.

Possible applications include coded automobile chassis numbers, automatic tolls, parking, copyright protection for video and computer software, documents, passports, ID cards, credit cards, badges, warehouse/stock handling, valuable items registration, insurance, shipping containers, luggage tags, cargo pallets, ammunition, arms, spare parts, aviation parts, customs, seals, blood samples, and laboratory applications. It is not surprising to see European firms way ahead of everyone else when it comes to advanced identification technologies. Scripture seems to indicate that the Antichrist will rise out of the European theater and use the technology which already is available (Daniel 2:29-45; 7:19-27; 9:27; Revelation 17:8-18).

Welcome to the Futurist Society

Since animal identification first was tested in 1987, the idea really has begun to catch on; however, selling this technology to the public has not always been easy. On May 1, 1989, Marin Humane Society in California announced that it would join other humane societies and begin using the biochip technology. Diane Allevato, Director of the Novato Animal Shelter in Marin County, cautioned, "The idea of implanting dogs and cats with identifying microchips is a concept we're taking slow." She added, "We want to make sure it's right for the animals, and that the community is willing to accept this new technology." Concerned citizens remarked that the implants were "unnatural and weird." "There's no doubt about it—injecting an animal with a computer chip is a pretty unnatural thing to do," responded Allevato. "But it's also unnatural, obscene really, that 15 million stray animals are destroyed in the country every year." On November 8, 1991, the Los Angeles City Council voted to implant pets, making Los Angeles the first big city to adopt the microchip program.

Since then, other major cities have endorsed the new technology. The American Kennel Club has endorsed the AVID chip already being used at the San Diego Zoo. The Canadian Kennel Club has endorsed the Destron chip, along with nearly 500 humane societies. Destron President, Jim Seiler, is enjoying his firm's success, but he also is aware of concerns which the public has. "Destron is only concerned with animal identification," says Seiler, "and is not considering human application." Mr. Seiler may not be considering human application, but others certainly are!

One such individual is Tim Willard, Executive Officer of the World Future Society, a Washington, D.C. based organization that claims 27,000 members worldwide, including *Future Shock* author, Alvin Toffler. In a disturbing article appearing in The *Mal-in Independent Journal* (April 4, 1989), Willard openly suggested using biochip technology on humans. "The technology behind such a microchip is fairly uncomplicated and with a little refinement could be used in a variety of human applications. Conceivably, a number could be assigned at birth and go with a person throughout life." Most likely the biochip would be implanted on the back of the right or left hand so that it would be easy to scan. Willard says it would be like a universal ID card, replacing all other forms of ID. "At the checkout stand at a supermarket, you would simply pass your hand over a scanner and your bank account would automatically be debited." Sounds convenient, doesn't it?

Remarkably, Willard goes on to suggest that a human microchip identification system "would work best with a highly centralized computer system." Now, Mr. Willard probably is not the Antichrist, but certainly such a mindset as his regarding this technology will applaud the real Antichrist when he comes! Notice how practical, humane, and efficient all of this is. Yet, most people still are very uncomfortable with this kind of technology. Sensing this, Willard comments, "While people over the years may have grown accustomed to artificial body parts, there is definitely a strong aversion to things being implanted. It's the 'Big Brother is watching' concept. People would be afraid that all of their thoughts and movements were being monitored." He adds, "People tend to be romantic about their independence and privacy." Mr. Willard, and others like him in the New World Order crowd always display their arrogance when it comes to sentimental notions like freedom, independence, national sovereignty, and privacy. After all, this is a New Age and we have to think globally and act locally.

In another article appearing in *The Washington Times* (October 11, 1993), Martin Anderson, a Senior Fellow at The Hoover Institution, makes some interesting observations regarding the National Health Security Card proposed by the Clinton Administration. The article is entitled "High-Tech National Tattoo," and in it he says the new health card is nothing more than a national ID card. This "smart card" would contain hundreds of pages of information, a digital photograph and signature, and a digital biometrically analyzed and stored fingerprint for positive identification. "The uses will be limited not by technology," writes Anderson, "but only by the imagination of government officials and their respect for our privacy." That's comforting to know, isn't it? Anderson continues, "Cost is not a serious problem. A state-of-the-art ID card can be manufactured in quantity for a dollar or two each. To make this tracking system work, every one of us must have a number that can be fed into the national computer banks. That is why the National Health Board, which would be set up by Mr. Clinton's program, would enforce unique identification numbers for consumers." One of the advantages cited by government officials would be to help cut down on consumer fraud. "This card could be used to crack down on welfare fraud, trace deadbeat dads who refuse to pay child support, supplant our social security cards, our draft cards, and our passports, maybe even to register voters and control voting fraud." All of this sounds good, but Donald McAlvany is not convinced. "The ulterior objective of these new government cards is to improve none of these things. Rather, they are a devious new means of further consolidating and computerizing all available information on each of us into a new electronically digitized, centralized government database that will ultimately lead to a complete loss of privacy, enslavement, and control."[4]

Privacy is always the main concern people have. "President Clinton and his aides are aware of how sensitive this issue is," writes Anderson, "and they are attempting to disarm the public by promising national privacy safeguards." It has been suggested that the government will establish a National Data Protection and Security Panel, but remember, the government once promised that social security numbers never would be used for identification purposes either. "The technology is now perfected," warns McAlvany, "and with the very significant year 2000 [less than] five years away, the Establishment is moving toward the National ID Card/people-control system at Mach 10 speed."

The technology for a national ID card is clearly available; however, Martin Anderson asks a very important question—what if we lose it? Jokingly, he says we can wear the card on a chain around our necks. But there is another solution, writes Anderson: "I hesitate to mention the idea because one of Mr. Clinton's White House aides may take it seriously. You see, there is an identification system made by Hughes Aircraft Company that you can't lose. It's the syringe implantable transponder." Of course, this is the same biochip now being used in animals. "It's sort of like a technological tattoo," says Anderson, "and far more efficacious than the numbers that the Nazis marked indelibly on the inner forearms of concentration camp prisoners....Of course, most Americans will find a surgically implanted government microchip repugnant. At least for the foreseeable future, the use of this ingenious device will be confined to its current use: the tracking of dogs, cats, horses, and cattle." Perhaps only for the foreseeable future—perhaps sooner than we think. Many futurists would argue there is no difference in principle between being forced to carry a microchip in a plastic card in your wallet or in a little glass tube in your right hand or forehead. "The principle that Big Brother has the right to track you is inherent in both. *The only thing that differentiates the two techniques is a layer of skin*" [emphasis added].

Whether or not you are familiar with Bible prophecy, that last sentence is very frightening. "Once you denigrate the idea of privacy," warns Anderson, "all kinds of innovative government controls are possible, things that didn't even occur to Aldous Huxley when he wrote his chilling novel, *Brave New World.*" But it never could happen here, right?

Not long ago, Jack Dunlap, a private investigator in Tucson, Arizona, tried to launch a new program called KIDSCAN. Concerned over lost children (not just pets), Dunlap proposed the same technology now being used on animals. "Each child whose parents signed up for KIDSCAN would get a computer chip planted under the skin and an identification number. The chip would transmit a signal that would bounce off a satellite and be picked up by police on a computer screen map. A parent with a missing child could call the police, give the KIDSCAN number, and have the child traced. Police everywhere would have the equipment, so you could find a child anywhere."[5] Anyone who has seen a missing child poster can understand the grief which parents must feel. Again, here is another example of how these programs are promoted for valid reasons, but the risks are always too great. Martin-Marietta Energy Systems originally showed interest, but this project never got off the ground.

In a more recent example of how far things have come along, the Food and Drug Administration passed a new ruling called the Safe Medical Devices Registration Act. This 1994 ruling requires that all artificial body parts have a microchip containing medical information, the microchip manufacturer, and the name of the surgeon performing the implant. Each year, six million medical devices are surgically implanted in people worldwide, everything from breast implants to chin implants. Lately, there has been concern that patients may forget or lose information regarding this implant. "No problem," writes Kathleen Wiegner,[6] "if the patient's implant carries an implant of its own—a microchip on which all relevant information has been encoded." The microchip being used in the U.S. is called "SmartDevice" and is manufactured by, you guessed it, Hughes Identification Devices, a subsidiary of Hughes Aircraft Company.

For the first time, implantable biochip technology designed for animals is being tested on human beings! Admittedly, it is not being used as a form of personal alphanumeric identification, but it is a giant step in that direction. Wiegner notes that medical personnel can decode the information on the biochip with a scanner. "The information on the chip would also be recorded on a computer-linked global registry," says Wiegner. Welcome to the Super Information Highway! LipoMatrix, Inc., a partial subsidiary of Collagen Corp. in Palo Alto, California, has been issued a patent for the use of SmartDevice in their medical devices and has begun putting them into their soybean oil breast implants. Meanwhile, SmartDevice biochips are already in 100 LipoMatrix breast implants being tested since October, 1994, on women in Germany, Italy, and Great Britain. Notice again how far advanced Europe is in their application of biochip technology.

Pressing Toward the MARC

In another example of Europe's lead in the area of identification technologies, the smart card was developed first by a French inventor, Roland Moreno, in 1974. Today, 23 years later, the Europeans have almost 150 million smart cards in use, compared with only a couple of million in the U.S. Three years ago, the Carte 1994 Conference was held in Paris. There was significant attendance from other EC countries, however, only a "smattering" of visitors from North America. "The Conference celebrated the 20th Anniversary of smart cards with the theme 'Smart Cards in the Year 2000.'"[7]

One of the more advanced uses of the smart card in the U.S. is by the U.S. military. The MARC card (Multi-Technology Automated Reader Card) is a smart card now being issued by the Department of Defense (DOD) to military personnel. According to an official release in 1994, "The DOD's test of MARC technologies and acceptance among a large beneficiary population will provide a great deal of information to the National Health Care Reform Team."[8] It seems that the Clinton administration first is trying out their prototype for a national ID card with a captive audience. And how fitting that it is called "The MARC Card"!

The MARC card uses different technologies: a standard three of nine bar code, magnetic stripe, embossed data, printed information (including a digital photograph), and an Integrated Circuit (IC) computer chip on the left side of the card. The combination of several media on one credit-card-sized device gives the MARC card its versatility—it can interface with a variety of technologies and systems, from standard imprinting machines to computer systems that use IC chips as data carriers. The DOD Information Technology Policy Board initiated the MARC project in response to a proliferation of single-use card programs in the military. How interesting that the MARC card and the national debate over health care came on the scene at the same time. McAlvany believes "it is a prototype for the National ID Card to be issued to every member of the U.S. civilian population."[9] The MARC card and its IC chip will be used to manage medical information on all U.S. military personnel worldwide. It also will store personal information regarding your educational background, police records, family and religious background, and other legal information. Although the MARC card looks like a credit card, it is a highly sophisticated smart card with powerful identification capabilities! The MARC card replaces the current meal card, and DOD project coordinators currently are evaluating it as a means of paying military personnel. It already has been tested for this purpose at Parris Island (Marine boot camp). "The military has long been in the forefront of such tracking technology," notes Peter LaLonde. "To speed the processing of personnel and supplies, for example, the DOD has married bar codes and smart cards with personal computers and portable readers."[10]

> As if they weren't "smart" enough already, an article in the January 8, 1996, *Government Computer News* is titled "The MARC Card Gets Smarter," with a subtitle of "DOD Considers Governmentwide Application of Automated Reader Cards."

> The Defense Department, which is preparing to expand its Multitechnology Automated Reader Card pilot to all

CHARLES R. WESTINGHOUSE
20/123456789   TAMC

RANK	SERVICE	STATUS	DATE OF BIRTH	BLOOD TYPE
1LT	USA	AD	19690615	O-POS

service branches, wants MARC to set the standard for federal smart-card technology.

We're looking at government-wide application of smart cards, the ultimate goal: 'A single standard, multiple-use card that can be used across the government' for applications such as payroll, employee records, health care, and personnel assignments…. MARC uses a 2K chip and contains seven application functions. Eventually an 8K chip will be standard for DOD-issued cards. Such cards could handle as many as 25 applications.

…The ability to erase data stored on the chip allows sensitive information to be removed before a soldier enters a combat area.

Doesn't that give you great confidence to know that people can access and revise anything about you? What if they mess up and just totally delete you? For those of you who have such great confidence in the accuracy of the military, I suggest you look up the meaning of the acronym SNAFU—never mind, I'll just tell you: Situation Normal, All Fouled Up! The above article also stated: "After MARC has been rolled out to active duty personnel, DOD intends to expand its use to include reserve and National Guard units, *then to*

DOD civilian employees, dependents, and retirees" (emphasis added). Is the MARC card being used as a prototype for a national citizen I.D. card for everyone? You'd better believe it!

A recent example of how the DOD has utilized high-tech identification systems is the method it has used to supervise the Haitian and Cuban refugees on Guantanamo Bay Naval Base in Cuba. In 1994, 50,000 Cuban and Haitian refugees flooded into this 45 square mile base between June and September. The United States Atlantic Command (USACOM), under the direction of the Joint Chiefs of Staff, implemented the Deployable Mass Population Identification and Tracking System (DMPITS), a system which has been tested since 1992. This highly sophisticated system utilizes all of the latest technology: a Hewlett-Packard 715 UNIX workstation sporting a two gigabyte internal hard drive; a 19-inch color monitor, keyboard, and mouse; an Identix TV-555 Touchview Fingerprint Scanner, and a Panasonic CCD color video camera. The system's server configuration includes an HP-735 workstation with 80M of RAM and a 525 GB external hard drive, a 9.6 KBPS analog communications modem, a flat-bed scanner, an HP LaserJet printer with 6M of memory, and a V.42 high-speed modem. And how is all this hardware put to use? With the AVID RFID transponder placed in a plastic wristband, along with an AVID RFID Tag Scanner! According to a firsthand report, "Military personnel place a black plastic wristband on the person's right wrist. It is secured using an aluminum metal pop riveter. Small children have the wristband attached to an ankle."

DOD systems designer, Mike Humphrey, Chief of Applications Programming for USACOM, said he got the idea to tag refugees with RFID technology from reading Auto*maticID. News,* an industry journal. Mark David, Editor-in-Chief *for AutomaticID. News,* remarking on the DMPITS operation, exclaimed, "It is an incredible application—one of the first to cross a controversial line and tag humans with RFID transponders."[11] Indeed it is, and the only thing lacking is "a layer of skin"! Reaction from the refugees was mixed. One woman said, "We have to wear it to get medical help at the hospital, and I have an injury. So it's okay." Others were not so compliant. Some managed to cut them off with homemade knives, while some actually chewed through the hard plastic! One man being interviewed was particularly upset, and for a very good reason. "In Revelation 13:16 the Bible says that the devil will mark us on our right hands. It says that we'll be marked with the number 666. It really bothers me that it's in the Bible."[12] It's remarkable that this response was published by the journal. But what should really bother us is the fact that our own government has a program already in place for the purpose of "mass population identification and tracking."

As you can see, the technology and applications are getting closer all the time to that day when biochip implants will be used on human beings. In his book, An *Illustrated History of the Gestapo,* Rupert Butler wrote, "All German citizens had to carry identification and could be stopped at any time by either civilian or military police." The day may not be far off when we can be stopped at any time and have RFID scanners waved over us as we approach the final stages of the biochip and I.D. technology of the New World Order system.

LUCID 2000™: If it's so important, why isn't it common knowledge?

"It is evident that the New World Order as conceived in Washington is about control and surveillance, not about values or a better life for the peoples of the world."—Richard A. Falk, World Federalist Association.

In his recent State of the Union Address, President Clinton announced, "The era of big government is over." The President then went on to propose government programs and solutions to a host of concerns in our society. Syndicated columnist John McManus rightly observed, "if the situation weren't so serious, that statement would be laughable. The day of big government isn't behind us; it looms larger almost daily." He concludes, "Returning to the Constitution is the answer." Indeed it is, but the New World Order crowd is more concerned about creating "a new civilization" and implementing more people-control.

Clinton's liberal colleague from California, Senator Dianne Feinstein (CFR, Trilateral Commission, Bilderberger member), has insisted that we need a national I.D. card. "She proposes, as part of legislation for tougher control of illegal immigration, a national identity card for every man, woman, and child in America," writes Ron Unz, Adjunct Scholar with the Center for Equal Opportunity in Washington, D.C. "Captivated by advanced technology, Feinstein says that such a card could include a magnetic strip or microchip containing a digitized form of each citizen's vital statistics, photograph, fingerprint, voiceprint, and retinal scan."[13] In a speech in Washington during 1995, the senator made her point. "Whether the card carries a magnetic strip on which the bearer's unique voice, retina pattern or fingerprint is digitally encoded, or whether it incorporates a digitized photo and signature integrated into the plastic card itself, it is clear to me that state-of-the-art work and benefits eligibility IDs can and must replace the Dinosaur Age documents now being used." Continuing, she pleads, "Is it really necessary to take three to four years to study the issue? Shouldn't we press forward with a single integrated system now, require everyone (not just immigrants) to obtain the new document within a reasonable phase-in period, and subject that document to annual renewals to minimize the effect of any residual fraud or change in eligibility status?"[14]

Notice that the solution to this "crisis" is enhanced government surveillance capabilities. What the senator needs to do is "take three to four years" to study the U.S. Constitution and her oath to uphold same.

In a shocking development, powerful groups and various government organizations are stressing the urgent need for a Universal Biometric Card in order to combat fraud and criminal activity, worldwide. This international I.D. system is known as LUCID 2000™. Let us learn more as we investigate the move toward this massive and highly technological system being proposed on a global scale.

LUCID 2000™ NET:
A Universal Information Identification System

For quite some time, now, even if people were familiar with the term "LUCID 2000"™, the exact title which birthed the familiar acronym remained a mystery. During my extensive interview with Dr. Jean-Paul Creusat, designer of the proposed program, I asked him to clarify this point. He responded openly to my inquiry and furnished much additional information in his response.

LUCID is an acronym that stands for Logical Universal Communication Interactive Databank, and within this databank there is a database that is composed of multiple entities that involve the medical, the criminal justice, the international justice system, the Department of Defense, the Department of Education, the Department of

Transportation, and the banking system, and other identification that is part of putting all in one universal card that will replace all the multiple cards that we are using.

The information contained herein has been taken largely from one source, the *NARC Officer* magazine. This is the official publication of the International Narcotic Enforcement Officers Association, Inc. The publication is distributed mainly among law enforcement officials around the world, including the International Criminal Police Organization (ICPO) known as Interpol. In other words, this concept study for a universal biometric card system has been going on since 1983 and we just *now* are learning about it— and you need to know about it!

According to its promoters, LUCID 2000™ is "a concept study for a future Universal Information Identification System via the LUCID 2000™ Net" (this is a reference to the Arpanet/internet protocols and infrastructure). The research and development of this system is "to help prevent, deter, and frustrate terrorism and international organized crime." The LUCID 2000™ system will be "an all-source fusion information center that will interface multilingual messages into a common communications network. The criminal justice will be enhanced by implementing…a 'Universal Computerized Identification Clearing House Resource Center' as a secure, uniform, interactive, and instantaneous tracking system from universal biometric cards through the LUCID 2000™ Net."

Sounds like a great idea, tracking down all the bad guys around the world, right? However, you will notice on the following page *little children* are to be issued powerful smart cards for positive I.D. It's a family affair, you see. As the senator from the left coast put it, "Every man, woman, and child in America."

The Ultimate in Global Surveillance

The project concept designer for the LUCID 2000™ system, Jean-Paul Creusat, M.D., is also the Medical Officer Investigator on narcotics control and the official representative of the International Narcotic Enforcement Officers Association (INEOA) to the Economic and Social Council (ECOSOC) of the United Nations (more will be mentioned later about this non-government organization [NGO]).

The first subproject for the LUCID 2000™ system was presented to various officials of the State of New York Law Enforcement Agencies on January 7, 1983. The second design was updated in November 1993 and presented on December 1993 to liberal Republican and criminal justice activist Congressman Benjamin Gilman (20th District-NY), who has expressed great enthusiasm for the project. The *NARC Officer* magazine (July/August, 1994) featured Dr. Creusat's article entitled, "Year 2000 & LUCID 2000™ System: A Millstone to Curtail Terrorists and International Organized Crime." A year later Dr. Creusat teamed up with Anthony S. Halaris in another article entitled, "LUCID 2000™ and the Counter-Terrorism Act of 1995." Mr. Halaris is an Information Systems Specialist and professor of Computer Science at Iona College in New Rochelle, New York. He is also president of Advanced Technologies Group, Inc. in New York. What these two technocrats are suggesting is nothing short of the Mark of the Beast! Their reasoning is very compelling because we *must* fight crime, terrorism, illegal immigration, and the like. In August 1993, during a speech on the topic of "Personal Security and Crime Control," President Clinton emphasized, "The first duty of any government is to try to keep its citizens safe, but clearly, too many Americans are not safe today. We no longer have the freedom from fear for all our citizens that is essential to security and prosperity." Of course, the solution is to disarm the American people so the *government* can "keep its citizens safe." New amendments were passed on September 13, 1994, to the Omnibus Anti-Crime Bill (H.R. 3355) which "marked a new beginning in America's fight against crime." Six months later on March 24, 1995, the Brady Handgun Violence Prevention Act (H.R. 1321) was introduced and later passed by Robert Dole and two other senators in a midnight session on the Senate Floor.

Now comes the Omnibus Counter-Terrorism Act of 1995 with draconian laws and restrictions for law-abiding gun owners. Apparently, this was orchestrated carefully to fight the expected continued acts of terrorism here at home in the U.S. (if you haven't noticed, the Clinton Administration and the liberal media have been making an onslaught of spurious allegations against all conservatives and Christians, "armed" with the act of terrorism in Oklahoma City, lumping us all into the category called "right-wing radicals.") Canada already has tough anti-gun laws, as well as other nations. What this is leading to is obvious: less freedom, more government control, and increased surveillance. Seems like the LUCID 2000™ system has arrived just in time!

"The vision is simple," writes Creusat and Halaris, "an unprecedented nationwide and, eventually, worldwide, electronic communications network that will connect the future 'Universal Computerized Identification Clearing House Resource Center' to the present and future Management Systems, providing secure, uniform, and interactive electronic communication."[15] The LUCID 2000™ system will operate 24 hours a day, seven days a week providing "a universal nucleus of contact for performing non-criminal justice background checks and tracking of positive identification requests for alias criminals (employment, administrative, immigration status, licensing, judicial, investigative, prosecutorial, custodial, fire arms purchase, etc.)." Antony Sutton, editor of *The Phoenix Letter*, asks, "What's an 'alias criminal'?...We applaud their ingenious use of the English language." Non-criminal justice background checks and alias criminals "means potentially everybody." Right, Tony. An "alias criminal" is obviously a "criminal" who hasn't been properly, or positively, identified yet...so all of us could be alias. That's why we need the LUCID 2000™ system with its automatic data processing and computer network. Welcome to the New World Order.

The Super Information Highway

In his first article in *NARC Officer* (July/Aug. 1994), Jean-Paul Creusat explains the problem of worldwide crime and his *perfect* solution: the microchip. "The international trade in illegal drugs has been estimated to be greater than the oil trade, second only to the arms trade; worth up to 300 billion U.S. dollars per year, with 100 billion dollars generated in the United States alone. Criminal organizations and criminal activities related to international illicit drug trade impose an inhuman toll on the quality of life worldwide, and more subtly, weaken faith in governments."

Mr. Creusat continues, "A new generation of international organized criminals is undermining International Security, compelling world governments to explore the new universal intelligence super highway system. As a method for assisting in the combat against this phenomenon, as well as other national and international challenges of the year 2000 and beyond, the project designer advocates the

L.U.C.I.D.© SYSTEM

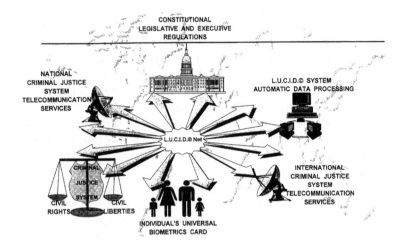

A Universal Information Identification System (L.U.C.I.D.©Net)

development and adoption of a system permitting an instantaneous read-out of individualized updated data satisfying selective requests from any branches of governments from developing and industrialized countries. The project designer refers to this future universal intelligence super highway system as LUCID 2000™.

"Born from the inspiration of the intricate geometrical structure of the DNA chain, where the genetic blueprint of life is contained in one molecule," writes Creusat, "LUCID 2000™ system will contain the equivalent capacity of millions of individual data integrated within one translucent device." And what is this little device? "The end product will be a 2.0"×0.5" thermolysis-proof translucent rectangular receptor/transcriber. The model proposal will be molded impartially within official cards or documents such as: health care, driver's license, identification, credit cards and bank cards, passport or refugee documents, and social security cards." Well, that just about covers everything, folks. Do you think you will be able to "buy and sell" or move about without this little translucent device? Don't count on it. During this interview, Dr. Creusat also revealed that their goal is to assign a LUCID 2000™

card to everyone at birth, with the footprint of the infant and the mother's fingerprint, to furnish unalterable, positive biometric identification. Some future world dictator is going to grab on to this technology just as the Bible predicted (Revelation 13:16-18).

In his second article (Sept./Oct. 1995), Creusat reveals that this little device is actually a "microprocessor," or "microchip" to be "inserted within a Universal Biometric Card which will store more than five gigabytes of personalized data." Five gigabytes of information—that is more than a *hundred* floppy discs the government wants to have on you! "The read-out of the device will be retrieved by operating read-out equipment involving two simultaneous steps," explains Creusat, "transcription and translation via a scanner light reader into a portable and/or fixed equipment unit." What is being described here is a potentially implantable biochip/microchip which can be read by radio frequency scanners (RFID technology), exactly what they are doing to animals now. It's easy to see why world governments would like this system.

"LUCID 2000™ will be capable of storing and updating 'up-to-the-second' personalized information systematically from an individualized master data bank [emphasis added]." This will include everything about you, in addition to photos, fingerprints, footprints, iris scans, textual data, DNA genotyping, human leukocyte antigen data, and so on—all digitized and permanently placed in a microchip within your mandatory biometrics card.

"This system," we are informed, "will be able to access and monitor demographic trends concerning shifts in labor force, tourism, immigration, and/or refugee status [remember the RFID transponders placed in the plastic wristbands of the Haitian refugees?] while also contributing to a user-friendly innovative classification judiciary back-up system connected to a universal judicial data bank." We are told "only selected users/authorities will be commissioned to update an individual's master data bank. Communication will be screened throughout all channels of department inquiries and inquirers, ensuring that only appropriate persons obtain access to the ultimate gates of clearance for viewing individualized data." The fact that the controls for this system will be tight is supposed to make us feel safer, but keep in mind that those tight controls also make it much easier for the government to control its people.

In 1986, the U.S. government established the Counter-Terrorist Center (CTC) which exchanges data with ten federal agencies: The Central Intelligence Agency, Federal Bureau of Investigation, Secret Service, Bureau of Alcohol, Tobacco, and Fire Arms, Immigration and Naturalization Service, National Security Agency, Department of State Diplomatic Security, Federal Aviation Administration, Naval Criminal Investigative Service, and Department of Energy. You can see that the trend is toward more and more centralized data to assist in law enforcement and surveillance. What is needed now is something on a worldwide scale. Mr. Creusat points out that on an international crimefighting scale "...some problems are viewed as law enforcement matters for the Department of Justice; however, other areas are handled by the Department of State, still others by the CIA, the DEA, the Customs Service, the Treasury Department or the INS." So what is the solution? "The LUCID 2000™ system, under the aegis of Universal Security, will be the future state-of-the-art technology, revolutionizing the capacity of world governments to deal with the challenges of record-keeping and law enforcement." Here in the U.S. "the LUCID 2000™ system will assist and facilitate investigations and prosecutions under the Bank Secrecy Act (Titles 18, 21, and 31 USC), the Continuing Criminal Enterprise Statute (21 USC, 848), and the Racketeer Influenced and Corrupt Organizations Act (18 USC sections 1961-68)." This last statute has been used repeatedly against Randall Terry and Operation Rescue members in the battle against the lucrative abortion industry in America. The government decides who is "corrupt."

So what's wrong with all this? Antony Sutton points out a few problems in his latest newsletter: "Law enforcement has no right to track or collect data on citizens who have not committed a crime unless there is evidence that they may have broken the law. This is protected under the Fourth Amendment. We the people did not delegate the right of privacy to the federal government in the Constitution, and it is protected under the Due Process Amendment." He further points out, "The authors own the LUCID 2000™ system, and one is President of Advanced Technologies Group that has a financial interest in Big Brother computer control systems. In brief, your loss of personal freedom is their future financial gain." Finally, the Department of Defense (DOD) has had a major hand in building a potential surveillance system of the civilian population (i.e., global positioning satellites [GPS], the high-tech MARC military smart card, the Deployable Mass Population Identification and Tracking System [DMPITS], and Arpanet/Internet infrastructure, etc.). Dr. Sutton comments, "The DOD has legitimate functions. Control of the population is *not* one of these functions." Indeed—you *are* absolutely correct. But the drive continues. In a moment you will see why, who, or what is pushing us toward permanent, positive identification.

The Lucid/Lucis/Lucifer Connection

As mentioned earlier, the project designer for the LUCID 2000™ system is Dr. Jean-Paul Creusat, who is also a member of the Economic and Social Council of the United Nations (ECOSOC). Perhaps this is a clue as to the name LUCID 2000™ and why it was chosen as the international symbol for government surveillance. According to *Webster's New Collegiate Dictionary,* the word lucid means "suffused with light; luminous; translucent; having full use of one's faculties; intelligible." It is also worth noting that since 1989 the Lucis Trust has appeared on the roster of ECOSOC of the United Nations.

And what is the Lucis Trust? It is a non-government organization (NGO) incorporated in 1922 and located at 866 United Nations Plaza, Suite 566-7, New York, NY 10017. The Lucis Trust has worldwide financial support for the Arcane School, the Lucis Publishing

Companies, World Goodwill, Triangles, Lucis Trust Libraries, and Radio Lucis—all of which draw exclusively from the New Age writings of Alice A. Bailey, a leading occultist at the turn of the century. As the name would imply, lucis also means "luminous; translucent; light-bearing; enlightenment." According to the literature of the organization, "This is a time of preparation not only for a new civilization and culture in a New World Order, but also for the coming of a new spiritual dispensation [i.e., New Age]." It's interesting to note this was written in 1986, and since then Gorbachev has coined the phrase "new civilization," while George Bush mentioned "The New World Order" well over 200 times, just during his term in office.

"A new civilization is emerging which embraces all peoples and is founded upon the spirit of brotherhood and right human relations," so say the light-bearing people. Their goal is "to *speed* this transformation in attitudes and behavior [emphasis added]." Of course, this is to be done with "the principles of the Ageless Wisdom" and "esoteric points of view" in order to assist in "the practical realities to be dealt with in the establishment of a New World Order." What this group really is trying to do is stage the Antichrist. "Today the reappearance of the world Teacher—the Christ—is expected by millions, not only by those of the Christian faith but by those of every faith who expect the Avatar under other names—the Lord Maitreya, Krishna, Messiah, Imam Mahdi, and the Bodhisattva...The coming world Teacher will be mainly concerned, not with the result of past error and inadequacy," say the Lucis Trust folks, "but with the requirements of a New World Order and with the reorganization of the social structure." Boy, will he ever be concerned about reorganizing the social structure! The world already is heading toward world government and the worldwide infrastructure for an Orwellian nightmare—but all of this has been predicted from the "ageless wisdom" of the prophetic books of the Bible.

The Bible says the devil will raise up an individual whose coming is in accord with the activity of Satan, with all power and signs and false wonders" (2 Thessalonians 2:9). Naturally, the evil one never appears to be "evil," but "good" and "enlightening," "...for even Satan disguises himself as an angel of light" (2 Corinthians 11:14). Ah, the word light! In the Old Testament, the devil (Greek), or Satan (Hebrew), is referred to as "Lucifer" (Isaiah 14:12 KJV). And what does *Lucifer* mean? "The morning star; light-bearing [from lux, Latin for light—note the spelling of L-U-X within the triangle of the Lucis Trust logo]; a fallen rebel archangel; used as the name of the devil."[16] The *real* force behind the worldwide drive toward permanent, positive I.D. *and* enslavement is none other than the devil himself (Revelation 12:7-17; 13:1-18; 17:11-18; 20:4).

Remember, the LUCID 2000™ system suggests the use of a *"translucent* device" with a scanner "light" reader? It is interesting to note that AT&T recently launched a new company called Lucent Technologies. According to company officials, this name was chosen among 700 names considered. Henry Schacht, Chairman, CEO, and CFR member, enthuses, "The word 'lucent' means 'glowing with light' and 'marked by clarity.' It suggests clear thought, brightness, and energy." AT&T is on the Board of Directors for the influential Smart Card Forum, which is financed by the biggest bank in America, Citicorp. This group is doing everything in its power to promote the use of integrated chip (IC) smart cards in banking, government agencies, the military, and medical facilities. Ultimately, this will lead to a cashless society.

AT&T now has split into three companies (a triangle?): they are AT&T (communication services), NCR (computer enterprises), and now Lucent Technologies (networks, equipment, and microelectronic components). "Lucent will be Wall Street's largest initial public offering, with an estimated value at more than $3 billion, topping the $1.85 billion spin-off of Allstate Corp. by Sears, Roebuck & Co. in 1993."[17] This has proven to be the case. On April 4, 1996, "shares in the record $3 billion sale rose 4½ to 31½ in midday NYSE trading of 30.7 million shares, more than four times the next most active issue."[18] A 19 percent gain from its initial public offering to the date of the news article? I guess it helps to have a little "enlightenment" when it comes to investing in stocks.

Seeking the True Light

The English proverb says, "The darkest hour is before the dawn." Certainly, we are entering the darkest hour of human history. Yet, the New Age/New World Order crowd insists we are entering an age of enlightenment and goodwill. "Humanity is not following an uncharted course," says the Lucis Trust literature. "There is a divine plan in the cosmos of which we are a part."

Unfortunately, most people are following the devil's plan, which is a counterfeit of the genuine article. Jesus said, "Enter by the narrow gate; for the gate is wide, and the way is broad that leads to destruction, and many are those who enter by it. For the gate is small, and the way is narrow that leads to life, and few are those who find it. Beware of the false prophets who come to you in sheep's clothing but inwardly are ravenous wolves" (Matthew 7:13-15).

Many today are deceived by the false prophets of the New Age and New World Order crowd. There *will* be a New World Order, but *only* when Jesus returns in power and glory (Matthew 24:29-31; 2 Thessalonians 1:7-10; 2 Peter 3:13). Jesus said to pray, "Thy kingdom come, Thy will be done on earth as it is in heaven" (Matthew 6:10). Someday, heaven is going to come down to earth, but until that day, the devil is running loose trying to construct a new Tower of Babel. No, the era of big government is *not* over, actually it is just beginning! When this so-called world teacher comes on the scene, the Bible says he will cause

> *all,* the small and the great, and the rich and the poor, and the free men and the slaves, to be given a mark in their right hand, or in their forehead, and he provides that no one should be able to buy or to sell, except the one who has the mark, either the name of the beast or the number of his name. Here is wisdom. Let him who has understanding calculate the number of the beast, for the number is that of a man, and his number is six hundred and sixty-six [666] (Revelation 13:16-18).

Each day we continue to press toward The Mark. I.D. technologies are advancing rapidly and someday will trap many because it will sound so reasonable and logical. There are men and women in high places who know exactly what they are doing. And what they want is control of your life. "These control ideas do not reflect American values, tradition, and philosophy—and certainly not the Constitution," writes Tony Sutton. "These planners are Hegelians. They believe the State is boss and individuals have to obey the State"[19] Ron Unz adds, "A national I.D. database represents the slipperiest of all civil liberty slopes." If that is the case, a worldwide I.D. database is the abyss!

Jesus said, "I am the light of the world; he who follows Me shall not walk in the darkness, but shall have the light of life" (John

8:12). Addressing His followers (in the Sermon on the Mount), He said, "You are the light of the world" (Matthew 5:14). Born-again Christians, not demon-possessed pagans, are the real "enlightened ones" who bear the "light" of the gospel. Jesus said, "I am the way, and the truth, and the life, no one comes to the Father but through Me" (John 14:6). It is my prayer that you will seek Him today and receive forgiveness and eternal life in His glorious New World Order (John 3:16)! To say that there is a deluge of "modern technologies" is almost an oxymoron, because they are changing so rapidly, nothing is "modern" for very long. Knowledge is expanding on all fronts. In one chapter I couldn't possibly give an in-depth study on the myriad of choices—virtual reality and the possible outcome of those under its influence, biogenetic research, splitting genes, cloning of mammals, and the number of new diseases/viral illnesses that coincidentally are immune to the standard treatment with antibiotics, with new ones springing up faster than the medical research teams can develop a cure. By the way, if some of these things sound familiar to you, I wouldn't be surprised. God's Word predicts them quite accurately, in great detail. My book, *The Mark of the New World Order,* contains much information and documentation concerning many of these topics, and my next book, *America's Identity Crisis and the Coming International I.D. Card* (currently in progress), will tell you where all these "Big Brothers" are located, and what they claim they will do in the near future— they don't even try to cover it up anymore. Just to whet your appetite, below is a quote of Senator Frank Church in James Bamford's excellent book, *The Puzzle Palace,* explaining the tyranny that could result from the National Security Agency's (NSA's) involvement in our lives.

> At the same time, that capability at any time could be turned around on the American people and no American would have any privacy left, such [is] the capability to monitor everything: telephone conversations, telegrams, it doesn't matter. There would be no place to hide. If this government ever became a tyranny, if a dictator ever took charge in this country, the technological capacity that the intelligence community has given the government could enable it to impose total tyranny, and there would be no way to fight back, because the most careful effort to combine together in resistance to the

> government, no matter how privately it was done, is
> within the reach of the government to know. Such is the
> capability of this technology....
>
> I don't want to see this country ever go across the bridge.
> I know the capacity that is there to make tyranny total
> in America, and we must see to it that this agency [the
> NSA] and all agencies that possess this technology
> operate within the law and under proper supervision, so
> that we never cross over that abyss. That is the abyss
> from which there is no return.

I couldn't have said it better myself! The Lord warns us of
coming events in His Word, because He doesn't want us to be
unprepared, or to have trouble overtake us by surprise. Remember
the Lord's admonition—we should be as cunning as serpents, but
harmless as doves. Therefore, we shouldn't be surprised when these
things come to pass, because it would seem that events are right on
schedule—on God's schedule, that is—according to the prophetical
passages in His Word. Another passage shares the good news that
we are to comfort one another with these words: when you see
these things begin to come to pass, look up, for your redemption
draweth nigh.

As these days get darker, it is my prayer that you will seek Him
who said, "I am the light of the world; he who follows Me shall not
walk in the darkness, but shall have the light of life" (John 8:12).
This life is found only in Jesus Christ. "For God so loved the world,
that He gave His only begotten Son, that whoever believes in Him
should not perish, but have eternal life" (John 3:16). Seek Him
today before it is too late. "For whoever will call upon the name of
the Lord will be saved" (Romans 10:13).

> The path of the righteous is like the light of dawn, that
> shines brighter and brighter until the full day. The way of
> the wicked is like darkness; they do not know over what
> they stumble (Proverbs 4:18,19).

God also tells us that men love darkness rather than light
because their deeds are evil. I pray that none of you find yourself in
that condition, but if you do, please settle your accounts with the
Lord...while there is still time. May God bless you.

▼   ▼   ▼

CHAPTER 5

False Peace: The Pseudo-Storm Shelter

J. Randall Price

Most people do not easily recognize the ways of deception. Like all delusions, if the appearance is proper, the words right, and the audience has displaced normal reservations in light of necessary (and expected) results, even seasoned statesmen can be deceived. In the ancient days of Israel's monarchy, a good king by the name of Hezekiah succumbed to political deception. After having survived an attack by the dreaded Assyrians, Hezekiah was over-confident that his empire was secure through its fortifications (many of which were accomplished under his administration). Hezekiah then gave Babylonian emissaries a complete tour of his kingdom (2 Kings 20:12-15). Naïvely trusting their show of concern and desire for peace (verse 12), he revealed to this foreign power the extent of his military might and even the wealth of his regime. As a result, the Babylonians, who later eclipsed the Assyrians as Israel's greatest enemy, destroyed the Israelite monarchy and took Hezekiah's heirs into captivity (verses 16-18). The king was deluded that he had done the right thing, even when warned by the prophet Isaiah concerning its dreadful consequences, because he thought,

"…there shall be peace and truth in my days" (verse 19). In our modern era another monarchy faced the same circumstances as that of Israel. In September of 1938 the British Prime Minister Neville Chamberlain met in Munich with German Chancellor Adolf Hitler. Secure in the reputation of his great empire "upon whom the sun never set," conscious of the expectations of his position and desperately wanting an "understanding" between their countries, Chamberlain returned from the meeting to proudly announce, "There will be peace in our time!" That "peace" led less than a year later to the Second World War in which 47 million people perished and Chamberlain's own city of London was practically demolished.

Pseudo-Peace at Any Price

The modern age has become intoxicated at the prospect of global peace as we begin the twenty-first century. Weary of wars, and believing that technology can rescue the future, there is today an unparalleled longing for "peace at any price" (so long as *our* country does not have to pay for it!). Yet, despite appearances to the contrary (since the nature of man and the conditions that foment wars have not changed), our planet is ready to pursue any process that may promise the coveted peace. While a good one-third of our earth is at war at any time, international attention has been focused on the one supposed obstacle to "peace in our time"—the Middle East conflict. Regardless of the irreconcilable religious agendas that precipitated and continue to provoke the conflict, the international community is driven by a desire to resolve the political situation. And, as in the case of Chamberlain, due caution and reasonable requirements for security have been abandoned in order to achieve "peace at any price."

For example, even though the Palestinian Authority acquired the biblical regions of Judea and Samaria, known popularly as the West Bank, as Israel's donation toward the peace process, the world has watched Palestinian "President" Yasser Arafat meet in the summer of 1997 with Iraq's Saddam Hussein (whom he supported in the Gulf War) and openly embrace and kiss the leader of the terrorist organization Hamas only weeks after and days before they launched terrorist bombings in downtown Jerusalem in the early fall of the same year. And though more have been killed on both sides *during* the peace process than before it was initiated, the world continues to urge on the peace process with Chamberlain's same naïve ambition. Why is peace in the Middle East, and especially between the Israelis and Arabs, deemed so vital? What is the agenda for this peace process, and what kind of peace is possible? Why has it been so difficult to achieve, and where will it ultimately lead us? These are questions we must examine within the context of Scripture and especially Scripture's predictions of the pseudo-peace that is to characterize the end of the age.

The Origin of the Middle East Conflict

The international media has presented a biased and incorrect image of the Middle East conflict as Israel's oppression of a displaced refugee people whose land they invaded. In truth, the conflict in the Middle East has persisted for thousands of years involving many nations. Jerusalem alone has been invaded or destroyed almost 30 times. However, the modern reference to conflict has its origin in the events that surround the creation of the State of Israel and the five wars it has had with Arab nations since. Jewish immigration prompted by the Zionist Movement in 1897 brought Jews to the land to live alongside Arabs who (then under Turkish rule) had been there since the Arab invasion of the country in A.D. 638. It should be remembered, however, that a resident Jewish population always existed in the Land throughout the past 19 centuries, despite the experience of persecution and pogrom. In the same way, Jewish communities still survive in Arab countries hostile to them such as Egypt, Iraq, and Syria. Throughout the early decades of the twentieth century as tensions mounted and riots occurred, usually over access to holy places, Great Britain, who had been granted mandatory jurisdiction over the country by the League of Nations (in 1922), after their conquest of the Turks in 1918, sought a solution to the conflict.

The Palestinian Problem

The British "solution," which violated both the terms of the Mandate and the Balfour Declaration (which had called for the establishment of a Jewish homeland in all or any part of Palestine) was to divide the country between the Arab and Jewish populations. On May 14, 1946 the British gave the eastern four-fifths of the land (known then as Transjordan) to the Arabs and to the rule of the Hashemite family. This created the Hashemite Kingdom of Jordan. Thus, Israel was left to occupy only 23 percent of Palestine (not 100 percent as the media portrays), while the Arabs received the remaining 73 percent. This territory was originally intended for the resettlement of Palestinian Arabs by the League of Nations, not to become an independent Arab state.[1] Interestingly, it was thereafter identified by its Arab occupiers as the nation of Palestine. Even as late as 1968, King Hussein of Jordan was still saying: "Jordan is Palestine and Palestine is Jordan."[2] Incidentally, in 1974, Yasser Arafat said much the same thing: "What you call Jordan is actually Palestine."[3] How different is the perception and rhetoric today! Today, Israel is called Palestine and Jordan is viewed as a distinct Arab nation such as Saudi Arabia.

In 1947, because of the British failure to resolve the mounting crisis between Arabs and Jews in the 23 percent of Palestine, the United Nations stepped in and established a temporary "peace" by partitioning this 23 percent of Palestine into a Jewish and Arab state. At this time the term "Palestinian" (the Anglicized form of the Latin name of Israel's ancient enemies, the Philistines), originally given to the country by the Romans after their conquest of the Jews, and revived by the British after more than a thousand years, was applied equally to both its Jewish and Arab population. For example, the well-known English language newspaper *The Jerusalem Post* was then called *The Palestine Post*.[4] However, this peace was short-lived, for when the United Nations narrowly voted to recognize the Jewish declaration of the *independent* State of Israel on May 14, 1948, the Arab world went to war against the Palestinian Jews, now able to call them "Israelis." Failing to overrun infant Israel, the attacking Arabs occupied what they could. Jordan annexed the biblical territories of Judea and Samaria (now known as the West Bank) in 1950, and Egypt took the Gaza Strip. But the Israeli victory had left displaced the Palestinian Arab population who had fled Israel's borders under Arab command and the promise that upon the defeat of the Jewish enemy they would reclaim their and the Jews' abandoned homes. Many of the Arab countries surrounding Israel could have easily absorbed their brethren, but refused. On the one hand, they did not want the economic and social burden of caring for an indigent people, while on the other, they wanted to create a problem for Israel which they knew could be an instrument for international criticism and eventual intervention.

Therefore, returning to Palestine, most took up residence in the Palestinian nation of Jordan in the Jordanian-occupied area known as the West Bank, while others chose to live within Israel proper and became citizens of Israel with the rights and benefits of Israeli citizenship. The former group of Arabs in the West Bank are the original "Palestinians," although today their ranks have been joined by a large number of Arabs who originally lived outside the borders of Israel. These came from Jordan, Syria, Lebanon, Egypt, Iraq, and other Middle Eastern countries allied with the original Arab League charter to remove all Jews from the land. Since the Palestinian "uprising" (Intafada) that began in 1987, the Israeli-Arabs (such as those of East Jerusalem) who comprise about 20 percent of the State of Israel have joined the ranks and now refer to themselves only as "Palestinians." It should be emphasized, however, that, except for Jordan, there has never existed at any time a Palestinian State. In contrast to what is popularly presented today, "Israel is being robbed of its political, historic, and geographic legitimacy while seeming to rob the Palestinians of a nation it already has."[5] Meanwhile, this newly-formed conglomerate of Arabs have sought to create what has never before existed by electing a president, adopting a flag, forming an army (read: "police force"), setting up diplomatic headquarters in East Jerusalem (the Orient House), and with Jordan's agreement, "declaring a state," all in violation of the stipulations agreed in the Oslo Accord which precluded any recognition of a Palestinian state or a "governmental presence" in Jerusalem.

The Cause of the Middle East Conflict

One of the major misconceptions concerning the Middle East conflict fostered by media reporting is that it is the result of a dispute over the ownership of land. Such a conflict, of course, is seen at the surface, with the Palestinians calling for a complete Israeli withdrawal from occupied territory (which according to Palestinian maps is all of the land!), and Israel arguing that the same territory is their ancient homeland and the inheritance given to their fathers by God (See Genesis 12:7; 13:15-17; 15:18-21; 17:8; 22:17). Seeking to create their own revision of history, Palestinians have now claimed descendency from the ancient Philistines, whom they say renamed Canaan "Palestine" in an attempt to pre-date the Israelites in the

Land![6] But the necessity of land should be understood in light of the statistical reality of Arab land at 4,600,000 square miles versus Israeli land (including the West Bank) at 34,000 square miles. Israel is content to live within this small amount of territory, even though the original covenant with Abraham included much more (about 200,000 square miles). However, the surrounding Arab nations deny Israel occupation in even this area, and despite the Oslo Accord to the contrary, the Palestinian Authority, in agreement with other Arab nations, continue as a provision of their charter a refusal to recognize the right of Israel to exist!

The real reason for the Arab-Israeli conflict is not political, but religious. The problem is Islam, which believes that it must subjugate the world by the sword, that all lands once in Muslim possession must never be relinquished or returned, and that the Koran proclaimed Israel as wretched and condemned and Jews as the friends of Satan worthy only of contempt and punishment. The Koran also teaches that Islam superseded both Judaism and Christianity, and therefore Islam cannot tolerate another religion sharing equal access or privileges with itself (such as at holy sites).[7] Many Muslims further teach that the Jews of today (and especially European Jewry) are really non-Semitic descendants of the Middle Age Khazar dynasty. Therefore, on religious grounds, it is impossible to negotiate a lasting peace with a perpetual enemy. The existence of a sovereign Jewish state is an affront to the Koran, and most Jews are not Jews at all and have no right to claim any inheritance based on the Bible. Because of these irreconcilable religious differences, the kind of "peace" understood by most Westerners and Europeans is impossible in the Middle East.

What Kind of Peace is Now Possible?

From the outset it is important to understand that peace between Israel and its neighboring Arab countries is possible so long as it is understood what kind of peace we can expect. Two types of peace are possible in the world today. The first kind of peace is that which exists between democracies. The peace between the United States and its neighboring countries of Canada and Mexico is an example of this type of peace. Even though Canada may protest the United States poisoning its environment with acid rain, and the United States may oppose the drug trafficking from Mexico, these countries do not go to war with each other over these issues. Democracies generally resolve their differences by non-violent negotiation and therefore do not require guarantees since there is no threat to the national security.

The second kind of peace that exists is that between democracies and non-democracies. When the nature of the regime changes, so must the nature of the peace. When political philosophies are inherently different, the type of peace expected will follow suit. In this case, agreements must be attended by guarantees of security and a balance of power that promotes détente. The type of peace that is being negotiated between Israel (the sole democracy in the Middle East) and its Arab non-democratic neighbors is of this second type. The Palestinian Authority was once at the top of the U.S. list of terrorist organizations because it employed terrorism as its means for achieving political ends. It used the terrorist tactic of "uprising" (*Intafada*) against Israel before the Oslo Accord and has continued to call for "holy war" (*Jihad*) throughout the first phase of the "peace process." It has also continued to openly embrace and support terrorist organizations such as Hamas. In addition, the Palestinian Authority has called for and implemented the death penalty for any Palestinian who sells family-owned land to Jews. Such use of terror is the way of non-democracies, but it is totally unacceptable in terms of negotiation with democracies. Therefore, in order to avoid confusion of expectations, it is imperative to understand that peace between democratic and non-democratic parties cannot be achieved on the basis of handshakes and non-violent negotiations, since only one side of the negotiators can ever be expected to honor these terms. The only possibility that a manageable peace could exist is if it exists with enforceable guarantees of security and a balance of military armaments.

The Issue of the Oslo Accord

The issue of the Oslo Accord was simple. The Israelis were to give the Palestinians territory for self-rule and the Palestinians were to curtail terrorism toward Israel from that territory. Israel never viewed their action as giving up territory for the creation of an independent Palestinian state, but as sharing sovereignty with their Arab neighbors west of the Jordan in order to create a defense against attacks aimed at the Israeli people. Israel's primary concern was the guarantee of security for its people who have continually been attacked by organized terrorists from these territories. The Oslo Accord did not deal with either the question of Palestinian statehood or the status of Jerusalem. Israel refused to consider the formation of a Palestinian state within Greater Israel (Judea and Samaria). They postponed the Jerusalem issue to a second phase of negotiation which ideally would build upon the foundation of the guarantee of security established by the first phase. Now that terrorism in Israel has demonstrated that the Palestinians are both unable and unwilling to honor their commitments to Israel's security, the second phase of negotiations has been frozen. Even so, it is clear that no government of Israel (whether Likud or Labor) will permit the formation of an independent Palestinian state nor change the present status of Jerusalem.

Problems for Present Peace

The Jewish construction of 6,500 housing units for its ever-growing immigrant population within Jerusalem's municipal boundaries at Har Homa has created an incident of international protest. Palestinians claim that this is in violation of the Oslo Accord and, as one CNN anchor put it, "an invasion of Palestinian territory by Israel." However, such construction is not prohibited by Oslo in areas under Israel's jurisdiction and 75 percent of the expropriated land for the project was Jewish-owned. Yet, when terrorist bombing was renewed in Israel, Palestinian Authority chief negotiator Feisal al-Husseni said, "the terror of the bulldozers [Jewish construction at Har Homa] has led to the terror of the bombs." How can there be negotiations with people who believe that a construction project can be equated with the murder of innocent people? Yet, rather than implement security procedures to control terrorism against Israel (in compliance with Oslo), Yasser Arafat turned his police force into a 40,000-man army (made up in many cases from known terrorist leaders) that is being trained to launch terrorism, not fight it. This has been demonstrated in recent riots in which members of this police force fired on Israelis, but not on its own fire-bomb throwing people. Arafat has continually given the green light to terrorist organizations sheltered within Palestinian territory to wage *Jihad* and liberate Jerusalem.

Other problems include negotiation with Syria over the Golan Heights, which is presently impossible because of Syria's preconditioned terms that Israel return the Golan Heights. Of course, if this were done there would be nothing to negotiate, since Israel would have lost its only bargaining chip and Syria would have what it wanted. No government could comply with such preconditions, especially with a country which continues to declare itself in a state of war and is increasing its armaments at an alarming rate.

The facts are that the so-called "peace-process" has been impossible from its outset and that the problems Israel has been enduring since the cessation of the Intafada and the handshake on the White House lawn (between Yitzhak Rabin and Yasser Arafat) have been the result of Israel's attempts to honor Oslo by giving the Palestinians control of Jericho, Gaza, and the West Bank. Are these problems of pseudo-peace part of the prophetic plan for Israel in the endtime? Gershon Salomon, an Orthodox Israeli and head of the Temple Mount and Land of Israel Faithful, believes the present conflict is a sign that his generation will see both the pangs of Messiah and the promised redemption. Concerning this he wrote in his newsletter:

> We are acting in a very critical time in the history of the people and the land of Israel. We always knew from the Scriptures and Jewish tradition that the time before the coming of the Mashiah and the complete redemption of Israel would be a difficult and complicated time. We call them "pangs of redemption." But I and my friends are completely committed to doing everything that we can to ensure that the prophetic plans of G—d will be fulfilled…We are committed to bring about the appearance of Mashiah ben David in our lifetime. If needs be we are ready to sacrifice ourselves for this. We have decided that we want to see the rebuilding of the Third Temple and the return of the Israeli Jewish nation to the boundaries which G—d promised us.[8]

If, as many Israelis believe, the present peace process is a pseudo-peace, it is necessary to consider what the Scripture says concerning the nature of such events in light of the prophetic program outlined for Israel in the endtime. Let us first consider what the Bible records concerning the real peace promised after the

Lord's return, and then, by contrast, the characteristics of false peace that will deceive the world prior to Christ's Second Advent.

The Promised Peace

While pseudo-peace processes may be attempted both before and during the Tribulation period, a time of true peace will eventually come to the region. The prophetic details concerning this promised peace are given largely by the prophets Isaiah, Jeremiah, and Ezekiel. Ezekiel refers to a "covenant of peace" (Ezekiel 34:25; 37:26) made between the Lord and the "sons of Israel" that will have several provisions: (1) it will involve secure occupation of the Land of Israel; (2) it will be everlasting (Ezekiel 37:26b); (3) it will establish and increase the Israeli population in the Land (Ezekiel 37:26c; compare verses 25 and 36:24, 28); and (4) it will secure the rebuilding of the Temple and return the Divine Presence (Ezekiel 37:26d-27; compare chapters 40-48). Isaiah, building upon these understood guarantees, adds in Isaiah 2 that this peace will also be universal and pervasive (verse 2), spiritual (verse 3; compare 11:9b), unparalleled, and will emanate from Jerusalem (verses 2,3; compare 27:13). Isaiah also depicts this peace extending beyond the political realm to the natural order (Isaiah 11:6-9a; compare Ezekiel 34:25), and as being inclusive of Gentiles as well as Jews (Isaiah 56:6,7). Jeremiah's details of this period of promised peace in Jeremiah 31 focus on its unconditional and spiritual nature. Here called the "new covenant" because it differs from the conditional and legal nature of the Mosaic Covenant which it supersedes, its provisions of national spiritual regeneration and restoration (verses 33,34) guarantees Israel's existence as a national entity.[9] This is enforced by the use of the stronger Hebrew term in verse 36 for a corporate body—*goi* "nation," rather than the weaker *'am* "a people." Thus, Israel must be preserved as a recognizable national entity, not simply as a distinguishable people for the fulfillment of this prophetic position. Although always known through the ages as the Jewish people, this national distinction was returned to Israel in May of 1948. Zechariah makes "peace" the hallmark of the coming age in contrast with the former time in which "there was no peace because of his enemies..." (Zechariah 8:10). Therefore, in the Millennial Kingdom, the time of promised refreshing (Acts 3:19), there

will be peace for agricultural activity, peace for Israel among the
nations, and peace within every Israeli city (Zechariah 8:12-19).
According to Revelation 20:1-9, this period of peace on earth,
whose security will be guaranteed by the righteous reign of the Messiah (Psalm 2:6-12), will persist for a thousand years before
becoming the permanent possession of the saints in the Eternal
State (Revelation 21:4, 24-26; 22:2,3).

The Characteristics of Pseudo-Peace

The Prophets Jeremiah and Ezekiel warned Israel on the eve of
the destruction of its monarchy: "...they have healed the hurt of
the daughter of My people superficially, saying, 'Peace, peace;'
when there is no peace" (Jeremiah 6:14; 8:11), "they have seduced
My people by saying, 'Peace!' when there is no peace" (Ezekiel
13:10,16). Israel made unwise and unworthy alliances with enemies who had the potential to fight for Israel, but whose plan was to
fight against her. In every case the move was away from trust in
God because of the fear of man (compare Isaiah 7:1-9). A similar
situation will occur when the day of the Lord commences with the
Tribulation period. During this time of human enthronement in the
Antichrist, security will be sought in his globalized governmental
system (Revelation 13:4,7,16,17). In 1 Thessalonians 5:3, we read
that at the very time they will be saying: "'Peace and safety!' then
destruction will come upon them suddenly like birth pangs upon a
woman with child; and they shall not escape." The deception and
disappointment of pseudo-peace is that those who believe they
have prevented future trouble have really only prevented themselves from escaping from it.

The Consequences of Pseudo-Peace

Pseudo-peace seems to offer the possibility for peace, but in
fact only makes more probable the necessity for war. The agreement with the Palestinians has effectively turned the calendar back
to 1947 when Israel was contained within its least defensible
boundaries, only nine miles in width in some places. It has
removed the necessary buffer zone between Israel and its hostile
Arab neighbors, made possible the establishment of an enemy army
in the territories under Palestinian authority who could cut off

access to vital water resources and invade Israel. While the world hopes for a "peace" in the Middle East, more seasoned analysts are now forecasting just the opposite. They see the peace process as part of a phased program devised to weaken Israel as a prelude to the next and perhaps final Arab-Israeli war. As one writer, comparing the similar context of history, has put it:

"Weakening Israel territorially or spiritually...will soon force it to face the choice Chamberlain faced when appeasement failed and Hitler invaded Poland: fight a desperate war or perish."[10]

The peace process has especially threatened Jerusalem, control of which has been the stated objective of the Palestinians since the beginning of official talks with Israel in Madrid. Since the end of the first phase of the Oslo Accord, the demand for Jerusalem as the capital of an independent Palestinian state has increased and been supported by terrorist attacks in the very heart of the city. This has led some newspapers to announce that "the battle for Jerusalem has begun!"

The Battle for Jerusalem

There is no doubt that the end of the conflict in the Middle East will be over Jerusalem. This is direction toward which all of the negotiations in the peace process have headed, and, as Arafat once announced: "Jerusalem is the essence of peace between us!" The biblical prophets also confirm that the resolution of the Middle East conflict will center in this city (Zechariah 12:2,3). When I spoke with Jerusalem's mayor Ehud Olmert a few days after Prime Minister Yitzhak Rabin's state funeral, he said to me that the Prime Minister had assured him just days before his assassination that he would never divide Jerusalem. Prime Minister Benjamin Netanyahu has repeatedly stated the same position, a position of strength which returned his Likud party to power. He has said: "I will never allow Jerusalem to be divided again. Never! Never! We will keep Jerusalem united and...we will never resurrender those ramparts."[11] And again: "Jerusalem has been the capital of Israel for 3,000 years since the time of King David and we don't expect to change that for the next 3,000 years!"[12] Renewed acts of terrorism have also provoked a renewed focus on the growing conflict over the holy city and the Temple Mount, the central stage for end-time events, but presently barred to Jews for religious purposes.

The Peace Process and Prayers at the Temple Mount

Likud's election manifesto declared that the Temple Mount is "the heart and soul of the Jewish people and the most holy focus of the Nation." According to Temple activists, it also promised to open the Temple Mount for Jewish prayers. In a letter from Prime Minister Benjamin Netanyahu to Yehuda Etzion, an activist on trial for resisting arrest when he was forcibly removed from the Temple Mount after attempting to pray there last September, Netanyahu is reported to have written:

> The right of the Jewish people to its holy place—the Temple Mount—cannot be questioned. I believe it is necessary to arrange for Jewish prayer at the site, especially given that we permit freedom of worship to all religions in Jerusalem...I believe we can do this properly when we return to govern the country.

The Israeli High Court did rule to permit Jewish prayers on the Temple Mount in the recent case of Yehuda Etzion. The Muslim reaction was predictable. In a sermon delivered shortly after the High Court's decision, the sheikh of the Al-Aqsa mosque declared: "We refuse to obey the decisions of this racist court. The rabbis will not enter Al-Aqsa, not [unless] over our dead bodies and shrouds." This was tested last Tisha B'Av (the day commemorating the destruction of the Temple in A.D. 70) when Chief Rabbi Israel Lau issued a call for all Israel to go to the Temple Mount and pray. The Muslims closed the Mugrabi Gate (the only entrance open to Jews) and thousands of Israeli Jews waited for hours outside. Muslims were permitted inside for prayers, but the Jewish worshipers were refused entrance by police who barred the entrance fearing the threat of Arab opposition.

The Peace Process and the Rebuilding of the Temple

If the "peace process" is to continue, the Palestinians have demanded sovereignty over East Jerusalem and the Temple Mount, though by next year a majority of Jews will live in East Jerusalem and most Israelis (whether secular or religious) continue to view the Temple as a unique symbol of Israel's independence and unity, if not of its promised future. The issue of rebuilding the Third Temple has also continually been at the forefront of Arab concerns.

In March of 1996, international newspapers published a photograph of Yasser Arafat holding up an artist's rendering of a restored Temple and telling his people to "get ready for the next battle" (for Jerusalem).

On September 25, 1996, the opening by the Israelis of an exit tunnel to the Hasmonean aqueduct which connects with the Western Wall Tunnel sparked a riot between Palestinians and Israelis. Palestinians heaved stones from atop the Temple Mount toward Israelis who were praying at the Western Wall as loudspeakers on the Mount called for Arabs to come and defend the holy places. Arabs came and by the end of the riot period some 58 had been killed. The Palestinians claimed that the newly-carved tunnel threatened the Muslim mosques on the Temple Mount. For this reason, Yasser Arafat described the action as "a crime against our religious and holy places...completely against the peace process."

The Palestinian-instigated riot, however, was merely a political tactic to turn attention to their demand for Jerusalem. The facts seem to support the Israeli contention: The Western Wall Tunnel, a 2,000-year-old underground passageway, used as a transit for priests during the time of the Second Temple, has been a popular tourist attraction since its official opening to the public in 1987. However, because the only exit for the tunnel at its northern end next to the Struthion Pool was through a private home, all tourist traffic had to exit back through the tunnel's entrance. This made it impossible to tour more than 30 people at one time, resulting in tour bookings literally around the clock. Therefore, as the Ministry of Religious Affairs contends, the Islamic *Wakf* (the Muslim authority which has jurisdiction on the Temple Mount) had an agreement with the previous administration to allow for the tunnel exit. The agreement was a deal to permit the Muslims a one-time use of the "Solomon's Stables" area for Ramadan prayers in exchange for permission to cut the tunnel. The Ramadan prayers were held last summer as scheduled, however, Feisal al Husseini, chief negotiator for the PLO, now says that no such agreement was ever reached with the Israeli government.

The real issue, according to Jerusalem mayor Ehud Olmert, is the control over Jerusalem: "The tunnel has no connection to the mosques—it is far away—this is about who will control Jerusalem." However, despite Israeli dismissal of the tunnel as an issue in the riot, it remained at the center of contention when I spoke with *Wakf* director Adnan Husseni in October. I even noticed that Arabic maps of the Temple Mount, with the new tunnel marked in red, were still being circulated from one of the *Wakf* offices. Even so, the *Wakf* reacted in an identical manner at Succot in October of 1990 when it was thought that the Temple Mount Faithful were going to bring a cornerstone for the Third Temple to the Mount. On that occasion, even though it was widely publicized to Muslim officials and the Arab press that the Israeli police would not allow the Temple Mount Faithful to enter the area, the riots were still conducted. However, Israeli intelligence reports later revealed that the reason for the attack at the Western Wall was to highlight the Palestinian plight and to gather worldwide Muslim support (then needed by Saddam Hussein) by focusing on the common Arab interest in Jerusalem.

Jerusalem's Importance to Islam

What is the common Arab interest in Jerusalem? Why has this one city been singled out as the key factor for the success or failure of the peace process? If we consider the religious status of Jerusalem for the Moslem, we find that it ranks only third after the Great Mosque of the Kaabah in Mecca and the mosque built upon the house of Mohammed in Medina. The Al Aqsa mosque on the southern end of the Temple Mount and the Dome of the Rock at its western side are the buildings that make Islam sacred to Muslims. However, it must be noted that Jerusalem is never mentioned in the Koran, that no Arab power ever made it a center of government or a site for pilgrimage, nor were the later significance of Mohammed's "Night Journey" and "Ascent to Paradise," associated with these structures, either in the Koran or as a part of early Muslim interpretation. Rather, the importance of the Al Aqsa and the Dome of the Rock lies in their being symbols of Islam's supersession of Christianity and Judaism. In A.D. 638 when Islam captured Jerusalem from the Byzantine Christian empire, it wanted to demonstrate its status as military conqueror of Christianity, that Mohammed was a greater prophet than Jesus, and that Islam superseded Christianity. Therefore, the Al Aqsa was built over the site of a Byzantine church which in turn was built over the site of Solomon's Porch where the Church was born on the day of Pentecost (Acts 3:11; 5:12), and the

Dome of the Rock was built over the site of the Holy of Holies within the Jewish Temple which had been defiled by Byzantine Christianity. This replacement theology of Islam can be further seen within the Dome of the Rock where inscribed verses from the Koran instruct Muslims that Christianity is false by saying "God had no son" and "Allah is the One God," and the Koranic teaching that Ishmael (Abraham's son claimed as the Arab progenitor), not Isaac (Abraham's son through whom the Jewish people came) was offered for sacrifice on the rock within the dome. This same concept of replacement can be seen in the fourth holiest place in Islam, the Umayyad mosque in Damascus, built in the city where Jesus' disciples were first called "Christians" (Acts 11:26) and over the site of the Basilica of St. John the Baptist. Nevertheless, apart from these apologetic purposes, Jerusalem holds no religious significance for the worship of the Moslem. As Shmuel Katz has observed: "Without Jerusalem, not an iota would be changed in the texture of Islam, or in the personal life of the Arabs or any other Moslem. He would continue to pray in the direction of Mecca, as he has always done."[13]

Jerusalem's Importance to Jews

On the other hand, in Judaism, Jerusalem occupies the most important place in its worship. The posture of Orthodox prayer from any point in the world is only towards Jerusalem, as mandated in the Bible (1 Kings 8:29,30, 38-44; compare Daniel 6:10). Since the destruction and exile of the Jewish people from Jerusalem in A.D. 70, Jewish prayers have included a petition to return to Jerusalem and rebuild. At Passover, Jews throughout the world end their commemoration of the Exodus with the prayer "Next Year in Jerusalem!" And whenever access was possible throughout the ages, the Western Wall of the Temple Mount was the chief center for pilgrimage and worship. No other city in Israel commemorates a special day of celebration over its liberation, but in May each year "Jerusalem Day" celebrates the unification of the city which occurred in 1967. Regardless of the religious affectations of Jewish people, there is a universal recognition and affirmation that Jerusalem remains the historic capital of Israel and the place from which the peace promised to the Jewish people and mankind will be realized. This realization is epitomized in many places around the city where there can be seen inscriptions of the familiar verse from the Psalms: "Pray for the peace of Jerusalem."

International Involvement

If, as Zechariah predicts, the nations of the world will one day unify in an invasion of Israel with the attack focused on Jerusalem, then we should expect to see international involvement in the Middle East situation mounting as we move toward the endtime. In this respect, China has traditionally supported Israel's Arab enemies and has especially close relations with Iran. Iran has for years been amassing non-conventional weapons, and China has agreed to build an atomic reactor for them. China has been interested in Israel's technological advances in agriculture since it struggles to feed its ever burgeoning population. Iraq, too, has continued to increase its armaments, despite the sanctions imposed upon it after the Gulf War, and recently Saddam Hussein received Palestinian President Yasser Arafat (who, with King Hussein of Jordan, had supported him in the Gulf War). Libya's Mohammar Khadafi has begun to build a mountain fortress containing an arsenal of chemical weapons that can be launched against Israel and even the United States. The Commonwealth of Independent States has continued to supply arms to these and other Middle Eastern Arab powers while eyeing Israel's considerable wealth of mineral resources in the Dead Sea and its immigrant intelligentsia. Such resources are desperately needed to revive the social and economic disasters that plague the former Soviet empire.

Arabs and the New World Order

At the same time, the Palestinians and the Arab League are hastening to position themselves to be part of the expanding New World Order that has emerged with the unification of Germany, the collapse of the Iron Curtain, and the rise of the European Economic Community. Essential to entrance in this network is a peaceful co-existence that fosters the overarching principle of unity. Yasser Arafat, recognized by Palestinians as "President" of an as yet non-existent Palestinian state, has listed acceptance by this community as one of his top priorities and motivation for making "peace" with Israel. He states:

> For many years I have been asking the Israelis to start
> making peace...There is a new world order. We want to
> be part of this new order, as Palestinians, and as an Arab
> nation.[14]

For this same reason Arafat demanded an International Force be stationed in the Palestinian territories to police the Israeli settlements nearby. Such an action drew the Palestinian state into the protective custody of the international community, while at the same time set Israel apart from it. The Arabs perceived this as an important guarantee for their security, since they had interpreted the establishment of diplomatic relations between Israel and the Vatican as a move against Muslim solidarity.[15] However, by coming under the indirect control of an international force, when the Russian-Arab alliance moves against Israel, the European community will be compelled to intervene. However, when the battle is turned to favor Israel, they will join with the Israelis, and their leader will perhaps claim credit for what is, in fact, a divine intervention.

It was incredible enough to believe Israel's nearly five million inhabitants could hold their own against 22 Arab nations of more than 200 million, but with the added numbers of Russia and her satellites, the world will be convinced that Israel's survival through this attack is indeed miraculous. For a time, the anti-Semitism that has spread through Europe will give way to an acknowledgment of this phenomena. However, once Israel asserts her independence from the rule of Antichrist, anti-Semitism will explode on a worldwide scale, and Israel will truly be "hated by all nations" (Matthew 24:9).

Arms Buildup in the Middle East

One of the most disturbing events occurring parallel to the supposed "peace" plan in the Middle East is the continual buildup of weaponry throughout the Arab League countries. Russia is one of the largest suppliers of submarines and other armaments to Iran, China has supplied reactors and nuclear technology to Iran and Algeria, and France has sold massive amounts of tanks to the United Arab Emirates. As a result of allied assistance during the Gulf War, the U.S. and Great Britain have made heavy concessions of fighter-bombers to Saudi Arabia.[16] It is also well known that Iraq,

Iran, Libya, Pakistan, Syria, and Algeria have all sought to produce or have produced nuclear and chemical/biological weapons in the last year.[17] Reports that Egyptians have located uranium sites concealed by Israelis in the Sinai have also caused recent concern.[18] One must wonder why there is an increased proliferation of arms pouring into these Arab countries if peace is truly a prospect.

What Could Happen Next?

If Israel is unsuccessful in its negotiations, and the "peace" process fails, it will be forced to engage in another war with its Arab neighbors, a conflict on a scale far greater than any it has yet seen. One writer summed up the situation as only trading land for time, adding a pessimistic prognosis for peace:

> But let us also be under no illusion as to what has happened, or what will happen hereafter. The Palestinian Arabs as a whole have not changed their minds one iota about what they regard as a great historic wrong, nor have they abandoned their hope of rectifying it.[19]

Let us consider, then, the events that may occur as we move down the road from pseudo-peace to a war in the Middle East.

The Road to Making Pseudo-Peace

Somewhere along the prophetic path that leads to the final pseudo-peace made by the Antichrist, will come a war between Israel and a Russian-Arab alliance (Ezekiel 38–39). This war, called the "Battle of Gog and Magog" in the context of Ezekiel, is placed between the chapters dealing with Israel's return to the Land and spiritual restoration (chapters 33-37) and the building of the Millennial Temple (chapters 40-48). Therefore, it could occur prior to the Tribulation or in either the first or second parts of the Tribulation, including at its end. Israel, at present, fits the description given in Ezekiel 38 of "living securely...without walls, and having no bars or gates" (verse 11). Only the old city of Jerusalem is walled, but the majority of Jerusalemites live in the new city outside these walls. Israel has also inhabited the "waste places" as predicted for this time in Ezekiel 38:12.

The Battle of Gog and Magog

During the end-time battle of Gog and Magog, Gog is depicted as a military leader that arises from "the northern region" (from Israel's vantage point) of Magog (ancient Scythia). Today this area is comprised of the former Soviet republics of Kazakhstan, Kirghiza, Uzbekistan, Turkmenistan, and Tajikistan. According to Ezekiel, other nations which align themselves with Magog to invade Israel are Rosh (Russia), Meshech and Tubal (territories in Turkey), Gomer (Germany), Togarmah (Turkey), Persia (Iran), Cush/Ethiopia (Sudan), Put (Libya), and Egypt (according to Daniel 11:40-42). While there is a difference of opinion among scholars as to the precise timing of this war, many now place it sometime before or during the Tribulation period (compare Ezekiel 37:8, 16; 39:9).[20]

Can it be only coincidental that the balance of power in this part of the world has for decades been concentrated in Russia and the Arab countries? Since the dissolution of the Soviet Union, six of the former southern republics have become independent *Islamic* nations: Azerbaijan, Kazakhstan, Uzbekistan, Kirghizia, Turkmenistan, and Tajikistan. All of these new nations, which are part of Ezekiel's prediction, have a militant Islamic movement and are virulently anti-Semitic. They all also have economic hardships which have forced alliances with other Islamic nations, and have nuclear weapons at their disposal.

In mother Russia there is also a strong anti-Semitism among nationalists. One of Russia's more prominent and radical nationalists, Vladamir Zhirinovsky, once proposed in a book entitled *The Final March to the South* a military strategy for world domination that is remarkably close to the prophetic sketch of the endtime one-world government divided into ten regions of power presided over by a supreme leader that arises from their ranks (compare Daniel 7:24; Revelation 17:12-13). Calling for a restoration of Greater Russia's primacy, he has threatened to even use atomic weapons to achieve his ends. His plan argues that it is Russia's destiny to capture the lands to the south, including Israel. His plan does not call for the destruction of Israel but its control. Richard Judy explains:

> Zhirinovsky sees the world as one of great powers destined to exercise hegemony over specific spheres of influence....Russia's sphere of influence includes...the

remainder of the Middle East not already included in Russia proper, plus East Africa and its horn...Iraq, also a friend of Russia, will exercise suzerainty over the Arabian peninsula (except for Israel, which quixotically will be permitted to exist)...Under Russian hegemony, the Muslims would be pacified and those threats [Islamic fundamentalism] eliminated...Russia would also guarantee (or co-guarantee) the security of the State of Israel.[21]

Russian control of Arab countries will perhaps give it the power to negotiate with Israel, although the thought expressed here is that Russia will invade Israel and control it by guaranteeing its security (by a covenant of peace?). This is similar to Daniel 11:40,41 and Ezekiel 38:8, which both picture a non-destructive invasion of Israel from the north.

It appears that the groundwork for this plan has even now been laid through the political and economic circumstances in Russia. Since Russia cannot produce a sufficient industry to survive economically, its only course has been to align itself with Third World countries. An axis has been formed at the present between Iran, Syria, Sudan, and Ethiopia to overthrow the U.S. and its allies. Russia has already forged alliances with some of these and others: Iran, Syria, Pakistan, Libya, and Turkey. In addition, the Central Asian Republics of Kazakhstan, Turkmenistan, Tadzhikistan, Uzbekistan, and Kyrghyzstan have signed a military assistance pact with the Russian Federation. These countries are all Islamic and have been confirmed to possess nuclear weapons. In the past year, Iran and Iraq have been arming themselves with weapons supplied by Russia and China as never before, an act which in itself calls for international involvement. Such events, combined with the downturn in the pseudo-peace process, has led Gershon Salomon, leader of Israel's Temple Mount Faithful, to announce publicly that he expects the soon-coming and unavoidable Arab-Israeli war to be none other than the prophetic battle of Gog and Magog:

I consider it my duty to warn my people and all the friends of Israel that a terrible war, the most terrible war of all the seven wars of Israel, is going to be perpetrated in this land against the people of Israel as a direct result of these terrible agreements and the giving away to the

enemies of G—d our Holy Temple Mount and the most
holy and important Biblical areas of Israel…According
to the prophetic plans of G—d these areas must be, and
will be, even more so than in the past, the land of G—d
and the people of Israel to carry the great mission in the
end-times…We read in the prophetic Scriptures of
Ezekiel and Zechariah about the terrible Gog and Magog
war which is going to come on the people of Israel in the
end-times, in the time of the redemption. When we see
these terrible, critical events in Israel we can understand
why, in this time of redemption, this terrible war of Gog
and Magog is going to take place…This war will not be
an easy time for Israel…but it will be the last war of
redemption of the people of Israel. This will be the war
when the Messiah, Mashiach ben David, will appear and
again be the eternal King of Israel. This war will also
open a new moral and spiritual page in the history of
Israel. After this war the people of Israel will not be the
same people… G—d is ready to make this a time of prophetic fulfillment, are we allowed not to be ready?…We
believe that a brave government committed to the historical vision of the people of Israel of the rebuilding of
the temple would soon give the order to renew the work
of finding the Ark [of the Covenant] and to place it in a
rebuilt Holy of Holies.[22]

If this expected pre-Tribulational war is that of Gog and Magog,
or some other war involving similar peoples, and it neutralizes the
pervasive political clout of Islam, Israel will emerge as a major
player in the end-time scenario and a force with which to be reckoned by all nations (compare Zechariah 12:3,9;14:2).

The Prophetic Process of Pseudo-Peace

Because the outcome of this coming Middle East war will result
in Israel gaining a new position of power in the Middle East, the
European leader (the Antichrist) will move to establish a balance of
power by making a covenant with the Jews (see Daniel 9:27). For
the first time in modern history there will be no Islamic opposition
to Israel's sovereignty over Jerusalem. It is possible that as a result
of the recognition of divine intervention in the war, Orthodox Jews
will be elevated in the eyes of the secular nation, and will take over

the government. These new spiritual-political leaders will announce that the victory of Israel has ushered in the long-awaited Messianic era of redemption. This will instigate the rebuilding of the Third Temple and the sacrificial system will be reinstituted (Revelation 11:1,2; Daniel 9:27).

Daniel's Prophecy of the Seventy Weeks (Daniel 9:24-27) clearly identifies a "prince that shall come" whose people destroyed the city of Jerusalem and the Sanctuary (Daniel 9:26). This future figure will make a "firm covenant" with the Jewish leadership ("the many") at a time when the Jewish Temple is (or can be) rebuilt and the sacrificial system reinstituted (verse 27). The relationship between these events in the same context imply that the restoration of the Temple and its services may be a result of the signing of this covenant. If so, the parallel of these events with the provisions in God's "covenant of peace" (to be made with Israel at the beginning of the Millennium), may also imply the Antichrist's attempt to counterfeit this predicted peace and deceive Israel and the world with a pseudo-millennium.

These events move Israel into the Tribulation period known in the Old Testament as the "Time of Jacob's Trouble" (Jeremiah 30:7) or "Time of Distress" (Daniel 12:1). The first half of this period, while certainly a time in which God's wrath is displayed on earth (Revelation 6:1,2), will nevertheless be a time in which Israel enjoys a pseudo-messianic era. However, this time of "peace" in the Middle East, which may be the political maneuver that propels the Antichrist into world ascendancy, is described by the Bible as a false peace (Jeremiah 6:14; 8:11). In 1 Thessalonians 5:3 we read: "For when they shall say, 'Peace and safety;' then sudden destruction cometh upon them, as travail upon a woman with child; and they shall not escape." It may be that during this time the False Prophet (Revelation 13:11-18), who will be Jewish (verse 11) may appear and eventually be accepted by many Jews as the Messiah (Matthew 24:24). This false peace will evidently end with the desecration of the Temple by the Antichrist and the worldwide persecution of Jews at the mid-point of this period. These events will usher the world into a time of Great Tribulation, described as a period when this pseudo "peace is removed from the earth" at the opening of the second seal judgment (Revelation 6:4).

How Will It Happen?

When we look at the mix in the Middle East today, there is con-fusion as to how the scenario posited in Scripture will happen. It is my opinion that the events concerning Israel during the Tribulation will be spearheaded by a minority element of religious Jews. They will enter into the contract with the Antichrist in order to secure peace and rebuild the Third Temple. From their ranks may come the 144,000 Jews who will understand the deception, receive the true Messiah, and bear witness to the gospel of His coming Kingdom to the world (Revelation 7:3-8). Many have wondered how the present religious minority movements in Israel (messianic and Temple movements) could influence world events. As the 1990 Temple Mount incident with the Temple Mount Faithful, which drew response from Saddam Hussein, and the Kach member Baruch Goldstein's 1994 mosque shooting have revealed, it does not require a majority to make a big difference in the Middle East. One writer has said concerning this disproportionate influence of minority organizations in Israel:

> Although small in absolute numbers, the power of these splinter groups to derail international initiatives and to reignite conflict on the West Bank is magnified by unin-hibited ideological fanaticism.[23]

Today in Israel there exists the Temple Movement, the Lubav-itchers with their continued hope in the resurrection of their pseudo-messiah Menchem Mendel Schneerson, (the Ultra-Orthodox anti-Zionist who awaits a divine intervention and the overthrow of secular Jewish government), and many other organizations who want to see Jewish sovereignty restored to all of the Land of Israel ('Eretz-Yisrael). Though at present these are splinter groups, a deceptive event of divine proportion could convince these groups to follow a single messianic figure and support the signing of a cove-nant that appeared to fulfill their biblical expectations.

Preparing for the Prince of Pseudo-Peace

But how will the world follow the figure of the Antichrist? Today, though the world is relatively stable, there exists a longing for someone to follow who will unite human hearts despite their cultural and religious differences. Modern media-enhanced figures have offered evidence that the masses can be moved to idolize and even "worship," be they rock stars such as John Lennon or political celebrities such as Princess Diana. The international outpouring of grief at the deaths of these famous people by so many from diverse cultural and religious backgrounds lay in the universal familiarity gained through media exposure. Though some seven billion people are thought to have shared in sympathy over "Princess Di," few, if any, of these had ever met her. It was the image they knew and had adored. Yet, something more may be revealed in these disproportionate displays of emotion. Perhaps we are also seeing the collective disappointment of a desperately seeking society cheated of a world-class figure whose projected image offered a rallying point for the planet.

However, once the spiritual checks and balances of the Holy Spirit working through the Church are removed at the Rapture, the great delusion will descend upon a world bereft of discerning leaders and in their place will arise the "man of sin" (2 Thessalonians 2:6-12). The world's penchant for following a charismatic figure will become fanaticism, and fearful of anarchy breaking out across the globe, the world will seek security in a leader who can effectively employ détente. When he reveals himself in supernatural proportions, the international media elite will join in projecting his image around the globe. And when this icon of pseudo-peace perishes, and then revives, the world which has been merged in grief and jubilation will passionately surrender itself to his leadership. Thus we read in Revelation 13:3,4: "And the whole earth was amazed and followed after the beast; and they worshipped the dragon, because he gave his authority to the beast; and they worshipped the beast, saying, 'Who is like the beast, and who is able to wage war with him?'" That future leader will be the one who resolves the Middle East conflict and finally makes peace possible. He will be internationally heralded as a superstar, man of the year, peace prize recipient, and even messiah. It is not hard to see how this will be possible given the modern climate of expectancy and the clamoring for any candidate who promises peace.

The True Storm Shelter of Peace

Failed promises of pseudo-peace have frustrated the deluded masses from time immemorial. God's Word in both testaments has preserved such thwarted hopes in its own record of man's desperation: "We waited for peace, but no good came…" (Jeremiah 8:15; 14:19), "and the path of peace they have not known" (Isaiah 59:8; Romans 3:17). But the Scripture also proclaims that the present desire for peace can be realized. Only Jesus Christ, the Prince of Peace (Isaiah 9:6), is able to "speak peace to the nations" (Zechariah 9:10), for with Him as the High Priest of His people is "peace and righteousness" to "turn many back from iniquity" (Malachi 2:6). However, Christ did not come into this world at His first coming to bring political peace (Matthew 10:34; Luke 12:51; compare John 18:36); this has been reserved for His return at the end of the age (Acts 3:20,21; Romans 16:20; 2 Thessalonians 1:5-10). Even so, Christ offered His personal peace as a storm shelter in contrast to the pseudo-peace of the world: "My peace give I unto you; not as the world gives, give I unto you" (John 14:27; 16:33). This peace is first of all a "peace with God" (Romans 5:1), since all men as sinners are at enmity with Him, being born into enemy camp (John 8:44; Romans 3:9-18). This spiritual peace is promised to the one who believes God's word concerning Christ, who died in the sinner's place on the cross that he might receive forgiveness from God and inherit eternal life (Acts 16:31; Romans 5:13; Colossians 1:20; Hebrews 13:20). Christ also grants a practical peace to safely weather all the storms of life (Galatians 5:22; Colossians 3:15; 2 Thessalonians 3:16), and assures us that as the God of Peace, His presence will be with us to make good His promise (Romans 15:33; 2 Corinthians 13:11; Philippians 4:9). This peace, which is beyond earthly understanding (Philippians 4:7) makes possible a new peaceful relationship between Gentiles and Jews (or for that matter, between Arabs and Jews), Ephesians 2:14-17. This, then, is the true peace for which the world seeks, and which may be found if sought in Christ alone. May you escape the deception of this age's pseudo-peace and find Christ's true peace which forever shelters from the storm.

▼   ▼   ▼

Part 2

▶

LAST-DAYS
LIGHTNING

CHAPTER 6

Israel: Island in the Violent Islamic Sea

Zola Levitt

"Israel is a good country in a bad neighborhood." So described the editor of the *Jerusalem Report* when I interviewed him for our television program one day. He made the point, which is manifestly obvious, that Israel would hardly have a single trouble in this world if it weren't for Islam.

Anti-Semitism is a kind of spiritual insanity that afflicts unbelievers everywhere. There are no truly biblical anti-Semites, but those pretending to a biblical faith—the cults, the sacramental churches, the Protestant "liberals"—all have displayed anti-Jewish sentiment through the centuries. And, of course, the patently unbelieving world has always been, to some degree, anti-Semitic. But all of these forces taken together do not equal the virulent hatred of the Jewish people that is manifested in the Moslem world. Truly, Israel is considered a cancer that must be excised out of the Middle East so that the Islamic countries can have their empire undisturbed and their god in charge of all surrounding lands (as well as other people's lands, if the truth be told).

At least that's the outward reason given for Islamic hostility toward Israel. In reality, deeper and more pedestrian motives can be assigned to the Moslems. After all, Israel has demonstrated that with a small patch of some of the worst land in the Middle East, having no oil or other natural resources to speak of, Jewish immigrants built a twentieth-century society in one generation. The Arabs, in some cases, have been working on their territory for thousands of years, and have reached a state of utter frustration. Egypt, to look at arguably the best of the Arab countries, is hardly able to feed itself. Having a population more than ten times that of Israel, its economy is less than ten percent of Israel's. The other Arab nations present an even more discouraging picture relative to Israel. Thus, simple economic envy and embarrassment are factors in Islamic hatred of the Jews.

There is also the irrational rumor that Israel means to conquer Arab territories and occupy their lands. There's never been an iota of evidence for this view. When Israel had options of pressing on to Cairo and Damascus at the end of the Six-Day War, they did not undertake these excesses, having no appetite for trying to administrate these hopelessly confused and overpopulated cities. Consulting the Israelis (rather than taking the media view, or the Islamic view, or the United Nations view, or the U.S. government view), one would find that they simply want to be left alone. Having been terrifically punished in so many countries for so many centuries, the Jews would simply like to live in peace—even an isolated peace.

With that said, it should also be recognized that the Jews in Israel are not the only Islamic targets. For centuries, Islam has taken territories and converted people, with the tongue or the teeth, throughout the eastern hemisphere. They are now making inroads into the United States and Western European nations. They are a force to be reckoned with. Dr. Walid Phares, a Lebanese who regards himself as a Phoenician, showed us a seventh-century Middle Eastern map on our television program. It was remarkable to see the vast territories given to peoples who today are minority populations. The "Hebrews" in particular lived in all of Israel, while the small group known as the Arabs were found only in Saudi Arabia. From that outpost, Mohammed's followers branched out to country after country, conquering and converting as they went, until they occupied a large proportion of the eastern world. Today their religion and customs prevail among something on the order of a billion people! And we should realize that we are only in the middle of their planned expansion, which includes the United States and the whole earth.

Politically, Islam is a force in this world and perhaps, should the Lord tarry, will make war on democracy all over the planet in the century to come. Spiritually, biblical people have serious questions about Islam. It is obviously the ultimate replacement theology, meant to supplant both Judaism and Christianity. And in many places, it has done just that. But its theology appears varied and confused. What would an Indonesian, who worships magic and totems along with Mohammed, have to do with a "Nation of Islam" Afro-American, whose platforms are based on a general aversion to whites and Jews? The Chinese Moslem (and there are more Moslems in China than there are ethnic Chinese!) counts Buddhists and Communists among his enemies, whereas the Arab Moslem probably knows nobody in either of those ideologies. The Koran is widely distributed among people who do not read, and is taught to them in the same manner that the Bible was taught to the Medieval church.

I visited the sumptuous Blue Mosque in Istanbul, a completely open and cavernous single room in which the worshipper is made to feel almost like a microbe. The stunning, vaulted ceiling several stories high looked down upon a floor that was empty except for an ornate throne, a "reader's chair." Access to this splendid and dominating pulpit was by a ladder-like series of rungs obviously reserved solely for the reader. The guide disclosed that from this chair, two or three stories above the heads of the massed congregants, the reader intoned the holy writ (the Koran). The whole picture was that of what the Book of Revelation calls Nicolaitanism, a term which seems to refer to the conquering of the laity or, in modern terms, the domination of the congregation by an all-powerful priesthood. I ascertained from our guide that the folks in the mosque did not have a copy of what the reader chanted, but merely took his word for the will of their god. There was no discussion, no questioning, no independent examination of their scriptures.

For biblical people, the Koran is like an Old Testament without a New. There is a heavy burden of law, but little grace. The Islamic believer is to be recompensed some great day in some other life, but forgiveness right now down here is virtually absent. While the

Koran champions the underdog and promises to recompense those who have been short-changed in this life, it is very unclear how that laudable goal will be accomplished. There has been much exploitation, rather, of the "spiritual payoff" philosophy. In the movie *Not Without My Daughter*, an Iranian character says that twelve-year-old boys kidnapped by army officers would be issued plastic keys marked "Paradise." They would then be utilized as human minesweepers ahead of the divisions fighting Iraq. The youngster "lucky" enough to step on a mine would have an immediate trip to heaven. In the Palestinian mode, 72 virgins will also belong to the young man who manages a heroic act such as blowing up a busload of innocent civilians. Terrorists who die in such despicable operations are considered martyrs, and a bittersweet celebration of their exploits is normally part of the honor given to such "heroes."

Christians are considered the enemy of the Moslems in many places. And in some countries, animosity has led to the slavery and murder of innocent people just because they follow Christ. In the Sudan, Christians are killed and their children sold into bondage. In Egypt, fundamentalist Moslem groups hunt them down. In all, untold millions of Christians are persecuted throughout the world by Islam, with barely a peep heard from the "free" Western world.

Israel and Islam

Where Israel is concerned, Islam is its most dangerous enemy. The propaganda machines of the Palestinians and the Arabs in general have made Israel seem so villainous in the eyes of the world that the tiny nation has become a pariah. But imagine for a moment that all of the Arabs would simply keep quiet about Israel, or even (just imagine!) say, "You have to hand it to the Jewish people; they built a modern nation in one generation and we haven't been able to do that anywhere." Who would then be Israel's enemies? What nations, other than the Arabs and other Moslems, have any real contention with Israel? In reality, this very small democracy would get along fine in this world without its perennial enemy. The anti-Israelism fostered by the Arabs has infected much of the world through the media and through economic control based on petro-dollars.

It is easy to see why the media consistently favors the Palestinian position over Israel's—extraordinary when you think about it, since much of the media is liberal and democratic, and yet it supports a dictatorship (or, if the truth be told, a police state) over a sister democracy. Apart from anti-Semitism, the answer lies in the terrific economic control that petro-dollars exert on the media. Let's keep in mind that the news providers are not running a public service business. They are profit makers, and profit-making businesses invariably cater to their best customers. Since manufacturers of oil-based products buy a great deal of the advertising in the newspapers of America and Western Europe, they have disproportionate sway over the editorial policies of those newspapers (or magazines, or television programs, or news services).

Petroleum products dominate advertising: gasoline, cars, cosmetics, plastics, every sort of household item, etc. It might come down on the grassroots level to a simple exchange between an advertising buyer and a seller, that might go something like this:

> Buyer: "We'll take a quarter-page ad (or a thirty-second spot) this month."
>
> Seller: "But you usually buy twice that. What's wrong?"
>
> Buyer: "The order comes from upstairs. There's just something about your editorial policies. Maybe those reports criticizing Arafat…"

You can be sure that the editorial policies will ultimately change, or the advertising provider is going to lose some real money.

As the media is swayed, so is public opinion. And Israel, a democracy with free elections and the homeland of a people who suffered greatly in the Holocaust and deserve some peace, becomes the bad guy. Whereas the Palestinians, under the leadership of an international terrorist who is building a typical Arab dictatorship (primitive, backward, and totalitarian), become the good guys.

More than economic pressures favor the Palestinians. There is the unrealistic public perception of the Arabs as the underdog and Israel as a mighty and powerful military machine. But if the facts are known, that's hogwash. There are four and a half million Israelis, compared to 200 million Arabs—the Palestinians have the support of the whole Arab world in their various quests. Considering Egypt alone, 60 million people are on Israel's border promoting the Palestinian cause against a nation less than a tenth its size.

There are tremendous political and religious pressures within the Middle Eastern Moslem countries. Despite the wars between them—Iran with Iraq in the 1980s, Iraq against Kuwait and Saudi Arabia in the Persian Gulf War, the various dictators who massacre their own people—the Western world tends to see them as purveyors of peace with an aggressive, warlike Israel. The leaders of many Moslem countries must maintain a delicate balance: they must appear to want peace, while somehow placating their militant citizens who want to annihilate Israel. The region is a seething cauldron, with tiny Israel poised on the edge of nonexistence.

In Egypt, pressures from Islamic fundamentalists have been highly influential in the past. The Egyptian government has never really been a friend to Israel, but at least it has honored the Camp David agreement forged by Begin and Sadat. It would be no surprise, however, if it were to turn against Israel and join its fellow Arab states in again striking out against the Jewish nation.

On the other hand, Turkey, the most European and democratic of the Islamic nations, recently deposed its fundamentalist Moslem prime minister. The Turkish army, a powerful political force, would not put up with his radical changes in that relatively organized and prosperous nation. It was less a matter of revulsion against religion than a simple threat to a free-market economy. This situation demonstrates the trouble that Islam and democracy have in co-existing. In Algeria, for example, when the results of an Islamic election victory were disallowed, the result was horrific terrorism by the fundamentalists.

Democracy and Islam would seem to be mutually exclusive. Individual freedoms and religious control don't mix. It's no accident that Moslem states are almost exclusively dictatorships. The new Palestinian Authority is no exception. While trying to maintain the appearance of a democracy, with elections and a representative legislature, it nevertheless cannot completely hide its true nature as a budding police state. Reports are reaching the Western world of torture, prisoners held without cause, and censorship of the press. A remarkable article, "Arafat's Awful Reign," appeared in the May 21, 1997 edition of the *Washington Post*. It was written by Fawaz Turki, a Palestinian living in America, who expressed his disillusionment with the new Palestinian state:

"We were wrong. All of us Palestinians were wrong about Yasser Arafat and the 'national authority' that he has foisted on the autonomous zones he now controls in the West Bank and Gaza.

"Not quite four years ago we watched this man on the White House lawn as he signed the Oslo Agreement and effusively shook hands all around. The overwhelming majority of Palestinians rejoiced at the spectacle. This was to be our first step toward statehood, our chance, at last, to be the determining force in our destiny.

"Those activists among us, democrats and patriots all, looked forward to building a community of laws and institutions, governed by a social contract between ruler and ruled, checks and balances, accountability.

"We had fought for independence, and lived through unspeakable suffering too long to settle for anything less. To end up creating yet another dreary *dawla*, or Arab state, known dismissively in Palestinian idiom as *istiqlal* (a term connoting frivolity, nepotism, coercion and violence) would have been a cruel terminus to our struggle, a fate worse than death.

"To be sure, we had no illusions about Yasser Arafat himself, this man of dubious background who had not read a half-dozen decent books in his life, nor grown with his job. We often cringed at his lack of élan, his vaudevillian ways and his penchant for one-man rule, just as we were scandalized by the excesses of his officials in the old glory days of the PLO, who had made a fetish of traveling on the Concorde with Samsonites full of cash.

"But we believed that once the institutional machinery for statehood was put in gear, it would be reasonable to suppose that the aggregate complex of popular culture would lead to stability and, finally, meaningful independence.

"We were dead wrong. No one could prophesy the true measure of the dissolution of civil society, of civilized norms, of human hope, that was to come.

"Yasser Arafat arrived in Gaza in 1994 with a group of men carrying not shovels but guns. He created nine intelligence services and a police force of well over 30,000 men, presumably more policemen per capita than any country in the world.

"The Palestinian Authority's first order of business was to pursue those figures regarded by any civilized society as central to the health of the body politic. The heretical editor was silenced, the human rights activist was hounded, the recalcitrant labor unionist was jailed, and the innovative intellectual was harassed and beaten.

"Those others, who represented through their literary effusions the adversarial current in the community, individuals whose necessary role in social life is to seek an articulation for the fragile plurality of human nature and conduct, have had their heads hit when they were lifted and their voices silenced when they were raised.

"To date, 14 Palestinians have died under torture at the hands of thugs (no other word will do here) from the dreaded intelligence services.

"Though the PA has scant respect for the life of the mind or for the value of dissent, its fear of them knows no bounds. There is a perversity in all of this that goes beyond one's repugnance at the use of repression to stifle the public debate. It tells us something about the semiliterate oafs who make up Yasser Arafat's ruling elite. For to silence, incarcerate, or torture to death a man because you disagree with his views is to pay tribute—a sinister tribute, to be exact, but tribute nevertheless—to the value of ideas in human affairs.

"With the Oslo Agreement, we were at last to free ourselves, if progressively, from foreign occupation, not because we had represented a military threat to Israel—truth be told, the PLO was as dangerous to Israel's existence as secondary smoke—but because the international community, including the United States, had to come round to that recognition. For Palestinians, expectations of progress, of personal and social enfranchisement, moved closer. Independence took on the urgent drama of concreteness, of a dizzying sense of total possibility. That was four years ago.

"The United States, notorious over the years for underwriting the survival of two-bit dictators around the world, has latched on to yet another one of these in the person of Yasser Arafat, whose woeful disregard for the human rights of his own people

Washington continues not only to wink at but to urge on him, presumably in the name of stability in the territories.

"One thing is plain: Yasser Arafat has unleashed destructive forces, dug up from the depths of the coercive tradition, that are destined to stifle our dream for living as free men and women.

"After our costly intifada against those who had occupied our homeland, it now appears that we have to wage another intifada against those who occupy our home. Damn the man."

If the author had written such an article in modern "Palestine," he might have been given a long jail term, or suffered a fatal "accident" at the hands of Arafat's police. Such is the price of freedom of expression in a typical Islamic country.

In his book *The True Believer*, Eric Hoffer noted that "the less justified a man is in claiming excellence for his own self, the more ready is he to claim all excellence for his nation, his religion, his race or his holy cause" (p. 23). He points out that people in any downtrodden group exhibit an almost insane jealousy of the successful people around them. In particular, they denigrate those successful people and want to take their possessions. The Palestinians and the Israelis present a microcosm of Islam versus democracy; the revolutionary fervor, the willingness to maim and kill in the name of Allah or land possession or whatever, and the cold, unending hatred seem to stem from this philosophy. We see it in ghetto America, in the underworld of the new Russia, and throughout the world wherever inequities persist. This is perhaps a better explanation of what is really going on in this world than all of the religious and nationalistic explanations.

Or, as Scripture succinctly puts it, in the end times many "shall betray one another, and shall hate one another. And many false prophets shall rise, and shall deceive many. And because iniquity shall abound, the love of many shall wax cold" (Matthew 24:10-12).

Perhaps the most powerful influence on Middle Eastern affairs is anti-Semitism, that remarkably persistent and virulent hatred of the Jewish people. Those who are openly antagonistic toward the Jews usually offer reasons that are easily seen to be false. They imagine that Jewish conspiracies rule the world (which are obviously not working out very well after centuries of trying!). They portray individual Jewish people as pushy, arrogant, over-talented, or whatever. In any case, the arguments don't justify the ongoing hatred of a people that has frankly been so persecuted that the whole world ought to weep, not hate.

Finally, there's that grain of envy the Jewish people have had to tolerate everywhere they've gone, simply because they are normally successful at what they do. Economically, Israel is such a powerhouse that those jealous of it would like to shut it down or hinder its progress. And the Western European countries can be counted on to support the Palestinian views. Germany must feel sheepish after the Holocaust, but other European nations are certainly as anti-Israel as any democracies can be. I myself encountered anti-Semitism from a police officer in the Paris airport, which was generated by the fact that I wore a Hebrew name badge. (Otherwise, I couldn't have been identified as Jewish.)

What is the difference between being anti-Semitic and being anti-Israel? People try to draw some kind of distinction between these two particular prejudices. But I have never been able to see how one can say, "I don't dislike the Jews, but I don't like what Israel's doing," a phrase one hears time and again in the liberal churches and the media. Can one really say, "I like the French, but I hate France," or, "I have many Japanese friends, but I despise their homeland." Frankly, when I hear this comparison, I feel I am hearing a distinction without a difference. People who oppose Israel do it in large part because they don't like Jews, and vice versa. Anti-Israelism and anti-Semitism are one and the same, for all practical purposes.

The Bible Tells Me So?

The Moslems, and especially the Palestinians, claim to believe in the Bible. They claim the biblical patriarchs and honor Jesus as a "prophet." They declare that Jerusalem is a holy city of Islam, and Israel is their own land. These claims, however, are completely false. Many people, even Christians, say that Allah is just the Arabic word for "God," therefore Christians and Moslems worship the same God. The ecumenical movement in America, a country that more and more embraces tolerance as the ultimate virtue, plays into the hands of Islamic ambition. The Bible and the Koran cannot both be true; there are too many contradictions between them, from the nature of God to who Jesus Christ is. Allah and the God of the Bible could never be the same. But the muddled spirituality of much of the world creates an ideal climate for the spread of Islamic falsehoods about Israel.

The Moslem claim to Jerusalem is based on a single verse in the Koran: "17.1 Glory be to Him Who made His servant to go on a night from the Sacred Mosque to the remote mosque of which We have blessed the precincts, so that We may show to him some of Our signs; surely He is the Hearing, the Seeing." Many people who uphold the Moslem's right to Jerusalem would be surprised to learn that this city is never once mentioned in the Koran. The "Sacred Mosque" mentioned in the verse above is Mecca. The "remote mosque" is not identified, and no distinguishing details are given to indicate where it could be located. It wasn't until much later that Moslems decided to use the verse to falsely declare that Jerusalem was this remote mosque visited by Mohammed, and that therefore it was rightfully their holy city. The Jews obviously have a prior historic claim, but if the Moslems claim Abraham and David as their own, have they not replaced the Jews? And therefore shouldn't they get the city?

In reality, the Koran substitutes Abraham's son Ishmael in place of Isaac in the sacrifice story, and there is a yearly Moslem holiday celebrating the sheep (in the Arab version) that was sacrificed instead of Ishmael. We must wonder how they can have it both ways. Isaac is buried in Hebron, but Ishmael is written up in the Koran. Should Hebron have been taken away from the Jews and given to the Moslems?

The claim to Christ himself is being edited still today. When Bethlehem was turned over to the Palestinians in December 1995, Arafat used the occasion to proclaim, "I declare Bethlehem free…and all the villages of this land blessed with the birth of the Palestinian Jesus Christ." A Palestinian banner at the festivities hailed Jesus as "the first Palestinian revolutionary." Palestinian spokeswoman Hanan Ashrawi stated on an episode of *The MacNeil-Lehrer Report*, "Jesus Christ was a Palestinian prophet born in Bethlehem in my country." Jesus is the most flexible deity this world has ever seen. He started out as a Jew, was turned into a Gentile, and now apparently has converted to Islam.

Ms. Ashrawi, who identifies herself as an Anglican, was quoted in the March 1993 issue of *The Colorado Episcopalian* as saying, "I am a Palestinian Christian…I am a descendant of the first Christians in the world, and Jesus Christ was born in my country—in my

land. Bethlehem is a Palestinian town." People who hold such views
are willfully ignorant of historical facts. The first Christians were
Jewish, as the New Testament makes clear. Jesus was born in
Israel—the name "Palestine" did not even exist until more than a
century after Christ's crucifixion. And Bethlehem was the town of
Ruth and David. It was Jewish then, and it was Jewish at the time of
the Messiah's birth. "Palestinians" did not enter the picture until
centuries later.

Such bald-faced lies and such purposeful duplicity ought to be
corrected at the outset, but media people in general are unbiblical
and wouldn't know how to combat such "public relations" ploys.
On the other hand, one would think an elementary school child
anywhere in America would be able to discern that Jesus was
Jewish and not a Moslem or an Arab. Historically, Jews have never
become Moslems, or Moslems Jews. Once again, the media's position on such matters is inexplicable.

Not content with claiming the Land and Jesus as their own, Palestinians are now claiming status as the actual Chosen People of
the Bible. An official Palestinian Authority television station aired a
program in the summer of 1997 that stated that the true descendants of the biblical Children of Israel are modern Palestinians.
One of the participants in the program stated, "God is my witness
that in my blood there is more of the Children of Israel than in that
of Ariel Sharon and Binyamin Netanyahu." Such a statement is
ludicrous, but there are few voices in the world to challenge it.

In an October 19, 1995 interview for our television series *Jerusalem 3000*, Faisal Husseini, the "Palestinian Representative for
Jerusalem," tried to tell me that the Palestinians actually predated
the Jews in the Land by many centuries. "We have been here 5,000
years," he said of a people that have been in existence since 1967
A.D. When I pressed him to explain, he told me that he counted the
peoples that belonged to ancient Canaan—the Canaanites, the
Jebusites, etc.—as all being Palestinians. I couldn't help but point
out in the close of that program that by that reasoning, I could
count the American Indians as Latvian Jews and determine that the
United States is my ancient homeland, after all.

It would surprise most readers to know that the Koran itself
gives Israel to the Jews, not to the Moslems. The following "Letter
to the Editor" appeared in the June 7, 1997, edition of the *Jerusalem Post International Edition*. It makes a most remarkable point:

the Koran, the very basis of Islam, states that Israel belongs to the Jews. All of the Islamic religious fervor fomented by Arafat is revealed as a smoke screen, a sham. This is hardly the first time in history that a dictator has covered his true motives with religious robes. But the following letter gives the most unimpeachable Moslem sources. For your convenience, we have quoted the relevant Koran verses after the letter:

> "Sir, Hamas member Abdel-Aziz Rantisi says, 'Islam does not permit giving up one inch of Palestine, and states that Palestine belongs to the Moslems, belongs to the Palestinian people, not to the Jews.'

> "This may be true according to the Islam of Abdel-Aziz Rantisi, but not according to the Islam of Mohammed. The Koran says God gave Israel to the Jews, and will restore them to it in the End of Days: 'Then We [Allah] said to the Israelites: Dwell in the land. When the promise of the hereafter comes to be fulfilled, We shall assemble you all together.' (Koran, sura 17, 'Night Journey,' verse 104).

> "Immediately preceding this verse, the Koran describes what happened to Pharaoh for oppressing the Jews and preventing their return to the Land of Israel (Koran, sura 17, 'Night Journey,' verses 100-103).

> Abdel-Aziz Rantisi and his Hamas associates would do well to consider what Allah did to Pharaoh, 'together with all who were with him.'"

> Koran 17:101—And verily We gave unto Moses nine tokens, clear proofs (of Allah's Sovereignty). Do but ask the Children of Israel how he came unto them, then Pharaoh said unto him: Lo! I deem thee one bewitched, O Moses.

> 17:102—He said: In truth thou knowest that none sent down these (portents) save the Lord of the heavens and the earth as proofs, and lo! (for my part) I deem thee lost, O Pharaoh.

> 17:103—And he wished to scare them from the land, but We drowned him and those with him, all together.

17:104—And We said unto the Children of Israel after him: Dwell in the land; but when the promise of the Hereafter cometh to pass We shall bring you as a crowd gathered out of various nations.

The "Palestinians"

The world has come to accept the term "Palestinians" for the immigrant Arabs who moved into Israel when the Jews started rebuilding their country there in 1948. But they have simply misappropriated the term. The Jews were called Palestinians before 1967, as were the Turks, the Bedouin, and anyone else who happened to live in Palestine. The Jewish newspaper *The Jerusalem Post* was previously called *The Palestine Post*, and its building in the Jewish capital of Jerusalem still bears that title. Again, simple historical fact is obscured or willfully overlooked.

To give you some background, the ancient Romans destroyed Israel in 70 A.D. and again in 135 A.D. The Emperor Hadrian changed the name of the Land in 135 A.D. to Palestine—"Philistia," after the Philistines, who were an Adriatic people. They were Greeks, not Arabs. This name change had nothing whatsoever to do with Arab peoples. The Moslems weren't to come on the scene for 500 years. The Romans renamed the Land in an effort to wipe out Judaism. It was another of those "final solutions" to the Jewish problem. The preposterous idea that Arab Moslems are the original Palestinians is nonsense. It makes the same sense as if white Americans (descended from European settlers) called themselves Seminoles or Cherokees.

However nonsensical, the term has served its purpose in giving the world the false impression that the immigrant Arabs have a legitimate, ancient claim to the territory. The history of the region is much more varied and complex than the simple version conveyed by most news reports. In this era of sound bites, news must be geared for the short attention span of the public. And so the media trumpets the cause of the "Palestinians" of "Palestine," and truth is left by the wayside.

Islam and the Antichrist

The terrorist acts of late summer 1997 served to demonstrate that the "peace process" had made little headway since its inception.

In fact, there were more Israeli deaths during this peace process than any comparable period before it! We were to believe that Hamas, the perpetrators of the bombings, were somehow different than the Palestinians of Arafat, the peacemaker, but that was hard to swallow. Arafat was appealed to in every way to stop the terrorism, but in the streets it was commonly known that he could not do that after all. Anwar Sadat of Egypt took an assassin's bullet for his advocacy of peace with Israel. If Arafat would have any effect against Hamas, it would be to his own peril.

In this manner, Islam began to take its place as an antagonist of Israel, a hallmark of the coming tribulation. The theme of the tribulation period is false peace, as we have observed, but coupled with an animosity toward Israel leading to the actual murder of Israeli citizens and invasion of the land. In this manner, the Moslems place themselves as perfect allies of the antichrist.

Any hope of restoring peace talks with Arafat following the terrorism seemed dashed by the opening meeting between Netanyahu and Arafat. The author spoke with David Bar-Illan, senior advisor to Prime Minister Netanyahu, the day after the 2:00 a.m., October 8, 1997, meeting. Bar-Illan, in government language, called the meetings "unsubstantive."

The Moslems, along with the other replacement theology adherents (such as Roman Catholics and liberal Protestants, who replace Israel with the Church in scriptural promises and prophecy), are wonderfully placed to assist the Antichrist in his domination of the upcoming world. In the Tribulation period, it appears that Islam will be a major ally of the Antichrist.

This would be ironic, since the Moslems claim knowledge of the Bible and respect for the ancient Hebrew prophets. And yet they give them no real credence, and consequently do not have an understanding of coming end-times events. They will join the other people who are caught in the Tribulation in not knowing what is going on; they will be taken completely by surprise. The Moslem veneration of the Bible means little since most Moslems evidently don't read it. They named a village in Israel "Nebimousa" after Moses and claim that he died there. If they truly respected Moses, they would understand that Jesus is the Messiah, since He said, "For had ye believed Moses, ye would have believed me: for he wrote of me" (John 5:46).

There is a reason that the Antichrist will be able to control virtually all of the nations on the globe (other than the Jews, and China and possibly other Communist dictatorships). That reason is religion. False religion is the Antichrist's ace of trump. He is a religious figure, keep in mind, not merely political. He is, of course, the ultimate false Christ: "For many shall come in my name, saying, I am Christ; and shall deceive many" (Matthew 24:5). For their own selfish motives, many people will take the number of the Beast, bow down to him, and serve his bidding.

That, of course, will involve the attempted annihilation of Israel. The Moslems, with their long history of hatred toward the Jews, will eagerly lend themselves to such a scheme. The Islamic mentality and worldwide base will give the Antichrist immediate control of a billion people in 150 countries. The false denominational Christians of the world, those who never truly gave their hearts to the real Christ, will now give their allegiance to this seeming "Christ." And the atheists and the "non-aligned religious," readily captured by Satan at any time, have no previous alliances— they would comprise enough with the others to easily make up 50 percent of the world. With the true believers taken out by the Rapture, the Antichrist would have the majority of mankind at his command. This is one possible scenario for how he will gain control.

As the Bible makes clear, he will first present himself as a man of peace. The Tribulation period will begin with a seven-year peace treaty, which is not the Oslo Agreement between Israel and Arafat, as some have mistakenly believed. Israelis will ally themselves with the Antichrist, although they won't accept him wholesale as their Messiah. The situation will be such that they will feel they need what he has to offer: security, protection, permission to rebuild the Temple, or some other combination of factors.

The peace will last for three and a half years, but then it will begin to fail. The Antichrist will exalt himself as God, blaspheming in the rebuilt Temple:

> "Let no man deceive you by any means: for that day
> shall not come, except there come a falling away first,
> and that man of sin be revealed, the son of perdition;
> who opposeth and exalteth himself above all that is
> called God, or that is worshipped; so that he as God sit-

teth in the temple of God, shewing himself that he is God" (2 Thessalonians 2:3-4).

When the Israelis see this, they will probably take Jesus' advice and flee: "When ye therefore shall see the abomination of desolation, spoken of by Daniel the prophet...then let them which be in Judea flee into the mountains" (Matthew 24:15-16). This will set in motion a chain of events that lead ultimately to Armageddon and the coming together of all the world's armies. One possibility is that the Chinese Communists, who did not ally themselves with the Antichrist, will see the Israelis bolt and will realize that the Antichrist is not the all-powerful being he claims to be—certainly not the God of Israel. They will then equip their 200-million-man army and, since they won't have the conveyances needed to transport these millions of soldiers, will march all the way to the Middle East. This operation will take practically the latter half of the Tribulation period.

The Antichrist will try to defend his stronghold, Israel, which he has occupied at the halfway point of the Tribulation. His forces will probably be comprised of Western European armies, and perhaps even American and Canadian troops, which allied with him early in the Tribulation. Who will fight on the Antichrist's side? It will be those false Christians and the non-religious who will now swear allegiance to the Antichrist. But would Christian, democratic America take part in such an endeavor? There are actually two Americas today: the worldly and the Christian. The Christian will be taken out in the Rapture, and with their influence gone, there will be no one left to stand against the tide.

With the billion Moslems who already follow him, the Antichrist will have quite a force with which to confront those who don't believe in him. Armageddon may well be a clash between the Antichrist's forces and those atheistic forces (Communists and other dictatorships and so on) who do not ever really subscribe to the Antichrist. The fight will possibly be about who controls the world from Israel. But the Lord will come back to stop the terrible slaughter: "And except those days should be shortened, there should no flesh be saved" (Matthew 24:22). And the Messiah's return will, of course, usher in the Millennial Kingdom, when all the world will recognize Him for who He is—not Allah, not the Antichrist, but the true living God.

Epilogue: What Do We Do Now?

Christian people always have the dilemma of knowing that pro-phetic events will certainly come to pass, and yet feeling as though they ought to do something about them. Obviously, true Bible believers want to protect Israel. And yet Israel is to be almost van-quished. True Bible believers would not stand for the division of Jerusalem, and yet Jerusalem is to become "a burdensome stone" to all nations. What do we do today about what's going on?

Our first task is to witness, and we should add the content of what we've learned about the Moslems to our witness. This nether force, this replacement theology, is considered a valid religion, along with Judaism and Christianity. That is wrong. It is in no way biblically valid, and while I cannot criticize every Moslem on earth for his behavior or his morals, I certainly do find much fault with the Koran and the entire system as it is written and practiced. We should loudly oppose Moslem "fundamentalists" because they are not really fundamentalists, but gangsters. Fundamentalists, such as Jewish or Christian fundamentalists, may be emphatic in their views, and even dogmatic, but they do not have a mandate to kill people who disagree with them. Moslem fanatics have killed 80,000 people in Algeria alone since 1992, not to mention the ongoing per-secutions of Christians and the four and half million Jews who would surely die if the Palestinians ever got enough weapons together to attack them in Israel. We should point out that the idea of fundamentalist Islam as some kind of equal partner in world reli-gions is simply a propaganda idea, and not one that should be given real credence in a world careening toward the Tribulation. A large number of radical Moslems are simply trying to gather up cash and land without regard for any serious motives of faith. (The Crusades of the Middle Ages are an example of this.)

With that said, step two ought to be Christian support of Israel. This is simply the reasonable position of a people who are going there to live for a thousand years in the Millennial Kingdom. (And that may begin seven years from today!) Believers in the United States should be especially concerned about their government's support of the current Middle Eastern "peace process" that is proving so detrimental to Israel. No government has the right to pressure another government to give up lands and concessions to a terrorist organization. America is seriously in danger of falling under the condemnation of Genesis 12:3—"I will bless them that bless thee, and curse him that curseth thee."

Number three: the Jewish people of all nations, whom God loves, deserve at least our support. They are too maligned by unbelievers for Christian people to let it pass. If you don't like the Jews, then in your own heart work on the idea that you are despising those whom God chose and loves, and those to whom the King of the Jews will return some great day. Keep in mind that the first thing that will happen to you in heaven will be a face-to-face interview with that King. And He will likely declare, as He says to the sheep and goats of Matthew 25:40:

> "Verily I say unto you, inasmuch as ye have done it unto one of the least of these my brethren [the Jews], ye have done it unto me."

We should always, as I say at the end of each of my television programs, "pray for the peace of Jerusalem" (Psalm 122:6).

As part of our love of the Jews and Israel, we should certainly extend our witness to the Chosen People. We have been remiss for nearly 2,000 years. Paul said the Gospel goes "to the Jew first" (Romans 1:16), but we have taken it last, if at all. Churches that send missionaries to Israel invariably do so to Arab villages and not to the Jews. We realize that the Jewish witness can be difficult, but it is still our Lord's command, and it is His very own mission. Did He not instruct His disciples in Matthew 10:5-6: "Go not into the way of the Gentiles, and into any city of the Samaritans enter ye not. But go rather to the lost sheep of the house of Israel." We should do no less than follow the example He himself set.

And finally, we need to tell all of the truths of this chapter and this book to all people everywhere just as fast as we can. The Tribulation seems to be almost upon us, if we are to believe the writings of the prophets. There's no time to lose. Even if you offend someone you witness to, you may well be instrumental in his salvation in the Tribulation. The Jew who rejects you now may well be one of the 144,000 to come. "And I heard the number of them which were sealed: and there were sealed an hundred and forty and four thousand of all the tribes of the children of Israel" (Revelation 7:4).

And if you are attending a "liberal" church (some born-again believers do for some reason), then make some noise. Get to be known as that "obnoxious" Christian who always stands up for the truth. Don't aim to be one of the nicest people in town, which has become some sort of Western Christian ideal, but be like Peter, Paul and the Lord Himself—someone who troubles the local population and makes them sit up and take notice. And if you are maligned, insulted and persecuted, well, "yours will be the kingdom of heaven" (Matthew 5:10). Even if you are crucified, you will have honored our Lord, who endured no less.

And above all, remember: pray for the peace of Jerusalem.

▼   ▼   ▼

CHAPTER 7

New Europe's
Eye of the Tornado

William T. James

Thunderstorms build quickly. Such was the case March 1, 1997, when skies over southwest Arkansas darkened, then began boiling ominously. Earlier warnings of probable severe weather issued by national, then local weather prophets proved accurate when gargantuan supercells burst high into the atmosphere along a cold front spanning the state from north to south. A quarter-mile-wide twister exploded from a wall cloud just above tree-top level, then raged into the small college town of Arkadelphia, killing four people and totally undoing a business district which will be years in the rebuilding process. Thankfully, that F-4 intensity tornado missed the apartment complex less than two blocks away—the apartment complex my son calls home while he attends a state university.

The monster storm hopscotched northwestwardly, missing my own home near Little Rock by less than eight miles. It mangled hundreds of homes and killed another ten people while injuring many others. Yet as deadly as that weather-beast was and despite all the tears and suffering it caused families and friends, the pain will fade with time. Mercifully, such memories inevitably do.

There is coming a storm of another sort, infinitely more dangerous. Within its building dynamic turbulence whirls cyclonic winds that are about to produce a vortex whose destructive force will be unparalleled in history. Unlike the storms and catastrophes of a nature which cause sufferings that fade and heal with the passage of time, the end-time storm will produce carnage that will burn agonizingly within the memories of its victims throughout eternity.

Ancient Forecasters Track Today's Gathering Storm

Those of us who live in the midwest and midsouth regions of the U.S. pay special attention when the experts begin posting thunderstorm watches and warnings. Most of us have, after one big storm or another, watched our local news telecasts presenting up-close looks at the utter devastation a tornado can produce. In many cases, we have only to drive a few miles from where we live to personally tour the ravaged area. Always in the back of our minds, if we are honest, is the thought, *"Well, we've dodged another one. I wonder if and when it will be our turn."*

Future storms are inevitable. We know they are coming, but the odds are in our favor. We convince ourselves that despite the storm clouds gathering on the western horizon and despite the predictions by the weather scientists and their Doppler radar technology, we will continue to escape unscathed. Statistics bear out our somewhat nervous confidence when it comes to thunderstorms, tornadoes, earthquakes, and other natural phenomena. Only a small fraction of the populations become victims.

God's Word tells us in graphic terms that there is coming a planetary upheaval of such magnitude that no one can escape its staggering effects. The mindset that says, "the odds are in our favor," will quickly change to panicked realization that the colossal storm is the biblically prophesied apocalypse.

Jesus himself forecast the greatest of all storms. He said, "For nation shall rise against nation, and kingdom against kingdom; and there shall be famines, and pestilences, and earthquakes, in various places" (Matthew 24:7) "and upon the earth distress of nations, with perplexity; the sea and the waves roaring; Men's hearts failing them for fear, and for looking after those things which are coming on the earth; for the powers of heaven shall be shaken" (Luke 21:25,26). God's prophetic Word depicts with powerful imagery the unleashing of divine judgment upon a rebellious earth. God's wrath is initiated when the first rider of the four horsemen of the apocalypse gallops into view following Christ's opening of the first seal. The apocalyptic storm then breaks upon rebellious mankind with wave upon wave of thunderous cataclysms, each storm front more devastating than the front that precedes it.

John the apostle, through his Patmos vision, forecasts that final storm in man's tumultuous history. He gives forewarning of 21 specific judgments in three series of seven each: the seals, the trumpets, and the bowls. We will deal with the first storm front that mankind will face, the Strimonikos that even now we can, if we attune our spiritual ears to God's end-time forecasts, hear rumbling in the western sky as we turn our thoughts toward Europe.

Daniel's End-Time Weather Bulletin

Nebuchadnezzar, king of Babylon and absolute master of the then-known world, served as a sort of early warning radar system in God's end-time storm forecast center. Of course, that supremely proud monarch had no idea that he was being used in such a capacity any more than Daniel the prophet fully comprehended that he was acting as God's geopolitical weatherman for a time in earth's history several millennia in the future.

The first end-time storm squall appeared on God's radar when Nebuchadnezzar had a dream so startling that his conscious thought processes refused to recall its details. Despite the partial amnesia, the agitated king knew the dream was profound and demanded that the so-called wise men of his kingdom tell him his dream and give its interpretation. He was infuriated when they could not do so and commanded they all be put to death. The king's edict of execution included Daniel.

The wise young counselor to Nebuchadnezzar inquired about the details of the king's violent actions. He requested and was granted an audience with the monarch.

Coming into the presence of the mightiest ruler ever to set upon an earthly throne—particularly when that king was angry— would have overwhelmed most men. Daniel's absolute trust in the God he loved above all else gave him strength and courage to ask for time to consider the dream-vision that was raging unsolved within Nebuchadnezzar's mind.

Having been granted his request, the great prophet, as he always did whether facing the smallest problem or one that seemed insurmountable, gathered about a circle of beloved friends who were his prayer partners and fell on his face before the Almighty. God's Holy Word records, "Then Daniel went to his house, and made the thing known to Hananiah, Mishael, and Azariah, his companions; That they would desire mercies of the God of heaven concerning this secret, that Daniel and his fellows should not perish with the rest of the wise men of Babylon" (Daniel 2:17-18).

Daniel's faith in the only God of heaven was justified that very night.

> Then was the secret revealed unto Daniel in a night vision. Then Daniel blessed the God of heaven. Daniel answered and said, Blessed be the name of God forever and ever; for wisdom and might are his, And he changeth the times and the seasons; he removeth kings, and setteth up kings; he giveth wisdom unto the wise, and knowledge to those who know understanding; He revealeth the deep and secret things; he knoweth what is in the darkness, and the light dwelleth with him. I thank thee and praise thee, O thou God of my fathers, who hast given me wisdom and might, and hast made known unto me now what we desired of thee; for thou hast now made known unto us the king's matter. Therefore, Daniel went into Arioch, whom the king had ordained to destroy the wise men of Babylon; he went and said thus unto him, Destroy not the wise men of Babylon. Bring me in before the king, and I will reveal unto the king the interpretation. Then Arioch brought in Daniel before the king in haste and said thus unto him, I have found a man of the captives of Judah, that will make known unto the king the interpretation. The king answered and said unto Daniel, whose name was Belteshazzar, art thou able to make known unto me the dream which I have seen, and the interpretation of it? Daniel answered in the presence of the king, and said, The secret which the king hath demanded cannot the wise men, the astrologers, the magicians, the soothsayers, reveal unto the king; But

there is a God in heaven who revealeth secrets, and maketh known to the king, Nebuchadnezzar, what shall be in the latter days. Thy visions in thy head upon thy bed, are these: As for thee, O king, thy thoughts came into thy mind upon thy bed, what should come to pass hereafter; and he who revealeth secrets maketh known to thee what shall come to pass. But as for me, this secret is not revealed to me for any wisdom that I have more than any living, but for their sakes that shall make known the interpretation to the king, and that thou mightest know the thoughts of thy heart (Daniel 2:19-30).

Earth's Geopolitical Weather Forecast for the Remainder of World History

The God of heaven alone is able to reveal secrets imprinted upon Nebuchadnezzar's mind about the stormy future of planet Earth. Daniel, through supernatural understanding given him by the God he loved above all else, unscrambled the geopolitical weather radar image and forecast the greatest of world kingdoms to come.

Nebuchadnezzar's dream presented a titanic, effulgent image whose appearance was awesome to the point of being terrifying. Daniel told King Nebuchadnezzar,

> "This image's head was of fine gold, its breast and its arms of silver, its belly and its thighs of bronze, Its legs of iron, its feet part of iron and part of clay. Thou sawest until a stone was cut out without hands, which smote the image upon its feet that were of iron and clay, and broke them to pieces. Then were the iron, the clay, the bronze, the silver, and the gold, broken to pieces together, and became like the chaff of the summer threshing floors; and the wind carried them away, that no place was found for them; and the stone that smote the image became a great mountain, and filled the whole earth" (Daniel 2:32-35).

Nebuchadnezzar's heart must have raced wildly with excitement, perhaps tinged with fear, when Daniel's recounting the dream in precise detail concluded. Surely the king leaned forward, his skin full of bumps like gooseflesh and his eyes wide in anticipation of what came next. Daniel's words spoke to the monarch and to everyone throughout human history who has an ear to hear God's omniscient forecast for manmade government upon this fallen planet.

> "This is the dream, and we will tell its interpretation before the king. Thou, O king, art a king of kings; for the God of heaven hath given thee a kingdom, power, and strength, and glory. And wherever the children of men dwell, the beasts of the field and the fowls of the heavens hath he given unto thine hand, and hath made thee ruler over them all. Thou art this head of gold. And after thee shall arise another kingdom inferior to thee, and another third kingdom of bronze, which shall bear rule over all the earth. And the fourth kingdom shall be strong as iron, forasmuch as iron breaketh in pieces and subdueth all things; and as iron that breaketh all these, shall it break in pieces and bruise. And whereas thou sawest the feet and toes, part of potter's clay and part of iron, the kingdom shall be divided; but there shall be in it of the strength of iron, forasmuch as thou sawest the iron mixed with miry clay. And as the toes of the feet were part of iron and part of clay, so the kingdom shall be partly strong and partly broken. And whereas thou sawest iron mixed with miry clay, they shall mingle themselves with the seed of men; but they shall not adhere one to another, even as iron is not mixed with clay. And in the days of these things shall the God of heaven set up a kingdom, which shall never be destroyed; and the kingdom shall not be left to other people, but it shall break in pieces and consume all these kingdoms, and it shall stand forever. Forasmuch as thou sawest that the stone was cut out of the mountain without hands, and that it broke in pieces the iron, the bronze, the clay, the silver, and the gold, the great God hath made known to the king what shall come to pass hereafter; and the dream is certain, and the interpretation of it is sure (Daniel 2:36-44).

The greatest of all human kings was awestruck in the presence of God's thunderous prophecy. The supremely arrogant ruler of the then-known world could do nothing other than prostrate himself before Daniel. We can know he was not worshiping Daniel because the words he used gave glory to Daniel's God. More than this, we can know that Nebuchadnezzar was not worshiping Daniel at this moment because Daniel said nothing to correct him when the king bowed before him. Daniel, whom the angel Gabriel later would call most "beloved" of God, would have certainly corrected the ruler of Babylon if such correction was warranted.

Nebuchadnezzar, though he would later erect a huge image of gold in a prideful attempt to thwart the prophecy symbolized by the dream image, was for the moment humbled before the God of heaven. When Nebuchadnezzar later erected that great golden statue (read Daniel 3), he determined to change God's forecast about the successive kingdoms to come. He thus tried to ensure that his kingdom would last forever. By forcing everyone everywhere to worship his great, golden image, he thought he could make himself a god.

Such is always the way with earthly rulers and with the rest of us as well. "The heart is deceitful above all things, and desperately wicked..." (Jeremiah 17:9). Mankind, like the grand deceiver, Lucifer, invariably believes he can put himself above the throne of God—or at the very least, alongside God's throne. This is why the great crushing stone will return from heaven at the time of Armageddon when mankind is battling for domination of planet Earth. The Rock of Ages, Jesus Christ, the King of Kings and Lord of Lords, will smite the final kingdom of earth as symbolized by the feet and toes of iron mixed with miry clay. The winds of history will sweep before Christ's majestic presence and remove the broken rebellious ones into the black abyss of outer darkness. And of the kingdom of God, the Lord Jesus Christ, there shall be no end (Luke 1:33).

Daniel's Specific Geopolitical Storm Forecast

God's early warning storm forecast center issued an alert to His prophet in startling fashion. Daniel reported that bulletin, saying,

> I saw in my vision by night, and, behold, the four winds
> of the heavens strove upon the great sea. And four great
> beasts came up from the sea, diverse one from another.
> The first was like a lion, and had eagle's wings; I beheld
> until its wings were plucked, and it was lifted up from the
> earth, and made stand upon the feet as a man; and a
> man's heart was given to it. And, behold, another beast, a

second, like a bear, and it raised up itself on one side, and it had three ribs in the mouth of it between its teeth; and they said thus unto it, Arise, devour much flesh. After this I beheld, and, lo, another, like a leopard, which had upon its back four wings of a fowl; the beast had also four heads, and dominion was given to it (Daniel 7:2-6).

Daniel seems to be reporting these three surrealistic animals presented in vivid imagery as part of a *single* vision. He separates then the first three beasts from the presentation of the fourth by reporting:

"After this I saw in the night *visions* [emphasis mine], and, behold, a fourth beast, dreadful and terrible, and strong exceedingly, and it had great iron teeth; it devoured and broke in pieces, and stamped the residue with its feet; and it was diverse from all the beasts that were before it, and it had ten horns. I considered the horns, and, behold, there came up among them another little horn, before which there were three of the first horns plucked up by the roots; and, behold, in this horn were eyes like the eyes of man, and a mouth speaking great things" (Daniel 7:7,8).

The fourth beast the prophet saw rolled through his mind in fantastic action scenes. The first three surrealistic animals seemed to fade into insignificance compared to the fourth astonishing beast, which apparently had no earthly animal counterpart.

The prophet then was given view of even more spectacular things to come. He saw, through vision imagery, the "*ancient of days*"—i.e., Almighty God Himself! He witnessed amazing activity around God's throne. Millions upon millions of heavenly beings performed indescribably remarkable things on behalf of the Almighty. Tens of millions of others stood in awed silence before the throne while the books of judgment were opened.

Daniel saw the horn dominating the dreadful fourth beast and heard it speaking great things. He saw the beast move swiftly across the pages of those last few years of human history and witnessed its being cast into hell. He saw the first three beasts of the vision fade into oblivion, their power and authority taken from them although they did not cease to exist entirely. God the Son was joined to God the Father and was presented His eternal kingdom. (Read Daniel 7:9-14).

Daniel struggled mightily within that supernaturally presented dream-vision. With trepidation, he approached a being who stood nearby while the spectacular scene before him continued.

> I came near unto one of them that stood by, and asked him the truth of all this. So he told me, and made me know the interpretation of the things. These great beasts, which are four, are four kings, who shall arise out of the earth. But the saints of the Most High shall take the kingdom, and possess the kingdom forever, even forever and ever (Daniel 7:16-18).

The heavenly being's explanation served only to whet Daniel's appetite for more information. The most troubling part of the vision for the prophet obviously lay in the terrifying nondescript beast. Daniel then said,

> Then I would know the truth of the fourth beast, which was diverse from all the others, exceedingly dreadful, whose teeth were of iron, and its nails of bronze, which devoured, broke in pieces, and stamped the residue with his feet; And of the ten horns that were in its head, and of the other which came up, and before whom three fell; even of that horn that had eyes, and a mouth that spoke very great things, whose look was more stout than its fellows. I beheld, and the same horn made war with the saints, and prevailed against them, until the Ancient of days came, and judgment was given to the saints of the Most High; and the time came that the saints possessed the kingdom (Daniel 7:19-22).

The heavenly observer who stood by Daniel responded,

> The fourth beast shall be the fourth kingdom upon the earth, which shall be diverse from all kingdoms, and shall devour the whole earth, and shall tread it down, and break it in pieces. And the ten horns out of this kingdom are ten kings that shall arise; and another shall rise after them, and he shall be diverse from the first, and he shall subdue three kings. And he shall speak great words against the Most High, and shall wear out the saints of the Most High, and think to change the times and the laws; and they shall

be given into his hand until a time and times and the
dividing of time (Daniel 7:22-25 KJV).

This fourth beast, dreadful and terrible as it is described by
Daniel and his heavenly observer-companion who interpreted the
fourth kingdom, whirled angrily from the great sea of human history. It overshadowed with its veracity and immense power all
former great empires. The beast system is prophesied to rage in this
world like an F-5 tornado slamming into a congested mobile home
community. God's forecast through Daniel's dream-vision is sure.
Even now, the thunderhead that will spawn the monster is boiling
on the geopolitical horizon.

John Tracks the Storm

John, the aged apostle and prophet exiled by Rome to the
Aegean island called Patmos, was given a stunning view of the
brewing end-time storm. Although many centuries had passed
since Daniel's prophecy was issued, God's omniscient radar continued to track the beastly storm's progression toward the climax of
history.

Much of the forecast was already fulfilled by the time John took
his shift as God's end-time weatherman. Precisely as Daniel prophesied, Nebuchadnezzar's magnificent Babylonian kingdom represented by the head of gold on the gigantic metallic image of the
king's dream came to its end. It lasted only 66 years. The Medo-Persian empire, represented by the arms and breasts of silver,
destroyed Babylon while that kingdom's reigning king, Belshazzar,
hosted a drunken orgy. The Greco-Macedonian empire, symbolized
by the belly and thighs of bronze, defeated the Medes and Persians
207 years later. That great empire, whose conquering hero was
Alexander the Great, was decimated by the Roman Empire after
about 269 years. The Roman Empire, in a state of decline at the
time of John's Revelation vision, was never defeated by outside enemies, but became divided and broke into pieces due to fierce intramural conflicts. Rome simply ceased to exist as a great empire 539
years or so after defeating the Grecian empire.

It appears that the great, broken iron empire of Nebuchadnezzar's dream is beginning to reform into the prophesied end-time
governmental power sphere. The feet of iron and miry clay seem to
be shuffling clumsily through the mix of today's aspirants to global

power. Even now, the ten toes of that great metallic image might be sprouting while new Europe lurches somewhat unsteadily toward the monetary union scheduled for January 1, 1999.

John Repeats Daniel's End-Time Tornado Warning

God obviously chose His prophetic weathermen with great care. Daniel is called by God's magnificent emissary, Gabriel, *"a man greatly beloved"* (Daniel 10:11). John the apostle is Scripturally dubbed *"the greatly beloved disciple"* (John 13:23; 19:26; 21:7,20).

John's vision of the end-time beast which God says will storm out of the sea of humanity to wage war upon the earth so closely resembles the fantastic beast of Daniel's earlier vision that there can be no mistaking that God wants the end-time generation alerted to the viciousness of the apocalyptic storm it faces. God goes into great detail in describing the fearsome creature. Not once, but twice. He entrusts this most important forecast of things to come to two men obviously very close to his heart. Each man, the Scriptures confirm, is associated not with God's anger but with God's deep, abiding love. This is an alert about a coming monster. God has given the warning because He loves His creation called man and wants him to seek refuge in His beloved Son, Jesus Christ, before the Tribulation tempest breaks upon the world.

John the apostle—awestruck and swept up in the stunning vision that would unveil the consummation of human history, spectacularly reveal the glorified Christ, and give dazzling glimpses into God's eternal, heavenly majesty—first reported this frightening encounter:

> And I stood upon the sand of the sea, and saw a beast rise up out of the sea, having seven heads and ten horns, and on his horns ten crowns, and upon his heads the name of blasphemy. And the beast which I saw was like a leopard, and his feet were like the feet of a bear, and his mouth like the mouth of a lion; and the dragon gave him his power, and his throne, and great authority (Revelation 13:1,2).

John saw Daniel's horrific vision-creature in its fully developed composite transformation, ready to do its satanically directed, murderous work upon planet Earth. All of the world empires of all history were manifest in the behemoth.

The Babylonian lion's mouth, the Medo-Persian bear's feet, the Greek leopard's body. But what about the Roman Empire? Where is revived Rome within this composite end-time creature that threatens to storm upon the world and break the earth into pieces?

It is a Roman Beast. One of God's angels who carried one of the seven bowls of wrath explained the fearsome animal. John recorded that the angel

> talked with me, saying unto me, Come here; I will show unto thee the judgment of the great harlot that sitteth upon many waters; With whom the kings of the earth committed fornication, and the inhabitants of the earth have been made drunk with the wine of her fornication.... I saw a woman sit upon a scarlet-colored beast, full of names of blasphemy, having seven heads and ten horns. And the woman was arrayed in purple and scarlet color, and bedecked with gold and precious stones and pearls, having a golden cup in her hand, full of abominations and filthiness of her fornication; And upon her forehead was a name written, MYSTERY, BABYLON THE GREAT, THE MOTHER OF HARLOTS AND ABOMINATIONS OF THE EARTH (Revelation 17:1-5).

John's angel companion then spoke about the strange sights and sounds while the stunned apostle watched.

> I will tell thee the mystery of the woman, and of the beast that carried her, which hath the seven heads and ten horns. The beast that thou sawest was, and is not, and shall ascend out of the bottomless pit, and go into perdition; and they that dwell on the earth shall wonder, whose names were not written in the book of life from the foundation of the world, when they behold the beast that was, and is not, and yet is. And here is the mind which hath wisdom. The seven heads are seven mountains, on which the woman sitteth, And there are seven kings: five are fallen, and one is, and the other is not yet come; and when he cometh, he must continue a short space. And the beast that was, and is not, even he is the eighth, and is of the seven, and goeth into perdition. And

> the ten horns which thou sawest are ten kings, who have
> received no kingdom as yet, but received power as kings
> one hour with the beast. These have one mind and shall
> give their power and strength unto the beast (Revelation
> 17:7-13).

Although the subject of the woman who sits astride the beast is
a topic to study in detail at another time, suffice it to say for now
that the woman symbolizes the apostate religious system prophesied to be the state-sanctioned church during the first half of the
Tribulation. A fascinating development involving a symbol depicting
a woman riding a beast has occurred in Europe recently. That
development is briefly addressed a bit further along in the chapter.
The most crucial thing to consider here is that the angel links this
astonishing beast to the Roman Empire as well as to the great
empires that preceded Rome. The *"five that are fallen"* are Assyria,
Egypt, Babylon, Medo-Persia, and Greece. The kingdom the angel
referred to when he says, *"one is"* was the Roman Empire which
was, of course, ruling at the time of John's Revelation vision.

God's messenger then lays out in graphic terms the beast's
Luciferian origin, intentions, and the swath of destruction it will
cut throughout end-time earth.

> And the beast that was, and is not, even he is the eighth,
> and is of the seven, and goeth into perdition (Revelation
> 17:11).

Kings and their *kingdoms* must be considered inseparable
within the terms of this symbology. With the Roman *king* or
kingdom being the prevailing power during John's time, the
apostle's vision forecast a seventh *king* or *kingdom*. This *king*
would reign for only a short period as compared to those great *kingdoms* which preceded his *kingdom*. However, a strange occurrence
is prophesied to then take place. This *seventh king*—called in Revelation 13:4 *"the beast"*—inexplicably *"is not"* (that is, he is no
longer on the scene). But suddenly he again appears. *"Even he is
the eighth"* (the *eighth king*).

The angelic messenger adds further, *"and is of the seven."* We
are told, in other words, that this *"beast"* which inexplicably was
no longer on the world scene has a second coming onto the world
scene.

The messenger angel indicates that this ruler is dramatically changed when he reappears. This person, who was of the seventh kingdom and now is the eighth ruler within the apostle John's beast-vision, *"goeth into perdition"*. He is now vicious and aggressively ungodly in his demeanor and comportment.

The Source of the Beast's Power

This revived emperor of the revived Roman Empire now becomes satanically charged with immense power. The angel tells Daniel, "And the ten horns which thou sawest are ten kings, who have received no kingdom as yet, but receive powers as kings one hour with the beast. These have one mind, and shall give their power and strength unto the beast" (Revelation 17:12,13).

Those coming *ten kings* who will receive power from Antichrist and will be of the same mindset as that last and most terrible ruler will give their total devotion and energy to accomplishing his satanically driven agenda. Having ripped asunder the apostate religious system symbolized by the harlot who rode the scarlet colored composite beast, Antichrist will declare himself God and will demand worship from all who dwell upon the earth.

Fading Roman Empire Spawns Prince that Shall Come

Much controversy has always swirled about the subject of Antichrist. Is he a person? Is the spirit of Antichrist simply a last-days godlessness that will pervade mankind? If Antichrist is a person, is he alive today? If so, who is he? Where does he come from—that is, what is his nationality, ethnic heritage, etc.?

These are fascinating questions to contemplate, but most often quite difficult to frame in a way that is conducive to orderly examination. The following dissection of this sometimes confusing character called Antichrist provides well-delineated and, I believe, Holy Spirit-directed thought in defense of the proposition that he is a man whose roots stem from the ancient Roman Empire.

In a recent broadcast, Gary Hedrick of The Christian Jew Hour (Messianic Perspectives) noted this regarding Daniel 9:26 ("And after threescore and two weeks [sixty-two weeks] shall Messiah be cut off"): "The Hebrew word [for 'cut off' or 'crucified'] literally carries the idea of a criminal execution. The Messiah shall be 'cut off,' but not for Himself.

"and the people of the prince that shall come shall destroy the city and the sanctuary, and the end thereof shall be with a flood, and unto the end of the war desolations are determined." This is the prophecy where Daniel pinpoints the time of Messiah's cutting off as A.D. 32 or 33. It's calculated from the terminus quo of 444 B.C. when Artaxerxes issued the command to restore and rebuild Jerusalem.

You can actually follow the time line all the way from 539 B.C....when Cyrus gave permission to the Jews to return to the land, but the actual terminus quo of the prophecy is 444 B.C.

Now here is the interesting thing, Hedrick continues:

He says that during the generation that's responsible for the cutting off of Messiah, Jerusalem and the temple will be destroyed. Jesus himself warned of that destruction in Luke 21:24 and Matthew 23:38. It happened in A.D. 70 when the Romans swept into Palestine, laid siege to the holy city, and finally destroyed it.

Now look at what Daniel says: "The people of the prince that shall come [that's the end-time Antichrist] shall destroy the city and the sanctuary." In other words, the people of the Antichrist will be the same ones who destroyed Jerusalem and the temple in A.D. 70...They will be Romans, they will be Japhothites; in other words, they will be Europeans and their political leader will be the Antichrist.

Since the book of Daniel associates the end-time kingdom of the Antichrist with the ancient Roman Empire, we assume his kingdom will be basically a resurrected Roman empire, geographically, politically and even religiously....[1]

Regarding this scriptural account, even more exciting than the proof that the Antichrist will indeed be a person who will come out of the revived Roman Empire is the proof that God's Word is absolutely true. So astonishingly accurate is the prophesied timeline in the Scriptures covered by Gary Hedrick in this presentation that the only argument Bible detractors have been able to manufacture throughout the centuries is the specious claim that another man named Daniel—other than Daniel the Old Testament prophet—wrote the timeline sometime after Christ's crucifixion. Daniel's prophecy of the four great world empires is now accomplished historical fact. His foretelling that there is coming a fifth empire that will be a derivative of the fourth can therefore be counted on as reliable. That prophecy, combined with John's Revelation vision detailing the rise of the *prince that shall come*, constitutes a geopolitical, socioeconomic storm forecast that this generation ignores at great risk. The apocalyptic storm is almost upon us!

New Europe's Tornadic Vortex

"*The love of money is the root of all evil*," said Paul the apostle (1 Timothy 6:10). While this generation of earth dwellers marches into the twenty-first century, who among us with any degree of conviction argue against that declaration? Some might debate that the desire for power is at the root of all evil. However, power and money are inseparable in this world of materialism, i.e., comfort, luxuries, and at the lowest end of things, hedonistic pleasures of every sort.

Two phrases that leap to mind concerning America's contemporary attitude about the pursuit of wealth are: 1) "it's the economy, stupid!" and 2) "show me the money." These are slogans made famous by politicians and kingmakers within the ranks of the media propagandists elite. Make no mistake. Powerful economic forces are fueling the ominous machinery of the new world order. The most dynamic of that machinery pulses at the heart of the metamorphosing European Union. It will soon begin generating a monetary whirlwind whose vortex will siphon the wealth of the world into the coffers of those who will become the ten kings of Revelation 17:12,13.

A Stunning Symbol for our Prophetic Times

Whereas America proclaims its love of money through shopworn Madison Avenue-type slogans such as "*It's the economy, stupid!*" and "*Show me the money*," new Europe expresses its opinion that money rules through a recently developed graphic symbol. The symbol is disturbingly blunt in its prophetic overtones.

A recent *U.S. News & World Report* article reports:

According to Greek myth, Europe was born w[...]
one of the Olympian gods, transformed himsel[...]
bull and coaxed a Phoenician princess named Europ[...]
climb on his back. When Europa mounted, Zeus hurri[...]
away to the island of Crete and begat Minos, the first
European king.

One day, the birth of a unified European nation may
inspire a similar tale. Once upon a time, the story will
go, Germany, economic powerhouse of the 15 nations of
the European Union, transformed itself into a bull and
coaxed the other 14 to climb on its back. Then it hurried
away to Frankfurt and begat the euro, Europe's single
currency.

So far, however, the modern seduction has not gone as
well as the classical, and it's no wonder. If the members
of the European Union, a federation of states founded in
1957, really do decide to jump on Germany's back and
adopt a single currency, their sacrifice will be
enormous....[2]

The article tells of the lost sovereignty and the autonomy the
individual states must suffer in the cause and the rights they will be
giving up. They will surrender their rights to independently balance
their own budgets and manage their own debts. They will give up
their individual monetary identities. Their currencies will cease to
exist.

The report then details plans for Europe's single currency:

This week in Dublin, EU leaders will be presented with
the winning design of the new currency notes, which are
slated to appear in July 2002. They will also try to
hammer out details about the conversion from the many
currencies to one—and the transfer of economic management from state central banks to a single European
Central Bank, which will set interest rates for all.

In theory, when the economic efforts of 370 million
people are combined this way, European goods and services will be better represented in the world economy by
an overarching institution capable of maintaining price
stability in all member countries at home and a single
stable currency abroad....[3]

)eans have adopted depicts a woman
red horned beast. And in May 1997,
iced. The likeness of Charles V, the
in Empire who assumed the Spanish
ingraved on one side.
ielf to Rome's glorious past in a sym-
Treaty is scheduled to make that
, 1999. At the same time, the EU,
beast symbol, reaches toward the
future with grandiose expectations of attaining geopolitical might and socioeconomic opulence equal to that achieved by ancient Babylon.

Europe's Iron and Clay Within the Maastricht Blender

Europe's nucleus leadership frantically strives toward constructing a union that can produce economic mastery over twenty-first-century earth. Of course, being *economic master* of the world means being *master*. Period. No doubt the atmospherics surrounding such a lofty sense of destiny created the supreme confidence that "the will to do" overcomes all obstacles.

The ten power brokers of Revelation 17:12,13 will impose Antichrist's beastly hegemony over the nations with severe punitive consequences for those who resist. The willful king of fierce countenance in Daniel 8:23-27 will tolerate no opposition and will ultimately demand worship.

While today's European leadership cannot command adherence to its edicts and directives as will the *ten horns* (or *ten kings*) of Daniel's and John's beast-visions, we can, if we examine the current European state of affairs, detect nuances of willfulness within European hierarchy. For sure, the *iron* elements of today's European Union are exerting increasing pressures upon the *clay* elements in order to mold new Europe to their specifications. They have their hands full in that regard. Mixing the *clay* nations, then blending them with the *iron* has, to this point, proved not doable. "...*they will not adhere one to another...*" (Daniel 2:43).

The main point of contention is money. Isn't that usually the case with human affairs at any level?

Germany and France comprise the heart of the reforming Roman Empire. The latter-day Roman system began regenerating with the Treaty of Rome in 1957. Germany, France, Italy, Belgium, Netherlands, and Luxembourg came together to create the *Common Market* at that time. When Greece joined as the tenth member January 1, 1981, many observers of prophetic matters believed the magic number had been reached. This was the *ten toes, the ten horns, the ten kings*, they educed. Alas, while this grouping is the matrix from which will grow earth's most powerful geopolitical entity, so many nations have been added and so many others are applying for membership to European Union and at such a dizzying pace that prophecy pundits no longer make such pinpoint assessments. Like the prophet Daniel and like John the aged apostle, we stand in wonder and awe while we watch the beast struggle to rise from the sea of nations.

And struggle it does! "*It's the economy, stupid!*" and "*Just show me the money*" might well be the slogans plastered upon the side of the beast-symbol of European unity upon whose back rides the woman symbolizing the nations of Europe. Monetary union apparently is to be the mixmaster—the blender—that will, the European *iron* nations believe, bring the cohesion necessary to new Europe's drive for dominance. Maastricht is the brand-name of the machinery they hope will stir their creation to life.

Daniel Singer, Europe correspondent for *The Nation*, writes:

> One conflict may conceal another, less visible but more fundamental. Attention today is focused on the struggle of many countries to join the European Economic and Monetary Union (E.M.U.), which is to be inaugurated on January 1, 1999. At that time marks and francs will be replaced by a single currency, the Euro. Admission to this exclusive club will be decided in the spring of 1998 on the basis of next year's [1997] economic results; hence, eligibility is really being determined now. There is much speculation about which candidates will be successful, about the rates in which the currencies will be converted into the Euro and the latter's strength in terms of the dollar.
>
> Yet hidden behind this Eurobattle is a deeper confrontation over the social shape and political future of Europe....[4]

Springer outlines the European blueprint for developing the economic muscles sufficient to wage vigorous competition in the rapidly changing arena of world trade:

> The Maastricht Treaty provided five criteria of economic and fiscal performance to determine whether a country is eligible for membership. Given the depressed state of the European economy, three of them (inflation rate, long-term interest rates, and currency stability) do not seem major obstacles to most countries. The two stiffest hurdles are the budget deficit, which must not exceed three percent of the gross domestic product, and the national debt, which should not top 60 percent of G.D.P. Of the fifteen members of the European Union, two— Britain and Denmark—have still not decided if they want to take part [in EMU]....[5]

Since this article was published, Britain, of course, has elected Tony Blair to replace John Major as prime minister. Blair has declared his intention to move Great Britain into EMU and to cooperate with the continental European leadership at every level of the monetary blending process.

> The odds on the chances of the thirteen starters fluctuate wildly. At times, the whole project is dismissed as infeasible on the theory that even the two main protagonists—Germany and France—will fail the tests....[6]

The writer explains that the deepest problem confronting European Monetary Union is the strict criteria of the Maastricht Treaty. Those criteria present bitter pills in the form of giving up socialistic addictions, pills which will be very difficult to force down the throats of Europeans.

Springer writes further:

> ...You must accept a slimming cure so your country can play in the big leagues and thus guarantee its future prosperity. Citizens are not being asked to tighten their belts briefly and then relax. Preparations are already being made to provide the E.M.U. with a "stability pact" to ensure that deficits will be kept low, preferably close to zero. The Germans insist that the rules must be strict, the exceptions few, the penalties stiff and more or less

automatic. The main purpose in this phase is to down-size the welfare state, and it is no secret that the next stage will be to attack workers' rights, or, as the current jargon has it, to "increase the flexibility of labor."[7]

Stringent Maastricht Treaty requirements that nations seeking membership in EMU tighten their belts with austere budgetary cuts have already sent political heads rolling. For example, French Prime Minister Alain Juppe decided not to continue in office, choosing to resign, saying the country needs a new team with a new prime minister. French President Jacques Chirac's governing party was soundly defeated in the first round of legislative elections of May 1997. Juppe was blamed for the center-right political element's poor showing. A report dated May 27, 1997, surmised:

> The late afternoon news rocked the political establish-ment still reeling from Sunday's stark repudiation of Chirac's governing party and the suddenly real prospect of a socialist-led opposition victory...More than six in ten French voters cast ballots against the majority coalition... The result was interpreted as a vote of no confidence...The electorate vented its anger against Chirac and Juppe's ineffectual management of the chronic unemployment crisis, their on-again, off-again efforts to shrink the social welfare system and their plans to push France into the new European order of smaller government, tighter budgets, a single European currency and the rigors of a competitive global marketplace....[8]

Despite the fact that lesser political heads among Europe's elite leadership will doubtless continue to suffer similar fates to Juppe's because working-class citizens continue to resist their austerity measure to meet the required Maastricht criteria, the power brokers remain undeterred. *The Nation's* Daniel Springer writes further about the European power elite's determination:

> The European Union is erecting a strange monetary structure. At the heart of it will stand the European Cen-tral Bank, modeled on the German Bundesbank, with strong powers and relative independence from elected representatives. This bank will not be checked by a strong European government or parliament, for which there is no prospect on the horizon. It will deal with

weaker institutions—the European Commission in Brussels and the Council of Ministers. This does not mean that the nation-states of Europe will now cease to matter as economic agents. Far from it. They keep plenty of power, notably control over taxation and expenditures....[9]

Springer then makes a fascinating statement that engenders thoughts of the final *ten kings* of Revelation 17:12,13:

But they will now be under close supervision from a mighty unelected watchdog, which will see that nothing is done by member governments that threatens profits or interferes with the working of the capitalist system....[10]

"It's the economy, stupid!"..."Show me the money"..."The love of money is the root of all evil." Money is power and power is money and never shall the two be separated. *Follow the money* and we will find at the very end of this earth system the seat and authority of earthly power which will ultimately energize the one called Antichrist.

While the prophetic Word of God omnisciently points to where the end-time economic power structure will reside and what the beastly results of its exerting its power will be, the current state of affairs makes precise predictions with regard to the *ten kings* scenario impossible.

The tornado's ominous vortex, however, rotates visibly within the boiling economic stratosphere above Europe today. A closer look at the dynamics within that turbulence gives glimpses of fascinating ongoing developments. The *iron* and *clay* of the feet of Nebuchadnezzar's gigantic dream-image whirl within the Maastricht blender. It seems the leadership realizes that to bring together elements which will not *adhere* one to another, those elements must be forced into the European monetary centrifuge. The cyclotron has been slow to start because of resistant nationalism, but is now beginning to spin vigorously.

An article in *Foreign Affairs*, a periodical published by the Council on Foreign Relations, provides some insights into new Europe's tornadic vortex:

Despite the aura of relaxed confidence pervading European capitals and financial markets as next year's [1997] deadline for meeting the convergence criteria for European monetary union approaches, the lines for a politically divisive battle are becoming clear. On one side stand German Chancellor Helmut Kohl, French President Jacques Chirac, the European Commission, and the vast majority of senior European politicians, who care far more about making European Monetary Union (EMU) happen on time than about how they get there. They worry that if monetary union is delayed once, it could be delayed more easily a second time, and a third, and so on until the great postwar drive for European union— and the Franco-German alliance at its center—fizzles out. On the other side stands the German "stability coalition," composed of the Bundesbank, the Federal Constitutional Court, [some popular German tabloids]...and opposition-controlled power centers in the Bundesrat, or upper house of parliament, and *Lander* governments. If Kohl and company worry that any delay would threaten European union, the stability coalition worries that rushing into EMU might cost Germany its sway over European economic policy, with control passing to a broad coalition of economically weaker southern European countries, led by a resurgent France.[11]

The article explains in-depth that Germany's stability coalition is concerned that France will manage to wiggle out from under the strict Maastricht requirements for those nations applying for membership in European Monetary Union. Great pressures exist in France and most other applicant nations because of the tremendous cuts that will have to be made to national budgets in order to meet the criteria for EMU. Voting constituencies of those nations vehemently resist cutting social welfare programs as demonstrated by the forced resignation of French Prime Minister Juppe in May 1997.

Even German chancellor Helmut Kohl, who most agree is Europe's most powerful leader at present, feels the pressure because both the German people and the stability coalition are monitoring closely as he navigates within the EMU turbulence. The article in *Foreign Affairs* continues:

Kohl faces a personal referendum on this issue in December, 1998, when he must stand for reelection. That means he will be going to the polls only weeks before formally—and irrevocably—handing over the Deutschemark to a gaggle of Europeans on January 1, 1999. If he condones flagrant cheating by French budgeteers, or too obviously looks the other way if France misses the deficit targets of the Maastricht Treaty on European Union by a wide margin, he risks turning the election into a referendum on giving away the Deutschemark....[12]

But the problems within the incohesive mix of *iron* and *clay* go much deeper than the rift between Helmut Kohl and the German stability coalition. The article says further,

The most important threat to Kohl and thus to the EMU comes not from bending the deficit or accounting rules for France, but from the attempts it would trigger from Spain, Portugal, and eventually even Italy—sometimes referred to as the "Club Med" countries—to use the same bent rules as a way of clambering into EMU in the first round...In the worst case, from the stability coalition's point of view, bending the rules for France would put the European Union on a slippery slope, with each country demanding just a slightly looser interpretation of Maastricht....[13]

Be assured that the European powers that be—and the world money powers that be, for that matter—will not allow European Union to continue down the slippery slope. Thus, powerful influence will more and more be applied to the Maastricht process as time progresses. The writer of the article in *Foreign Affairs* offers advice to the European:

In an ideal world, Kohl and Chirac would slowly let out the truth that France will not hit the deficit targets, but that monetary union will go ahead regardless. Thus they would publicly acknowledge that monetary union is first and foremost a political matter. It would complete the great postwar drive for a permanent Franco-German alliance before their generation fades from the scene and takes its searing memories of world war to the grave. Continuing to ignore the problems ahead and insisting that all is well is flirting with disaster...Kohl and Chirac should make the 4 percent deficit for France into a political non-event by talking it to death. Simultaneously, they should disarm the stability coalition, for whom that kind of talk is heresy, by quiet negotiations with southern-tier countries. Financial incentives, ex officio membership for those countries in all central bank councils, and a pledge not to begin using the euro until all countries are in EMU should go a long way toward making a two-step EMU politically acceptable for Spain and company....[14]

The writer then addressed the reality of the situation:

But this is asking a lot of politicians. So if the politics of confession don't fly, there is another way for Kohl and Chirac to make monetary union happen. One fine Saturday morning, the sooner the better, they should make monetary union a fait accompli by announcing a permanent link between the Deutsche mark and the French franc. The benefits of such a link would soon spread far beyond solidifying the Franco-German core and would create an extra-Maastricht dynamic for EMU that would break through the increasingly dangerous adherence to the arbitrary and irrelevant deficit target agreed to in Maastricht in 1991....[15]

The language used in the *Foreign Affairs* article sounds eerily prophetic in summarizing New Europe's prospects.

Despite the threat of unanticipated consequences, French and German currencies ought to be linked as a necessary next step in the process of creating an EMU. Otherwise this politically important opportunity might be lost as the flagging credibility of the Maastricht criteria precipitates cataclysmic turbulence in the financial markets. Fortunately, a unique confluence of opportunity, political incentive, and personal leadership is now in place to pull off this endgame coup.[16]

However, it is not mere *good fortune* that brings *opportunity, political incentive and personal leadership* into *unique confluence* for an *endgame coup*. The author of confusion is stirring the incompatible ingredients of iron and miry clay, creating a tremendous vortex that holds them together. Satan's is a purposeful whirlwind to which fallen mankind has sown seeds of avarice and greed—a tornadic end-time wind this earth system is about to reap.

United Europe vs. United States: Current Facts and Troubling Prospects[17]

Most experts in the field of global economic affairs seem to believe that a single European currency will be the most important development in the international monetary system in decades. Their contention is well founded because as much as $1 trillion of investment internationally may shift from dollars to euros, according to the figures they analyze.

The Group of Seven (G-7) and the United States' governmental brain trust seem to have underestimated what the rise of the euro will mean for the volatile global economic system. Yet it is essential, according to the experts, that all world monetary players—especially Europe, the United States, and international financial institutions—be prepared for the Euro's coming impact.

Changes are swiftly moving Europe into the leadership position. The EU's GDP (gross domestic product) amounted to $8.4 trillion in 1996 while the U.S. GDP was $7.2 trillion. The European Union's external trade was $1.9 trillion in 1996 as compared to $1.7 trillion for America. Presently, the Euro core group of nations accounts for 18 percent of world product output and 19 percent of world trade. The full European Monetary Union accounts for 31 percent of world product output and 20 percent of world trade. The euro's implementation is expected to cause each of these categories to increase by at least 50 to 100 percent immediately and eventually by 65 to 200 percent.

The euro, it is estimated, could attain a 20 percent to 30 percent share of world finance if European Monetary Union included only the core nations. They could reach a 25 to 50 percent share if the entire European Union becomes involved.

Such a revolution in world economics could produce a major diversification of portfolios around the globe from dollars to euros. Official reserve shifts from dollars to euros would most likely range from $100 billion to $300 billion. Total private portfolio diversification would mean much larger monetary amounts would be shifted from the dollar base to the euro base—probably between $500 billion and $1 trillion.

Again, according to the experts, substantial euro appreciation and dollar depreciation could take place in the international portfolio situation during the transition to a dominant European Union. While most believe that such a shift will take considerable time, there is plenty of experience in the history of world financial markets and major currencies to show that unexpected shocks can produce rapid changes.

According to an article in *Foreign Affairs*,

> ...the availability of a more attractive alternative to the dollar could reduce the ability of the United States to finance its large external deficits. With more than $4 trillion in external liabilities and an array of alternative assets available to international investors...the United States policy autonomy already faces considerable limits....[18]

Indeed, the January 1, 1999, date for the birth of the euro looms ominously!

Analyzing the Strange Mixture

Those who analyze present-day Europe are often frustrated by the on-again, off-again efforts at unification. They know great history-making things are in progress that will likely produce a world superpower. However, they do not know, indeed, cannot know that supernatural forces are shaping a new Europe from which will spring the colossal *ten kings* superstate that will serve as Antichrist's power base. They cannot understand the supernatural aspects of the process because rather than being the enlightened ones they believe themselves to be, they are in darkness, spiritually speaking (1 Corinthians 2:14).

Understanding the strange mixture of iron and clay nations and the process currently underway to force them into cohesion can be accomplished only through spiritually attuned senses. Dr. Daymond Duck's analysis, I believe, comes from Holy Spirit-directed prayer, study, and thinking about this profound matter involving biblical prophecy. He writes:

> Daniel predicted that the Roman Empire, represented by the legs of iron, would crack and break into pieces

(nations). The pieces would bruise (fight wars and oppress people).

That is exactly what happened. The Roman Empire fractured into the nations of France, Germany, England and so forth. They fought many wars. England and France warred, Spain fought England, Germany fought England, France, Russia and other nations, ultimately culminating in World Wars I and II. *Wars and rumors of wars* continue to this very day. "It shall break in pieces and bruise" (Daniel 2:40).

Duck then puts the feet and toes of Nebuchadnezzar's great man-image under the microscope of the Bible and history.

What about the fifth Gentile world kingdom? Daniel said the last kingdom will be divided. It is difficult to say exactly what he meant, but it seems likely he is saying it would organize into two divisions at first. And later on, it would have ten subdivisions. It is probable that the two feet implies two primary divisions at the outset. And the ten toes most likely represent ten secondary divisions that would come afterwards.

This is not far-fetched. Notice, the statue had two arms of silver which represented two groups of people—the Medes and the Persians. The statue had two legs of iron which represented the Roman Empire that split into two divisions—Eastern and Western. This historical pattern suggests the Revived Roman Empire will come on the scene with two main divisions. Then, when it reaches its final form, it will have ten subdivisions.

But it will not come strictly out of the old Roman Empire. It will be an odd mixture of iron and clay; an incohesive alliance of old Roman Empire nations and non-Roman Empire nations.

And most of its power will come from the iron nations that were in the old Roman Empire. They will give the kingdom its power by transferring their weapons, resources, and military to it.

The kingdom will lack uniformity. It will be "partly strong and partly broken" signifying a mixture of strong nations and weak nations, strong established democracies from Western Europe and weaker ex-Communist countries from Central Europe.[19]

The writer's fascinating observation becomes doubly so in light of developments beginning early in 1997. NATO (North Atlantic Treaty Organization), which despite its name is becoming more and more Euro-centered, began and is continuing to entertain applicants for membership even from among former Soviet bloc nations, including Poland, Hungary, and the Czech republic. More startling than that development, Russian president Boris Yeltsin signed an agreement with NATO in May 1997, giving his nation a say in NATO decision-making.

Despite the diplomatic mask portraying unity and understanding, however, the agreement brought with it the usual double-talk and dual interpretation spin-doctoring.

U.S. News & World Report, May 26, 1997, states:

> The documents that Boris Yeltsin and Bill Clinton were each loudly praising had the same title, but that was almost where the similarity seemed to end. "The binding nature of this document is for all to see," the Russian president told a television interviewer. "If Russia is against some decision, it means this decision will not go through. This is of capital importance." At almost the same time, Clinton was at the White House announcing the "historic step" that gives Russia "a voice in, but not a veto over, NATO's business."[20]

How long can it be before the feet of Nebuchadnezzar's gargantuan metallic monster begin smashing everything and everyone in their path? How near are we to the time when the composite beast with seven heads and ten horns begins stamping the residue of broken nations with its terrible, clawed feet?

The Mechanics of New Europe

To quote Dr. Dave Breese, Europe today has many organizations in place that "form a governmental entity that resembles one of the many-headed monsters of the apocalyptic visions of the Bible."[21] That is a powerful conclusion reached by one of the world's foremost prophecy scholars and geopolitical observers. He gives us a look into the vortex of new Europe's descending funnel cloud.

The following is an excellent organizational overview of European Community inner workings:

"The Treaty of Brussels" (signed in 1965, becoming effective in 1967) established four governmental branches.

The Legislative

The European Commission, based in Brussels, Belgium, initiates all policy for the European Community. Its members are chosen for four-year terms by their governments, and the Commission President is chosen by consensus of the heads of the [15] European Community countries.

The Advisory

The European Parliament meets one week a month in Strasbourg, France, but maintains administrative offices in Brussels. With 518 members, it forms one giant advisory board, with each member giving his opinion as to what is good for their own nation.

The Administrative

The Council of Ministers consists of the heads of [15] European Community governments. They set European Community policy. In some cases, the European Parliament can veto their actions. In many cases, the [15] national parliaments have to approve their actions. But in spite of all these limits, this is where things really happen.

The Judiciary

The European Court of Justice is based in Luxembourg. It adjudicates disputes between the European Community institutions, and between the European Community and its member nations. Europe has put together the machinery to run a united community.

A Common Defense

The European Community Conference on Security and Cooperation has called for a new collective security organization for post-Cold War Europe. They seek a new entity, considering NATO outdated.

In October 1991, France and Germany proposed a 50,000 member army that would become the precursor of an EC army. Until an EC army comes into reality, this force would serve as the European Community's defense arm, with possible headquarters in Strasbourg, France. As a matter of fact, German and French troops have already begun to cooperate in joint military exercises.

Money Talks

The Unity Treaty of 1992 calls for a European Central Bank to replace national central banks late in the 1990s, when Europe switches to a common currency. Germany, France, and the other EC nations are committed to replacing their currencies with the ECU in this decade, no later than 1999.

A common currency would mean tremendous savings for the European economy. Currently, Europe wastes an estimated $17 billion a year converting currencies, all of which would be saved when they go to the ECU [euro].

Further, there's the question of potential: When the ECU replaces all of the European currencies, it will hold 46% of all international bonds, as compared to the dollar's 31%. When the ECU takes control, its government bond market will be the world's largest financial market!"[22]

New Europe's tornadic vortex has already begun siphoning the economic undergirdings of many nations. Markets are powerfully influenced by this brewing, brooding monster's looming presence. But as Dr. Daymond Duck points out in his book, *On the Brink*, the forming European Union is only part of a larger prophetic geopolitical power structure to come.

The New World Order

Duck writes:

> The new world order is not the same thing as the EC. But the EC is the model intellectuals and world leaders are using. They want to divide the world into trading blocks. The EC, NAFTA and the Pacific Rim nations are examples. If they succeed, the EC will become the dominant

force in the new world order and cause it to take on dev-
ilish overtones. The implications are so horrendous,
Christians are wise to be wary.[23]

Anyone today who mentions *the new world order* is immediately suspected of being *a conspiracy theorist*. Sometimes mention of such things as the United Nations, the World Bank, the
Bilderbergers, the Council on Foreign Relations, the Trilateral
Commission, the International Monetary Fund, etc., when used in
conjunction with talk of a *globalist agenda*, brands one as a *conspiracy nut* or a *kook*.

Clearly, there are those who carry these themes to the fringe
and go about their daily lives with a fanatic militia and/or surviv-
alist mentality. Evidence abounds, however, pointing to the fact
that there is reason to worry about trends toward governmental
overinvolvement in day-to-day human affairs. The globalist conferences held over the past several years in Rio de Janeiro, Venice,
Cairo, Beijing, Istanbul, Rome, and New York City lend credence to
concerns that there exists a globalist agenda dead set on bringing
everything and everyone into one world configuration. They want
uniformity under central global authority in monetary matters,
education, environmental control, law, family values and relations,
and everything else. God's prophetic Word says the time will come
when one world religion will also be instituted.

Daymond Duck writes that the globalists want "a world charter,
the United Nations to have a standing military, the United Nations
to have authority to cross borders and attack nations, a world
income tax and much more." He says, "They used buzzwords like
'collective security, interdependence, global harmony, integration,
a democratic world, a new civilization, global citizenship, a world
perspective,' and 'the international community....'"[24]

Duck says further, "They think in terms of human rights, eliminating war, promoting world peace, establishing a fair and benevolent government, eliminating famine, sharing wealth, stopping the
proliferation of nuclear weapons, protecting the environment and
such."[25]

Of course, all of this is about building a power structure from
which a globalist elite can lord it over the rest of us. This is because
such grandiose plans come not from the mind of God but from the
mind of Satan, who controls the thinking processes of fallen mankind.

Ten Kings Spawn From European Storm

Growing conjecture about the ten kings of Revelation 17:12,13 sparks interesting debate among astute observers who are students of biblical prophecy. The European Union continues to increase in number of member nations. Thus, the question has arisen, since the EU has eclipsed the magic number *ten* (membership presently stands at 15 nations), does this mean that the ten kings of Revelation 17:12,13 might come from a source or sources other than European Union, which might ultimately include 30 or more nations?

There seem to be some legitimate reasons for considering that possibility. For example, the Scripture says, "...those horns which thou sawest are ten kings who have received no kingdom as yet...". They will be leaders whose kingdoms did not exist at the time John received the vision. It is therefore reasonable to infer that several different geographical configurations for that end-time power sphere arrangement are possible by the time Antichrist comes to power.

The rest of the Scripture says these kings "...receive power as kings one hour with the beast...". The reference "as kings" might be construed as meaning they will not be kings over particular nations. Rather, "like" kings, they are given charge over these power spheres for a short time under Antichrist's overall dominion.

Some excellent scholars in biblical prophecy believe these ten kings represent ten economic spheres of influence, or trading blocs, into which a large portion of planet Earth will be divided by the time the Revelation 17:12,13 prophecy nears fulfillment. Other scholars who are equally well studied hold to the belief that the ten kings will be the kings or rulers over ten actual nations geographically located within the region encompassed by the old Roman Empire. These nations will have unified by the time the Revelation 17:12,13 prophecy is played out.

This is to offer no speculation one way or the other with regard to which view is correct or as to whether there is another scenario more plausible. Regardless, it is unmistakably clear that Rome was at the heart of the Empire. It is equally clear that Antichrist will be descended from the people indigenous to that region (read Daniel 9:26).

We have already seen earlier that Titus, the Roman general, destroyed Jerusalem and the temple precisely on schedule in 70 A.D. following Christ's crucifixion. Titus and his troops were *"people of the prince that shall come.*" They were Roman. They were European. Therefore, the ten kingdom confederation of Revelation 17:12,13, regardless of how it is finally constituted, will have sprung from the very heart of Europe.

The "prince that shall come" will descend from the stormy economic chaos of his time like the terrible funnel that struck the tiny town of Gerald, Texas in May 1997, killing seven people and injuring many more. Antichrist will be far more deadly than that killer storm. However, most people will believe him to be a peacemaker and a problem solver—a breath of fresh air in their degenerating, decaying world.

The people of Europe, indeed, the people of the world, cry out for a leader who can bring peace, prosperity, and love for all mankind to this deeply troubled world. Paul Henri Spaack, former secretary general of NATO and one of the founders of the movement toward European union, once voiced the European longing for such a leader: "What we want is a man of significant stature to hold the allegiance of all people and to lift us out of the economic morass into which we are sinking. Send us such a man, then be he god or devil, we will receive him."

Based upon consideration of the many issues, events, and prevailing conditions dynamically shaping the world today, that man must even now be rising within the political power structure of new Europe.

He is given many names in the prophetic Scriptures. *The little horn, the king of fierce countenance, the prince that shall come, the wicked one, the man of sin, the son of perdition*, and others. He will come promising peace, but it will be a false peace which will quickly prove to be a prelude to global war, famine, pestilence, and death.

Thankfully, Christians today are not to be looking for Antichrist, but for the Lord Jesus Christ—the stone who will smash the Beast's kingdom to pieces at Christ's second advent.

Before that time when the world's worst tyrant takes the reins of the coming global order, Jesus will shout, *"Come up here!"* (Revelation 4:1) to all who truly trust in Him alone for their salvation. Considering developments in Europe and around the world, that stupendous moment must indeed be near.

▼   ▼   ▼

CHAPTER 8

The Deadly Chinese Typhoon

Noah W. Hutchings

A movie, *Mission Impossible*, based on a TV series of the '70s, opened in June 1996, in theaters across the United States. In the movie, undercover agents are presented with a seemingly impossible mission. Because of their improbability of success, the participants are given the option to accept or reject the assignment. In January 1996, I was presented with a similar proposal. My mission: To provide the underground churches and home churches in China with Bibles and teaching materials.

News coming out of China indicated that since I had last been there in the fall of 1991, government policies in relation to all three levels of church establishment or witness (self, home, and underground) were more severe and restrictive. The plan to provide home churches and underground churches with Bibles and needed printed items originally called for getting all this material into the country by commercial shipping avenues. However, one month before we were to leave for China it was learned that this avenue would no longer be open to us. Four recipients of Bibles and Christian publications for home churches and underground churches had been arrested and were in prison. Due to the time factor, the only other option appeared to be taking the printed matter with us. I had been arrested in 1987 trying to get a shipment of Bibles past the customs and immigration officials at Guilin in the south, and because new China policies against Christians and missionary efforts were now even more restrictive, I had serious reservations about the success of our mission.

Early on the morning of June 8, my wife, Kim, and I left Oklahoma City by United Airlines. Tour members had been instructed to bring only one suitcase. A second suitcase was packed with Chinese Bibles, Illustrated Bibles, Condensed Bibles, New Testaments, tracts, etc. Weight limit per suitcase was 44 pounds, but some of the suitcases with printed material weighed between 70 and 100 pounds. However, God was with us and all the suitcases were accepted by the airline.

The flight to Tokyo was over ten hours, the layover was three hours, and then the flight to Beijing was another three hours. Beijing arrival time was 10 p.m. It had been a very, very long day, and Oklahoma City was a half-world away. I called the members of our tour together in preparation for immigration and customs inspection. Four members of our tour had left the previous day for Shanghai with Bibles and literature for the home and underground churches in the central section of the country. Eight additional members left the group to fly to Shanghai on June 8.

The day before I left for the tour, I was given an entrance visa for 18 tour members to get us through immigration. However, when I presented the entrance visa to the immigration officer, I was informed in no uncertain terms that my tour group could not get into China without also having an exit visa. The tour members had to be verified by an official, and the visa had to be stamped with the date of entrance along with the expected exit date. So now my problem became not only to get the contraband Bibles and Christian literature past customs, but also to get my entire tour group past immigration.

Had we traveled all this way just to be turned back by Satan? Had the devil won?

I tried every reason and argument known in attempting to get the tour members past immigration, but to no avail. Our national guide, a young man whom we called Leonard (not his Chinese name) expressed dismay at our not having an exit visa. Finally, our local guide (whom we called Jack) was located. Jack called the China Immigration and Customs office. An arrangement was agreed upon whereby a new exit visa would be issued for $4 per tour member.

Although waiting to see if we could even get into the country was somewhat traumatic, the Lord worked it to our advantage. We had been held up so long that we were rushed through immigration without our luggage ever being checked, and along with our luggage went suitcases filled with precious Bibles and teaching materials in the Chinese language. We checked into our Beijing hotel about 12:30 a.m. None of the luggage with literature was assigned to my room, because being the tour leader, I would be the first to be checked. I also cautioned the tour members not to say anything about our mission. It is well known that hotel rooms may be bugged by the Secret Service. It is also best not to say anything about the country that might be negative.

Church History in China

The status of the church and/or Christian missions in China is directly related to the political and economic past.

While Nestorian Christianity did make a presence in Xion, and possibly other areas of southwest China in the eighth century, Christianity was considered a foreign religion, suffered persecution, and vanished.

Going back into history 4000 years, we find that China was ruled by emperors in succeeding dynasties: Song, Tang, Qing, Ming, Zhou, to name just a few. Emperors ruled by provincial, city, or war lord alliances.

In the nineteenth century the Roman Colonial powers of Europe, plus the United States, discovered China to be a land of golden commercial opportunity. Commercial land holdings and enclaves were established on the mainland. China neither needed nor wanted much of what was manufactured or grown by Europe or the United States. In order to prevent a huge trade deficit, Spain began to sell opium to the Chinese. England followed in the opium trade market and soon Chinese men became drug addicts in increasing numbers. In 1839 Lin Zexu pleaded with Queen Victoria to stop the opium traffic to China, but warned: "Your Majesty has not before been thus officially notified, and you may plead ignorance of the severity of our laws. But I now give my assurance that we mean to cut off this harmful drug forever...." Europe demanded more and more tea, silk, and spices, but the only thing England had to trade that the Chinese wanted was opium. A series of opium wars ensued in which kegs of opium were thrown into the sea from British ships. This eventually led to the Boxer Rebellion, in which Christians and business representatives were killed or held prisoner. A number of nations, including England and the United States, sent armies to the rescue, captured Beijing, and burned much of the Summer Palace.

Out of the confrontations between China and the West, which the West always won, the French, British, and the United States received land and trade concessions in Shanghai and at other ports. The British also received Hong Kong.

In the wake of Occidental commercial expansion also came Christian missionaries. The main religions of China had been Buddhism and Taoism. In spite of commercial and aggressive associations, Christianity became widely accepted and churches were founded. However, some prominent Chinese, possibly influenced by cultic doctrines, seized upon the new converts to promote their own political programs. Hong Xiuchuran, who declared himself to be the brother of Jesus, started the Taiping Rebellion which raged between 1850 and 1864. The goal of the revolution was to free women and promote the Kingdom of Heaven on Earth. Approximately 20 million were killed in this rebellion. To put the casualties of this civil war into perspective, this would be more than 20 times that of the number of Americans who were killed in all of the following wars: Revolutionary War, War of 1812, Mexican War, Civil War, Spanish-American War, World War I, World War II, Korean War, Vietnam War, and Persian Gulf War. Therefore, it is understandable that even today some oriental governments are reticent to welcome Christian missions or church growth.

If the nineteenth century was traumatic and turbulent to China, the twentieth century was even worse. Greed, corruption, and foreign vested interests so weakened the rule of the Ch'ing Dynasty that it was unable to govern. Sun Yat-sen, in the revolution of 1911–1912, overthrew the last emperor. The new George Washington of China desired to establish some form of a republican political entity. He was a professed Christian, yet he was practically deserted by the church and the governments of Europe and the United States, who waited to see if China really wanted a democratic form of government. Sun Yat-sen could not wait, so he turned to Russia and the new communist regime of Lenin. In Sun's army there were two young rising stars, Chiang Kai-shek and Mao Tse-tung. Chiang was sent to Moscow to be schooled in how communism could be brought to China. However, Chiang had a Christian wife, and he himself professed to be a Christian. There was nothing in communism to Chiang but chaos and evil. Mao, possibly to please Sun, espoused communism, and China was again embroiled in a long civil war.

It appeared that the nationalist forces under Chiang Kai-shek had won, so Mao and his beaten army fled to the west. After the long march, only a few thousand survived. In 1937, the Japanese invaded China and quickly occupied Beijing and then Shanghai. At nearby Nanjing, Japanese soldiers who killed more than 100 defenseless citizens each were given prizes. When I was in Nanjing in June 1996, I was told the army actually killed more than 300,000 defenseless men, women, and children. While an accusing finger is pointed at the United States for dropping atomic bombs on Hiroshima and Nagasaki, where an estimated 200,000 were killed (doubtless saving millions of lives by shortening the war), no one today outside of China remembers the terrible crime of the rape of Nanjing.

Chiang Kai-shek was criticized for trying to fight on two fronts. He was under pressure to join forces with the communists and fight a united war against Japan. Chiang's philosophy was: "The Japanese are a disease of the skin; communism is a disease of the heart." Mao profited from Chiang's refusal to join forces with him, or form a coalition government at the insistence of the U.S. State Department. After the Japanese surrender and the end of World War II, the U.S. State Department was riddled with communist sympathizers and promoters like Harry Dexter White. Some in the military (like General Joe Stilwell and General George Marshall), held ill will for Chiang, so the balance of power was thrown to Mao, and the nationalist forces had to flee to Formosa (now Taiwan).

In 1950, the churches of China were confronted with a government like that of Russia—hostile to all religions, and especially Christianity. In order to survive as a collective entity, many churches throughout the nation formed what is known as the "Three Self Church Alliance." The meaning the name of the new association tried to convey was that the churches in the alliance were self-governing, self-supporting, and self-motivated. All foreign identifications or ties with Baptists, Presbyterians, Methodists, Catholics, etc., were immediately severed. Even today, the only foreign association tolerated is the World Council of Churches, which has a history of social gospel theology, as well as being infiltrated with communists or their sympathizers.

No system of political communism has survived for more than 70 years without imploding. In 1965, Mao found his economic policies failing, his critics increasing, and his policies of encouraging women to bear more children producing him with an additional 300 million young mouths to house, feed, and educate. He offered to resign, but with Mao gone, the entire government would fall. So Mao was convinced that it was a remnant of the capitalists, religionists, and counterrevolutionists in China that were causing his problems. For the next ten years, the rivers of China ran red with the blood of millions as the so-called Red Guard pillaged, murdered, raped, and burned. Even the Three Self churches were closed. Pastors and church workers were killed, sent to prison, or sent to labor camps. In talking with people throughout China, I have yet to find anyone who did not have a mother, father, brother, sister, or friend who died in the Cultural Revolution. It is probably conservative to say that at least 50 million died in this unspeakable period of hell on Earth.

In 1987, on my third mission to China, our national guide, secretary of the China Tourist Agency and daughter of the governor of a province in South China, changed our flight to land in Guilin rather than in Shanghai. Subsequently, because of the change, I was caught with a rather large shipment of Bibles and tracts. After the Bibles were confiscated and I was forced to sign an arrest warrant acknowledging my "guilt," we proceeded and did the best we could. One of our efforts which the Lord blessed was to win our young national guide to the Lord. As usual, we had Scripture readings, devotionals, and prayers on the bus. A local guide kept challenging me to read also from Mao's Little Red Book because he said that Mao was greater than Jesus. Finally, I told him, before the group, that Mao was given credit conservatively for killing 60 million people, but Jesus never killed anyone; Jesus came to give life, not to take it. Therefore, based on the number of victims, Mao would be greater than Jesus? The guide never bothered me after that.

The Mission

The Tiananmen Square protests of 1989 resulted in the killing of approximately 3000 students. However, this student revolution was not just in Beijing; it was throughout most of China. It was a nationwide student effort to get the government to allow graduates to open job opportunities with competitive salary offers between employees and employers. This would have been an important step toward an open market economy, and the leaders vowed that what happened in Russia would not happen in China. In 1991 when I returned to China, there was a feeling among students, teachers, and Christians that the United States had failed to back them with even moral and political support. The United States had lost face.

Now, during our 1997 tour, after a full American breakfast, we boarded our bus to tour Tiananmen Square and the Forbidden City, our first visit to these cities since 1991. The Forbidden City was the palace buildings and complex for emperors of the Ming and Ch'ing dynasties. It was so named because any foreigner caught inside the city walls was to be executed. Thousands of tourists daily tour these sites, so our presence was hardly noticed.

I had been advised not to attempt to witness or pass out tracts. On previous visits, our tour group would line up across the square and furiously pass out Bibles and tracts for ten minutes and then disappear in the crowd. Although I knew that this time, due to increasing government persecution of Christians, this would not be possible, I had to test the attitude of the people in 1996 toward our country and their willingness to listen to the gospel. Consequently, I found the Chinese people on the square to be open, friendly, and willing to listen or take anything offered. On the square I gave two families (husband, wife, and child) a small thumbnail tract containing only a few Bible verses. They gladly received the tract, took my picture, and shook my hand. I thought that I had given the tract without being observed. Next, we went to the Forbidden City, which is across the street from Tiananmen Square. I followed the same procedure, and even sent Kim, my wife, into one of the buildings to pass out a few tracts. She returned to report that she experienced no problem and the people gladly received the Scriptures. In the meantime, I thought I had talked to two additional couples without being observed and I passed on to them another small Scripture tract. Later, our national guide, as we neared the end of touring the Forbidden City, informed me that I had been observed by the secret police and would be arrested when I departed through the huge exit gate. Evidently, I was either being followed or our national guide had reported me to the police. Another member of our tour group was also placed under arrest with me. Evidently, some tracts had been given out without my knowledge, and she had passed some of those out that morning.

A large black limousine was waiting for us, and we were taken to the police station just off Tiananmen Square. In an adjoining room, another prisoner was being interrogated. The yelling was so loud that finally our interrogators had to ask for quiet so we could be questioned. I had been arrested before and the law I had violated had been explained; therefore, I did not ask that it be read to me again. The law simply states that it is against the laws of China to bring into the country and/or distribute books or literature that promote propaganda harmful to the people. On other occasions I had argued that the Bible is not harmful, but would, in fact, make better citizens for the government. However, since I had lost the argument before, I did not try to justify myself on these grounds. I anticipated it would be useless.

In the course of questioning I surrendered what few tracts I had left in my pocket. The police in China are experts in interrogating. I had to be careful and not contradict myself or be caught in an untruth. The police were mainly interested in finding out if I had brought in other material. They wanted to know if the four small tracts I had given out were printed in China, or if I had brought them from the United States. They were very interested to find out if I had local contacts, friends, or co-conspirators. They also wanted to know if I had additional "religious propaganda" in my hotel room. I could honestly reply that I had none in my room, but they sent two men to check my room anyway. After approximately an hour and a half, the police evidently concluded that they had gotten all the information they could get out of us, so they set down the charges on paper and asked us to sign and acknowledge our guilt. We signed the paper and were released. When I asked the police to take us back to our tour group, they indicated it was not their responsibility to do taxi service. Had the police known that in another room at the hotel we had thousands of Bibles, Condensed Bibles, and Children's Illustrated Bibles, the charges would have been much more serious. We probably would have had our visas canceled, been taken to the airport, and sent back to the States. I doubt if the government of China would have risked a confrontation with the United States by keeping us in jail, but in China you never know. Even our guides said they never know how to advise tourists over such matters, as the rules change from day to day. I doubt that many Christian organizations (I know of only one other) would risk taking Bibles for distribution to the underground church.

God Makes the Impossible, Possible

That evening several of the brethren met to consider our remaining problem. We still had Bibles in our possession at the hotel, our contacts in the Beijing area had been arrested, and there was no apparent way to contact the home churches or the underground churches. I had established a friendship on former visits with the elder pastor at a Christian Men's Church, a Three-Self church. It was decided that the following day I would attempt to call this pastor to contact a representative of the home or underground churches. If no other options were available, we would try to get the pastor to receive the material himself. However, subsequent information we received indicated that this would not have been possible.

At this time I was not fully aware of the details regarding suppression and control of Christians in China that had been decided on, and reported to the Communist Party, on January 14, 1996. In attempting to stay clear of possible problems with the local Beijing communist authorities, I asked our guide to call the pastor and set up a meeting. Jack appeared reticent and explained that the government might be suspicious of a foreigner trying to get in contact with a local church. This was something that I had not encountered before. Nevertheless, Jack got the number for me, and advised that I should call after 9 a.m. However, when I called the church after 9 a.m., a government agent answered the telephone. The agent was loud, antagonistic, and definitive. He shouted at me that I would not be allowed to see a pastor at the church. When I attempted to reason with him, he simply shouted "Impossible! Impossible!"

The rest of the tour group had departed by bus to the Great Wall and the Ming Tombs and would not return until evening. Two tour members were left behind to assist me, so I took a taxi to personally go to the church. However, when we arrived at the church we were confronted with the same problem. After trying for 30 minutes to get through to the pastor, we gave up and returned to the hotel. When we met with the tour group that evening, I had to report our failure. We were to depart Beijing for Nanjing (Nanking) the next morning. Due to the weight limitations on China's domestic airlines, there was no way we could take the Bibles and other materials with us. Plus, we couldn't leave them at the hotel because they would be traced to us. Suddenly, we realized the Bibles and materials posed a great danger to all of us. Again I prayed and turned the matter over to the Lord; the battle was His. I confessed that we were helpless, so He would have to take care of it.

About 11:00 p.m. my telephone rang and woke me up. A member of our tour, Mercedes Ford from Washington, D.C., was on the phone. She informed me that someone speaking broken English had called three times asking if we had something for him. She finally realized that it might be someone asking about the material we had for the underground church. Contact was made quickly in the lobby. The suitcases were carried downstairs and shuttled passed the security people in front of the hotel. The security personnel were evidently busy with another matter and did not even notice the suitcases. The underground church men were overjoyed, and shouted "Hallelujah!" with a Chinese accent. "Mission impossible" had suddenly become possible, because "with God all things are possible" (Matthew 19:26).

I was pleasantly surprised as we boarded our flight to Nanjing. A sparkling clean Boeing 737 was our carrier. On previous domestic flights I usually said a prayer, closed my eyes, and tried to ignore the stench as we flew from one city to the next. Flights were usually on outmoded British Tri-Stars that were overcrowded and poorly maintained, with not enough room for even the service people to move freely in the aisles. Odors from overflowing toilets pervaded the entire airplane. At least half of the flights were on old 1940s or 1950s foreign, propeller-driven planes. Often wrecked planes were dragged off the runways, but left in open view of passengers. I remember one flight from Wuhan to Shanghai in 1985. When we left Wuhan at midnight it was so dark we could not see the twin-engine propeller plane of indeterminate age or origin that we were boarding. After we were seated, it became obvious that this was not a passenger aircraft. Once in the air, the engines began sputtering and chugging as if they might expire at any moment. Two German business representatives, evidently in China for marketing opportunities, sat across from me. I asked one of the German gentlemen if this were not an old World War II Russian cargo plane. He replied, "Not only that, but it is one we shot down over Stalingrad."

On every flight we took in China on our 1996 tour, we boarded an almost-new airplane. Most of the airports are now improved and up to U.S. standards. The in-flight service personnel are outstanding—bright, charming, well-dressed, and polite. Every flight departed and landed at almost the exact minute as scheduled. All this reflects the growing economy which the taxpayers of the United States help build and maintain through the "favored nations trade" policies of our own government, from Nixon to Clinton.

This was my first visit to Nanjing. On previous trips to China we had gone to nearby Shanghai. Nanjing is a former capital of China, but it cannot compare to the modernized cities like Beijing. However, we enjoyed our visit to the city, and I was especially interested in visiting the only Christian seminary in China. On former visits to China I had heard about a great Christian seminary in Nanjing where young Chinese men called to the ministry can learn in complete academic freedom. What a sad travesty. Total personnel on campus, including students, teachers, staff, and attendants, was 150, meaning that there could not have been more than 100 students to train for the ministry to serve 1.3 billion people. No staff member of the school met us, even though our guides had made an appointment. A student met us at the main gate. Evidently, the staff members were afraid to talk to us. The student was not very communicative, appearing somewhat reticent to even answer questions. We finally did get him to open up to some extent, and he confided to two of us that they were in a most tenuous position with the government, and often had to wear two faces.

Our student guide through the "seminary" also related in a quiet voice that some students, and even pastors, were in prison for attempting to minister to house churches. I asked the student guide about the financial support of the seminary, and he indicated that funds came from the Three-Self churches and limited tuition fees. However, it is believed that most funds come from the government. Thus, the government—through fund allotment—can better control the policies and size of the seminary. The library at the seminary was confined to one 18' by 18' room. It housed a few good reference books, but for the most part it was a pitiful excuse for a school library. The student said we could send books to the library, but that, based on past experience, the government mail service would most likely not send the books on to the school.

Before we left for Xion, we visited the gigantic tomb and memorial to Sun Yat-sen. The men who had gone to Shanghai joined us at Nanjing; therefore, missionary commitments for Beijing and Shanghai had been fulfilled.

Xion was the capital of China when the Great Wall was built and the Terra Cotta army was made. Both the Great Wall and the Terra Cotta army should be numbered among the Great Wonders of the Ancient World. Xion, on the banks of the Yellow River in central China, is removed in distance enough from the stronger, governmental-controlled eastern China cities to allow more freedom concerning one-on-one evangelism. On a former visit to Xion, one of our tour members had passed through a company of soldiers at attention and handed each one a tract. I received a reprimand from the commanding officer, but it was mostly in a pleasant manner.

We did not have an abundance of Christian literature left in our possession, but we felt freer to distribute what we did have. We held Sunday morning worship service at the hotel. Some Australians who were staying at the hotel came to worship with us, and our national guide, Leonard, was present. I had insisted that we also attend service at a local church, and we were scheduled to visit a Catholic church. We informed our guides that as conservative evangelicals, we would not be in conformation to a Catholic church. Having gone to a non-Catholic church in Xion before, I insisted that we go to that church. As far as I know, there are two churches in Xion—one Catholic and one non-Catholic. Approximately 300 were present at the service, which had already begun when we arrived. Church services in China, as established by English and American missionaries, follow much the same order as worship services in our churches, with opening hymns, announcements, prayer, offering, message, closing hymn, and prayer. The audience remains quiet except during congregational music.

Churches in China usually have five pastors, two of which may be women, as was the pastor delivering the sermon at this service. It is possible that one or two of the five pastors regularly report to the government. Two Wycliffe translators reported to me that since the government crackdown on churches this year, regular sermons have to be pre-approved by the government, and the same sermon is sent to all Three-Self churches on a weekly basis. Pastors are forbidden to speak on prophetic subjects; one pastor who did was removed from his church and forbidden to ever preach again.

The pastor at the church appeared to be sincere and delivered her message in a clear and forthright manner. Most sermons I have heard from church pulpits in China have been from the Gospel of John. At the conclusion, the congregation sang "Nearer My God to Thee" in Chinese. All hymns in Chinese churches, at any level, are taken from 1940 American or English church hymnals. As the service was dismissed, people crowded around us and our tour members did the best they could to communicate. In central China and west China, the number of Chinese who speak English are fewer than in the east.

At the hotel in Xion, Pastor Robert Fultz, a member of our group, won two girls in their late teens to the Lord, and we were all gratified with the testimony we had given. However, we were later informed that Christians in Xion were under heavy persecution, and that we were most fortunate not to have been arrested.

Our flight from Xion to Guilin was pleasant and uneventful. On each flight I got acquainted with a Chinese man or woman in an adjacent seat. The Chinese are easy to talk with, open for any discussion, most eager to hear about the U.S., and welcome any information or witness about our testimony and faith in Jesus Christ. I took down several addresses and promised to send them a Bible when I returned to the States. Entering Guilin Airport, one of the few airports in China that has not been updated, brought back bittersweet memories of former visits to the city. I had hoped to find some evidence of the present circumstances of our former national guide, Chiang, and my underground pastor friend, but I was unsuccessful. In China people just disappear, and then no one will acknowledge that the person ever existed.

Our time in Guilin was short, and our boat trip along the Li River through the most fantastic scenery on earth took one full day. Our guide, Stew, encouraged me to try to get a visa to come back to Guilin next summer for a two-month stay. I have wanted to get away and write a book on Revelation, but whether I could get a visa to go back to Guilin next year is questionable.

Our flight from Guilin to Canton in a new 757 was pleasant, smooth, and uneventful. We only had five hours for touring in

Canton, and at that time we had planned to return to Hong Kong and complete our mission. We also planned to keep an appointment with Dr. Lamb and his church, one of the most courageous ministries in the world today. At mid-afternoon, our tour group caught a hovercraft and made the three-hour trip to Hong Kong by sea.

A huge electric clock on Tiananmen Square in Beijing counted the days and the hours until Hong Kong reverted to China in July, 1997. More billionaires live in Hong Kong, more skyscrapers tower above Hong Kong, and there are more banking and business centers in Hong Kong than perhaps any other city in the world. Under British tutelage, Hong Kong has become the business and communication center for Asia and the South Pacific. Per square foot, the most valuable real estate in the world has been Hong Kong and the connected islands. When all of this property is given back to China as a free gift, the already exploding economics of China will explode even more.

The homes of billionaires on Victoria Peak and the other mountain peaks overlooking Hong Kong were worth millions or hundreds of millions of dollars. Under the communist government of China, all property belongs to the state. We would assume that when China reclaimed Hong Kong in 1997, these homes were worth nothing. This is just another example of the truth of Scripture—we can't take it with us. One million in Hong Kong had applied to leave, and an additional 5000 were applying every day. Immigration staffs can process only 5000 applications a day. The greatest tragedy about immigration applications is that no one but the very rich have anywhere else to go.

Another coming tragedy about Hong Kong is that this city had been the missionary doorway to China and southeast Asia. There are many Christian missions in Hong Kong, as well as Christian schools, Christian orphan homes, Christian churches, and most importantly, Christian publishing houses and printing establishments. Christian institutions in Hong Kong will be the first to be closed or come under harsh regulations and persecution.

The day before we left Guilin for Canton, our contact man was arrested, his passport canceled, and he was put on a plane for Hong Kong. We had planned to complete our mission by returning to Canton from Hong Kong with Bibles and Christian literature for home churches and the underground church in the south. The arrest of our contact once again complicated this effort. We attempted to use our extra visa or get a new one-day visa, but to no avail. We hoped to be able to return to Hong Kong in late winter of 1997, or early spring, 1998, to complete our mission. We accept this as God's will. God knew how to manage events in Beijing, beyond our understanding, to get the Bibles and literature to the right people where they were most needed. There is a reason we were delayed in getting back into China from Hong Kong, and this reason will be revealed in due time. I am a strong believer that the truth of Romans 8:28 is absolute—all things do work for good to those who love God, to those who are the called according to His purpose.

China Today

The Economy: China's economy is indeed exploding, growing by as much as 18 percent a year. It is difficult to classify China's economic system other than to say it is government-controlled frenetic capitalism. Wages have not increased greatly in the past ten years. Average wages for skilled employees, including teachers and engineers, is about $60 a month. However, there appears to be a "government permitted" rich class rising to the top. The government has also relaxed its restrictions on automobile ownership, so more cars are now on the road, including some American models. Growing traffic congestion is encouraging widening of streets and the building of new highways. Massive government high-rise apartment projects are much in evidence.

The Government: It is difficult to classify the present political complexion of the government of China. It appears to be more fascist than communist. There is certainly no freedom in the will of the people upon the governmental process. Our national guide observed that if China had not changed its attitude on capitalistic motivation and market enterprise, China today would be worse off than North Korea. Four times as many people live in China today than in the United States, on the same amount of ground. What would we do in the United States if we had four times our present population? As distasteful as the despotic dictatorship of China is, or as atheistic and repressive (and even though the living standards of the Chinese people in general are much below that of the people of the United States and Europeans), someone is apparently doing a pretty good job of housing and feeding 1.3 billion Chinese people. If there is any widespread hunger in China, I have failed to find it. However, the rulers of China and the encompassing bureaucracy, whether it be fascist or communist, are deathly afraid that what happened in Russia may happen in China. Block leaders and spies through the land keep the government informed about what is happening, down to each block, each house. Even the policemen in China are not trusted with guns. Only military personnel, who are under strict control, are allowed guns. Mao's slogan was that political power comes out of the end of a gun. Another Tiananmen Square is not on the foreseeable horizon.

The People: The Chinese citizen today appears to be reasonably pleased with his or her present status. The economic realities of life have improved year by year and month by month since 1981. They have learned to live and be satisfied with their living standards and governmental regulations (such as one child to the family). Most Chinese dress neatly and appear to have a newfound pride in themselves. Whether out of fear or patriotism, few criticize their government. Boys don't wear long hair or earrings, and girls and women dress smartly, with modesty and good taste. The younger generation sports a new attitude and demeanor, and out of pride more than boasting, they say China will surpass the United States by the year 2000.

I have found the young people in China to be the most intelligent, open, and basically honest of any I have met in any nation, including our own. The Chinese in general are a delightful people. On our last tour I was startled to see 200 couples at the Temple of Heaven jitterbugging to the tune of "Bugle Boy of Company B," a World War II American song.

Our Chinese Guides: Our local Beijing guide, Jack, appeared to be a fine young man, but more serious than most. He came to our aid in the Beijing airport and fulfilled his duties in an expert manner. He was deeply touched by our Christian love and spirit, and when we left, he almost wept when he said goodbye, and told us that he would never forget us. Of course, we did witness to him and gave him a Bible and salvation tract. Although we could not legally witness outside the tour group, we could witness to our guides.

Our guide at Nanjing was a female in her mid-thirties. She was very much Chinese and scoffed at those who wanted to go to the

United States. She contended that the Chinese in China were much better off than the Chinese in the United States. Although we did give her a Bible and tracts, it is doubtful that she read them.

Our guide at Xion was a male in his late twenties. Well-educated and speaking almost perfect English, he was a firm believer in atheistic evolution. Though he was most courteous, helpful, and kind in every way, he expressed no interest in our prayers, devotions, or literature. He shared that after seven years he and his wife had finally decided to have their one child, and the doctor had told him it would be a girl. He related that friends and relatives had come by to mourn for him in that he would never have a son, but he said that he liked girls and he would keep her as his own. Many Chinese couples abort the baby when they know for sure it will be a girl, or they get rid of the female baby as soon as it is born. If they have, and keep, a second child, they lose their jobs, their housing, and are fined heavily by the government. This is why there are 32 million abortions a year in China.

Our guide in Guilin was a delightful young man who reminded me of actor Red Buttons. While most Chinese appear happy, inwardly they are empty and spiritually hungry. He remarked on the bus how much better off he was, but he was not happy. This gave me an opportunity to give him my pamphlet on the Chinese word for happiness. I had several long conversations with him, and he said that he would consider becoming a Christian. His English name is Stew. Remember him in prayer. He wanted me to return to Guilin for an extended visit in 1997.

Our guide in Hong Kong was another female in her mid-thirties. She indicated that she was looking for a rich, foreign husband so that she could escape from Hong Kong before the communists take over in 1997. She was concerned about what would happen to the people and institutions. The average apartment rent in Hong Kong is $1,000 a month, but under Chinese wage scale, educators and technicians make only $80 a month. She stated that the mindset of most of the citizens of Hong Kong was to "eat, drink, and be merry, for tomorrow we die."

Leonard, our national guide, although a communist, seemed to be under deep conviction. He attended our devotions and services for the tour members. He also brought others to our services, or to us individually, to hear the gospel.

Military: The absence of military presence in the cities and highways on this tour was a mystery. On previous trips to China, I had seen soldier movements in trucks or with both light and heavy armor everywhere. On this trip, the only soldiers I saw were one small contingent on Tiananmen Square and one company at Xion. Chinese naval, air force, and marine units were on maneuvers in the straits between Taiwan and the mainland. However, I saw no military aircraft in the sky and no evidence of the army in the cities or in the country. Wherever China is hiding its military forces is puzzling.

Expanding economies to support empirical intentions often means aggressive military machines preparing for war. In all outbreaks of Chinese or Mongolian aggression in the past, the thrust has been to the West and not East (Attila the Hun; Genghis Khan and the Golden Horde invasions of Russia, Ukraine, Persia, Turkey, Eastern Europe, etc.). China is the only nation that can raise a 200-million man army, and historical precedents suggest it will be an army from China that will cross the Euphrates and move toward Jerusalem.

China's Spiritual Intentions: The reproduction of an article from our local daily newspaper reflects the government of China's attitude and concern about Christianity deterring national programs and intentions. Below is a recent *Bible in the News* article I wrote which further explains the government's intentions to challenge God:

"Christians Under Attack"

Persecution of Christians in China is more severe than since the Cultural Revolution. Why?

In answering this question we refer to a news release, January 23, 1996, dateline Hong Kong. On January 14, Ishmael Amat, a member of the Communist Party's Central Committee of the Nationalist Affairs Commission, and chairman of the China-Turkey Friendship Association, outlined in a public address China's new plan over the next fifteen years to conclude, "a final effort once and for all to squash growing interest in spiritual activity in China."

According to Amat, who speaks for the State Security Bureau, missionaries in China will be "criminalized," meaning that any proselytizing, or approaching any Chinese citizen with a religious message outlawed by the state, will result in criminal punishment. Criminal punishment in China means imprisonment or execution. In this public announcement by Amat, he made clear that these new efforts will be made only against Christians, or non-Chinese traditional religions. He stated that "Islam and Buddhism are considered Chinese religions" and will be exempt from inclusion in new criminalism. New appraisals will also be made against foreign teachers who might be Christians. Amat stated that the ban on any published or disseminated religious material will continue, that all places of religious worship or activity must be registered with the government, and that "patriotic preachers" would be dealt with. Buddhists and Moslems will not be interfered with, but Christians will be punished. Yet nothing is raised in protest by pastors in the United States or Congress, or our President. It is interesting to note that *The European*, July 24, 1996, Europe's most widely read newspaper, reported that Norwegians protested China's President Zemin's visit to their country over the arrest of a Tibetan monk Gyasto. Why are there not protests over the persecution of 70 million Christians in China?

Ishmael Amat, by name, implies that he is a Moslem, or at least of Arabic racial origin. He is heading China's effort to become aligned with Turkey (biblical Togarmah), one of the conspirators of Gog in Ezekiel 38. Revelation 9 foretells that a two-hundred-million man army will march from the east to fight at the Battle of Armageddon. China is the only nation capable of raising such an army. Is it possible that our recent arrest in China brought us into the maelstrom of the prophetic scenario for the coming Great Tribulation?

What Can We Do About China?

"The Lord is…not willing that any should perish, but that all should come to repentance. But the day of the Lord will come as a thief in the night…" (2 Peter 3:9,10).

The soul of a Chinese person is just as precious to God as the soul of an American, and there are four times as many souls in China as there are in the United States. America is flooded with churches; Bibles and salvation tracts are available in thousands of bookstores, and Christian programs on radio and television stations can be heard at any hour of the day. Our guide Leonard came to me one day and asked if it were possible for any American to buy a Bible. As we left Canton and boarded the hovercraft to take us to Hong Kong, I gave Leonard my Bible. His last words were, "If you get on a shortwave station with your program that can be heard in China, will you let me know?"

As we have gone through the cities in China and looked out at the millions of people so open to the gospel, it is difficult not to rush out and start preaching and distributing salvation tracts. Yet this is not possible at this time. The most effective salvation message we distributed in China, and one that brought the most rewarding response, was my pamphlet with the Chinese word for "happiness" on the cover. We take three Chinese words, "happiness," "create," and "Garden (Paradise)," and explain in both English and Chinese the gospel.

China Tomorrow

In 1971, the Cultural Revolution had bled China dry; the nation was in a state of fear, shock, and economic collapse. On February 27 of that year, Dr. Henry Kissinger, the titular head of the Council on Foreign Relations, sent his famous "Shanghai Letter" to President Nixon. This communiqué opened the way for President Nixon to visit Mao, resulting in granting China "favored nation status," and opening world markets to Chinese-produced products. Had this not happened, as our guide Leonard stated, China today would be in a worse condition than North Korea. The twenty-fifth anniversary of the Shanghai Letter was celebrated in a CFR presentation on C-Span with Dr. Kissinger presiding, February 27, 1997.

Why the Shanghai Letter? The most obvious reason was political, as the United States and Russia were still in the grips of the Cold War. The secondary reason was, of course, economic. According to the April 30, 1989, edition of the *New York Times*, Kissinger and Associates represent 30 multinational corporations, including American Express, H.J. Heinz, ITT, Lockheed, and ing. Goods with the label "Made in Hong Kong" began to appear in increasing quantities in United States' merchandising outlets, and usually the only thing made in Hong Kong was indeed the label. The products were made in China, leading to verification of the 1984 Hong Kong Accord with England, releasing all three sections of the island kingdom back to Beijing on July 1, 1997. Only one section had been covered in the 100-year lease.

Not only are Chinese-made goods flooding American markets, but American companies are using cheap labor in China to produce shoes, sports equipment, clothes, furniture, household items, etc. (check the labels when you buy and see how many items are noted, "Made in China").

Since 1980, the Chinese economy has been growing from 10 percent to 18 percent a year. Now with the reclaiming of Hong Kong, it will doubtless continue to expand. With the decline in U.S. military power, China emerges into a position of world leadership. China now has a new face which will command the attention of the nations of the East, including Malaysia, Indonesia, Thailand, Singapore, Philippines, Vietnam, Cambodia, Laos, Burma, Korea, and even Japan and Taiwan. These nations include approximately 50 percent of the world's population.

The reported promises of the Beijing government in relation to Hong Kong—one nation, two Chinas—can only apply to economics. Politically, the government of China must control absolutely and there can be religious freedom, according to the Central Committee's declaration of January 14, 1996, only to Buddhists and Muslims.

The Euphrates River is the acknowledged boundary between the East and the West. From the Word of prophecy, we read in Revelation 9:13-16:

> And the sixth angel sounded, and I heard a voice from the four horns of the golden altar which is before God, Saying to the sixth angel which had the trumpet, Loose the four angels which are bound in the great river Euphrates. And the four angels were loosed, which were prepared for an hour, and a day, and a month, and a year, for to slay the third part of men. And the number of the army of the horsemen were two hundred thousand thousand (two hundred million)....

As noted by the late Mao Tse-Tung, only China—of all the nations in the world—can raise an army of 200 million. But China will not be alone in its march to the West:

> And the sixth angel poured out his vial upon the great river Euphrates; and the water thereof was dried up, that the way of the kings of the east might be prepared. And I saw three unclean spirits like frogs come out of the mouth of the dragon, and out of the mouth of the beast, and out of the mouth of the false prophet. For they are the spirits of devils, working miracles, which go forth unto the kings of the earth and of the whole world, to gather them to the battle of that great day of God Almighty (Revelation 16:12-14).

Almost every prophecy in the Bible relating to the Battle of Armageddon indicates that armies of all nations will be involved, and this prophecy certainly includes the nations of the Orient. Deception (2 Thessalonians 2), seducing spirits (1 Timothy 4:1), false miracles (Revelation 13), are the entities with which the Antichrist will gather the nations at the last battle of the Tribulation.

The drying of the Euphrates could be both literal and representative. The headwaters of the Euphrates are at Mt. Ararat. The Syrians have built a huge dam on the Euphrates near Aleppo. Turkey has also built several dams, and according to Dr. Halit, our guide in Turkey, the world's largest dam is being planned between Mt. Ararat and the Syrian border. Therefore, the drying up of the Euphrates would be a relatively simple matter. However, to bring an Oriental army led by China into Israel would take considerable dispersion of historical positions.

The fourth plague on Egypt described in Exodus 8 was an invasion of frogs. Leaving the Nile, frogs covered the land, crept into beds, fell into the food, and no one could walk without stepping on frogs. Stench from their decaying bodies filled the nation. This describes the demonic spirits that will cover the world during the Great Tribulation. The Jamison, Fausset & Brown commentary says of Revelation 16:13:

> "Three frogs were the original arms of France, the center of infidelity, socialism, and false spiritualism." China's Central Committee has chosen Buddhism and Islam over

Jesus Christ, and let us consider the spiritual deception that has gripped other nations of the Orient:

Burma—89 percent Buddhist
Bangladesh—83 percent Muslim; 16 percent Hindu
Cambodia—9 percent Buddhist
India—80 percent Hindu; 14 percent Muslim
Indonesia—87 percent Muslim
Laos—85 percent Buddhist; 15 percent animist
Pakistan—97 percent Muslim
Singapore—29 percent Buddhist; 16 percent Muslim; 13 percent Taoist
Japan—Buddhist and Shinto
Sri Lanka—69 percent Buddhist; 15 percent Hindu; 8 percent Muslim
Thailand—95 percent Buddhist; 4 percent Muslim.

The only two nations in the Orient where Christians are in the majority are South Korea and the Philippines; however, in the Philippines, 80 percent of the church membership is Catholic.

The Orient is like a volcano that remains dormant until it erupts with disastrous consequences. The Huns, a nomadic race that inhabited the region east of the Caspian Sea and western China, suddenly roared into Europe and devastated southeastern Europe. The Huns, under the leadership of Attila (406–530 A.D.), called the "Scourge of God," ravaged and almost conquered both the Roman Empire and the Byzantine Empire. Genghis Kahn united the Mongolian tribes of northeast China and through a succession of military campaigns conquered all the nations between the China Sea and the Mediterranean Sea, including much of Russia and India. The Tartars, called the Golden Horde, under the leadership of Batu Khan, conquered Russia and eastern Europe. The Mongolian Tartars ruled Russia from the beginning of the thirteenth century to the beginning of the sixteenth century.

Most Oriental empirical savagery has been unleashed toward the west with Russia, Asia Minor, and Europe bearing the brunt of the onslaughts. The reason for the western direction of Mongolian military campaigns is the lack of a naval force to move east and south through the island kingdoms of the Pacific Ocean. However, in the first half of the twentieth century, the Japanese, another Mongolian nation, did build a navy that almost destroyed the United States naval forces at Pearl Harbor, Hawaii. The Japanese armies and naval forces conquered much of China, Philippines, and the South Pacific islands between Australia and China before being turned back by the Americans and finally defeated. Had Germany's campaign against Russia been successful, then the United States might today be governed by a Golden Horde from Japan.

Modern China encompasses much of the ancient Mongolian lands and peoples. Although the Chinese in the past three millennia have been mainly concerned with the protection and consolidation of their own peoples and lands, China has in recent decades indicated a propensity to move aggressively where its own self-interest is involved. The Korean War, Tibet, the Vietnam War, and the Cambodian Civil War are examples.

As we look at China today, we see the forming of a huge empirical vortex being fed with political motivation, national identification pride, spiraling economic fires, and a swelling mass which continues to increase in spite of restrictive family-size laws. China's military capabilities include nuclear weapons which would deter, at least initially, an atomic response. Limited naval forces dictate that when China moves militarily, along with Pacific Rim allies, it seems reasonable that its 200-million-man army will follow the invasion routes traveled by Attila the Hun and Genghis Kahn.

The satanic conspiracy that will certainly bring all nations into Israel to fight against the Lord Jesus Christ at His coming will victimize the millions of Christians in China. However, we are promised in 1 Thessalonians 4:13-18, that when that day comes there will be a great escape for those who know Jesus Christ as Savior and Lord.

"Wherefore comfort one another with these words" (1 Thessalonians 4:18).

▼　▼　▼

CHAPTER 9

The Russia, Muslim, Magog Whirlwind

Chuck Missler

One of the most provocative aspects of our strategic horizon is the disturbing misinformation—and the ostensible threat—of the largest (and most disenchanted) military establishment on the Planet Earth and its current designs on the volatile Middle East.

Premature Burial?

Among the many myths promoted in the media—and in the bizarre foreign policies of our current administration—is the notion that the "Evil Empire is dead." "The cold war is now over" and everything seems to be "under control." But is it really?

America now faces an adversary who has a crumbling economy—about 10 percent of that of the United States—which is attempting to support a military several times the size of the U.S., whose society has been seized by crime bosses, and whose military establishment has been disillusioned and unpaid. This is hardly the stuff from which stability comes.

Russia's Strategic Dilemma

With its economy in shambles (about $720 billion GDP),[1] Russia is desperately dependent upon its export of raw materials and armaments. Its residual strength results from its reservoir of the world's largest reserves of a wide variety of industrial raw materials. (Russia's oil and natural gas output accounted for about 20 percent of the world total, and energy exports accounted for nearly one-third of domestic production.) The Kremlin is critically in need of cash and their need for an extended power base is desperate. What are their alternatives?

Westward Prospects

Prospects westward are clouded by the German-dominated European Union. Now exacerbating these pressures are the recent addition of three Warsaw Pact countries, Poland, Hungary, and the Czech Republic, into NATO. (While France failed in its attempt to have Romania and Slovenia also included, this is viewed by some as possible in the future.) None of this, needless to say, is welcomed by the Kremlin. The western horizon clearly consists of competitors for containment rather than viable partners for development.

The Kings of the East

The Russian prospects eastward are clouded by the emergence of an inevitable enemy across an indefensible land border: China.

China's economy is predicted to eclipse the economy of the U.S. before President Clinton's term of office expires. China already accounts for 25 percent of world output and 50 percent of foreign exchange. The nation has raised more investment capital in the past five years than Japan has raised since World War II. (The U.S. supplies them $36.5 *billion* per year—over $100 million *per day*— to feed its spectacular growth.)

Across an indefensible land border is the growing challenge of China's immense population growth. China's population is growing at between 16 million and 20 million per year at a time when agricultural land to sustain the country's 900 million rural and 300 million urban population is diminishing. The excess rural labor pool is already somewhere between 120 to 150 million. Some estimate that within ten years there will be nearly 70 million urban unemployed in China.

While a growing strategic alliance between Russia and China is the official policy, this marriage of convenience appears to be serving China more than Russia. And it is increasingly coming under criticism by the Kremlin's critics. General Lev Rokhlin, chairman of Russia's Parliamentary Defense Committee, launched a serious attack on Yeltsin's defense policy which included a focus on China. He warned that China's ascendancy in the Asia-Pacific region posed a long-term threat to Russia's sparsely populated, resource rich, eastern territories. "Russia could lose its Far East region and Siberia right up to the Urals," he warned.

The rise of China has resulted in an arms race in the Pacific second only to that of the Middle East.

The Southern Opportunity

Clearly, the only option available to strengthen Russia's power base is to the south: the radical Islamic countries of the Middle East. With approximately 30 percent of its own population Muslim, intrigues to the south appear to be a manifest destiny.

And what better way to enlist Islamic support than to resolve the Muslim's primary "bone in the throat"—the nation Israel? With the ultimate collapse of the so-called "Peace Process," an incursion into the incendiary Middle East would appear irresistible.

The Ezekiel Passage

The present intelligence horizon would seem to fit the famous prophetic passage in Ezekiel 38 and 39. In fact, it is the author's opinion that the more one knows about the textual details of the Ezekiel passage, and the more access one has to the current intelligence assessments in the Middle East, the more it appears that this prophecy may be about to take place!

Ezekiel 38 and 39 describe an attempted invasion of Israel by the people of "the Land of Magog" and their allies. This passage is well-known among Bible students for two reasons: (1) it is the occasion in which God dramatically intervenes on behalf of the nation Israel and decimates the invading forces; and (2) the passage appears to describe the involvement of nuclear weapons.

God's intervention includes a seismic event felt the world over.[2] The left-over weapons will provide all the energy needs of Israel for seven years,[3] and they hire professionals to clear the battlefield, burying any remains east of the Dead Sea—*downwind.*[4] It is interesting to note that the field procedures in Ezekiel include the instruction *not to touch* any bones found that the professionals might have missed; rather, the finder of such a bone should set up a sign by it and let the professional come and deal with it.[5] That protocol is rather consistent with contemporary Atomic/Biological/Chemical ("ABC") warfare procedures!

The Magog Identity

To understand the prophecies of Ezekiel 38 and 39, one must identify the people described in the text as from the "Land of Magog." Fortunately, the identity of these ancient tribes is now relatively well understood and numerous sources as well as recent archaeological discoveries have clearly confirmed this identification.

Magog was one of the sons of Japheth[6]. There have been controversies with respect to Gog and Magog,[7] but the traditional experts and most reputable sources have identified the descendants of Magog as the ancient peoples known as the Scythians.[8]

One of the earliest references to Magog was by Hesiod, "the father of Greek didactic poetry," who identified Magog with the Scythians and southern Russia in the seventh century B.C.[9] Hesiod was, in effect, almost a contemporary of Ezekiel. Another of the major sources on the ancient history of the Middle East is, of course, Josephus Flavius, who clearly identified Magog:

> Magog founded the Magogians, thus named after him, but who were by the Greeks are *called Scythians.*[10]

Another first-century writer was Philo,[11] who also identified Magog with southern Russia.

But most of our information comes to us from Herodotus of Halicarnassus, who wrote extensively in the fifth century B.C. and is known as the "Father of History." He wrote the earliest important historical narrative, in which he described the background and the course of the great war between the Greeks and the Persians in the fifth century B.C. After the Peace of Callias (449 B.C.), Herodotus was free to travel throughout the Middle East, visiting Egypt and Mesopotamia. Many scholars have, from time to time, been critical of Herodotus' accounts,[12] but numerous archeological discoveries have clearly confirmed Herodotus' reports in general, and his Scythian accounts in particular.[13]

Herodotus recounts many bizarre and savage practices of the descendants of Magog known as the Scythians: they drank the blood of the first enemy killed; they carried the heads of their victims to their chiefs; they scalped their enemies and used these scalps as "napkins"; they used the skins of their victims to cover their quivers; they drank from the skulls of their victims; they practiced blood brotherhood by drinking each other's blood mixed with wine. The Scythians "bathed" in the vapor from heated hemp seeds. When their king died, they sacrificed one of his concubines and several servants. After a year, they commemorated his death by sacrificing fifty servants and fifty horses.[14] Rough bunch, these Scyths.

The descendants of Magog terrorized the southern steppes of Russia from the Ukraine to the Great Wall of China from the tenth century B.C. to the third century B.C. The ancient writers refer to the Great Wall of China as *Sud Yagog et Magog:* "the rampart of Gog and Magog."[15]

The 15 republics which comprised the former Soviet Union embraced 110 different ethnic groups, but the Russian Federation is the largest—covering 11 time zones—and consists principally of descendants of the ancient Scythians. The total number of Russians living in the non-Russian republics of the former Soviet Union is estimated to be 25 million. In the Ukraine, 12 million out of the 52 million population is Russian; in Central Asia, where 40 percent of the expatriate Russians live, 10 million of the 55 million population are Russians. In Kazakhstan, Russians make up 43 percent of the republic's 18 million population.[16]

The tortuous path from the horseback archery of the early Scyths to the nuclear missiles of the modern Russia includes many centuries of turbulent history. The depth and intensity of this background has endowed these vibrant people with the beauty of Pushkin, Dostoyevsky, and Tchaikovsky, but has also resulted in the cruelty of Ivan "the Terrible," the intensity of Lenin, the brutality of Stalin, and the deceits and intrigues of Gorbachev.

Military Preparedness

Despite its current economic decline, Russia still possesses 1,270,000 active armed forces, 800 inter-continental ballistic missiles, 540 missiles in 34 operational ballistic missile nuclear submarines, 66 strategic bombers, 16,800 main battle tanks, 87 tactical submarines, 166 principal surface combatant ships, and 1,775 combat aircraft.[17]

While we continue to reduce (as well as dilute and distract) our military establishment, Russia continues to prepare itself for the advent of a nuclear war. As we decommission our strategic assets, 90 of Russia's 176 silos are being retrofitted with next-generation missiles. It is building a new underground command post inside Kovinski Mountain east of the Urals, and Russia's new Yamantau Complex is almost the size of the Washington Beltway—except it's underground.

About every 14 to 16 months Russia actually *practices* a preemptive strike against the U.S. heartland. The last one, (as of this writing) in October of 1996, exercised its entire triad (land, sea, and air arms). A surface-to-surface SS-25 was launched against its practice target, a Typhoon ballistic missile submarine launched an SS-18 from the Arctic which hit its target in Kamchatka (just east of Alaska), and two cruise missiles (with a range of 2,500 miles after their air launch) were successfully deployed from bombers participating in this "training" exercise. There's nothing like staying in practice.

Russia's military is nevertheless in shambles. Russian officers are reportedly living on the edge of survival and penury. Between 1990 and 1993, 95,000 officers under the age of 30 resigned their commissions. We hear that no servicemen's allowances have been paid at all in 1997. Their demoralization is a major political reality. This, of course, is *not* stabilizing!

The Allies of Magog

So the deadly embrace with Islam continues. Russia's principal ally southward is Iran. (This is precisely the profile predicted by Ezekiel.)[18] Yeltsin has signed a military assistance pact with Iran which could turn out to be the "hooks in the jaw"[19] of the Ezekiel passage.

Iran's strategic goal is the destruction of Israel. This is seen by Tehran as the means by which Iran can establish itself as the undisputed leader of the Islamic world. Iran's continued progress to upgrading its arms technology—chemical and biological as well as nuclear—has prompted disturbing rhetoric from both the U.S. and Israel, and Tehran is fearful of another preemptive strike. (The 1981 preemptive strike by Israel against Iraq's Osiraq nuclear facility drew criticism from the U.N., but it is disturbing to imagine what the results of the Persian Gulf War might have included had Israel *not* done so.)[20]

Syria

The massing of the Syrian forces next to the Golan Heights is in the papers daily. In Syria, the military represents some 15 percent of the working population and accounts for over 50 percent of public expenditure. The Syrian military has grown from 132,000 in 1973 to more than 400,000 today. Of some temporary effect is the current treaty between Israel and Turkey, which provides Israel limited use of Turkey's air bases—and thus access to the northern border of Syria. But this treaty may prove to be short-lived.

Turkey

The "Meshech and Tubal" of the Ezekiel passage is an allusion to what we know as Turkey, which is clearly moving away from its Ataturkist, secularist principles, toward a more Islamic orientation. In the years immediately after World War I, Kemal Ataturk transformed Turkey from a theocratic autocracy into a Western-oriented democracy by the strength of his own will. In 1922 he abolished the Sultanate, in 1924 he abolished the Caliphate and the religious courts, and in 1925 he made it illegal to wear the fez, a symbol he regarded as backwardness. Having stripped away the trappings of Islam, Ataturk then embraced Western ways. In 1925 Turkey took the Western calendar, in 1926 it adopted the Swiss civil code, in 1928 the country switched to the Latin alphabet, in 1931, the metric system, in 1934 all Turks were obliged to take a surname, and in 1934 women were given the vote.

Following World War II, Turkey joined all the main Western institutions: the UN in 1945, the International Monetary Fund in 1947, the OECD in 1948, the Council of Europe in 1949, and NATO in 1951. In September of 1959, Ankara applied for associate membership of the

European Economic Community (the forerunner of the European Union), which was granted in September 1963.

All this was to change, however. It has become painfully clear that Turkey's 70-year experiment has been wasted: its recent rejection for full membership in the European Union is seen as a deep affront to a people who have sacrificed their own past in favor of attempting to become Western. It has been left no option but to turn again to the East, and Islam, for its future.

Coincident with their rejection by the E.U., the opening up of Turkic Central Asia by the demise of the Soviet Union has provided an attractive and viable horizon of Eurasia, from the Adriatic to the Great Wall of China. And this, too, has given Turkey and Iran a manifest destiny.

Some Missing Players

Provocative indeed are the *omissions* in the list of Magog's allies in the Ezekiel passage: Egypt and Arabia. Egypt is conspicuous by its absence of mention, Saudi Arabia ("Sheba and Dedan") is nervously on the sidelines, gainsaying the ostensible invasion by Magog and its allies.[21]

The leadership of the House of Saud is currently on a slippery rock, highly fearful of its adversary to the north, Iran. Saudi Arabia's income from crude oil, refined products, and liquefied petroleum gas was around $35 billion in 1995, down from a peak of $116 billion in 1981. The costs of two Gulf wars (supporting Iraq against Iran and then everyone against Iraq) has emptied the Saudi treasury. The war against Saddam Hussein cost Saudi Arabia $50 billion.

(In May 1991, the kingdom had to take out its first-ever foreign loan: $4.5 billion. At the same time the Saudi treasury borrowed $2.5 billion from local banks. By August 1994 informed sources indicated that the Saudis were close to asking for a deferment of the next repayment. Humiliation was avoided only by a timely rally in the price of oil. The repayment terms of the country's $9.2 billion debt to the U.S. has already been renegotiated.)

In Summary

The Middle East is a cauldron ready to boil over. Egypt wants the southern Negev; the Palestinians want all of Israel and Jordan;

Syria wants all of Lebanon, Jordan, Israel, and the West Bank; Turkey wants part of Iraq; Iran wants part of Iraq and hegemony in the Persian Gulf; Iraq wants Kuwait and whatever parts of Saudi Arabia it can get; Yemen also wants part of Saudi Arabia; and everyone is desperate for water. This is not a stable neighborhood.

The decisive fulcrum in the Middle East is Israel. It is Israel that prevents Egypt and Syria from bearing down on Saudi Arabia. For many years it was Israel that prevented Syria from taking control of Lebanon. It was Israel that prevented Syria from occupying Jordan in 1970, and it is Israel that prevents the Palestinians from gaining a base from which to destabilize Jordan.

Israel is currently contemplating a territorial retreat in order to secure peace treaties with neighboring states which are ruled by brutal dictators which have a history of military interventionism. The ruling regimes are without exception reliant on military backing for their continued hold on power, and this ensures a continuing necessity for high military expenditure. The general instability of this situation is heightened by the rising influence of radical Islam and the declining Arab economies.

The Men Who Would Be Gog

A Russian presidential election is scheduled for the year 2000 and the rival candidates are visibly positioning over what they view as the political carcass of Boris Yeltsin (who has announced that he will not even seek a third term). Each of the "Men who would be Gog"[22] are clearly postured as militaristic, nationalistic, and intent upon a strategy of external adventurism. Washington is clearly less comfortable with any of these alternative leaders, but it is not likely to be any more successful at controlling Russia's internal politics than they were in meddling in Israel's.

The political instability in Russia continues as Yeltsin's rivals become increasingly outspoken. General Lev Rokhlin appears to be joining General Aleksander Lebed, the former security chief, Communist Party chief Gennady Zyuganov, and the maverick "Mad Vlad," Vladimir Zhirinovsky, in the stampede to position themselves for the next presidential election in the year 2000. All of them are extremists, and not nearly as comfortable for Washington as Yeltsin seems to have been.

Israel's Allies?

The long-term implications of the retrenchment of the United States is also problematic. The reduction of military forces are scheduled by 1999 to reduce the army from 14 active duty divisions to 10, warships from 443 to 300, and active air force fighter wings from 16 to 13. (Actual funding plans will not even support the scheduled levels.)[23] America's share of gross world product has declined from over 40 percent in 1945 to only 22 percent lately. It isn't possible for a country with just 4.7 percent of the world's population on 6.3 percent of the world's land mass to support 38 percent of the world's military budget. America's inevitable retrenchment is the strategic reality of the coming decade.

The potential role of the European Union with respect to the Middle East is also problematical. It is highly likely that the pro-Islamic orientation of the dominant member states would prove adverse to Israel. The reasons for this pro-Arab orientation are historical (colonial links) and geographical (the proximity of North Africa to Europe), as well as the result of immigration policies which have produced a European Muslim population of 15 million, the largest religious minority in France, Germany, Britain, and the Benelux countries. In Britain, more attend services in mosques than go to church.

Furthermore, the fear of coordinated terrorist attacks within the heartland of both America and Europe compound the complexities of any intervention in the Middle East. FBI and CIA officials say that hundreds of Islamic radicals and members of Mideast terrorist groups, including the Hamas, Hezbollah, Islamic Jihad, the Algerian Islamic Salvation Front, and the Jordanian Muslim Brotherhood are using the United States as a base from which to co-ordinate attacks in their home countries.

A further disturbing hint appears in Ezekiel chapter 39, verse 6:

> And I will send a fire on Magog, and among them that dwell carelessly in the isles: and they shall know that I am the LORD (Ezekiel 39:6).

God apparently sends "fire" down, not only upon Magog and his allies, but on some distant people living in the "isles" or "coastlands." Who are they "who dwell carelessly [securely] in the isles"? The word for isles could be an idiom for remote continents. Could this be an allusion to the United States? Is the "fire on Magog"—*and these others*—a result of a nuclear exchange?

For a deterrent to be effective it has to be credible. Not just the technology, but the executive decision process. Could this all be a result of a gigantic miscalculation? Or shall we just wait and see?

It is particularly disturbing to observe President Clinton's refusal to implement an anti-missile defense system despite Congress' repeated insistence to do so. One can't help but wonder why?

Is Ezekiel 38 on the Horizon?

The continuing positioning toward the inevitable invasion of Israel—as detailed by Ezekiel in chapters 38 and 39—now appears to be on the near horizon. This author is of the opinion that we are being plunged into a period of time about which the Bible says more than it does about any period in history—including the time when Jesus walked the shores of Galilee and climbed the mountains of Judea. As we examine similar passages detailing the end-time events in Israel, Jerusalem, Babylon, Europe, and other topics, it seems they are *all* being positioned for the final climax.

What does this mean for *you*?

It is, indeed, an exciting time to do our homework! Have you done yours?

▼   ▼   ▼

CHAPTER 10

America's Perilous Times Have Come

Tim LaHaye

America was once the freest, safest, most honorable, moral, and happiest nation of people on earth. That was when it was the most God-fearing country in the world, because that is how it was founded. That was also when the conscience of the nation was set by its churches. Not one, but hundreds of churches and denominations, most of whom took the Bible seriously and believed the Ten Commandments were the best civic code ever devised.

Gradually, that began to change because secularizers took over the entertainment industry (which today has more influence on the nation's conscience than do our churches), "progressive" (or socialistic) educators took over our schools from K through Ph.D., liberals took over our media and through their biased reporting have for the most part taken control of our government through the electoral process. Add to that the takeover of our judicial system and legal profession by ACLU-type thinkers and members who have demanded unlimited freedom without accountability to or recognition of God, and you have a culture that is out of control. For the past 60 years, God and His commandments have been opposed and expelled from the public square, bringing on the anarchy, crime, welfare abuses, and "perilous times" predicted by the apostle Paul for the "last days."

This takeover of these powerful agencies of influence by a relatively small number of people who have either rejected God or expelled His control over our lives has made this country the pornography, crime, violence, rape, and drug capital of the world. Once we exported freedom, responsibility, and morality from our shores to the other countries of the world. Hollywood and the moral midgets who control it now use the most powerful vehicle to the human mind ever invented (film, because it combines both the eye and ear-gates to the mind), to export depravity, corruption, and degradation until some countries will no longer let our "entertainment" be shown legally. The founders of this great land would be appalled at the moral cesspool our country has become because a handful of unelected, godless antagonists of moral values have virtual control over the communications industry. The result? "Perilous times"! Read 2 Timothy 3:1-7. List the 18 conditions the prophet foretells for the last days and then examine your daily newspaper and you will agree: They are already here!

In our nation's capital we now have more violent deaths each year than days of the year—more than 399 in 1996. From coast to coast our nation is witnessing an explosion of cruel and utterly conscienceless acts.

David Johnstone, a young father visiting San Francisco on business, was walking down a street when he drew the attention of three teenagers. The boys shot David in the back. The bullet severed his spinal cord, nicked his lung and kidney, perforated his colon twice and finally lodged in his liver. He died within a month of the shooting. This angry, uncivilized action by three hostile teens left a wife widowed, and left fatherless a 14-year-old daughter and an 11-year-old son.[1]

How did the San Francisco community respond to this heartless murder? It was determined that the teenage killer was himself a victim—after all, he had never met his father and had been abandoned as a baby by his drug-addicted mother. Certainly none of us would envy such a childhood, but the man was guilty of murder. But according to the San Francisco jury, the criminal was simply living according to his conditioning; he was a mere victim of circumstance.

How twisted can thinking become? Our legal system would have us consider the murderer a victim. We acquit the criminal and punish the innocent victims who often cannot speak for themselves. Taught that he is helpless and powerless to resist his impulses, a convict has no hope for change. Such thinking is based on a refusal to accept the doctrine of sin, which leads behaviorists no alternative but to conclude that mankind is naturally good but can be corrupted by his environment and experience. Taken to its natural conclusion, behaviorism teaches that no one is ever responsible for his or her action. People who do wrong are not to be blamed—they are just responding to what life has handed them. Is it any wonder crime is escalating?

Whenever a nation turns its back on God or begins to live as if He does not exist, it begins to show up in its citizens' disregard for human life. At one time almost every American believed in God, and that belief was reflected in the way people treated each other. Today's humanist elite, who exercise more and more control over the media, education, and to a great extent, our government, are largely driven by humanistic values and an agenda that is neither God's nor that of the people they are supposed to serve.

Devaluing Life in America

Unless one acknowledges that life comes from the hand of God, life really doesn't have much meaning. Nowhere in our country is that philosophy more apparent than in the legal accessibility of abortion. Every day, babies are aborted as a result of the government's policy of granting a woman the right to terminate the life of her unborn child. Each year 1.4 million such "choices" are made, totaling between 30 and 40 million such deaths since abortion was declared legal by the highest court of the land in 1973.

Is it any wonder that a nation that has legalized the slaughter of innocents in the name of "choice" and convenience is witnessing wholesale teenage slaughter? Godless humanism cheapens all life. Our current crime wave is merely the public manifestation of an empty belief system.

Destroying the National Conscience

The next generation may be worse than the present one. A Washington Metropolitan Police captain, deploring the increase in preadolescent slayings in recent months, said: "Earlier in the year, we had a twelve-year-old who killed his mother and stepfather because he was told they were going to have to move and that he'd have to go to another school."[2] When children would sooner kill their parents than change their residence, you know a society's in trouble!

Chuck Colson, founder of Prison Fellowship, describes the problem well:

> Twenty years ago, in the midst of Watergate, there was a battle for the government of the United States. Today there is a battle for the soul of America. And that battle makes Watergate look like child's play. Look at the headlines from recent days:
>
> *Dartmouth, Massachusetts: Three schoolboys stabbed a ninth-grade classmate to death, then traded high-fives and laughed.*
>
> *Washington, D.C.: An unsupervised eight-year-old boy in a homeless shelter swung a twelve-week-old baby around a room, bashing his head repeatedly against the floor, "like Robocop." The baby was killed. The boy explained, "I was just playing."*
>
> This is the face of crime today—crime without reason or remorse. We are witnessing the most terrifying thing that could happen to a society: the death of conscience in a generation of young people.
>
> The bone-chilling words of Adolf Hitler appear at the entrance of Auschwitz. Hitler wrote: "I want to raise a generation devoid of conscience." It is an irony that the world rose up and defeated Hitler out of moral conviction, and now we in America, through our indolence and apathy, are achieving exactly what Hitler failed to do."[3]

Moral barbarians are educating our youth. In a 1988 television special on education titled *America's Kids, Why they Flunk*, Barbara Walters courageously confronted parents with news they did not want to hear. Noting that our nation's children are not getting an education, she bemoaned the plummeting test scores by students, many of whom couldn't locate the United States on a world map. A significant number of the high school students she surveyed thought the Holocaust was a Jewish holiday. Then she said something profound: "The real crisis is one of character. Today's high school seniors live in a world of misplaced values. They have no sense of discipline. No goals. They care only for themselves. In short, they are becoming a generation of undisciplined cultural barbarians."[4]

Barbara Walters is right in her conclusion that we're raising "a generation of undisciplined, cultural barbarians," and we shouldn't be surprised. An old truism states: A stream never rises above its source. It is unrealistic to teach an atheistic, relativistic, evolutionary philosophy of life claiming that "man is the measure of all things" and then expect our children to graduate from high school being anything but undisciplined, greedy, self-centered individuals who have a hard time maintaining long-term relationships and who have no sense of right or wrong. No wonder they will not maintain their wedding vows or take responsibility for their children or most other actions. Raised as they are today, they have no moral compass and are often hostile to those who do.

Rousseau: A Classic Example

Jean Jacques Rousseau, the atheistic Swiss philosopher, is still quoted often on college campuses today. Many current theories of education are based on the concepts of this eighteenth-century skeptic whose philosophy did much to degrade France. One of his basic beliefs was the "perfectibility of man." He was not the first, of course, to hold such an unfounded and flawed theory. Pythagoras, four centuries before Christ, had the same idea when he said, "Man is the measure of all things." Instead of a God-centered worldview, humanists of every age have embraced a man-centered approach to life.

History opposes the humanist, for it invariably teaches that apart from God's grace, man is a moral barbarian. Rousseau was no exception. He never married the mistress with whom he lived in Paris, even though she bore him five illegitimate sons—all of whom he abandoned in a Paris foundling home. That educated barbarian may be a respected leader of today's educational elite who have adopted his Enlightenment theories into modern secular humanist education, but he obviously lacked a moral conscience.

It takes a healthy conscience to be a man or woman of character, self-discipline, commitment and godliness—qualities that the

Bible upholds. But where God is despised, so are His values. And when this happens, society is at great risk.

Morality cannot endure where right and wrong do not exist. True right and wrong cannot exist where God is not acknowledged. How long can a nation survive without morality?

Godly Morality Key to America's Future Well-Being

Pat Buchanan, syndicated columnist, commented on the superiority of America's religious-based culture when he said,

> The root of any culture is the "cult" or religion. The religion of the West, and of most Americans, is Christianity. And Christians believe the Founder of their faith is the Son of God, whose teachings, true for all time, are contained in the "greatest book ever written."[5]

As George Washington accurately observed in his "Farewell Address," national morality cannot prevail apart from religious principle:

> And let us with caution indulge the supposition that morality can be maintained without religion. Whatever may be conceded to the influence of refined education on minds…reason and experience forbid us to expect that national morality can prevail in exclusion of religious principle.[6]

Can we make a better, more harmonious world without God's assistance? Has this generation evolved morally to the point where it no longer needs divine assistance?

Just read your morning newspaper, and you'll find the answer there. Mankind needs God. We need his moral standard. Just as you and I cannot survive long without oxygen, so morality is doomed without God.

Our major institutions today are inhabited by a generation of humanistic barbarians who claim to be working for freedom and justice for all, but instead, their efforts are degrading our society. Do our leaders in government, the media, education, and the entertainment industry realize what destruction they are wreaking? Maybe, maybe not. They are the mind-benders of this society. But regardless, the harsh reality remains: We are producing Hitler's dream—a generation devoid of conscience.

Mankind's Deadliest Century

> Contrary to its promise, the twentieth century has become mankind's most bloody and hateful century, a century of hallucinatory politics and of monstrous killings.[7] —Zbigniew Brzezinski

The late great American novelist, Walker Percy, considered this century the most savage, inhuman, and murderous mankind has ever known, labeling it "the century of death." Zbigniew Brzezinski, national security advisor to President Jimmy Carter, went so far as to call it the "Century of Megadeath", writing:

> This century's wars have extinguished no less than approximately 87 million lives, with the numbers of wounded, maimed, and otherwise afflicted being beyond estimates. These staggering numbers are matched and morally even overshadowed by a still more horrifying total, one that justifiably stamps the twentieth century as the century of megadeath: the number of defenseless individuals deliberately put to death because of doctrinal hatred and passions.[8]

Night after night we hear about the slaughter of more victims in Bosnia, Rwanda, and other parts of the world. Senseless slaughter has become so routine that we scarcely feel the pain unless it strikes someone we know. Still, we are shocked by the cruel carnage when people are murdered as they walk to the market on a Saturday morning or ride a city subway. We are horrified to think that violent death may lurk just down the street.

As shocked and horrified as Americans are at such news, we seem to forget that another kind of destructive and gratuitous slaughter is occurring, *legally*, in our own cities and towns. This second slaughter involves what Dr. Bernard Nathanson has called "the silent scream," so named after witnessing the gaping mouth of a writhing fetus during an abortion. Have we forgotten our unborn?

Why have we allowed our national conscience to be quieted as innocent children have been destroyed by their mothers and doctors before their eyes have seen the light of day? In defiance of logic and instinct, we abort our babies, and yet we are shocked to find murderers in our midst. How can we teach relativism and expect our children to be morally upright?

The proabortion Allen Guttmacher Institute, the research arm of Planned Parenthood, reports that anywhere from 36 to 53 million abortions were performed worldwide in 1987 alone.[9] We condemn Hitler, Stalin, and Mao for the atrocities their regimes committed toward their fellowman, but are our "civilized" leaders any better than them? In terms of numbers, we cruelly extinguish more lives annually than any of them did in their entire regime! When it comes to abortion, this modern Holocaust may be hidden and the scream may be silent, but there is One who sees and hears. To Him will we all one day give an account.

Murdering America's Future

Speaking on behalf of the unborn child in the United States House of Representatives in June 1993, Congressman Henry Hyde made a persuasive case against abortion: "An abortion forecloses the future for generations and generations."[10]

In addition to killing the aborted children themselves, we're annihilating any descendants they might have had. Hyde said further:

> Think for a moment, I say to my colleagues. If you can, exercise your moral imagination, and think about the other party of the abortion decision, the unborn being, the child who might write the book, the child who might compose the symphony, the child who might discover the cure, the child who might lead his country in a time of peril. That child has no one to hear, "I want to be born." Answer that cry of the heart with your vote today.

The Collapse of Rome

In his book, *How Should We Then Live,* the late Francis Schaeffer related historian Edward Gibbon's observations on the state of the Roman Empire prior to its demise. The characteristics he listed are strikingly similar to those of contemporary American life:

> Five attributes marked Rome at its end: first, a mounting love of show and luxury (that is, affluence); second, a widening gap between the very rich and the very poor (this could be among countries in the family of nations as well as in a single nation); third, an obsession with

sex; fourth, freakishness in the arts, masquerading as originality, and enthusiasms pretending to be creativity; fifth, an increased desire to live off the state.[11]

More than ever before in our nation's history, we are seeing an ever-enlarging government that has stepped in to provide for our education, welfare, retirement, mail, and now, even our health care. In days past, the church and strong social structures of communities did much to meet the needs of those in their vicinity. Today, however, having replaced a love of God with love of pleasure, we are substituting commitment to our fellowman with taxes to our government—relegating to government the duty of caring for our fellowman.

Is government really the solution to our personal and national woes? Does more government help a problem or exacerbate it? President Abraham Lincoln had this to say on the subject: "You cannot help men permanently by doing for them what they could and should do for themselves." Excessive government fosters dependence—not independence.

Certainly we see the day that the lofty goals of Roosevelt's "New Deal," Johnson's "Great Society," and other similar government initiatives, led directly to the undermining of the people and institutions that they were intended to bolster. Welfare, while perhaps initially helping some, ultimately destroyed initiative, drive, and industry among the indigent. And our government, despite its litany of failures, increasingly insists upon playing "almighty Provider," while simultaneously discouraging social involvement on the part of religious organizations.

There is a growing and legitimate concern today that the government of the United States is stepping over the constitutional bounds that were established to limit its role in society. In addition to the fact that government intrusion is taking more and more taxes, we ought to be concerned about our individual rights. We're learning through experience that individual rights decrease in direct proportion to increases in government interference.

Putting themselves in the place of God, government authorities are more and more often determining which beliefs and practices are permissible and which are not. Society is being conditioned to look to government, not God, for guidance. There is an attitude that "Big Brother" will take care of us. As columnist Joseph Sobran puts it, there is a trend for people to see their "rights," not as coming from the Creator, but rather as being founded upon state sufferance and, therefore, dependent upon the whims of the state.[12]

Who benefits when government grows beyond its legitimate bounds? Thomas Sowell, economist and senior fellow at the Hoover Institution, says, "The only clear beneficiaries of activist government policies are the people in government, whose egos are allowed full play, to use the rest of the people as guinea pigs for their bright ideas and social experiments."[13]

William Buckley Jr. is equally forthright in his opposition to activist government: "Enthusiasts for government will list the benefits of government: free schooling, healthcare, the lot," he writes. "Well, the slave masters also provided food, lodging and medical care."[14]

Government Over God

Like a virus multiplying in its host, expansive government is controlling domains over which it has no legitimate authority. One such domain is that of religious faith and expression. America's foundation is being systematically undermined and demolished. What is intended to replace it? A faulty and fallacious "new politics of meaning" embraced by a very select and secretive political elite interested in furthering their vision of social utopia.

Our nation's problem is not that we have lost our political moorings—that is a mere symptom of a systematic malaise. Rather, we have lost our national conscience founded upon a reverence for God. The fruits of our departure are the love of entertainment and indulgence, an obsession with sex, bizarre art, and an ever-burgeoning state.

The current generation knows little about significance, but much about "safe sex." What will our coming generation be like, given the dramatic decline we've experienced in a few short years? One young observer makes this pitiful forecast:

> Anyone with an interest in the future of American society need only turn on MTV, watch "Beavis and Butt-head" and understand what the next century will be like.
>
> The founding principle will be nihilism. Rampant disregard for other living things (e.g., hitting frogs with a baseball bat)

will be in. Taking responsibility for one's actions will be out.[15]

I am afraid that short of God's great mercy and our imminent repentance, America will surely go the way of the nations, leaving behind shattered lives and decrepit monuments of our failed dreams.

What can we do? Is man basically good? Is he morally neutral, or is he what the Bible declares him to be—created in God's image but fallen and in need of redemption? If ever there was a time in history in which man's nature was clearly manifested, that time is the twentieth century. Those living in this century have witnessed war upon war, brutal leader after brutal leader, crime upon crime, and even disease upon disease.

Determined to improve matters without the touch of the Master's hand, we are like the beggar who lost his wallet in Times Square but went to another part of the city to find it because the lighting was better there. We foolishly refuse to recognize the truth that unless we return with all of our heart to the Lord Jesus Christ, we will never recover the moral ground we have lost as a nation and worse, we will have some weighty accounting to do on the Day of Judgment.

What we can do as individuals may seem limited. But each of us must assume responsibility for the part we play in building up or tearing down society by the way we live, the way we speak out or stay silent, and the way we try to be "salt and light" wherever we are.

Fond Remembrances of Things Past

Why has America prospered and become the world's leading nation? One reason is that our country was founded by religious people. Even as the pilgrims settled at Plymouth Rock in 1620, their motivation for braving the hardships of this untamed new world was their desire for religious freedom and the opportunity to raise their children in their faith.

During the seventeenth and eighteenth centuries, America was *not* a secular state. Religion was not only indulged, it was promoted by the colonial governments. Although personal faith was not required for citizenship, almost every state constitution required that candidates for public office acknowledge a belief in God and in future rewards and punishments. For example, the constitutions of

Pennsylvania and Vermont stated: "And each member, before he takes his seat, shall make and subscribe the following declaration, viz.: 'I do believe in one God, the creator and governor of the universe, the rewarder to the good and the punisher of the wicked.'"[16]

Even more interesting is a fact brought to light by the well-known Presbyterian pastor and television minister Dr. James Kennedy in a sermon on the subject of church and state:

> In reading over the constitutions of all fifty of our states, I discovered something which some of you may not know: there is in all fifty, without exception, an appeal or a prayer to the Almighty God of this universe.... Through all fifty state constitutions, without exception, there runs this same appeal and reference to God who is the Creator of our liberties and the preserver of our freedoms.[17]

I find it strange that all the constitutions of all the states acknowledge God, yet our youngest citizens cannot offer public prayer to Him in our public schools. At a time when a frightening number of our nation's youth have chosen to adopt the cultural values of barbarians instead of those of our founding fathers, it is time to examine whether we have been subtly secularized by those who do not share those values. Certainly the founding fathers would not object to acknowledging God and His values, for they proudly admitted they were a religious people.

Our founding fathers showed no reluctance in savoring Christianity, the commonly practiced religion of their day. Evidently, they didn't see this act as imposing a religion on people, but rather as promoting morality in the fledgling nation.

It would be difficult to exaggerate the influence of the Bible and the church on the writing of the amazing document we call the Constitution of the United States. It could never have been produced by an amoral or biblically illiterate people.

John Jay, like Thomas Jefferson, was out of the country at the time our Constitution was written. He was our envoy to England, Jefferson our envoy to France. Jay returned home just in time to become one of the three men who wrote the *Federalist Papers*, without which the new Constitution would never have been adopted by the states. He was selected by George Washington as the first chief justice of the U.S. Supreme Court.

John Jay believed not only that Americans were a religious people, but he also believed—like many others who were influential people in our nation's founding—that America was a Christian nation. His words seem almost foreign in view of today's secularized climate: "Providence has given to our people the choice of their rulers," wrote Jay, "and it is the duty, as well as the privilege and interest, of a Christian nation to select and prefer Christians for their rulers."[18]

It is easy for any unbiased investigator to see that this nation was founded by religious people, most of whom were Christians. Our nation's laws and our public schools were established according to Judeo-Christian principles (laws and principles that came down to us from Mount Sinai and the Mount of Olives), and public policy reflected the Christian worldview ingrained in our national conscience.

The Good Old Days

If you're fond of looking back on the good old days of 40 or 50 years ago, you're in danger of being ridiculed by those who have a running romance with this new-and-improved, politically correct generation. Admittedly, some things about the good old days really weren't so good. For example, once it took six to eight weeks to travel across America. Who wouldn't prefer jetting across the country? Both my wife, Beverly, and I are very grateful that it's possible to speak in Florida on Friday and Saturday and in California on Sunday. Without any question, most technological progress beats the old days' alternative.

But in those good old days, there existed in this country a wholesome kind of lifestyle that certainly was superior to what we have today. Such expression's as "A man's word is his bond" or "You are your brother's keeper" lent themselves to a richer, more humane way of life. Marriage was most often a commitment for life, divorce rates were low, and single-parent families were rare. Children usually grew up with the security of both parents at home.

Our streets were safe day and night. Murder, rape, and mayhem were the exception, not the rule. There was, in fact, a "Christian consensus" in this country that produced the basic respect for one's fellowman, making life safe and enjoyable.

But today, in certain big cities, when you say good-bye to your loved ones each morning, you have no assurance that you will see them again. Ask any of the nine families in New York City who experienced the loss of a loved one when an armed madman shot blindly through a subway train as people were on their way home from work. In a single moment of time, countless families' lives were changed forever.

Or consider the Washington, D.C., parents of a 17-year-old honor student whose jealous boyfriend blew her brains out in a "lover's quarrel." They would probably trade modernity for the good old days when our streets were safe.

America's cities have become a battle zone. Twenty-three thousand people are murdered on our streets every year. And crime isn't limited to adults. Our schools report more than a quarter of a million acts of violence each year, making violence a parent's number one fear as children go off to school.

In his report on the cultural decline of America, Dr. William Bennett pointed out that the major problems in public schools in the 1940s were talking in class, chewing gum, skipping school, and not getting homework in on time. But in the 1990s, our schools' top problems are guns in the classroom, forcible rape, and gang-related violence. I think another top problem is a school curriculum that includes sex education materials explicit enough to make a stevedore blush. Some of these courses contain teaching diametrically opposed to the values of the parents, who pay the salaries of the teachers and the cost of sex education materials with taxes but have virtually no control over what is taught in school.

What were American schools like in the good old days? Until 30 years ago, each school day began with prayer—something like this prayer that was banned in *Engle v. Vitale* in 1962:

> Almighty God, we acknowledge our dependence upon
> Thee, and we beg Thy blessings upon us, our parents,
> our teachers, and our country.

I remember my elementary school teacher keeping order in the lunchroom. Before anyone opened his or her lunch pail, a simple prayer of thanks was said by a student or the teacher.

God was openly acknowledged and called upon in public schools and in public life. Family, schools, and government were committed to Him at the beginning of the school day. Students learned to acknowledge God and to be thankful for what they had. And God watched over our families, protecting our nation from the ravages of crime, abuse, and sexually transmitted diseases (STD's), and we enjoyed high esteem in the sight of other nations, according to God's promise in Psalm 91:14-16: "I will protect him, for he acknowledges my name. He will call upon me and I will answer him; I will be with him in trouble. I will deliver him and honor him. With long life will I satisfy him and show him my salvation."

The recent shooting of three boys in their Washington, D.C. high school hallway by another student and the violence committed against patrolling police officers have moved many in Congress to call for prayer in schools. Even D.C.'s former mayor has called for the return of prayer to our schools in the hope that it would return peace to the classrooms, like it was in the good old days before secularists destroyed the Judeo-Christian moral consensus in this country.

In 1993 a federal appeals court in Houston, Texas ruled that while the Constitution bars school officials from initiating prayer, it does not stop students from praying. Lawmakers in at least nine states are following Texas' lead: Legislatures in Georgia, Alabama, Tennessee, Mississippi, and Virginia have passed measures authorizing student-led prayer at school events. Similar bills are pending in South Carolina, Louisiana, and Oklahoma. (The Florida legislature killed its version of the bill.)

What can we do? There are attempts to return to our roots of righteousness, but never has the battle against such a return been so vigorous. America has not always been a sterling example of justice and well-being for all, for sin is a force to be dealt with in every society. Nevertheless, righteousness was never resisted as fervently as it is today. Habitual sin was not openly promoted as a lifestyle in previous generations as it is today. While the vices committed today are nothing new ("There's nothing new under the sun"– Ecclesiastes 1:9), in the good old days people viewed vice as a shameful thing. Today shame is related to the religious right as those who would impose their moral values on others.

Just think a moment—when is the last time you heard anyone say, "Aren't you ashamed of yourself?" Shame is the natural result of a quickened conscience that was instrumental in the forming of our great nation. It is time for individuals, families, and churches to allow another voice to be heard, uncompromised by our own inconsistencies. We can't criticize the effects of public television if we keep the TV sets turned on all day. We can't criticize non-Christian or anti-Christian teaching in public schools if we don't support Christian, private schools or make our voices heard before school boards and in the voting booth.

The Tragic State of the Nation

Depending on their training and temperament, people feel varying degrees of guilt when they do wrong. If they are raised in a relativistic culture that has no place for right and wrong but believes that whatever seems good to the individual is okay, their natural conscience will be weakened or even "seared." In the fourth chapter of 1 Timothy, the apostle Paul refers to people who will fall away from the faith as being "seared in their own conscience as with a branding iron" (4:2).

As the church has ceased to be the most influential guide in the molding of our national conscience, every moral value of the past has been assaulted. The evidence surrounds us—consider profanity, for example. Not too long ago, the "d word" was rarely used in public. But today the "f word" falls off the tongues of adults as if it were part of proper speech.

At first the entertainment industry ignored morals; now morality is openly attacked. Once our nation looked to religious leaders like Billy Graham, Bishop J. Fulton Sheen, and Rabbi Tannenbaum to set community standards. But today, filthy-mouthed "comics" like Roseanne Arnold or talk-show hosts like Howard Stern are imitated as though their standards of right and wrong were "gospel."

Clearly a widespread assault is being waged on the morals of millions of school children by adults who insist that all moral values should be replaced by the "new morality." This "new morality" is based on relativism (nothing is absolutely right or wrong; choices depend on your situation), which inevitably deals a death-blow to the social conscience.

A pastor friend of ours told us about a 21-year-old college girl from his church who came to ask his advice. When the pastor learned that the girl was living with a young man, his face revealed his deep disappointment and surprise. At this, the young woman nonchalantly replied, "Pastor, being a virgin is no big deal anymore."

We know we are in bad shape when people who have been reared in the church feel no remorse for their immoral lifestyles.

Just a generation ago a woman living with a man who was not her husband would certainly not have been respectable.

According to the latest surveys, our society has made promiscuity morally acceptable, for 51 percent of girls and 67 percent of boys are said to be sexually active before they graduate from high school. After high school, unless they marry young, the promiscuity level goes off the chart. STD's and the incurable AIDS plague are evident that chastity is a thing of the past for most young people. There is, however, a growing positive movement to restore virtue and chastity among our young people. Both Protestant and Catholic churches have launched national campaigns to urge young people to remain chaste until marriage.

While religious leaders and parents are encouraging young people to engrave the biblical mandate for sexual purity in their conscience, government officials and educators are, through neglect or in the name of avoiding religion-based moralities, accommodating promiscuity, causing the consciences of our youth to be seared. Some government agencies provide free condoms for teens, with or without parental permission. The government, while allowing abortion clinics to operate, is mostly silent about the need for courses that stress abstinence before marriage or teach why and how young people should say no.

Our government has deceived these young people by lying to them, telling them that sex before marriage is safe if you simply use a condom. Many girls will carry the scars from this message to their grave.

Silence, Sin of Omission

America owes her life to her churches. Unfortunately, when the moral war broke out for the cultural soul of America, fewer people took their relationship to the church seriously, and the heavy artillery of communication lay in the hands of secular people. The entertainment industry could get its amoral message to the average American home, but the religious leaders' message was either filtered or excluded. By the 1970s and '80s, it was regularly ignored or distorted. And now the media has learned to intimidate religious leaders into near silence by accusing them of being "political." That, of course, is foolish. Their efforts have silenced the churches; meanwhile, that silence continues to quiet the conscience of our nation.

America has been known around the world as a nation to be admired for her morality. She has been the land of opportunity because of the freedom and safety provided by her moral values which were reflected in our nation's laws and public policy. The churches, or the religious people, were for centuries the conscience of the nation.

Today the churches have lost most of their influence as they have piously or passively withdrawn from the public arena. It is estimated that 38 percent or more of the population professes a "born-again experience with Jesus Christ." It is doubtful that 10 or 12 percent of our elected public and governmental officials make that claim—and both our laws and our public policy reflect that deficiency. For we have spurned the Judeo-Christian ethics of our fathers and become an amoral country. Our national conscience has been seared. The moral failures of some so-called Christian leaders caused some to hold all Christianity up for ridicule, weakening the voice of Christians. But the biggest problem, for the most part, has been the silence of our churches.

What has happened to the churches and the godly influence they once had? During the sixties the church greatly influenced the civil rights movement. Where is the church of the nineties? A *USA Today*/CNN/Gallup Poll taken in March 1994 found that 69 percent of those polled said that religion as a whole is losing its influence on U.S. life. Only 56 percent felt that way in a 1974 Gallup Poll. Yet the recent polls find that 70 percent belong to a church or synagogue and 66 percent attend services at least once a month.[19]

If church membership and attendance has remained stable for the last ten or fifteen years, why, then, has the influence of religion diminished? It certainly seems obvious that America is in desperate need of a spiritual awakening today.

Will the church sit back idly while our nation euthanizes our already seared national conscience? Or will she rise up and make a moral difference by the way she votes and participates in bringing, through her influence, moral changes in her communities? The answer to that question will determine whether or not America is a secular country or "one nation under God" during the twenty-first century.

America's Failing Family Life

In May 1992 Vice President Dan Quayle gave a speech on family values. He raised typical themes, including the breakdown of the American family and the need for a concerted effort to strengthen this threatened institution. Attributing social anarchy to family breakdown, the vice president stated that if we don't succeed in "restoring basic values, any attempt to fix what's broken will fail....When families fail, societies fail. The anarchy and lack of structure in our inner cities are testament to how quickly civilizations fall apart when the family foundation cracks."

Then the vice president made a comment the media would never let him forget. Despite the accuracy of his comment, the media took him to task for the following words as though he had committed a horrible crime:

> It doesn't help matters when prime time TV has Murphy Brown—a character who supposedly epitomizes today's intelligent, highly paid professional woman—mocking the importance of fathers by bearing a child alone, and calling it just another "lifestyle choice."[20]

To the surprise of few, the media/entertainment pundits found the vice president's comments anachronistic and inaccurate. Their reaction was a perfect example of what film critic Michael Medved refers to as the media/entertainment industry's "circling the wagons mentality."[21] The truth undoubtedly stung, and they weren't about to let a painful comment go by unpunished. In unison they cried out against the vice president's preference for two-parent families, as if single-parent families were equally successful and worthy of praise.

It certainly doesn't take the current experts' consent to confirm the age-old truth that a child develops best when loved and nurtured by his father and mother in the same home! Common sense makes that fact quite clear.

In recent days our nation has been forced to confront the fact that the decline of traditional family values has directly contributed to unprecedented illegitimacy, "absentee fathers," and escalating rates of crime, violence, and welfare dependency. Family patterns are cyclic. When a boy has no father or stable role model, or if his father is in prison or a drug dealer, it is almost inevitable that he will grow up with a distorted view of manhood. He repeats what he sees, and the cycle is perpetuated.

Between 1983 and 1992 the number of *minors* arrested for murder in the United States increased 128 percent, while the number of *adults* arrested for the same crime rose by only 8.6 percent.[22] These statistics reveal that our society is becoming more murderous, but more specifically, they show us that this problem is exacerbated among minors. Experts cite child abuse, neglect, and family breakdown as some of the primary contributors to the "plague of violence by young criminals today."[23]

Dr. Ken Magid, an expert on psychopathic children who have never developed a conscience, writes in part:

> Factors are at play that, for the first time in the history of this country, are interfering with the basic bonding needs of America's infants. Society is in the midst of a profound demographic revolution. In the way that it affects the lives of our children this revolution is as significant as the industrial revolution that changed the course of history at the turn of the century....Without suitable answers, these problems could result in a national attachment crisis, thus putting our future generation of children at high risk.[24]

Our children do not feel valued or loved by parents because they spend too little time with them. Fathers are all but nonexistent in too many families. Democratic Senator Patrick Moynihan has been a welcome spokesman against the dangers of the escalating illegitimacy among the black population. As he well stated, "Either there is a rebirth of moral responsibility in this area, or we are on the way to ruin."[25]

Are more government programs the solution to the breakdown of the family in America? Or does the answer lie in listening to our conscience, that neglected voice that tells us that families are important, that children need their mother and father, and that children are to be prized and loved and taught the principles of God's word, for those truths are the way of life?

When governmental agencies invade family life, the incursions sometimes inflict bizarre results.

Last summer a couple from our former pastorate told me how four of their children were taken by force from their home because a counselor extracted a statement from their five-year-old that falsely accused their father of molestation. It took eight months and thousands of dollars in lawyers' fees to get their children back. During these eight months the children—one was only 3 years old—were bounced around from one foster home to another. By the time the youngest was returned to her parents, she was emotionally devastated.

America has been deceived. Government programs to promote daycare, healthcare, and domestic partnerships will not mend our broken families. Bryce Christensen, editor of *The Family in America*, a publication of the Rockford Institute Center on the Family in America, accurately assesses our national problem, drawing a strong biblical conclusion:

> The erosion of religious faith, the rise of commercial hedonism, and other cultural trends weakening marriage, lie beyond the direct control of government leaders in a free republic....Only through an elevated spiritual vision can Americans transcend the modern notion of wedlock as simply a working contract between two individuals and so restore the older understanding of marriage as a divinely ordained union within which husband and wife truly become "one flesh" (Genesis 2:24; Matthew 19:5).[26]

We cannot continue to neglect our national conscience in the area of our families. Just as a conscience is a safe guide only when God is the guide of the conscience, our families will be safe and strong only when they follow the biblical patterns of marriage and child rearing that have been proven successful through generations.

A Troubled Nation in Transition

Few historians are eager to point out that America, the nation founded on more biblical principles than any other, has had one of the most humanitarian governments in the history of mankind. Few nations have done as much to rescue whole regions of the world from would-be dictators as America has on at least two occasions. After conquering our enemies in World Wars I and II, we signed peace treaties with them, financed their economic reconstruction, and occupied them peacefully until they were back on their feet again. Today they are our greatest business competitors on the world market, and they enjoy unusual freedom.

No country in recent history, perhaps in all history, has been so benevolent. The 350 million souls in Europe, the hundreds of millions in the Philippines, Japan, Korea, and other countries in Asia enjoy freedom today because the United States has "policed" would-be tyrants for the past half century.

Credit largely belongs to the Judeo-Christian roots of our country, which had such a dominant humanitarian influence on our nation that government policy was affected. Those policies were established when our nation was known as a Christian nation. Most evangelical Christians would prefer to say that our country was "Christianized," that is, the influence of our Christian founding fathers and the churches of this nation resulted in the building of hospitals, orphanages, schools, and colleges. Benevolent practices were common at home and abroad, and they were a sign of how deeply Christians had influenced this country.

In one sense the pre-World War II era of American history was "Christian" because the United States was heavily influenced by Christians. But as the secular influences on the media and education began to have their effect, largely excluding all Christian thought, our status as a "Christian" nation has gradually changed. This change accounts for much of the breakdown in the family, and marriage, and our citizenry's transformation into self-centered, greedy, selfish, even barbaric individuals.

Even though Frenchman Alexis de Tocqueville was but a visitor to our land, he understood America because he had gone to our churches. In 1848 he knew that the Christian influence on America was enormous. In those days our nation recognized and spoke freely of its moral conscience. Moral absolutes were evident in our laws, education, and government policy. Virtually all Americans accepted them, with the obvious exception of a handful of atheistic socialists who were the forerunners of today's secular humanists, whose influence was felt for many years to come.

Why We Are Losing Our Rights

Dr. Bill Bennett calls ours a devalued culture. The secularizing influences in government, education, media, and entertainment have debased, polluted, and demoralized the public square. They seem to be winning because Christians aren't paying attention. When 52 percent of the eligible Christian voters didn't even go to the polls in 1992—and of those who did, 18 percent voted their "pocketbooks" instead of morals—no wonder Christians have no more say in the present government than they do. Morally committed

Christians could easily have made the difference in the future of America simply by voting.

They certainly did in 1994, when they went to the polls in unprecedented numbers and gained conservative moralist control of both houses of Congress for the first time in 40 years. Fifty-two percent of the evangelical Christian community went to the polls and voted for the most pro-life and pro-moral of the candidates. In 1996, however, due to overwhelming bias in the media, a half-hearted pro-family candidate on the right and some evangelical leaders who muddied the waters by giving the impression that the president was one of us (when in fact he had not appointed a single evangelical of note to any position of consequence during his first four years in office), only about 42 percent of the Christian voters went to the polls and an unprecedented 24 percent of those voted for the most liberal of the candidates. Even his outrageous veto of the Ban against Partial Birth Abortion, which even pro-choice Senator Kay Baley Hutcheson said was "not abortion, it is murder!", didn't shock enough apathetic Christians to get another 10 percent to the polls, which would have changed the outcome and the future of America for years to come.

Mobilizing a majority of truly religious citizens to vote only for public officials who are similarly committed to moral values will not save anyone's soul, but it will provide a climate of civic decency and religious freedom in which the gospel can be freely presented. Secularists will not rest until they have removed every acknowledgment of God from our society and subjugated religious practice to government's heavy hand.

Christians have no need to fear sharing the gospel of Jesus Christ in a free society. What we seek is the survival of our nation's religious liberty, protected by the Constitution that established the belief that government has no authority to dictate what or how we believe but must instead leave matters of faith in the hands of its individual citizens.

Secularist Change Agents Oppose Jesus Christ

The one figure in all of history most hated by secularists is Jesus Christ. Some ignore Him, others deny He ever lived. Some secularizers not only hate our Lord but also detest His fixed moral standards. They seem intent on doing everything they can to oppose His standards of morality.

Probably the most confusing group of secularizers are those who call themselves religious humanists. Usually, religious secularists take one of two forms: Either they undertake the destruction of religion as a lifelong quest, or they hold a mystical view of God that is nothing like the true God of the Bible. Their view is more pantheistic and New Age. Their basic view is that man is the center of the universe, morals are relative, and each man must do his best.

Whatever its denominational preferences, the church is a teaching vehicle that communicates the God-centered philosophy of the Bible. That philosophy, called "the wisdom of God" by the apostle Paul, is diametrically opposed to the wisdom of man or the "wisdom of the world" (1 Corinthians 1:18-25)—secularism. Let me describe the two philosophies standing in opposition to each other. One is based on the writings and thinking of man. The other is based on the Bible—the revelation of God's will for man.

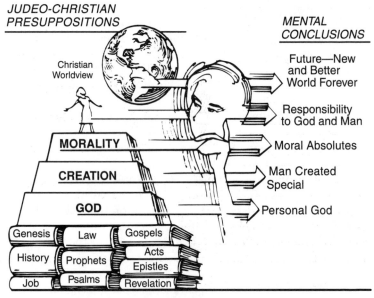

The Beliefs of the God-centered Man.

1. GOD—There is a personal God who created all things.

2. ORIGIN—God created man uniquely for himself.

3. MORALS—God has given mankind a human conscience and a moral code, the Ten Commandments. When people disobey the commandments, they feel guilty. When they obey God, their conscience approves their behavior, and they feel good about themselves.

4. PURPOSE—Man's purpose in life is to be a "servant"—first to God and then his fellowman. Man's ultimate happiness comes through serving—not being served.

5. THE WORLD—It is a temporary habitat to be used by man while he is on this earth "propagating" (teaching) the gospel and preparing for the next and eternal world that will be even better, for it will be ruled by Christ.

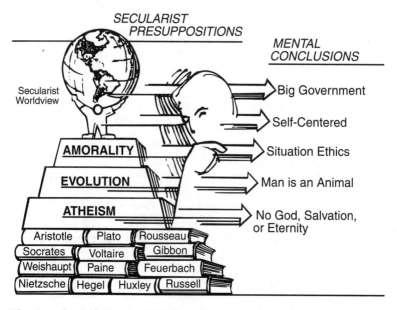

The Secularist's Basic Beliefs.

1. GOD—Secularizers deny God's existence, despite the absence of evidence to support their atheism. The order and design of the universe clearly indicate the existence of a creator-designer. Atheists, as the apostle Paul said, who refuse to acknowledge God, have been given over to a depraved

mind (Romans 1:28). And as the psalmist said, "The fool has said in his heart, 'There is no God'" (Psalm 14:1). To believe that this world—with all its precision and interrelated and coordinated forces—came into existence independent of a super intelligence and power is foolishness. The anti-intellectual belief in a creator-less creation is the cornerstone of the atheist's belief system.

2. ORIGIN—The theory of evolution offers the secularist an explanation for man's origin independent of God. For them, evolution replaces the divine force with natural forces. Evolution is *at best* a theory, for it has never been witnessed and even their fossil evidence is not undisputed. Evolutionists, nevertheless, persist in teaching their beliefs to our nation's children, making one wonder if it is because it conveniently denies the existence of a creator.

3. MORALS—One of secularism's cardinal doctrines is that moral absolutes do not exist. They reject the Ten Commandments and feel every individual should make up his own mind about how one should live, despite the fact that wherever "situational ethics" have prevailed, social havoc has resulted.

4. PURPOSE—Secularizers believe man should be free of all restraint, that there is sufficient good in him that he should be allowed to express his selfish desires and independent spirit. But history reveals that such autonomous thinking leads to moral slavery, hedonism, violence, sexual promiscuity, divorce, sexually transmitted diseases, pregnancy outside marriage, violence, and death—both physical and spiritual.

5. THE WORLD—It is a treasured resource that must be protected by a humanitarian government. Since secularists do not believe in God, they look for government to care for man from the cradle to the grave. And since they do not believe in life after death, their unspoken creed is, "Eat, drink, and be merry, for tomorrow we die." The modern version is, "Get all the gusto you can get!" Because they do not believe in the next world or eternal life, they have neither hope nor purpose nor understanding of their need of salvation.

No wonder the Bible calls secularism "foolishness." When you look at these two philosophies side by side, you can't help but be struck with the dark hopelessness of secularism. Secularism damns both the hearer and the teacher in this life and the one to come.

The Secularized Multitudes in the Valley of Decision

When Jesus saw the multitudes, He felt compassion for them because they were "distressed and downcast like sheep without a shepherd" (Matthew 9:36). Throughout America today, millions of people are blindly following secularist leaders. These multitudes, who basically believe in God but have never taken Him or His plans for their lives seriously, have been severely influenced by their secularist teachers.

They don't share the secularist view of God and life after death—they may even try to reconcile evolution and creation by adhering to "theistic evolution." Or they may avoid thinking about it altogether. Some of these victims of secularism may leave the church and adopt the social lifestyle of the world. Some even become hedonists or moral barbarians and never return. Others, if they marry, may return to the church when they begin to have children, and are confronted with the responsibilities of parenthood.

One thing they almost never do is make any kind of social contributions to their country. Since they were educated—or indoctrinated, depending on your point of view—by secularists, they usually accept liberal moral values for themselves and for society in general. When it comes to exercising the responsibilities of citizenship by voting, they either don't investigate a candidate's moral values or they say, "I don't think I should impose my moral values on others." Why not? Secularists have never hesitated to impose their relativistic "values" on the rest of us!

Our nation began with a deep sense of high moral values. It has been the influence of secularization that has changed our laws to allow such sins as abortion and gambling, but has forbidden school children to pray.

Sadly, the effects of secularism couldn't have happened without the help of a lot of people who stood by and allowed it to happen. Because of the absence of Christian votes and voices, a minority of people have gained control of our most influential agencies, among them, education, the media, and the entertainment industry, and

AMERICA'S PERILOUS TIMES HAVE COME

now have the power to determine who gets elected to the government.

If before the next election enough Americans wake up to the fact that their voice counts and that they should elect to government office only those who have a deep commitment to traditional moral values, we may yet see the social change our nation needs. Any nation that mocks the laws of God by legalizing immorality will experience God's wrath and judgment as it speeds down the road to Sodom and Gomorrah.

Maybe, just maybe, there are enough strains of moral sensibility left in the masses of America to bring about a revival in righteousness. If not, we all will discover shortly that we are on a collision course with wholesale corruption and anarchy.

A Time for Action

The church must get serious about sin. My wife and I have been Christians and active in churches for 50 years. It pains us to say that Christians do not always live out their beliefs about the Scriptures.

The Lord Jesus Christ has called His church to holiness. The Christian is called to live by high standards. Recent surveys indicate that the conduct of the church isn't too different from that of the world. George Barna has assessed the state of Christianity in the nation:

> Most Americans—about four out of five—describe themselves as "Christian." Some equate the term with a general belief in God. Still others say it has to do with religious practices such as attending church or "being religious." Much of the spiritual dimension of the concept has been lost while the population has been immunized to the Christian faith.
>
> There is an interesting contradiction here between what most of us say we believe and what we do (or don't do) in response to those beliefs.[27]

It is time that religious people become serious about holy living. For example, many of the filthy television shows that are corrupting the minds of the secularized society are being watched in Christian homes. Two or three hours in church on the weekend will not lessen the 20 or more hours of pollution viewed during the week. To renew our national conscience, people of all faiths are going to have to purify their minds and live their beliefs.

We must boycott sleazy advertisers. We can get serious about restoring our national conscience by ceasing to patronize those who sell or advertise that which is immoral. Almost all religious people (and many moral non-religious individuals) recognize that pornography is harmful to any society. ACLU lawyers sold the Supreme Court the felonious idea that the First Amendment gives pornographers a right to produce and market sleazy filth. But freedom is not an absolute right; it comes with responsibilities. Legalizing pornography has produced an industry that has morally degraded our culture and many individuals as well.

Can you imagine what would happen in six months if all the religious people in our country politely informed store proprietors who sell such materials that they would take their shopping else-where? Pornography producers would definitely feel the impact.

Such a concerted program, if proclaimed from the pulpits and over Christian radio and television and in the religious magazines, would eventually motivate the people in the pews to get serious about moral indecency in our communities that we would stop sub-sidizing it. The same could be done with advertisers of products who subsidize morally degrading films and television shows by sponsoring them.

The serious threat of a boycott by Christians would certainly cause producers to think twice about advertising on immoral, anti-family programs. The trouble is, we religious-minded people are just not serious enough about morality. If we were, we would stop patronizing those who contribute to the moral destruction of society. It is one thing to look at the moral devastation surrounding us and deplore it as if we could do nothing to halt the moral hemor-rhaging of our society. It is quite another to get serious and to do something about it.

The entertainment industry also needs to be cleaned up. We have already seen that the entertainment industry has more influ-ence on the moral climate of our country than the church or any other agency. There is no possibility that it will clean itself up *unless it is forced to do so!* The people who make up that industry don't seem to understand how morally degrading and harmful their programs are.

The religious people in this country need to send a message the entertainment industry will understand, by patronizing only those movies and watching only those television programs and buying only those music albums that do not flaunt or promote immorality.

During the past 50 years the media has abused its freedoms and by its irresponsibility has hastened the moral chaos in our country.

Pondering America's Future

As a nation, we have squandered the blessings of God and the legacy of our Christian forefathers' prayers. When we show more concern for ice-trapped whales and snail darters than we do for our unborn babies, we deserve anything but God's blessing. We condemn the innocent and pardon the guilty. We have forgotten the pledges and vows of our forefathers in our quest for convenience and comfort.

Many people in the Lord's work have given up on the future of America. Some even see in our present moral decadence a fulfillment of prophecy found in 2 Timothy 3:1-6:

> In the last days, difficult times will come. For men will be lovers of self, lovers of money, boastful, arrogant, revilers, disobedient to parents, ungrateful, unholy, unloving, irreconcilable, malicious gossips, without self-control, brutal, haters of good, treacherous, reckless, conceited, lovers of pleasure rather than lovers of God; holding to a form of godliness, although they have denied its power; and avoid such men as these. For among them are those who enter into households and captivate weak women weighed down with sins, led on by various impulses.

Our Optimism About America's Future

At the risk of alienating some of my less optimistic brethren, I still believe God has a plan for this nation's future. There are four reasons for my optimism. Please weigh them carefully.

1. *God is a merciful God.* The place where I more seriously take issue with those who forecast gloom, doom, and despair for the future of America is the subject of whom God holds accountable for the sins of His country. Will God judge the 250 million citizens of our land or those who have indoctrinated and educated people, leaving them with the kind of moral values they hold—those in the entertainment industry, education, media, and government? In the eyes of God, who is most deserving of His judgment—the evil shepherds or the sheep they are leading astray?

I still believe that even as morally dark as America is today, we could yet experience a moral, spiritual revival—not because we deserve it, but because God is a merciful God, abundant in loving-kindness. Just as He spared the wicked city of Nineveh in the days of the prophet Jonah, so He may yet spare America. As God Himself said, "And should I not have compassion on Nineveh, that great city in which there are more than 120,000 persons who do not know the difference between their right or left hand, as well as many animals?" (Jonah 4:11).

If God would save Nineveh because of 120,000 innocent boys and girls "who didn't know their left hand from their right," why would he not also save America? We have 45 million children, many of whom "don't know their right hand from their left" or don't know right from wrong because they have been brainwashed by secularists who taught them "there are no moral absolutes."

I believe that our merciful God will yet spare America because of who and what He is. But there is another reason, a principle of his Word that he has honored for over 3500 years.

2. *The Abrahamic covenant!* Many believe that God will save America because of His promise to Abraham made thousands of years ago. God performed a biological miracle on the bodies of Abraham and Sarah, and created a new nation of people called the Hebrews, or the Jews. A part of God's promise was "to make you a great nation, I will bless you and make your name great; and so you shall be a blessing; and *I will bless those who bless you* and *the one who curses you I will curse*. And in you all the families of the earth shall be blessed" (Genesis 12:2,3, emphasis added).

In my opinion, one of our nation's most worthwhile accomplishments has been its consistent regard for the plight of the Jewish nation. During the eighteenth century in both England and the United States, a more detailed interpretation of Bible prophecy arose that was called premillennialism. Premillennialists believe that the return of Christ will occur before the Millennium, a position held by most evangelicals today. As a result of the Reformation, the Bible was taken out of the dark ages and translated for the common people. This caused them to take a closer look at the Scriptures referring to the millennial period, which they interpreted literally. Consequently, Christians began to see that a future restoration of the nation of Israel was part of the prophetic teachings of Scripture. Gradually, they began to recognize that God was not through with the Jewish nation and that there would be a regathering of the nation of Israel. As early as the middle of the eighteenth century, Christian groups began calling for the restoration of the Jews to their biblical homeland—Palestine.

Jews were soon welcomed to New York and other cities in America, where they were treated to unprecedented freedom. They had a significant part in the industrial revolution of this country. Jews have enjoyed more freedom in America for a longer period of time than in any other major country since they were driven from their land centuries ago. Even England has not always been as charitable to the Jews as America. Some have been bold enough to suggest that the decline of the British Empire resulted from her mistreatment of the Jews or her accommodating policy toward the Arabs during the thirties and forties.

America has committed many sins for which we may well deserve judgment. But as a nation, we have been a consistent friend of the Jews and the nation of Israel.

3. *The strong hand of Providence in America.* God will spare America because, as the framers of our Constitution believed, His hand was on the founding of our nation. Anyone familiar with the history of this country knows that it is a miracle nation. Without "the strong hand of Providence," as George Washington called it, we would never have survived in the first place. Among this country's first settlers were Christian Pilgrims who claimed they would never have made it through that first long, cold winter without divine intervention.

Recently, my wife and I took our granddaughter to the site on the Delaware River where God supernaturally arranged a fog through which General Washington was able to lead seven thousand troops and eighteen hundred wounded soldiers to safety during a British siege that would have effectively destroyed any chance of winning the Revolutionary War. Our fledgling country's victory was a miracle, as was victory in the War of 1812—and the list goes on. God had a plan in founding this nation and a great part of His plan, no doubt, involved using the United States as a beacon and bearer of the gospel. No other country has so cooperated with God's world-wide plan of getting the gospel to people of "every tribe and tongue and people and nation" (Revelation 5:9).

Politically, America has been an inspiration to freedom-loving people throughout the earth. Without it the world would be enslaved today by either Adolf Hitler or godless communism.

4. *There are more Christians in America than any country on earth.* During God's conversation with Abraham, found in Genesis 18, God agreed to spare Sodom and Gomorrah if he could find within it ten righteous souls. As you recall, ten could not be found. And while we're not blind to the glaring evils of our nation, there is no other major country on earth with as many Spirit-filled, Bible-believing Christians. Gallup polls tell us that 60 to 70 million of us claim to have been "born again." Frankly, could it be that this 60 to 70 million may be what is preserving America from God's destruction today? The judging hand of God has never fallen on any nation in history that had the percentage of Christians this nation possesses. Consequently, I do not think God will destroy America, but we might expect Him to discipline her. Nations, like many individuals, can rarely be trusted with great blessing. The "good life" in America is not conducive to faith in God. In the Old Testament, the nation of Israel had that same problem—that's why they went through the cycles found in the book of Judges. They strayed from God and His moral values, and God sent a nation to humble them and bring them back to Him. Time after time God heard their cry and sent them a deliverer.

America may even now be experiencing the judgment of God, for certainly we are faced with disasters of all sorts. We have already seen the plagues of AIDS and other sexually transmitted diseases. Our nation has experienced the worst two years of natural phenomena in history, with devastating hurricanes in Florida, floods in the Midwest, deadly blizzards in the northeast, and earthquakes in southern California. Add to that riots, our unprecedented crime wave, and the ever-present threat of nuclear proliferation and terrorism. No one can say with certainty that these problems *are* definitely God's judgment. But neither can anyone say with certainty that some of them are not!

What the Church Can Do to Help Save America

Thank God we have many Christian leaders who have raised their voices in opposition to America's secularist movement, which would stifle all dissent in this country the way they have stifled dissent in the public schools. Christian leaders have been joined by courageous Catholics, as well as some conservative Jews and other religious leaders, in their observation of the dangers of the amoral culture infecting our nation.

Ever since our San Diego church was denied an application for approval to build a new auditorium, I have realized the importance of the Christian's responsibility to vote. The application was denied by six secularists who hated churches. That was in 1970, but since then we have seen similar illustrations of secularist discrimination that stymies the growth of churches all over the country. In Virginia, we saw a fine church refused a building permit on 76 acres of land just three miles from a music center that attracts enormous crowds and creates unbelievable traffic problems. The reason is simple. Secularizers approve wild rock concerts in their communities, but they disapprove of churches. We keep hoping such acts of governmental discrimination against Christians and churches will prompt pastors by the thousands to wake up and get their members out to vote on election day.

It isn't a matter of asking all Christians to become politically active, of which some of our critics accuse us. The real issue is responsible Christian citizenship. The Christian who doesn't vote has lost his right to complain about how the secularists run his community or country.

What Christians Must Do: Combine Our Hope with Action

For 25 years, Bev and I pastored a wonderful church in San Diego, California. During that time, I earned the reputation of being controversial because of my political activism. I accept that reputation as a badge of honor. It came because every time we had an election, I would organize an ad hoc group of 18 well-known ministers in the area and print their names on a letterhead which I had printed up called "San Diego Council for Good Government." After our committee interviewed candidates, we would endorse those with the clearest commitment to the moral values we shared. We never endorsed candidates through our churches, nor did we fund them with church money. Instead, we raised money privately and sent letters to the ministers of this city who privately distributed them at their discretion. Consequently, four of the five representatives from that part of California today are conservatives with strong voting records on the moral issues.

Our activities may have been considered controversial to People for the American Way and other leftist secularizers, but we acted within our rights and responsibilities as citizens concerned for the welfare of our country and our state. And it certainly didn't hurt the soul-winning endeavors of our church, which grew ten times larger during our 25 years there. Actually, our activism combined with our soul-winning program and practical Bible teaching enhanced the church's growth.

We want to see moral values return as the official public policy of our land and to guarantee the perpetuation of religious freedom for all churches and synagogues. The secularizers want to profit financially by the sale of smut and sleaze on television or video or in print—regardless of how many people are injured, killed or offended. If Christians and their ministers are too afraid of being considered controversial to raise their voice in warning and encourage Christians to become responsible voting citizens at election time, they will eventually preside over the death of Christianity in this country.

As Dr. Francis Schaeffer said toward the latter years of his life, "He that will not use his freedom to preserve his freedom while he still has his freedom will lose his freedom, and neither his children or his children's children will rise up to call him blessed."

There is still time to restore America's conscience. God could still send our nation one last spiritual revival and moral reformation. It will take two things in order for this to happen: 1) A miracle of God; and 2) The prayerful participation of millions of Christians.

Let us join hands to make this a reality.

▼   ▼   ▼

CHAPTER 11

Energy, Ecology, Economy: A Foreboding Forecast

Christopher Corbett

Massacre: Murdering hundreds/thousands of people (or trees!) at a time.

From glossary of widely-used children's book "Rescue Mission Planet Earth" published by the United Nations.

"They killed trees to make my bed," complained the six-year-old Tucson girl to her parents.

"Our class used to sit in the desert to write and do other school activities," wrote one of her older schoolmates in a letter to the *Arizona Daily Star*. "But now they're using that land just for people to live in homes they don't really need."[1]

Don't really need?

"My two daughters came home from school angry with my husband and me, saying we were destroying the planet," reports one mother in Arkansas.[2]

And on and on it comes.

The 1990s have seen a flood of "save the planet" sentiment aimed at children and adults, rushing at us in torrents in movies, television, and especially school curricula. But behind the deluge lies a movement of seismic proportion to bring the world under religious, economic, and political domination. Indeed, within the velvet glove of most grade-school ecology lies the seductive caress of New Age religion—and the iron fist of politico-economic control.

These are issues Christians certainly need to be concerned about as they fulfill our Lord's command to be "salt" and "light" in a dark, deceived world. Parents especially need to protect their children from satanic deception which hides behind a mask of concern for the environment.

But these issues also have fascinating implications for Bible prophecy. The Bible portrays the end of this age as one in which ancient Babylonian worship of "the creature rather than the Creator" (Romans 1:25) is rampant, and in which centralized, suffocating political and economic control over individuals, families, and nations reaches a global dimension (Revelation 13:4-9).

It's a close fit to today's trends. Of course, extreme care must be taken not to engage in idle speculation. This discussion falls into the category of plausible "stage setting" for prophetically foretold events; I am not saying these are "signs," only trends. With that caution noted, however, when you compare the biblical scenario with the current partnership of power politics and New Age ecology, it makes you wonder whether the stage is being set for movement toward the prophetic climax.

The Most Attractive Crusade in History

No serious Christian should take stewardship of the environment lightly. The earth, though fallen, is God's gift to us and should be treated with care. This is taught repeatedly in the Scriptures, and violated repeatedly by governments and corporations worldwide. Turning a blind eye to these threats can result in damage and injustice to millions of human beings. But responsible stewardship and conservation have little to do with today's popular environmentalism.

Ever since the first "Earth Day" in 1970—born out of a late-1960s counterculture which was steeped in New Age mysticism and a rejection of a biblical worldview—the environmental movement has been dominated by two forces. One is the political left calling for more government power; the other is the religious far left raising the banner of pantheism.

What are the "up front" claims of the environmental movement? Considering the saturation of its message in our culture, any well read, aware consumer of information will be familiar with at least one or more of the following:

Global Warming. We are told that gases emitted from automobiles, smokestacks, factories, aerosol sprays, and even lawn and gardening equipment have so affected the atmosphere that it is causing a "greenhouse" effect that is warming and polluting the biosphere. This is not only having an adverse effect on animal species, but at worst it threatens to melt large portions of the icecaps and flood coasts throughout the globe.

Ozone Holes. We are told that the thin layer of ozone in the upper atmosphere, which protects us from harmful ultraviolet rays from the sun and helps regulate the world's temperature, is being quickly eaten away by industrial gasses. The effects will be a rapid increase in skin cancers, global warming hazards, and other major problems.

Acid Rain. We are lectured that industrial gasses are poisoning clouds with overly acidic precipitation—"acid rain"—which pollutes rivers and streams, kills fish, kills trees, leads to greater soil erosion, and contributes to various other maladies.

Deforestation. We are told that forests and jungles are being cut down or burned out at such a profound rate that the entire interdependent ecosystem is in jeopardy. According to many environmental activists, deforestation is wiping out numerous species of animals, ruining the soil, and contributing to atmospheric problems since plants transform carbon dioxide to oxygen. The biggest problem, they say, is the reduction of the South American rain forest.

Species extinction. We are told that tens of thousands of animal species—from microscopic insects to large mammals—are being wiped out, threatening the interdependent ecosystem and committing a general affront against nature.

Contamination of air and water supplies. We are told that pollution by waste and pesticides is poisoning the water we and other creatures consume and the air we breathe, causing sickness, death, and extinction.

Overpopulation. We are warned that people are reproducing faster than the food supply and causing starvation and other socio-economic crises.

Driven by these dire scenarios, the environmental movement is presented by its evangelists as the most attractive crusade ever. What could be more important? More historic?

The planet is dying, we're breathlessly reminded. Our "cosmic lifeboat," "Spaceship Earth," is in trouble, just like Apollo 13. *Now* is the decisive moment to intervene. If we fail, we face mass starvation, disease, suffocation, and deluge. If we succeed we can return the Earth to an Edenic balance where all these evils will be escaped and paradise restored. Even better, the process of rescuing the planet will transform human thinking about our race and help us "spiritually evolve." We will be, as the popular slogan states, "One Planet, One People."

Who could resist? Fortunately, there are some who can. But only those who see the religious and political dangers lurking behind the crusade—and who have learned that much of the panic is nothing but manufactured fear-mongering.

Debunking Eco-Hysteria

Before unveiling the iron fist behind the velvet glove of today's environmentalism, let's pause to look more closely at the glove itself.

What about global warming? Is it real? Is it dangerous? According to studies done by Oak Ridge National Laboratory in 1990—and replicated by other prestigious institutions—even the most pessimistic measures and projections show that current temperatures are "well within the natural range of known temperature variation."[3]

Satellite data shows no evidence of warming over the past 14 years.[4]

Dr. Robert Balling, Director of Climatology at the University of Arizona, states:

> Some individuals are absolutely convinced from their very limited reading that we are headed for disaster via global warming. Strangely, no amount of evidence seems to shake this crowd....They care more about their [own

version of the] environment than they care about science.[5]

Why this "crowd" seems "strangely" impervious to the evidence may become clear in a few pages.

But what about the other environmental "crises"?

Ozone holes? It turns out that the scare headlines emanating from NASA and other government-funded agencies turn out to be much ado about nothing: fluctuations of a tiny percent of the ozone layer around the earth are fluctuations that the majority of scientists believe to be natural, not produced by man-made gasses. Yet the scares have resulted in the banning of air-conditioner chemicals that once provided inexpensive relief from the summer heat to millions of people around the world. As the costs go up, the poor suffer most.

Acid rain? Yes, some exists, but not anything close to the horror stories told to children and unwary consumers of news documentaries. As environmental researchers Michael Sanera and Jane Shaw put it, the most extensive study ever done found that "the much-feared acid rain has harmed only a small number of lakes" and less than .01 percent of forests.[6]

Deforestation? A concern, but hardly a crisis. Sanera and Shaw compared scare stories in school textbooks to true figures of deforestation and found the textbooks to be grossly inflating the numbers. And experts on forestation and deforestation point to historical and sociological studies showing that intense periods of deforestation by nations in a building mode slack off when the boomlets inevitably stabilize; in fact, replanting soon appears, and financial interests of timber corporations prompt wise long term forest management. Michael Coffman, Ph.D., and professor of Forest Science at the University of Idaho, asserts that American forests have been *increasing* since the turn of the century! The same is likely to happen with Brazilian rain forests—without eco-hysterical pressure.

Species extinction? It turns out that most of the scare statistics count microbes and fungi which most scientists dismiss as nonessential. Many species die out naturally. No one agrees on how many species actually exist, or how many are disappearing.

Contamination of air and water? Again, a legitimate concern, but not a crisis. The Council on Environmental Quality reported in 1992 that air had been getting cleaner since 1975. Studies also show that government regulation often boomerangs. During the energy scare in the 1970s the federal government adopted tougher standards for weatherization of all buildings. Not only did this fail to make a significant dent on energy costs, but it has now been cited as a bigger factor in the rise of asthma cases than has the quality of air outside of buildings, since more dust and mite particles were trapped inside of structures due to the regulations.

Overpopulation? There is no such thing. Scare statistics are common, but not backed up by hard data. You could fit the entire world's population very comfortably into the state of Texas. The problem is *regional food shortage*, and that stems from religious superstition and totalitarian economic and military problems. Just think about it: two of the most population dense cities in the world are Tokyo and Singapore, yet nobody starves there. But in some of the least population dense places, such as East Africa, starvation is rampant. Population isn't the problem, and population control isn't the answer.

1960s Radicalism in 1990s Classrooms

Unless the hysteria is exposed, however, we risk losing a whole generation of impressionable children to the unifying pied piper of ecological salvation and spiritual oneness. TV programs such as Ted Turner's *Captain Planet* have done much to spread the environmental gospel. Yet those conduits are modest in comparison to the flood tide of ecology-minded school curricula.

A quick look at today's classroom dogma exposes the ideological bias and fanatical zeal of its creators. "Save the planet" education has become a multi-million dollar industry flowering from the seed planted on that first counterculture "Earth Day" in 1970. As described in one investigative article printed in *Investor's Business Daily*:

> Earth Day speakers [in 1970] advanced the view that growth and crass consumption threatened the Earth's survival. Major changes were needed, they argued, and schools were a great place to start.

In this view, it was not enough for schools to convey appreciation for nature. Through lectures, films, field trips and community service projects, schools had to mobilize pupils politically.[7]

That political focus resulted in classroom books like *50 Simple Things Kids Can Do to Save the Earth*, which gave children the following message:

> Kids have a lot of power. Whenever you say something, grown-ups have to listen...They don't always tell you this, but it's true. So if saving the Earth is important to you, then grown-ups will have to follow along.[8]

From a biblical standpoint, this would hardly reinforce respect for parents, even if the cause were just. But the problems go even deeper. Jonathan Adler, director of environmental studies for the Washington D.C. based Competitive Enterprise Institute, comments:

> Most of what passes for environmental education is a pastiche of bad facts with a shrill tone. Teachers are taking advantage of students' natural curiosity about the world and transforming them into activists.[9]

But then, why wouldn't kids become activists? Madison Avenue has come to your local school, telling your children the world is about to end. Environmental alarm-clanging is a multi-million dollar industry, and much of that budget is aimed right at the minds of children starting in kindergarten.

Fountains of Deception

Where does the push come from? The answer is that almost all of it comes from politically-partisan groups from the left, often funded by powerful individuals, left-wing foundations, and rich corporations (including corporations which themselves pollute the environment yet can get special exemptions or are so rich they can afford the regulatory costs, unlike most small businesses).

Figures published in 1994 reveal that Greenpeace USA, a major promoter of environmental fear and activism, had a membership of 1.6 million and a budget of $41 million. Next in membership came the heavily activist World Wildlife Federation, sporting 1.3 million members and a budget of $88 million. Then there is the World Wildlife Fund, weighing in at 1.2 million members and $56 million.[10] Much of the budget went to educational products.

And that's just a sample.

In 1994, the National Audubon Society, whose president was outspoken in his views against constitutional protection of private property rights, began to develop curricula for grades one through six. Their stated goal was "to give youngsters a basic understanding of endangered wildlife, *and encourage their involvement in efforts to strengthen the Endangered Species Act*" (emphasis added)[11]. Completely overlooked was the fact that it is a hotly debated point within the scientific community whether the endangerment of wildlife is anything close to a crisis, and the additional fact that many observers sympathetic to protecting the environment see the Endangered Species Act as a power-grab by the federal government, not an ecology-focused measure.

How radical is the National Audubon Society? It's not just a bird-watching club anymore. One fund-raising letter from the Society stated,

> If nothing is done by us, our descendants will have few options. We can project with some accuracy the eventual end of the natural world as we know it. That is, no trees. No wildlife. Climate changes so radical the tropics have migrated to the North Pole.[12]

Others getting into the act include the far left organizations such as the Sierra Club and Zero Population Growth, for example, which contribute heavily to politicians who lean toward weighty national and international government control.

Lobbying by these groups and others, such as the North American Association for Environmental Education (NAAEE), have started a "green wave" of *mandated* environmental education in grades K-12 in twelve states (as of 1996), including California, Illinois, and Pennsylvania. And in states where the curricula is not "mandated," it is usually present anyway.

But the biggest financier of "save the planet" education is the federal government itself. The main funnel is the Environmental Protection Agency (EPA). Since 1990, the EPA's education division has given more than 1200 grants for such education in "schools, colleges and universities, state and local agencies, and nonprofit groups. The maximum grant is $250,000, with most no more than $25,000." The one exception was a whopping $5.3 million grant to the NAAEE to develop even more grassroots environmental education.[13]

That's "green" education. But the grassroots seeding of this ideology has powerful friends in the highest places.

Apostles of Planetary Salvation

At the national level, the undisputed champion of high-pressure environmentalism is former Tennessee Senator and later Vice President Albert Gore. Gore is author of the 1992 book *Earth in the Balance: Ecology and the Human Spirit*, which quickly became the manifesto of the environmental movement at just the time when Gore was helping Bill Clinton climb to the Presidency.

Once in office, Gore successfully placed his chief advisor on environmental matters, Carol Browner (who assisted him in writing *Earth in the Balance*), as head of the EPA. Not only that, but the EPA was elevated to cabinet level status and beefed up with additional funding for enforcement of its tens of thousands of complicated regulations.

If Al Gore is the American champion of environmental power politics, his international counterpart is even more formidable. That champion is Maurice Strong, billionaire Canadian industrialist and veteran United Nations assistant.

It is impossible here to describe—or overstress—Maurice Strong's power and influence. Or his connections to other men and women of titanic sway. The *New Yorker* magazine said of Strong: "The survival of civilization in something like its present form might depend significantly on the efforts of a single man." Strong, of course. He was called the "Custodian of the Planet" by the *New York Times*.[14] He has repeatedly been a candidate for U.N. Secretary General.

A cover story on Strong in *National Review* said,

> The adventures of Maurice Strong & Co. illustrate the fact that you don't have to be a household name to wield global power....Among the hats he wears are: Senior Advisor to UN Secretary General Kofi Annan, Senior Advisor to World Bank President James Wolfensohn, Chairman of the Earth Council, Chairman of the World

Resources Institute, Co-Chairman of the Council of the World Economic Forum, member of Toyota's International Advisory Board. In 1997, he was put in full charge of the important effort to reform the U.N.

Strong's career includes a stint as head of a U.N. commission which advocated forming a "green police force"—a global army—which would cross borders to enforce global environmental mandates. Then Strong organized the Earth Summit in Rio de Janeiro in 1992, called the largest gathering of leaders in world history, to lay the blueprint for eventual global authority by the U.N. over every conceivable ecological feature on the planet.

What drives eco-hysteria champions like Gore and Strong? The answers are as obvious as they are troubling.

The Caressing Hand of New Age Religion

The guiding spirit behind today's environmentalism is Eastern pantheism in its various forms. While there are some authentic Christian evangelicals—many of them politically liberal though spiritually sincere—trying to redeem the environmental left from pantheism, they are swimming against a very stiff tide.

"Deep Ecology," as it is called, is built on the "Gaia hypothesis" that the planet is a living entity (and that, in fact, inanimate matter is not truly inanimate). Gaia is the name of a Greek earth goddess. With its roots in ancient paganism, this hypothesis was first articulated as such by highly regarded British scientist James Lovelock, and touted by Al Gore and other popularizers of environmental radicalism.

Driven by this divine decree, saving the planet becomes a theological and spiritual quest, a holy crusade. If we don't defend the planet ourselves, prophesy the faithful, then "Mother Earth" will defend herself by wiping the "virus" of humanity (as some radical environmentalists refer to people) from her sacred body. Lovelock, who is cited favorably by Gore and many other writers, has stated:

> Gaia is Mother Earth. Gaia is immortal. She is the eternal source of life. She does not need to reproduce herself as she is immortal. She is certainly the mother of us all, including Jesus....Gaia is not a tolerant mother.... If we men hinder [her] we will be eliminated without pity.[15]

Lovelock's hypothesis finds restatement again and again in environmental literature. More importantly, it dovetails with the drift of the entire culture toward Eastern mysticism, known as the New Age Movement, which is taking hold in the West in popular culture and even many liberal Protestant denominations and Catholic bodies.

It is also becoming the religion of the powerful. Consider Albert Gore.

Who Is Albert Gore's God?

In the mid-to-late 1990s Gore represented himself as an evangelical Christian, giving interviews in magazines such as *Christianity Today* (one highly positive interview, weeks before the 1992 election, mentioned little of Gore's controversial religious statements), using lots of theological jargon, and making the most of his membership in the Southern Baptist Convention. He has done much to build bridges between theologically liberal Protestants and politically liberal evangelical groups concerned about the environment.

But who is Albert Gore, really?

There is no reason to doubt that he is zealously spiritual. But words like "God" and terms like "faith in Jesus Christ" can have different meanings to different people, as any student of the cults will attest. So what does Gore mean when he uses theological terms?

In reality, there is little evidence that Gore is evangelical. Gore was raised as a liberal Protestant, attending St. Alban's (Episcopal) Boy's School in Washington, D.C., and Vanderbilt (United Methodist) Divinity School in Nashville, Tennessee. Back in Washington as an adult, he attended a liberal mainline Presbyterian church, and only became a Southern Baptist after marrying his wife, who attended Mt. Vernon Baptist. Even then, Mt. Vernon was part of the small "moderate" wing of the denomination.[16] This wing's leading publication has printed articles and ads which labeled creationists as "Neanderthal" and biblical inerrancy as "heresy." They are very comfortable with Al Gore.

His book *Earth in the Balance* sheds more light into the interior of Gore's theology.

In its pages, Gore lauds the ancient European religion whose worldview, as favorably described by Gore, "was based on the worship of a single earth goddess, who was assumed to be the fount of all life and who radiated harmony among all living things."[17] Paul considers this kind of idolatry to be inspired by demons (1 Corinthians 10:20). What does Gore think of it? While lightly acknowledging its barbaric side, he writes:

> Still...it seems obvious that a better understanding of a religious heritage preceding our own by so many thousands of years could offer us new insights into the nature of the human experience.[18]

Gore also seems to lament the demise of this goddess worshiping religion, noting that "the last vestige of goddess worship was eliminated by Christianity," which he calls a religion with "distinctly masculine orientation."[19] In Gore's politically correct religious and political spheres, this is not a complementary tag. He then proceeds to laud numerous cults, religions, and religious figures who come from a pantheist worldview.

But that's the tame side of Gore.

In an article in the admittedly conservative, yet highly-regarded magazine *Crisis*, writer Mark Tooley of the Institute for Religion and Democracy notes:

> [With] audiences outside conservative Christian circles, Gore sometimes is less careful. In 1991...he unveiled his enviro-theology at the "green" Episcopal Cathedral of St. John the Divine in New York City. On the annual feast day of St. Francis, the cathedral celebrates an earth mass, whose music has included the taped cry of a timber wolf and the aquatic grunts of a humpback whale. Prayers to Ra, the Egyptian sun god, and other ecologically safe deities are not uncommon.

> Amid the "wonderful sights and sense and sounds" of the "environmental cathedral" on the feast day of St. Francis, Gore hailed St. John the Divine as a "think tank for restoration ecology." As the senator spoke, an elephant, a camel, a vulture, a swarm of bees, dogs, cats, parakeets, plants, and other living creatures patiently awaited their annual blessing from the cathedral dean.

This service is remarkable in part because it celebrates the re-awakening of a truer expression of what our relationship to the other living things of the earth really is," Gore solemnly intoned. "The cause of environmental integrity and justice must occupy a position of utmost priority for people of faith.[20]

Other statements by Gore at this service boggle the sensibilities of any knowledgeable Christian:

And if God is within us, is God not also within other living things? Is God not also in the rest of creation?... We are not separate from the earth. God is not separate from the earth.[21]

Of course, this is a simple blurring of the categories of God's transcendence and immanence (nearness). Christianity teaches that God is both transcendent and immanent. Indeed, His transcendence rescues Christianity from the pantheism that results from focusing exclusively on His immanence. God is present every-*where*, but He is not every*thing*—He is, in fact, "separate" from the earth. Gore either ignorantly or purposefully obliterates that distinction, heading toward end-times Babylonian creature worship and luring many naive Christians with him.

Who Is Maurice Strong's God?

What of Maurice Strong, Gore's counterpart of the green gospel in international power politics? Where does the "Custodian of the Planet" stand on spiritual issues?

As Chairman of the U.N. Earth Summit, Strong used a strong pantheistic theme to operate as ideological background music to the policy-making affair. Strong opened the Summit by referring to the earth as "sacred" and nature as "divine." In the opening pageantry, a Viking ship labeled "Gaia" was paraded before the delegates.

The truth is that Maurice Strong is a committed adherent to New Age, pantheistic mysticism. He is a member of the Baha'i faith, which proclaims that all religions are one and that a messiah will come to demonstrate this reality.[22] According to a profile in the May 1990 issue of *West* magazine, Strong's wife, Hanne, is an occultist who claims to speak with disembodied spirits. Christians recognize this activity as demonism.

In 1978 the Strongs purchased a ranch in Colorado of several thousand acres. Following a series of mystical experiences, the Strongs established Baca there—a retreat community for New Age exploration, frequented by the likes of Shirley MacLaine, and visited by Henry Kissinger, the World Bank's Robert MacNamara, and the presidents of corporations like IBM, Pan Am, and Harvard University, as well as being the home to some of more prominent, and radical New Age think tanks like the Aspen Institute.

The Strongs intend to make Baca a model for harmonizing all the world's religions. Hanne says, "this place will have a key role in the future of mankind."

The Iron Fist of Economic Control

Remember the Crusades? The Inquisition? Remember the massacre of Jews in medieval Europe? These are just examples of what can happen when religious zealotry marries political power. It's also what makes the current eco-hysteria a serious threat to Christian beliefs and political freedom, and may link it to the coming of the creature-worshiping, heavy-handed world ruler described in 2 Thessalonians and Revelation.

In his best-selling book, Gore sounded the note of imminent planetary destruction unless *major* changes were made in the economic and even religious actions of the human race. The primary culprits are western nations, especially the United States. The primary remedy must be a paradigm shift in western thinking in which economic and technological development would be reworked under a new governing consensus.

Massive shifts of resources would be necessary. Sacrifices would be many. And government would have to take a leading—that is, *commanding*—role in "facilitating" such sacrifices by businesses and families. Throughout the proposal which climaxes his book—a "Global Marshall Plan" to save the Earth, named after the Marshall Plan which rebuilt Europe after WWII—Gore repeats the mantra: "Governments should... Governments should... Governments should..."

Gore was instrumental in turning his views into policy via the Clinton Administration. The Interior Department has used environmentalism to assert regulatory control over private property in an unprecedented manner, culminating in 1997 with the American Heritage Rivers designation which would overlay federal regulations upon thousands of acres of private land without the consent of the citizens' elected representatives in Congress. Under Clinton-Gore, private property across the United States has been designated as "wetlands"—the kiss of death for any unfortunate owner who had invested in the land. The definition of wetland was so vague that it included many pieces of property with small, shallow, seasonal puddles. The pattern repeated itself as the federal government used protection of wildlife (including microbes, rats, and tiny fish) as grounds to overlay federal control over private property and render it useless to owners.

Effectively, government has found a way to subvert property rights (a right which the Bible endorses) and other legal protections without seizing the property outright.

Getting Rid of Ecological "Jews"

But the real showstopper was the EPA, led by Gore's protégé Carol Browner. The litigation tactics used by Browner, an activist attorney-politician from Florida, were described by the head of Florida's largest business trade association with these words: "She kicks the door open, throws in a hand grenade, and then walks in to shoot who's left. She really doesn't like to compromise."[23]

As head of the EPA, Browner announced drastically tougher laws on soot and smog, with draconian mandates forcing cities and businesses across America to comply or face crippling fines. Even many of the EPA's own consulting scientists objected to what they said were twisted interpretations in the research used to justify the new regulations.

An editorial by two researchers, published in the *Wall Street Journal*, stated, "In pushing through the new air-quality standards, the EPA is clearly going against the bulk of scientific opinion. The agency has opted to ignore the advice of its own Clean Air Scientific Advisory Committee....Most members of the advisory committee advised against lowering the ozone standard, concluding that it would provide only marginal public health benefits. Only four of the 21 members supported EPA's proposed standard for particulate matter."[24]

Even more astonishing, the cost for the measures was esti-mated to be $90 to $150 billion per year—affecting mostly the poor who can least afford consumption taxes, increased utility fees, and refitting appliances. Yet these costs were not shown to be offset by projected health benefits.[25]

Why, then, would Gore, Browner and company proceed? Remember, the key behind today's environmentalism is not ratio-nality. It is Babylonian creation-worship saturated with the wine of Roman power. It is, perhaps, the pattern foreshadowing the reign of the Beast of the Book of Revelation.

Conservative commentator William Lind puts it in stark but accurate terms:

> Totalitarian ideologies are dangerous precisely because they are masters of disguise. They don't come to power by promising Gestapos and gulags. What they promise sounds good: peace, land and bread was the Bolsheviks' slogan in 1917. By the time people see the real agenda—unlimited power for a privileged few—it's too late.
>
> How might totalitarianism disguise itself today, in this country, in order to be attractive and win converts? We don't have to theorize in order to answer that question. The answer is all around us, in the ideology of environ-mentalism....
>
> Environmentalism offers totalitarianism a perfect justifi-cation, because everything we do affects the environ-ment. Therefore, environmentalism can claim the right to control everything we do. If we demur, then it is only right that we be cut off....The label of "polluter" is an even more useful justification for liquidation than the labels "capitalist" or "Jew."[26]

If you believe Lind is paranoid, remember that Gore has branded any political opponent who opposes the EPA standards as engaging in "environmental *jihad*" (holy war) against the planet. And President Clinton attacked his political opponents in darker terms: individuals who *knowingly* push measures which would "kill people" through "poisoning" the air and water. Gore and Clinton achieved major political victories using such labeling tactics. The

Environmental Jew has clearly been given his public badge of shame.

Eco-Tyranny's Global Bear Hug

The United States is being transformed from within by environmentalism. But America and other nations are also under siege from outside their walls.

To see why, look no further than Maurice Strong. This powerful "Custodian of the Planet" is a socialist who envisions causing a collapse of developed nations and creating a "green" police force to invade nations to enforce global mandate. How do we know this? He says so.

In 1976, the billionaire Strong told *Maclean's* that he was "a socialist in ideology, a capitalist in methodology."[27] As head of the U.N. Environmental Program in 1987 he promoted his idea of the green police and the concept of "sustainable development." Sustainable development means the *minimum* development required to sustain *all* life on earth. In other words, the United States would have limits—caps—on its gross national product. These caps would be determined by a formula dictating how much each person really needs to sustain himself. Anything over the sustainable limit would be sent to nations who are under their sustainable development levels. In Strong's words:

> It is clear that current lifestyles and consumption patterns of the affluent middle class—involving high meat intake, consumption of large amounts of frozen and convenience foods, use of fossil fuels, ownership of motor vehicles and small electrical appliances, home and work-place air-conditioning, and suburban housing—are *not sustainable*. A shift is necessary toward lifestyles less geared to environmental damaging consumption patterns.[28]

Strong also has openly mused about the possibility of engineering an economic collapse of western nations.[29]

But is Strong a lonely kook, tilting at windmills? Hardly.

As head of the U.N.'s monumental reform effort, Strong is busy "reforming" the U.N. after the pattern of his Commission on Global Governance, which advocates funding global governing structures with a new global tax.

According to Inge Kaul, top U.N. strategist, the world would need to be softened up to the idea of a global tax. Indeed, as alien an idea as it might seem to the public, a global tax has long been a dream of one-world planners in the U.N. The plan is to start with a tax on currency exchange, sold to the American public, in the words of one of its proponents, as "a tax on Wall Street, not Main Street."[30] But it wouldn't stop there. The U.N. has discussed taxes on:

- all overseas travel expenses,
- satellite communications,
- ocean fishing,
- international phone and computer communications,
- currency exchange,
- postage,
- fossil fuels and non-renewable energy.[31]

At a 1995 summit in Denmark, U.N. official Kaul estimated that "a global tax on non-renewable energy...could generate $66 billion per year." Other estimates went as high as $300 billion per year.[32] The irony of such suggestions is that, through 1995, U.S. taxpayers had already paid the U.N. $30 billion since 1945, funding a quarter of its budget.[33]

Strong and other recognized international power-brokers such as David Rockefeller and high-ranking U.N. official Jim MacNeill call for an expanded Earth Charter (the initial one was signed at the 1992 Earth Summit), with "an Earth Council, perhaps the [U.N.] Security Council with a broader mandate, [to maintain] the inter-locked environmental and economic security of the planet."[34] Former French Prime Minister Michel Rocard says:

> Let's not deceive ourselves.... International instruments must be transformed into instruments of coercion, of sanctions, of boycott, even...of outright confiscation of any dangerous installation. What we seek, to be frank, is the legitimacy of controlling the application of the inter-national decisions.[35]

The U.N. clearly has designs on what to do with the money it craves. Past U.N. Secretary General Boutros-Ghali in a major address in 1992, and again in an article in the Council on Foreign Relation's *Foreign Affairs* magazine, has called for establishment of a permanent U.N. operated global army. CNN lauded this proposal for what it called a "Planetary Police."[36]

Of course, such concepts are often couched in more polite terms for mass consumption. Yet behind the velvet jargon on your TV screen and the pages of your newspaper lies the iron fist of globalist demand-based economics. This flies in the face of a biblical concept of property rights, individual initiative, national sovereignty, and voluntary charity towards those outside one's own borders.

Is There Hope?

What is a Christian to do, standing under this waterfall of deception? Is there hope to stand against it? Is there hope that the trends can be turned around?

The answer is yes. We know from scripture that *ultimately* Babylonian creature-worship and Roman political domination will come under the False Prophet and Beast of Revelation. We know that the trends mentioned in this chapter point in that direction. But we also know that, in each generation, God is willing to delay judgment on societies who heed the warnings and repent.

In Jeremiah chapter 18, verse 8, God asserts that "if that nation against whom I have spoken turns from its evil, I will relent of the disaster that I thought to bring upon it." This principle was demonstrated in God's withholding of judgment on Judah (2 Kings 22-23) and Nineveh (Jonah 3:9-10). Eventually both nations were judged, but not in the generation of those who repented. Eventually our world will be judged, but it may be in God's plan that Christians in this generation will be a catalyst for revival and repentance which delays the coming wrath.

Christians must arm themselves and their families with the truth, and then saturate and enlighten their surrounding culture with this truth. This truth includes the totality of Bible doctrine and its worldview application to every issue in life.

Specifically concerning the issues in this chapter, however, Christians should develop a mature view of environmental stewardship, protection and responsible use of private property, the necessity for decentralized government power which restrains the propensities of the sin nature—both of the governed and the state, and the special role of nations as the divine framework within which man is to live. (For more details, see the chapter "The U.S. and other U.N. Serfdoms" in *Foreshocks of Antichrist*, Harvest House, 1997).

It is also necessary to learn—and teach our children—the true facts of environmental stewardship to combat the twisted science used to generate fear by those who hunger for excessive power. I recommend such books as *Facts Not Fear: A Parent's Guide to Teaching Children About the Environment* by Michael Sanera and Jane S. Shaw (Regnery, 1996), *Saviors of the Earth? The Politics and Religion of the Environmental Movement* by Michael S. Coffman (Northfield, 1994), and the many fine books by Dr. Dixie Lee Ray and Dr. Julian Simon. And there are many others.

Yes, there is hope—the hope of those found obedient whether the Lord comes tomorrow or delays His coming as we spread His truth to open the eyes of our generation.

▼   ▼   ▼

Part 3

▶

History's Deadliest Storm/ God's Eternal Grace

CHAPTER 12

The Shout Heard Around the World: Overview of the Rapture

Thomas Ice

Some opponents of pretribulationism have insisted that it has human rather than biblical origins. Some say that if pretrib is taught in the Bible, then it is a view that should also be found throughout the history of the church. In the past few years more voices from the Church's past testifying either to some form of pretribulationism, some form of a two-stage advent of Christ, or to statements containing various pretrib elements have been discovered.

I believe that pretribulationism is our "blessed hope" spoken of in the New Testament. Regardless of when a significant group of believers began to realize that the Bible teaches pretribulationism, that teaching has been part of God's Word all along. Many Christians throughout the church's history have believed many important elements that compose the pretrib doctrine without necessarily understanding it to the extent that others have come to understand it in the last 200 years. Nevertheless, hosts of believers down through the centuries have understood many key pretrib elements: that Christ could return at any moment without signs preceding;

that Christians will not go through the time of wrath known as the tribulation; that there are two stages involved in Christ's return. In the last few years, a number of discoveries have been brought to light and presented to the Christian public. But what guidelines should we follow in finding examples of a pretrib rapture and pretrib elements from historical documents?

Criteria for Finding Pretribulationism

Pretrib rapture critic William Bell has formulated three criteria for establishing the validity of a historical citation regarding the rapture. If any of his three criteria are met, then he acknowledges it is "of crucial importance, if found, whether by direct statement or clear inference." I believe that at least two of Bell's standards have been met by some of the examples I will supply below. The standards are as follows: 1) "Any mention that Christ's second coming was to consist of more than one phase, separated by an interval of years," and 2) "any mention that Christ was to remove the church from the earth before the tribulation period."[1]

The Early And Medieval Church

The early church was clearly premillennial in its view of prophecy, with only a few dissenters. Irenaeus (circa A.D. 202) stated in the strongest possible terms that premillennialism was traditional orthodoxy (*Against Heresies* 5.32.1).[2] Pretribulationism is not *clearly* represented within the extant writings of these early fathers. However, before one draws the conclusion that it is totally absent, it is possible that a few ancient statements do represent *elements* of a fuzzy form of pretribulationism.

The early church was often subjected to persecution for its faith, and as a result, tended to confuse Church Age trials and tribulation with the specialized tribulation of the seventieth week of Daniel. At the same time, they often spoke of a belief in an "any-moment" return of the Lord. Expressions of imminency abound in the Apostolic Fathers. Clement of Rome, Ignatius of Antioch, *The Didache*, *The Epistle of Barnabas*, and *The Shepherd of Hermas* all speak of imminency.[3] Furthermore, *The Shepherd of Hermas* speaks of the pretribulational concept of escaping the tribulation:

You have escaped from great tribulation on account of your faith, and because you did not doubt in the presence of such a beast. Go, therefore, and tell the elect of the Lord His mighty deeds, and say to them that this beast is a type of the great tribulation that is coming. If then ye prepare yourselves, and repent with all your heart, and turn to the Lord, it will be possible for you to escape it, if your heart be pure and spotless, and ye spend the rest of the days of your life in serving the Lord blamelessly.[4]

Early church historian, Larry Crutchfield, notes, "This belief in the imminent return of Christ within the context of ongoing persecution has prompted us to broadly label the views of the earliest fathers, 'imminent intratribulationism.'"[5] Crutchfield notes concerning Irenaeus (ca. A.D. 120–ca. A.D. 202):

He seems to have believed that there would be an interval between the rapture of the saints and the final venting of the Antichrist's wrath upon earth. His reference to the church being "suddenly caught up" and to the Antichrist's "sudden coming" provide at least some... sense of imminency (*Against Heresies* 5.29.1-2). While the evidence is not conclusive, it suggests at least the possibility that Irenaeus held to a remote/imminent, intratribulational rapture of the church.[6]

There appear, scattered throughout the church fathers of the first three centuries, statements that are not only strongly premillennial but which also reflect a possible undeveloped belief in pretribulationism or a two-stage coming. For example, Frank Marotta has noted the following statement from the *Apocalypse of Elijah*, an extra-biblical writing (A.D. 150–275):

Now those upon whose forehead the name of Christ is written and upon whose hand is the seal, both small and the great, will be taken up upon their [angels'] wings and lifted up before his wrath.[7]

Marotta adds, "Even the editor of this work (almost certainly a liberal) heads verses two through six with 'the removal of the righteous' and verses seven through fourteen with 'Natural disasters which follow the removal of the righteous.'"[8]

Victorinus (died A.D. 304), Bishop of Petau, who wrote an early commentary on the book of Revelation, gives an explanation of Revelation 6:14 which includes his belief that "the Church shall be taken away" sometime in the future when the passage is fulfilled. Again, regarding Revelation 15:1, he says, "these shall be in the last time, when the Church shall have gone out of the midst." Here he speaks of something that will have happened previously, apparently looking back to his statement in Revelation 6:14. This could reflect elements of pretribulationism. It seems even more likely in light of the fact that Victorinus was said by the anti-Chiliast Jerome to have been a known premillennialist; yet his commentary was clearly amended in the passage regarding Revelation 20 to read as if he were Augustinian (i.e., amillennial). An American editor of Victorinus has concluded:

> This confirms the corruption of the manuscripts. Indeed, if the Victorinus mentioned by Jerome be the same as our author, the mention of Genseric proves the subsequent interpolation of his works....It is evident that the fragment which is here preserved,...is full of the corrections of some pious disciple of St. Augustine who lived much later.[9]

After Augustine (died A.D. 430), there were clear efforts to redact premillennialism out of earlier church writings on the part of some copyists—Victorinus being an established example of such attempts—in a sincere but misguided attempt to bring these writings in line with what they thought should be the orthodoxy of the day. There can be no doubt that some during the Middle Ages either destroyed texts or changed them from their original autographs.

Another example is seen in the fact that during the Middle Ages, the last five chapters of Irenaeus' *Against Heresies* were lost. It just so happens that those were the ones that contained the heart of his eschatological thought. Wilber Wallis explains:

> The premillennial scheme seems to have disappeared completely after it was condemned as heretical at the Council of Ephesus in A.D. 431. This disappearance was probably aided by the suppression of the last five chapters of Irenaeus' *Against Heresies* after the rejection of premillennialism and the loss of the Greek original. The reappearance of the full text of this ancient presentation

of premillennialism in 1571 (later reconstructed from the Armenian and Syriac manuscripts) may have had something to do with the reemergence of premillennialism in the seventeenth century.[10]

In light of such revision and suppression, it is entirely within the realm of possibility that the early church could have had clearer and more numerous pretribulational statements in their writings. Such a supposition is strengthened in light of the recent rediscovery by North American Evangelicals of Pseudo-Ephraem (fourth through seventh century) and his sermon known as *On the Last Times, the Antichrist, and the End of the World* or *Sermon on the End of the World*. Latin copies of these texts were compiled and edited by C. P. Caspari[11] and have more recently received attention from the late Cal Berkeley Professor, Paul J. Alexander.[12] Pseudo-Ephraem's sermon contains a clear statement about the church's removal before the tribulation as part of a two-stage coming.[13]

> Why therefore do we not reject every care of earthly actions and prepare ourselves for the meeting of the Lord Christ, so that he may draw us from the confusion, which overwhelms all the world?...For all the saints and elect of God are gathered, prior to the tribulation that is to come, and are taken to the Lord in order lest they see the confusion that is to overwhelm the world because of our sins.[14]

Pseudo-Ephraem demonstrates that a belief in the rapture was understood very early in the history of the church, assuring us that others had a similar understanding, since the sermon had to have had some circulation to have been preserved to our day, and that some of the previously vague statements could also have been expressions of an early and undeveloped pretribulationism that was under attack and censorship. The tribulation for Pseudo-Ephraem was three and a half years instead of seven, but in spite of this, it should be viewed as pretrib because the sermon viewed the entire tribulation as 42 months, three and a half years, and 1,260 days. This is a gathering (rapture) to the Lord that is said to occur "*prior to the tribulation*" (Section 2), while the sermon proceeds in a chronological manner so that the final paragraph (Section 10) speaks of the second coming at the end of the tribulation. "And when the three and a half years have been *completed,*...will come the sign of the Son of Man, and coming forward the Lord shall appear with great power and majesty,…and also even with all the powers of the heavens with the whole chorus of the saints.…" Further, in the previous paragraph (Section 9) the sermon reads as follows when commenting on the two witnesses who "are the servants for the heralding of the second coming of Christ." Here we have a clear reference, as demanded by William Bell's pretrib rapture criterion, of the promise of removal of all believers before the tribulation (the rapture), which is then clearly separated by an interval of time (three and a half years), followed by the second coming at the end of the sermon.

The Reformation

Once premillennialism began to be revived in the early seventeenth century within various Reformed traditions, there was a corresponding increase of statements that some believe reflect pretribulational views, in spite of the fact that historicism was the near-unanimous approach to prophecy. As many Reformed scholars adopted premillennialism, some began to see the rapture as a distinct event from the return of Christ to the earth.

It has been claimed that some separated the rapture from the second coming as early as Joseph Mede in his seminal work *Clavis Apocalyptica* (1627), who is considered the father of English premillennialism. Scholar Paul Boyer says that Increase Mather proved "that the saints would *'be caught up into the Air'* beforehand, thereby escaping the final conflagration—an early formulation of the Rapture doctrine more fully elaborated in the nineteenth century."[15] Whatever these men were saying, it is clear that the application of a more literal hermeneutic was leading to a distinction between the rapture and the second coming as separate events. Suffering under the disadvantage of a historicist prophetic framework, they appear to be struggling with how to coordinate these different events into a prophetic scheme. About 200 years ago, a clearer understanding of a pretrib rapture came about by casting off historicism and adopting futurism. When that occurred, blended with a revived premillennialism, a belief and understanding of pretribulationism exploded across Christian circles.

However, even before the 1800s, others began to speak of the rapture. Paul Benware provides the following summary:

Peter Jurieu in his book *Approaching Deliverance of the Church* (1687) taught that Christ would come in the air to rapture the saints and return to heaven before the battle of Armageddon. Philip Doddridge's commentary on the New Testament (1738) and John Gill's commentary on the New Testament (1748) both use the term *rapture* and speak of it as imminent. It is clear that these men believed that this coming will precede Christ's descent to the earth and the time of judgment. The purpose was to preserve believers from the time of judgment. James Macknight (1763) and Thomas Scott (1792) taught that the righteous will be carried to heaven, where they will be secure until the time of judgment is over.[16]

Frank Marotta believes that Thomas Collier in 1674 makes reference to a two-stage coming, but rejects the view, thus revealing his awareness that such a view was in circulation hundreds of years ago. Marotta writes of Collier:

> Because he raised the question of the saints being raised at Christ's "first appearing in the clouds of heaven," instead of later on "at the entrance of the thousand years," it is apparent that Collier certainly *considered* the idea of a pretribulation rapture.[17]

It would not be long after Collier's day that pretribulationism would become much more well-known.

Morgan Edwards

Morgan Edwards, an important early American Baptist scholar, clearly taught some form of pretribulationism. Edwards founded the first Baptist college in the Colonies, Rhode Island College, which we know today as Brown University of the Ivy League. It was during his student days at Bristol Baptist Seminary in England (1742–44), that Edwards wrote an essay for eschatology class on his views of Bible prophecy. This essay was later published in Philadelphia (1788) under the following title: *Two Academical Exercises on Subjects Bearing the following Titles; Millennium, Last-Novelties.*[18] Upon reading the 56-page work, it is evident that Edwards published it with only minor changes from his student days, thus, we can date Edwards' pretribulationism as originating in the early

1740s. The pretribulationism of Morgan Edwards can be seen in the following statement from his book:

> II. *The distance between the first and second resurrection will be somewhat more than a thousand years.*
>
> I say, *somewhat more* because the dead saints will be raised, and the living changed at Christ's "appearing in the air" (1 Thessalonians 4:17); and *this will be about three years and a half before the millennium*, as we shall see hereafter: but will he and they abide in the air all that time? No: they will ascend to paradise, or to some one of those many "mansions in the father's house" (John 14:2), and *so disappear during the foresaid period of time.* The design of this retreat and disappearing will be to judge the risen and changed saints; for "now the time is come that judgment must begin," and that will be "at the house of God" (1 Peter 4:17)…"[p. 7; emphasis added; the spelling of all Edwards' quotes have been modernized.]

What has Edwards said? Note the following:

• He believes that at least 1,003.5 years will transpire between resurrections.

• He associates the first resurrection with the rapture in 1 Thessalonians 4:17, occurring at least 3.5 years before the start of the millennium (i.e., at least 3.5 years before the second coming of Christ at the start of the millennium).

• He associates the meeting of believers with Christ in the air and returning to the Father's house with John 14:2, as do modern pretribulationists.

• He sees believers disappearing during the time of the tribulation, which he goes on to describe in the rest of the section from which the rapture statement is taken.

• He, like modern pretribulationists, links the time in heaven, during the tribulation, with the "bema" judgment of believers.

The only difference, at least in light of the above statements, between current pretribulationism and Edwards is the time interval of 3.5 years instead of 7.

Edwards says in his introduction that his views are not those normally held in his day and because he was approaching eschatology with a literal hermeneutic. Such an approach is said by modern pretribulationists to be the primary determinate factor leading to pretribulationism. Edwards explains:

> I will do my possible: and in the attempt will work by a rule you have often recommended, viz. "to take the scriptures in a literal sense, except when that leads to contradiction or absurdity." Very able men have already handled the subject in a mystical, or allegorical, or spiritual way.

It is clear from the above comment that Edwards was taught literal interpretation by his teachers, but they did not apply it consistently throughout the whole Bible. Edwards was determined to apply in practice what he had been taught in theory, even though it contradicted the common practices of his day in the area of the study of Bible prophecy.

Edwards expands on and repeats his earlier rapture statement later when he says,

> Another event previous to the *millennium* will be the appearing of the son of man in the clouds, coming to raise the dead saints and change the living, and to catch them up to himself, and then withdraw with them, as observed before [p. 7]. This event will come to pass when Antichrist be arrived at Jerusalem in his conquest of the world; and about three years and a half before his killing the witnesses and assumption of godhead....

Edwards clearly separates the rapture and the second coming, as is evident from the following statements:

> 8. The last event, and the event that will usher in the *millennium*, will be, the coming of Christ from paradise to earth, with all the saints he had taken up thither (about three years and a half before)...[p. 24] millions and millions of saints will have been on earth from the days of the first Adam, to the coming of the second

> Adam. All these will Christ bring with him. The place
> where they will alight is the "Mount of Olives, which is
> before Jerusalem on the east." Zechariah 14:4 [p. 25].

Of interest is the fact that Edwards wrote 42 volumes of sermons, about 12 sermons per volume, that were never published.
Other than his historical writings and ecclesiastical helps, his essay
on Bible prophecy was his only other published work. It is significant that this essay, from his youth, was published and not something else. This indicates that there was some interest in his views
on this subject. Such an interest would have surely risen out of his
bringing it to the attention of those to whom he ministered. Yet, on
the other hand, the book only went through one printing, showing
that it could not have been a widely held view. It could also reflect
the fact that Baptists were not a large denomination at this time in
America. Nevertheless, Edwards' work on Bible prophecy did have
some circulation, and it exposed early Americans to many of the
ideas that would come to dominate Evangelicalism a century later.

J. N. Darby and the Rapture

In spite of earlier developments of pretribulationism, there can
be no doubt that Brethren scholar John Nelson Darby is the foun-
tainhead of the modern formulation. However, the last few decades
have seen several attempts by anti-pretribulationists to say that
Darby clandestinely pilfered at least part of his pretrib ideas from
questionable sources. These claims cannot be sustained.

The Lacunza Theory

Baptist evangelist John Bray of Florida contends that Darby got
his idea of a two-staged coming from the Jesuit priest Emmanuel
Lacunza, who wrote *The Coming of Messiah in Glory and Majesty*
in 1790.[19] Lacunza's book was first published in Spanish in 1812
and then translated into English and published around the middle
of 1827. Supposedly, Darby read this book and then thought up
pretribulationism. There are a few problems with such speculation.
As will be noted below, the idea of a pretrib rapture first came to
Darby in December 1826. Edward Irving says he wrote the foreword to his English translation of Lacunza on Christmas Day, 1826,
before it was released in printed form later in 1827. Neither Bray
nor other Lacunza theorists have been able to show any historical

evidence that Darby was influenced by this source. Finally, if Lacunza's view of a 45-day interval between some events relating to the second coming constitutes a two-stage coming and thus an element of pretribulationism, then why not make the case that amillennialists such as Jerome (A.D. 342–420) or The Venerable Bede (A.D. 673–735) of England were also pretrib sources, since they held a similar view on the 45-day interval from Daniel 12:12?

The Irvingite Influence Theory

Anti-pretribulationist Dave MacPherson has developed and disseminated the false notion that Darby was involved in a plot in which he secretly got his idea of the rapture from the Irvingites and more specifically from the prophecy of a 15-year-old girl named Margaret Macdonald.[20] Dr. John Walvoord has noted concerning MacPherson's attempt at historical research:

> The whole controversy as aroused by Dave MacPherson's claims has so little supporting evidence, despite his careful research, that one wonders how he can write his book with a straight face. Pretribulationalists should be indebted to Dave MacPherson for exposing the facts, namely, that there is no proof that MacDonald or Irving originated the pretribulation rapture teaching.[21]

There are at least four major reasons why MacPherson's speculations are not true: First, it is doubtful that Margaret Macdonald's "prophecy" contains any elements related to the pre-trib rapture.[22] Second, no one has ever demonstrated *from actual facts of history* that Darby was influenced by Macdonald's "prophecy" even if it had (which it did not) contained pre-trib elements.[23] Third, Darby clearly held to an early form of the pretrib rapture by December 1826 or January 1827, as will be shown below. These are a full three years before MacPherson's claim of 1830. Fourth, there is no evidence that Irving or any of the early Irvingites ever held to pretrib views. This has been noted recently by Columba G. Flegg, who has produced one of the most extensive critical analysis ever on Irvingite doctrine. He declares that Irvingites were still primarily historicist, while Darby and the Brethren had become futurist. Further, Flegg notes that the Brethren teaching on the rapture and the present invisible and spiritual nature of the church—

were in sharp contrast to Catholic Apostolic teaching... There were thus very significant differences between the two eschatologies, and attempts to see any direct influence of one upon the other seem unlikely to succeed— they had a number of common *roots*, but are much more notable for their points of disagreement. Several writers [referring specifically to MacPherson] have attempted to trace Darby's secret rapture theory to a prophetic statement associated with Irving, but their arguments do not stand up to serious criticism.[24]

The Development of Darby's Views

Brethren writer Roy A. Huebner claims and *documents* his belief that J.N. Darby first began to believe in the pretrib rapture and develop his dispensational thinking while convalescing from a riding accident during December 1826 and January 1827.[25] If this is true, then all of the origin-of-the-rapture conspiracy theories fall to the ground in a heap of speculative rubble. Darby would have at least a three-year jump on any who would have supposedly influenced his thought, making it impossible for all the "influence" theories to have any credibility.

Huebner provides clarification and evidence that Darby was not influenced by Margaret Macdonald, Lacunza, Edward Irving, or the Irvingites. These are all said by the detractors of Darby and the pretrib rapture to have been bridges which led to Darby's thought. Instead, he demonstrates that Darby's understanding of pretribulationism was the product of the development of his personal interactive thought with the text of Scripture as he, his friends, and dispensationalists have long contended.

Darby's pretrib and dispensational thoughts, says Huebner, were developed from the following factors:

1. "he saw from Isaiah 32 that there was a different dispensation coming...that *Israel and the Church were distinct*."[26]

2. "During his convalescence JND learned that he ought daily to expect his Lord's return."[27]

3. "In 1827 JND understood 'the ruin of the Church.'"[28]

4. Darby also was beginning to see a gap of time between the rapture and the second coming by 1827.[29]

5. Darby, himself, said in 1857 that he first started understanding things relating to the pre-trib Rapture "thirty years ago." "With that fixed point of reference, January 31, 1827," declares Huebner, we can see that Darby "had already understood those truths upon which the pre-tribulation rapture hinges."[30]

German author Max S. Weremchuk has produced a major new biography on Darby entitled *John Nelson Darby: A Biography*.[31] He agrees with Huebner's conclusions concerning the matter. "Having read MacPherson's book..." says Weremchuk, "I find it impossible to make a just comparison between what Miss MacDonald 'prophesied' and what Darby taught. It appears that the wish was the father of the idea."[32]

When reading Darby's earliest published essay on biblical prophecy (1829), it is clear that while it still has elements of historicism, it also reflects the fact that for Darby, the rapture was to be the church's focus and hope.[33] Even in this earliest of essays, Darby expounds upon the rapture as the church's hope.[34]

F. F. Bruce, who was part of the Brethren movement his entire life, but one who did not agree with the pre-trib rapture, commented on the validity of MacPherson's thesis:

> Where did he [Darby] get it? The reviewer's answer would be that it was in the air in the 1820s and 1830s among eager students of unfulfilled prophecy...direct dependence by Darby on Margaret Macdonald is unlikely.[35]

John Walvoord's assessment is likely close to the truth:

> any careful student of Darby soon discovers that he did not get his eschatological views from men, but rather from his doctrine of the church as the body of Christ, a concept no one claims was revealed supernaturally to Irving or Macdonald. Darby's views undoubtedly were gradually formed, but they were theologically and biblically based rather than derived from Irving's pre-Pentecostal group.[36]

Conclusion

Detractors of pretribulationism often want to say or imply that our view cannot be found in the pages of the Bible and must have come from a deviant source. Of course, we strongly object to such a notion, and have taken great pains over the years to show that the New Testament not only teaches pretribulationism, but holds it forth as our "blessed hope," a central focus of faith. It is also clear to me that when the church recognizes the four biblical foundations supporting pretribulationism (consistent literal interpretation, premillennialism, futurism, and a distinction between Israel and the church), that the biblical view of pretribulationism is recognized.

As believers in the imminent return of Christ, we need to let this precious truth and hope impact our daily lives as we anticipate our Lord's return. We, like those who have gone before us, need to realize that such a blessed hope should teach us that we should live chaste lives, giving ourselves to evangelism and world missions until the bride hears her groom shout, "come up here!" Church historian Kurt Aland characterizes the impact that belief in an imminent coming of our Lord (a key element of pretribulationism) had in the life of the early church:

> Up until the middle of the second century, and even later, Christians did not live in and for the present, but they lived in and for the future; and this was in such a way that the future flowed into the present, that future and present became one—a future which obviously stood under the sign of the Lord's presence. It was the confident expectation of the first generations that the end of the world was not only near, but that it had really already come. It was the definite conviction not only of Paul, but of all Christians of that time, that they themselves would experience the return of the Lord.[37]

Aland then contrasts it with the condition of the church in our own day and at another time when she is not motivated by the imminent return of Christ:

> At first, people looked at it as only a brief postponement, as the Shepherd of Hermas clearly expresses. But soon, as the end of the world did not occur, it was conceived of as a longer and longer period, until finally—this is today's situation—nothing but the thought of a postponement exists in people's consciousness. Hardly any longer is there the thought of the possibility of an imminent

Parousia. Today we live with the presumption—I would almost say *from* the presumption—that this world is going to continue; it dominates our consciousness. Practically, we no longer speak about a postponement, but only seldom does the idea of the end of the world and the Lord's return for judgment even occur to us; rather, it is pushed aside as annoying and disturbing—in contrast to the times when faith was alive. It is very characteristic that in ages when the church flourishes, the expectation of the end revives—we think of Luther; we think of Pietism. If we judge our present time by its expectation of the future, our judgment can only be a very negative one.

…Only when the imminent expectation of the Parousia diminishes, only when life is no longer lived in constant reference to the Last Day and no longer takes its direction from the Last Day was an organization of the church as an institution even possible or necessary. This took place in the second half of the second century.[38]

While Brethren theologian J.N. Darby may have restored the pretribulational rapture doctrine into the life of the church, he did not originate it. Pretribulationism is found first in the New Testament and at times throughout the history of the church. Oh that we would recapture for the church in our day this "blessed hope" which would help stir her to life with the mighty implications of such a truth. This cannot be accomplished when there are those who are disturbing the faith of some by the misuse of the history of the rapture. Maranatha!

▼ ▼ ▼

Cyclone of Apocalypse

Dave Breese

This Amazing Age

We live in one of the most remarkable ages in the history of the world. It is a notable time for many reasons, the first of which is the remarkable technological developments which make yesterday's cutting-edge technology decidedly crude by today's standards. The tide of progress continues to roll, bearing the promise of even more amazing developments for the days to come.

This is also a remarkable age because of the rise of iniquity in our time. By any standard in which wickedness can be statistically measured, the percentage of the increase of abominations is greater than ever before. It seems like every week someone invents a physical, moral, or spiritual absurdity that soon develops into a frightening cult. Add to this the staccato gunfire of drive-by shootings and the emergence of the drug culture and we have before us a complicated society. A great number of "answers" are being presented to solve the problems of our time. Unfortunately, none of them work, partly because God has made life deliberately precarious so that we should be forced to trust in Him. There will, therefore, never be a solution to the concerns of society short of the glorious return of Jesus Christ.

The third—and perhaps the greatest—reason that this is a remarkable age is because of divine forbearance. Many ask why God allows these things to happen, why He doesn't just kill the devil or pull every shred of iniquity out of the world. But perceptive readers know that the answer to that question is that God has made man a free moral agent with the power to choose. God refuses to interrupt that power lest man be turned into a mindless automaton with no power of choice.

In the midst of this rise of iniquity, God continues to show His forbearance. Nevertheless, the Scripture announces that man is storing up wrath for himself against the day of wrath and revelation of the righteous judgment of God, who will "render to each one according to his deeds" (Romans 2:5,6). So the fund of human iniquity and consequent divine judgment is building in a kind of cosmic bank. While this is the day of grace and God is not moving in devastating judgment, it is also the time that iniquity is being recorded in a book that will one day be opened. Do we see the opening of that book today? We think so and we certainly must allow for that possibility.

When we think about divine forbearance, we are stating in another way that this is the day of grace. It is not the day of judgment but rather a time in which this Scripture is being fulfilled: "God sent not His son into the world to condemn the world; but that the world through Him might be saved" (John 3:17). So the day of divine condemnation is not upon us now. Be sure, however, that it is sure to come. Because of His moral universe, nothing that is an exception to the perfect will of God will go unrecognized and unpunished.

Is there a day, an era, a period in history that will be particularly characterized by divine judgment? The answer is yes. It's called the Tribulation. Grace will end one day and after that will be the day of divine judgment.

The event that will punctuate that change is a remarkable time called "the rapture of the church," the time in which the Lord Himself will descend from heaven with a shout, taking His own—members of the body of Christ—to be with Him. That is the time when this relatively calm and peaceful generation will be subject to the cyclone of the oncoming Tribulation. At that time, man, having sown the wind, will reap the whirlwind. This very picture is given to us in Scripture. To face a cyclone is not a pleasant experience. God also gives us another picture which presents the surprising, over-whelming nature of the oncoming of the Tribulation.

In the early pages of Revelation (chapters 5 and 6) we see the picture that should not be forgotten. First of all, we see a discussion in heaven concerning the question "who is worthy to judge the world?" The answer, found in the Word of God, is "Worthy is the Lamb that was slain to receive power, and riches, and wisdom, and strength, and honor, and glory, and blessing" (Revelation 5:12). So Jesus Christ is accounted worthy to pass judgment upon the world.

The nature of the judgment becomes most pronounced with an account of the rise of four horsemen of the apocalypse: "And I saw, and behold a white horse: and he that sat on Him had a bow; and a crown was given unto him, and He went forth conquering, and to conquer" (Revelation 6:2).

Here we have a picture of the false Christ, the diminutive Christ. Here is presented to us the rise of Antichrist. Indeed, during the days of the great Tribulation, the Antichrist will organize world politics, world religion, and many other things to become master of the earth. His dreadful presence, empowered by Satan, will be felt strongly in the world. The Revelation picture continues, "And there went out another horse that was red: and power was given unto him that sat thereon to take peace from the earth and that they should kill one another" (Revelation 6:4).

So the rider on the red horse, denoting war and death, breaks upon the world as a frightening picture indeed. He steals peace from the earth and turns the world into a system of deadly anarchy.

> And when He had opened the third seal, I heard the third beast say, Come and see. And I beheld, and lo a black horse; and he that sat on him had a pair of balances in his hand. And I heard a voice in the midst of the four beasts say, A measure of wheat for a penny, and three measures of barley for a penny (Revelation 6:5,6).

The rider of the black horse signifies the rise of economic manipulation, indicated by the balances carried in the hand of this deadly rider. This economic manipulation worsens to the point that, finally, it will take a day's pay to buy a loaf of bread. What a picture! With this begins the Tribulation.

> And I looked, and behold a pale horse: and his name that sat upon him was Death, and Hell followed with him.

> And power was given unto them over the fourth part of
> the earth, to kill with sword, and with hunger, and with
> death, and with the beasts of the earth (verse 8).

This dreadful fourth rider has power over a quarter part of the
earth to produce death and hell on earth. It is difficult to imagine a
picture more grim than that set of judgments that will come upon
the world, initiating the days of the Tribulation. Here we have a
whirlwind with pain, suffering, and death inflicted on masses of
people. When we think about the direction that our present world
is taking, we can certainly learn why such a judgment will be
brought upon us.

This dreadful picture is followed by the account in Scripture of
this awful period of the Tribulation. If we want to know the
direction in which the world is going, that direction is ahead of us.
We are to anticipate not a utopia or a perfect world, but an era of
devastating divine judgment.

The Tribulation Trilogy: The Tribulation Begins!

If someone were to suggest that we are living in an amazing age,
would you agree? Certainly, all you have to do is compare the
morning papers with what the Bible says to discover a remarkable
consonance between the Word of God and what is happening.

But if these times are amazing, a time is coming that can only
be called "awesome." That day is so indescribable that we can
hardly put into words what the Bible says it will be like. Listen to
what Jesus said:

> For then shall be great tribulation, such as was not since
> the beginning of the world to this time, no, nor ever shall
> be. And except those days should be shortened, there
> should no flesh be saved; but for the elect's sake those
> days shall be shortened. Then if any man shall say unto
> you, Lo, here is Christ, or there; believe it not. For there
> shall arise false Christs, and false prophets, and shall
> show great signs and wonders, insomuch that, if it were
> possible, they shall deceive the very elect. Behold, I have
> told you before. Wherefore, if they shall say unto you,
> Behold, he is in the desert; go not forth: behold, he is in
> the secret chambers; believe it not. For as the lightning
> cometh out of the east, and shineth even unto the west,

so shall also the coming of the Son of man be. For wherever the carcass is, there will the eagles be gathered together (Matthew 24:21-28).

With these few verses, Jesus began His stunning answer to a question pressed upon Him by His disciples. They wanted Him to tell them about the future, and in particular, about the world at the time of His return. In this passage alone, the Lord spends two whole chapters describing what will happen during the days of the Tribulation, and then the Great Tribulation. When added to the many other revelations that the Bible offers about this awesome day, a breathtaking picture comes into focus. It will be the time of Jacob's trouble. It will be the time of the worst carnage and the most despicable situations and the most overwhelming impact of the judgment of God that the world will ever see.

If you think that God doesn't see, that He doesn't notice, that He won't judge the world one day, think again. The judgment of God during the Great Tribulation will be absolutely indescribable.

The Coming Tribulation

Notice what the Bible says about the beginning of the Tribulation, remembering that we live in the Day of Grace, not the Day of the Tribulation. The Day of the Tribulation will be a seven-year period that begins the Day of the Lord. The apostle Paul specifically wants the Church to understand that the Day of the Tribulation, the Day of the Lord, has not yet begun:

Now we beseech you, brethren, by the coming of our Lord Jesus Christ, and by our gathering together unto him, That ye be not soon shaken in mind, or be troubled, neither by spirit, nor by word, nor by letter as from us, as that the day of the Lord is present...for that day shall not come, except there come a falling away first, and that man of sin be revealed, the son of perdition (2 Thessalonians 2:1-3).

Then the apostle Paul gives us some characteristics that the world will attain that will give fair warning to a future generation (perhaps this generation) that the Tribulation is about to begin.

The Bible does not teach that man is going to bring to pass a perfect society. It does not teach that utopia will be fashioned by clever human beings. Rather, it teaches that we live in a deteriorating world. One day, that deterioration will get so bad that it will turn, literally, into the judgment of God. So to think that the world is getting better and better is to have a false view, false optimism about life. To be realistic, we must remember that the Bible says there is coming a day called the Tribulation.

Do we have that settled? I hope so. And I hope that we each have seen through the flimsy theories of the spiritualizers who say, "Well, this is the Tribulation, because problems happen to us," and all of that. Listen: The sum of all the problems people have endured from the beginning of time until now are almost nothing compared to what will happen during those days of the Tribulation!

Now, when we begin to think deeply and soberly about that, which we should, we start to ask, "How will we know that maybe we are getting close to it? If that day is indeed drawing near, what are the signs that could alert us?" That is exactly the question that was asked of Jesus by His disciples. Matthew 24 says:

> And as he sat upon the Mount of Olives, the disciples came unto him privately, saying, "Tell us, when shall these things be? And what shall be the sign of thy coming, and of the end of the age?" (Matthew 24:3).

The disciples had the opportunity for a private conversation with the Lord Jesus. He responded to their inquiry by telling them several things. First of all, He said that when we think about moving into the future, there are at least two conditions that we will face at all times. One, we will face the possibility of spiritual subversion, spiritual warfare.

> "For many shall come in my name, saying, I am Christ; and shall deceive many" (Matthew 24:5).

And the second perennial condition, He said, will be:

> "...ye shall hear of wars and rumors of wars; see that ye be not troubled..." Matthew 24:6.

Now, do we have spiritual warfare and physical warfare moving strongly across the world? Of course. More than 40 physical wars in our world are currently being fought, in addition to a great deal of spiritual warfare, contending with principalities and powers, something even more than physical forces. Perhaps you've been involved in this kind of contention. Perhaps you'd be one who would say very quickly, "We have experienced this type of spiritual warfare." It's going to happen. Look for satanic opposition. Look for events that will show that the devil is frustrated by your spiritual production. Be involved in spiritual warfare. Those conditions have always been with us, and will increase as we come to the end of the Church Age.

The Beginning of Sorrows

Then, almost like a road that leads into the Tribulation, there will come a specific period of time which Christ called "the beginning of sorrows." He said:

> For many shall come in my name, saying, I am Christ; and shall deceive many. And ye shall hear of wars and rumors of wars; see that ye be not troubled; for all these things must come to pass, but the end is not yet. For nation shall rise against nation, and kingdom against kingdom; and there shall be famines, and pestilences, and earthquakes, in various places. All these are the beginning of sorrows (Matthew 24:5-8).

The period of time called the *"beginning of sorrows"* is best described as that bridge of events that takes us out of the Church Age and into the Tribulation. That Beginning of Sorrows, Christ said, will have five characteristics:

> nation shall rise against nation, and kingdom against kingdom: and there shall be famines, and pestilences, and earthquakes.... (Matthew 24:7).

Do we see nation rising against nation (the word *"ethnos"* means racial animosity, racial warfare, among people)? Yes! At the root of almost every war going today, like those in Africa, and the Middle East, and Ireland, lies racial animosity.

And then kingdom (*"archon,"* rulers, political things) shall rise against kingdom. I've been mystified many times by the question, "Why do people fight with one another? What is the real reason someone packs a rifle or a knapsack and gets into an airplane and goes off to kill as many people as possible? To take over real estate? What is that? Why do people do this?" Well, James, of course, answered the question by saying:

> From where come wars and fightings among you? Come
> they not here, even of your lusts that war in your mem-
> bers? Ye lust, and have not; ye kill, and desire to have,
> and cannot obtain; ye fight and war, yet ye have not,
> because ye ask not. Ye ask, and receive not, because ye
> ask amiss, that ye may consume it upon your lusts
> (James 4:1-3).

People go to war because they don't know how to get God's provision for themselves and for their nation, so they decide to take it
from somebody else. It is totally irrational. Usually, thousands or
even millions die in the process. Millions died in World War II, tens
of thousands in recent wars. When it's all over, what do you have?
Perhaps a surrender, or a cease-fire, or economic sanctions, or a
blockade. But before too long, you're back to square one as if
nothing happened. It is totally silly, but it is done. Such wars will
increase, Jesus said, as we move toward the end of the age.

Famine, pestilence, and earthquakes were three more things.

Famine: people without enough to eat. By the way, in a world
like ours, if people are hungry, it isn't generally because there is no
food. It's because the supply of food has been interdicted by some
political intervention. Food is a weapon of warfare in today's abra-
sion between nations.

Pestilence: pestilence is sickness that is out of control. Daily on
television you hear of this: the AIDS epidemic, the Ebola virus,
alcoholism out of control, and other forms of disease. What do we
do about this? The world doesn't know.

Earthquakes will also characterize this time called the Beginning of Sorrows.

Do we live in the Tribulation now? No we don't. This is a different age. In this age, we have a set of principles that are really
quite astonishing, operating between God and man. God deals with
man by grace. The Bible says about the coming of Jesus Christ:

> For God sent not his Son into the world to condemn the
> world, but that the world through him might be saved
> (John 3:17).

Consequently, I'm sure you have shared the frustration of
many who have wondered why wicked people do not immediately
come under the judgment of God. It seems as if there is a strange,

almost illogical forbearance. "God ought to have stricken them dead," we think, but He has not.

Some who desire the vengeance of God, ask, "Why doesn't God do something? How come He hasn't come back and ended the terrible situation going on in the world today?" I think we must remind ourselves why we have such a terrible situation in the world at all! The Bible says about Adam and Eve:

> Wherefore, as by one man sin entered into the world, and death by sin, and so death passed upon all men, for all have sinned (Romans 5:12).

The reasons for the problems of the world are not lack of education, lack of knowledge, lack of economics, or the lack of clever ideas. They're not even crooked politicians. At the root of all the problems of the world is the fact that the world is corrupted by sin, and every person in it is a sinner.

> For all have sinned, and come short of the glory of God (Romans 3:23).

Sin not only exists, but it is progressive. The Bible says:

> sin, when it is finished, bringeth forth death (James 1:15).

The implication is that sin grows and grows, like a terrible contagion, which it is. Finally, people drop into total dissipation, so that they cannot resist the dreadful force of sin.

When the world goes past that point of no return, then it's time for the Tribulation. Until then, God speaks to the wickedest of people and says, *"By grace are ye saved. Come unto Me. I will give you rest."* You have every right from God to talk to Godless sinners and tell them, "Okay, Jesus came not *'to call the righteous, but the sinners to repentance'* (Matthew 9:13). And God deals with you by grace. So if you will believe the gospel, the message that *'Christ died for our sins according to the scriptures; And that he was buried, and that he rose again the third day according to the scriptures'* (1 Corinthians 15:3,4), you can be saved."

You can tell that to the wickedest of people, and God will save them, because believing in Jesus Christ is the one single prerequisite for salvation.

But there is coming a time when that will no longer be true. The Bible says that man is treasuring up

> wrath against the day of wrath and revelation of the righ-
> teous judgment of God, Who will render to every man
> according to his deeds (Romans 2:5,6).

So there is coming a day, subsequent to this, in which divine
vengeance is the way that God will deal with a lost mankind.
There's a lot of difference, then, between this day, and the day of
the coming Tribulation. What will be the line of demarcation? How
will we know that we have moved from the Day of Grace to the Day
of the Tribulation?

The Rapture of the Church

The answer is a tremendous event called the Rapture of the
Church.

> For the Lord himself shall descend from heaven with a
> shout, with the voice of the archangel, and with the
> trump of God; and the dead in Christ shall rise first;
> Then we who are alive and remain shall be caught up
> together with them in the clouds, to meet the Lord in the
> air, and so shall we ever be with the Lord. Wherefore,
> comfort one another with these words (1 Thessalonians
> 4:16-18).

You see, Jesus Christ is not simply coming at the end of the
Tribulation, which He will do. But before the Tribulation, at the end
of the Day of Grace, He is coming to take all believers out of this
world.

> Behold, I show you a mystery: We shall not all sleep, but
> we shall all be changed, In a moment, in the twinkling of
> an eye, at the last trump; for the trumpet shall sound,
> and the dead shall be raised incorruptible, and we shall
> be changed (1 Corinthians 15:51,52).

The Rapture ends the Day of Grace and begins the Day of the
Tribulation. So the Tribulation does not just gradually come upon
the world, as does the Beginning of Sorrows, but it will be marked
by an instantaneous and cataclysmic event—the removal of the
Church from Planet Earth. So remember, the Rapture is important
for many things, but its chief importance is that it marks the end of
the epoch of grace and the beginning of the dispensation of the

Tribulation. That fact is a source of comfort and help and solace for every Child of God.

The Fury Unleashed

When the Church is taken out of the world, the wrath of God will finally be unleashed. God will be perfectly free to work His judgment upon people. Why has God not sent His judgment upon the world already? Answer: the Church is here. We protect the world. Society is still around because we are still here. The presence of the Church in the world forestalls final judgment by God. God has spoken to every Christian, and reminded us:

> For God hath not appointed us to wrath but to obtain salvation by our Lord Jesus Christ (1 Thessalonians 5:9).

> We are "justified freely by his grace" (Romans 3:24).

> There is, therefore, now no condemnation to them who are in Christ Jesus...(Romans 8:1).

But watch for that moment when the Church is taken up, and the wrath of God falls upon a wicked world.

I have viewed the Tribulation as a sort of historic necessity, given the attitude of men today. People today, in their arrogance, say, "We don't need God. We can run the world." Atheism is prevalent in our world. Millions of people are atheists, and they say, "We are masters of our own destiny." The average academician is an atheist, and he's teaching our young people that there is no God, and they are autonomous, and they can manage their own destiny. There's even a theory going in the world of academia that evolution has brought us to the place where we can control our own evolution. Name the future that you want, and you've got it.

Well, God has a way of giving us the opportunity of having our own way, does He not? God, in the final analysis, has given men a free will. They can choose what they will believe in the life that they will live, but they've got to pay the consequences. Well, God speaks in a sense to the world that remains after the Rapture, and He says, "Now, you've been so smart, you've been so presumptuous, you say you can run the world, have it your way." Man's day then comes to pass, in which autonomous man is in charge of the world.

Will that be a good thing for the world? Will you be happy and overjoyed to see that scoundrel, who once served as your ward committeeman, now sitting on some throne somewhere as the master of Earth? Will you be ready to place your faith in the philosophy of your con-artist neighbor, who wrote a book on how to run the world under a religion of his own invention? How will it be, when the whole world is in violation of the statement of Scripture which says:

> There is a way that seemeth right unto a man, but the
> end thereof are the ways of death (Proverbs 16:25).

How will it be when the world is in violation of the statement of the Bible which says:

> For other foundation can no man lay than that which is
> laid, which is Jesus Christ (1 Corinthians 3:11).

How will it be, when there suddenly is only man to depend upon? I've listened to many a lecture on a university campus, and, of course, seen and heard many of the same things you have heard and seen on television, and I've been absolutely astonished at the arrogance of people who think they know it all. Their haughtiness approaches a strange insanity.

Take, for instance, one subject, among the dozens that we could refer to. About the matter of marriage, the Bible says:

> Therefore shall a man leave his father and his mother,
> and shall cleave unto his wife; and they shall be one flesh
> (Genesis 2:24).

That shall be a new entity, a marriage, man and woman. Well, they are now passing laws excusing and even advocating same-sex marriages. Now look: that's not just a clever sociological opinion. That's insanity. That's perversion. But a world that pretends to be sophisticated says, "Well, isn't that a nice new idea about what marriage ought to be?"

Now everybody in his right mind, who has not been subverted by becoming an expert on the subject, and who still thinks straight, knows this is insanity. But he is disquieted by the fact that it's these kind of people, with dislocated minds, who aspire to run the world in the days to come.

Are they going to master the world? The answer is no. They are going to bring to pass a day in the history of mankind so shameful, so frightening, so terrible, so fatal to masses of people that the Bible says:

> Except those days should be shortened, there should no flesh be saved... (Matthew 24:22).

You see, man, having treasured up mounds of sin, will come under the fury of an offended God. You ought to read the classic early American sermon, "Sinners in the Hands of an Angry God." Jonathan Edwards put it rather well. An angry God has planned a day of vengeance. It's called the Tribulation. Please miss it, by being a part of the Rapture of the Church.

The Day of Wrath

The Wrath of the Antichrist

One of the characters that will play a telling role during the days of the Tribulation is this monster called the Antichrist. Listen for just a moment to what the Bible says about him. Paul writes to the people at Thessalonica:

> Now we beseech you, brethren, by the coming of our Lord Jesus Christ, and by our gathering together unto him, That ye be not soon shaken in mind, or be troubled, neither by spirit, nor by word, nor by letter as from us, as that the day of the Lord is present (2 Thessalonians 2:1,2).

Remember, the Day of the Lord is that period of time that comes after the time of the Church Age, after the Day of Grace. Don't let anyone tell you that the Day of the Lord is going on now.

> Let no man deceive you by any means; for that day shall not come, except there come the falling away first, and that man of sin be revealed, the son of perdition (2 Thessalonians 2:3).

Do not let anyone tell you that this is the time of divine wrath. That day shall not come until there is a falling away first. The word is *"apostasia,"* meaning "to stand away from where you used to stand." It is translated "apostasy." The apostasy will first come, before the Day of the Lord comes.

Then, Paul says, will the *"man of sin be revealed, the son of perdition."* Here Paul introduces a character that will be of consequence during the days of the Tribulation. And what does he call him? The great benefactor of mankind? No. The *"man of sin"* will be revealed, the man whose fundamental nature is sin. He is the embodiment of sin.

> the son of perdition, Who opposeth and exalteth himself
> above all that is called God, or that is worshiped, so that
> he, as God, sitteth in the temple of God, showing himself
> that he is God (2 Thessalonians 2:3,4).

This vast, presumptuous impostor will present himself to the world as "the man with a plan." The revealing of that man will introduce the days of the Tribulation. I have an opinion. God tells Christians a lot of details about the man of sin that the world doesn't know about. And I do believe the implication is that we, if we are perceptive, will be able to recognize the oncoming of the man of sin. While the world does not suspect that he is the Antichrist, he will be obvious enough to perceptive Christians so we will be able to say, "There he is," and prepare for the almost immediate Rapture of the Church.

The wrath of the Antichrist, which contributes to the day of wrath, the Tribulation, is also described in many other locations in the Word of God. Revelation 6 gives us the picture of the horsemen of the Apocalypse. It says the rider of the first horse is on a white horse. He will present a great plan to the world. And this rider on the first horse goes forth *"conquering, and to conquer"* (Revelation 6:2).

This cruel monster of a person, the Antichrist, will make great gains until he becomes master of Earth. If you think that the Antichrist's rise is possible now, you are thinking correctly. So one source of wrath, during the *"day of wrath and revelation of the righteous judgment of God,"* will be the wrath of the Antichrist.

The Wrath of Nature

We want to suggest also that that will be a time in which nature itself turns against man. The rider of the fourth horse of the Apocalypse rides upon the pale horse, and the Bible says:

> And power was given unto them over the fourth part of
> the earth, to kill with sword, and with hunger, and with
> death, and with the beasts of the earth (Revelation 6:8).

The suggestion is that the beasts of the field, maybe even
domestic animals now, will be a part of that whole spirit of the devil
that turns against humanity. The very animals of which we are
familiar will be enrolled on the side of the devil.

Imagine a house cat that suddenly becomes very vicious, and
exercises some kind of killer instincts. Nature itself will seem to
rebel against mankind, engined by the power of Satan. There's
quite a chapter in the Book of Revelation that talks about one of the
impacts of nature against man. One of the characteristics, the Bible
says, of the final days, will be that nature joins this rebellion and
comes down upon man. Actually, Revelation 6 gives us quite a
description:

> And the heaven departed as a scroll when it is rolled
> together; and every mountain and island were moved out
> of their places. And the kings of the earth, and the great
> men, and the rich men, and the chief captains, and the
> mighty men, and every slave, and every free man, hid
> themselves in the dens and in the rocks of the moun-
> tains, And said to the mountains and rocks, Fall on us,
> and hide us from the face of him that sitteth on the
> throne, and from the wrath of the Lamb; For the great
> day of his wrath is come, and who shall be able to stand?
> (Revelation 6:14-17).

Earthquakes will characterize that time. But what I would have
us notice is, the wrath of the Lamb is so terrible and strikes such
fear in the lives of people that they consider an earthquake that
actually covers them up to be preferable to the wrath of Jesus
Christ.

Think of "gentle Jesus, meek and mild," being what characterized the days of His earthly ministry, but also remember something
else: In the day of His judgment, He is the one whose *"eyes were
like a flame of fire"* (Revelation 19:12). He is the one whose countenance is as the sun which shines in its strength. Yes, He is the one
who is going to be the ultimate Judge of mankind. So devastating
will that judgment be, that even the rebellion of nature will seem
comforting and sanguine by comparison to the wrath of Jesus

Christ, and facing the days of His wrath during those hours of the Great Tribulation.

So the wrath of God is going to be poured upon the world. In fact, the Bible uses those very illustrations. There will be the series of trumpet judgments, and then the bowl judgments in which God's judgment is poured upon the world in absolutely devastating fashion. One should tremble at this prospect of the wrath of God coming upon the world. But that's the way it will be, during the days of the Great Tribulation. Therefore, once again, do not think of the future of man as being a sweet and sanguine thing, but the future of man is to fall under the wrath of God.

Once again, we should remind ourselves that there is one interdiction of that wrath, one way to avoid the wrath of God. What is that?

> There is, therefore, now no condemnation to them who are in Christ Jesus, who walk not after the flesh, but after the Spirit (Romans 8:1).

If you are a Christian, having believed the gospel, you may have been ten times a sinner before that, but if you will believe in the finished work of Jesus on the cross, and trust Him as your personal Savior, you are not to fear the wrath to come. Why? Because you have a date with destiny. You're going to be taken home to heaven, to be with the Lord Jesus. When thinking of divine wrath, remember, it is Calvary that saves us from that awful eventuality. In times like these, that should not only bring reassurance, but motivate us to become articulate witnesses for Christ, so that we may help others escape the coming wrath.

The Wrath of Satan

We are also told that there will be the wrath of Satan himself. Listen to what the Scripture says:

> For the devil is come down unto you, having great wrath, because he knoweth that he hath but a short time (Revelation 12:12).

We have the statement in Scripture that the clock will be ticking against the devil and his plans. He will realize this. He doesn't have an omniscient or an omnipotent mind, but he'll be smart enough to realize that that clock is ticking! He'll come to the point where he realizes that if he's going to make that big play for the world and ever hope to capture everything, he'd better get with it now. So he comes forth with *"great wrath, because he knoweth that he hath but a short time."*

Now, because he is angry to the point of irrational fury against God, what does he do? Well, the Scripture indicates several things. First of all, he puts together and attempts to manage and run a world government. All of the nations of the world are enrolled in his cause. But I particularly am interested in the fact that he will have a set of sinews that he wants to hold that world government together, and that set of sinews is a world religion.

In fact, Revelation 13 tells about a religion that Satan organizes. That religion has several characteristics. It will be satanic. The Bible says it will cause people to worship the devil who is behind it all (Revelation 13:4). Secondly, it will be humanistic. They will worship the beast (Revelation 13:4). That's the Antichrist. The Antichrist will offer himself, wearing a white robe, and present a great plan as the religious modulator of all mankind. They will worship a human being. Thirdly, it will be universal. The Antichrist will organize a religion as big as the whole world. The whole world will be called upon to worship him (Revelation 13:8). Fourthly, it will be ecumenical. It will be the kind of theology that everyone can believe.

We all should be concerned about bad theology. Bad theology may only seem silly when it is first heard, but if given the chance to carry the day, it can quickly become fatal! Bad theology will characterize the religion of the Antichrist and the attempt of Satan to organize a world religion, because it will produce a "lowest common denominator" type of religion. People are getting together today, saying, "Unity and understanding and love—that should be the whole story of religion. That should be the basis on which we put together a world religious movement."

Any cooperative program must be characterized by good theology. That's hard to come by in today's world. But the world then will have a low common denominator, such as "God is love," or "life has a lot of possibilities," and all will be called upon to believe that and make it the sole basis of their worship.

Also, Revelation 13 says the religion of the Antichrist will be phenomenalistic. That means he will give you something that will satisfy the sight of your eyes. I've noticed something that concerns me, and that is, that so many religions, even Protestant religions, want to be so obvious, so phenomenalistic, and to have great visible and material things, such as vaulted buildings, for you to see.

Well, the Antichrist is going to use that big-time. He causes fire to come down from heaven in the sight of all the people who are worshiping him (Revelation 13:13). They look and say, "Wow. Look at that. He can control the forces of nature. He must be the man to believe in." This fire from heaven will be impressive.

Chapter 13 tells us that the prophet of the Antichrist will be empowered to work miracles, in order to give credibility to the things he is saying to people (Revelation 13:14). So his phenomenalistic religion will be hugely successful. Also, the Bible says that religion will be idolatrous. He will make an image. That image will be able to speak like a man (Revelation 13:15). That image will say, "Worship me. I represent to you the great man who runs the world." That idolatrous copy of the person and the personality of the Antichrist will be set up in the Temple. The setting up of that image gives us the last characteristic of that evil world religion, and that is, it will be terribly cruel. Whoever does not worship that image is put to death (Revelation 13:15).

The Wrath of God

Finally, the greatest wrath imaginable will be the very wrath of God. The Bible does not simply tell us that God is love. It also tells us:

> It is a fearful thing to fall into the hands of the living God (Hebrews 10:31).

It tells us that it is not a sanguine activity to just get along with God on any basis. But you must be His friend, or else His fearful wrath will come upon you. The time of the Great Tribulation, particularly the last 3½ years of it, is the time of divine wrath. Lesser forms of it impact upon the world during the first half of the Tribulation, but the last half of the Tribulation, that is the wrath of God! Those are the days of which Jesus was speaking when He said:

> Except those days should be shortened, there should no flesh be saved....(Matthew 24:22).

We've already read the passage from Revelation 6 where the kings of the Earth and the great rulers cry to the mountains and rocks, and say:

> Fall on us, and hide us from the face of him that sitteth
> on the throne, and from the wrath of the Lamb; For the
> great day of his wrath is come, and who shall be able to
> stand? (Revelation 6:16,17).

When will we learn that there is no sin that is forgotten? When will we learn that everything is recorded before God?

> All things are naked and opened unto the eyes of him
> with whom we have to do (Hebrews 4:13).

When will we learn that? Well, mankind will certainly learn it in the days of the Tribulation. We will certainly learn that nothing is forgotten by an omnipotent God. And when the wrath of God is come, the Bible asks the question, *"who shall be able to stand?"*

It's worth emphasizing at this point, that everything in the world that is not of God will be washed away one day. Every house, every car, every nation, every political system, every everything that is not centered in the Person of Jesus Christ, and does not admit that He is Lord—it all will be gone one day, and the wrath of God will be poured out on the world.

The Bible gives us the offer of being in the Lamb's book of Life. That is a marvelous act of love. But do you know what else it says? That very verse says:

> This is the second death. And whosoever was not found
> written in the book of life was cast into the lake of fire
> (Revelation 20:14,15).

I did not write that, but God did. There is not only a heaven to gain, but there is a hell to shun. And that hell is only shunned by believing in Jesus Christ, and trusting in Him as personal Savior. When the wrath of God comes upon the world, then it will be too late. Then, those who are lost will be lost forever. And those who are saved will be saved forever, when the great day of His wrath comes upon the world.

"When I recall that God is just," said Abraham Lincoln, *"I fear for my country."* The justice of God still reigns across the whole world. That justice will come upon the world in absolutely smashing fashion in that day of divine wrath.

So remember again. The Day of the Lord is not some happy circumstance for those who do not know the Lord. The Day of the

Lord is blood and fire and vapor and smoke, and divine wrath poured upon every soul of man that doeth evil, the Bible says.

People used to talk about how they looked forward to the Day of the Lord, back in the Old Testament, because that would make life easy. It would be a time of deliverance. Many of the prophets had to remind the people of Israel, "Don't you look forward to the Day of the Lord, because the Day of the Lord will overtake you as a thief in the night. The Day of the Lord will overtake you as judgment that you could not foresee, and the very things in which you have placed your affection will all be gone!"

Those same powerful words must be said to this generation. This generation must hear that there is coming a time of divine judgment upon the world that will embrace every man and every woman. It will cover everything done in the body. The Day of the Lord will be that exacting.

Therefore, what should we do? We should avoid the Day of the Lord and that great judgment by doing one primary thing: *"Believe on the Lord Jesus Christ, and thou shalt be saved"* (Acts 16:31).

> There is, therefore, now no condemnation to them who
> are in Christ Jesus.... (Romans 8:1).

One of the great stimulants to being a Christian, to having everlasting life, is to see the oncoming Day of the Lord. How do I avoid that day? I believe the gospel. I say that wonderful "Yes" to Jesus Christ. I trust Him as my personal Savior. When I do that, I am delivered from the wrath to come, and I have God's gift of life everlasting. Be sure that you are in that great plan by knowing Jesus as your very own.

Except Those Days Be Shortened...

Prophecy and the Promise

Remember again two verses that Christ tells us about the Tribulation:

> For then shall be great tribulation, such as was not since
> the beginning of the world to this time, no, nor ever shall
> be. And except those days should be shortened, there
> should no flesh be saved; but for the elect's sake those
> days shall be shortened (Matthew 24:21,22).

Now, when we read of all that's going to happen during the Tribulation, we get a little explanation as to why these days will have to be shortened. For instance, just before Christ said that, He said:

> When ye, therefore, shall see the abomination of desolation, spoken of by Daniel the prophet, stand in the holy place (whosoever readeth, let him understand), Then let them who are in Judea flee into the mountains; Let him who is on the housetop not come down to take anything out of his house; Neither let him who is in the field return back to take his clothes. And woe unto those who are with child, and to those who nurse children in those days! (Matthew 24:15-19).

This describes quite an eventful time in the history of the world which will be a terrible time of opposition to those who know the Lord. But in the midst of it, also, Jesus says:

> And because iniquity shall abound, the love of many shall grow cold. But he that shall endure to the end, the same shall be saved (Matthew 24:12,13).

This is a good time to drop a note that will be helpful in our thinking. Endure to the end. That's the basis of salvation during the days of the Tribulation. Christ is not talking about the Church, and the Gospel of the Grace of God, and preaching salvation by endurance for Christians. Rather, He is speaking about resolute, intrepid people who endure the opposition of the devil and the Antichrist and society during this day approaching the Tribulation. Then, when the Tribulation is done, having endured, they will be the first to go into the Kingdom. Notice also that Jesus said:

> And this gospel of the kingdom shall be preached in all the world for a witness unto all nations; and then shall the end come (Matthew 24:14).

We should then remember that the Gospel of the Kingdom and the Gospel of the Grace of God are two different things. The Gospel of the Kingdom says, *"the kingdom of heaven is at hand"* (Matthew 4:17). When one believes this, he becomes a part of the Kingdom of Heaven. He becomes a proselyte to the Jewish nation, the inheritors of the Kingdom of Heaven. He will be a part of that group that inherits the Earth forever. That's the result of believing the Gospel of the Kingdom.

But the Gospel of the Grace of God produces a different result: you become an inheritor of eternity.

> Whether Paul, or Apollos, or Cephas, or the world, or life, or death, or things present, or things to come; all are yours, And ye are Christ's, and Christ is God's (1 Corinthians 3:22,23).

Think of the Scripture that says: "He that spared not his own Son, but delivered him up for us all, how shall he not with him also freely give us all things?" (Romans 8:32).

That is what is inherited by the believing Christian in the world today. I beg of you, please learn the difference between the Body of Christ (which is the Church) and Israel (God's chosen people). The human destiny of Israel is to inherit the world, but the destiny of the Church is to inherit the universe. If we have that clear, we'll understand these chapters. So first of all, consider the prophecy that the days of the Tribulation will be shortened, and the promise by Jesus Christ that they will be.

The Anti-God Conspiracy

As the effect of the Tribulation grows, a thought will come into the mind of the Antichrist. He says, "I've got control of the United States, except for a few little pockets of resistance. I've got control of Canada. I've got total control of Latin America. I've got great control of Europe. I've got other nations of the world that are in my retinue. I can say almost without fear of contradiction that I control the world. Except, the contradiction is those irascible people in Israel. Those Jews that will not be converted to my cause, those Jews that profess to believe in Jehovah God—what am I going to do about this?"

And so he conspires to produce a tremendous action to destroy the nation of Israel and the city of Jerusalem. He raises a military contingent from all of the nations of the world. Then he calls that military contingent to the conquest of Israel, and particularly the siege of the city of Jerusalem. It's quite a picture. If you want to know what the Bible says about this, consider Psalm 2 and Zechariah chapters 10–12. It is described in Scripture as being mounted by the Antichrist to destroy the remembrance of God in the world. Psalm 2 says:

> Why do the nations rage, and the peoples imagine a vain thing? The kings of the earth set themselves, and the rulers take counsel together, against the Lord, and against his anointed, saying, Let us break their bands asunder, and cast away their cords from us. He who sitteth in the heavens shall laugh; the Lord shall have them in derision…Yet have I set my king upon my holy hill of Zion. I will declare the decree: The Lord hath said unto me, Thou are my Son; this day have I begotten thee (Psalm 2:1-4,6,7).

The second Psalm is a great source of reassurance that God is in control of every situation at every time. But He particularly resists this great conspiracy against the people of Israel mounted by the Antichrist, whereby the Antichrist hopes to destroy the final remembrance of God in the world.

It's an interesting thing to see, and it does, of course, give us insight into the heart of wicked men at all times. If a person does not know Christ as personal Savior, the chances are that he will move through successive periods of degeneration, until finally he becomes a reprobate.

By this time, the world has a reprobate on the throne, the Antichrist, the man of sin, the son of perdition. And it is this reprobate idea that says, "I can be the king of the world. I can be the lord of the universe, and nothing can stand in my way." "Oh, no you won't," says the Bible. "It won't happen."

I thought of this one time when I was in Germany. I was out at Berchtesgarten, and looked up at what they called the "Eagle's Nest" at the top of this great mountain. That was the small palace that Hitler built for himself. He went up there only a few times after he built that palace, and looked out. Because it's the highest mountain in the area, you can see almost forever, 360 degrees. I'm sure that he looked out those windows, and said, "I control it all. The 1,000 year Reich, it will be mine. Nothing can stand in my way. Those idiot people that couldn't resist, they have all been done away with. Now I will be the master of all I survey."

Being a megalomaniac, he told himself how he could be the master of the universe. Did he become the master of the Earth, the world's Antichrist of his day? He did not. God, who sits in the heavens, laughed at this posturing little moral and spiritual pygmy. And of course, the end of Hitler was not Berchtesgarten, and overcoming and overwhelming the world. The end of Hitler was a flaming corpse in the government building in Berlin, as Russian guns were going off in every direction, and the place was having the daylights burned out of it.

That was presumption. And there's coming a day when the very same thing is going to happen to the Antichrist. He will be destroyed. He will be discomfited. The end of his mission will be in the gigantic defeat of his forces in the environs of the city of Jerusalem.

How will the Antichrist be destroyed? You may be very surprised at the answer to that question, because you, if you are a Christian, are personally involved. The destruction of the Antichrist and the deliverance of the people of Israel will take place because of a very particular group of people, who accompany the Lord in the accomplishment of that tremendous mission.

The Final Invasion

Did you know that there will be an invasion of this Earth from heaven, an invasion not just of Jesus coming alone, but with a mighty, mighty army with Him at its head? I can tell you now that nothing will be able to stand in the path of that invasion. Listen to where this is described in Scripture, lest you suspect that I'm inventing these things as we go along.

> And I saw heaven opened and, behold, a white horse; and he that sat upon him was called Faithful and True, and in righteousness he doth judge and make war (Revelation 19:11).

So, we have a white horse coming from heaven. The name of the rider is *"Faithful and True,"* and who is that? Jesus Christ the faithful Witness, the true Witness. *"In righteousness he doth judge and make war."* Who is the final Judge of history? Christ is. Who has the responsibility of righting every wrong? Christ does. He judges and makes war.

> His eyes were like a flame of fire, and on his head were many crowns; and he had a name written, that no man knew, but he himself. And he was clothed with a vesture

> dipped in blood; and his name is called The Word of God. And the armies that were in heaven followed him upon white horses, clothed in fine linen, white and clean. And out of his mouth goeth a sharp sword, that with it he should smite the nations, and he shall rule them with a rod of iron; and he treadeth the winepress of the fierceness and wrath of Almighty God (Revelation 19:12-15).

Think of that description of the wrath of God, represented by the faithful and true Witness, who is Jesus Christ.

> And he hath on his vesture and on his thigh a name written, KING OF KINGS, AND LORD OF LORDS (Revelation 19:16).

There's no doubt that this is Jesus Christ. The picture that John sees is Jesus Christ coming back from heaven, riding on a white horse. Now, there's an element in this return that has interested me for a long time:

> And the armies that were in heaven followed him upon white horses, clothed in fine linen, white and clean (Revelation 19:14).

Since the beginning of the Tribulation, where will the Church have been? In heaven. The Church will have gone through an experience called the Judgment Seat of Christ, and the Marriage Supper of the Lamb. At that time, it is *"clothed in fine linen, white and clean."* But then the announcement is made to Christians, the Church in heaven with God, that there's still a very serious piece of unfinished business that needs to be done in the world. That is to depose the Antichrist, and to pronounce the judgment of God upon the devil. They will be instruments in bringing that to pass.

So Jesus Christ comes back, not alone, but He brings the Church with Him. How do we know this? Well, Jude quotes Enoch as saying about Jesus: "Behold, the Lord cometh with ten thousands of his saints" (Jude 14).

Now a saint is a Christian. There is no such thing as Saint Somebody, or Saint Somebody Else, as unique Christians who are awarded sainthood through the vote of some committee. Rather, all of us who have been saved by grace, given the gift of imputed righteousness, are *"hagios"*—the holy ones, by virtue of the holiness of

Jesus Christ. We are saints. These are saints returning with the Lord Jesus, the saints of God, *"ten thousands of his saints."*

By this time, the armies that surround the city of Jerusalem have every reason to expect that they will conquer the place. Yet, they look up, and see a massive military contingent coming back from heaven, sweeping down out of the skies, and taking them out of the way like nothing! They will be utterly destroyed. That army will be scattered all over the place. There will be millions who die. And there will be a special thing that is done with reference to the devil and the Antichrist. The Scripture says that the Antichrist will be thrown into the lake of fire (Revelation 19:20), and the devil will be thrown into the bottomless pit (Revelation 20:1-3). He is kept prisoner there for 1000 years.

You may say, "That's a lot of arrogant presumption. Christians returning with Jesus Christ? Who do you think you are to say that?" Well, the Scripture says that. In fact, did you know that the Bible says that the saints, that is, Christians, shall judge the world? Did you know that the Bible says that the saints shall judge angels (1 Corinthians 6:2-3)?

The devil, as you know, is an angel. Therefore, the devil will be a part of this group that is judged by you, and by me. There are people who have been done to death by the activity of Satan. But they will see him again, standing in judgment before them. We will be a part of that tribunal that makes right everything that is wrong in the world.

As a part of the army of Jesus Christ we will return to conquer. We will inherit the universe. The Bible says:

> Whether Paul, or Apollos, or Cephas, or the world, or life, or death, or things present, or things to come; all are yours, And ye are Christ's, and Christ is God's (1 Corinthians 3:22,23).

It's no small thing to be a Christian. It is to be an inheritor of the universe. But I'm sure that you get the picture. A mighty invasion, the saints come back, and the saints do away with those armies that are in the process of conquering the nation of Israel. Israel is delivered by the Church; it is the Christians who will deliver the nation of Israel.

The Tribulation Ends

Then, of course, finally, we must mention that the Tribulation ends. Remember Jesus said, "And except those days be shortened, there should no flesh be saved..." (Matthew 24:22).

Well, the days were ended. How? By this invasion from heaven, in which Christ comes again. We are the ones who shorten the dreadful days of the Great Tribulation. We are the ones who relieve the siege of the city of Jerusalem. And we are the ones who say to the world, "Here is the Lord; now you are free."

During the Tribulation, there will have been many who have accepted the Lord, and believe the Gospel of the Kingdom. And what will happen as a result of that faith for them? When the Tribulation ends by the return of Christ, He will come, and not only deliver the nation of Israel, but He will set up His Kingdom. Where will the capital of that Kingdom be? Jerusalem, the Holy City, called the *"city of the great King"* (Psalm 48:2) in the Old Testament. He will establish His throne there, and He will reign over the world for 1000 amazing and remarkable years.

We call this the Millennial Reign of Jesus Christ. During that Millennial Reign, there will be peace. No one will be able to make war. There will be prosperity. Everyone will have his own possessions. There will be the opportunity to confer with the great King. In fact, the people who do not come to do obeisance to the great King, will not receive rain where they are. And the world will know a marvelous array of riches for every person that will be beyond description.

Why do you suppose God does this? God does this because He wants the world to know the prosperity they could have known all of the time, had they elected to believe in, and to follow Jesus Christ. Why do we have problems in the world today? It's because man chose to live in sin, rather than to pursue the righteousness of God.

Well, the righteousness of God will be imposed upon the world during those Millennial days, and people will see the blessings, the benefits, the peace, the prosperity that could have been theirs all of the time. People of the nation of Israel will say, "Look at what we missed when we would not let Jesus Christ reign over us." And they said that, didn't they? *"We will not have this man to reign over us"* (Luke 19:14). Then Christ said, "All right, as a result of that, something will occur in your nation that will be terrible indeed."

> O Jerusalem, Jerusalem, thou that killest the prophets,
> and stonest them who are sent unto thee, how often
> would I have gathered thy children together, even as a
> hen gathereth her chickens under her wings and ye
> would not! Behold, your house is left unto you desolate
> (Matthew 23:37,38).

So the house of Israel has been desolate from then until now. But Israel will be restored. The hours of desolation will be gone. And Israel then will be the greatest nation in all of the world, with Christ her Messiah ruling her as King.

Now, the Millennial Reign will show to Israel the prosperity and blessing that it could have known for thousands of years preceding this. Israel, with a vengeance, will embrace her great King.

And then, of course, the coming of Christ to establish His Kingdom has tremendous implications for you and me, members of the Church which is His body. The universe will then belong to us! We will be thinking of plans and fantastic possibilities that reach out into the wideness of eternity. Where do you think you will serve? Will God send you to oversee operations on some distant planet? We can't even begin to imagine: "…Eye hath not seen, nor ear heard, neither have entered into the heart of man, the things which God hath prepared for them that love him" (1 Corinthians 2:9).

Out of the Tribulation will come fantastic results. One of those great results will be the Church arriving at the place of its true destiny, and becoming, with Jesus Christ, rulers of the universe. Look forward to that day. Don't let the tiny things of this present moment mean that much, because God will wipe away all tears. God will do away with all these frustrating things that plague us today. And we shall live in the light of God's glorified Son. It will be wonderful beyond description. Don't miss it.

Where Will You Be, During the Tribulation and Beyond?

God tells us these things in the Bible, because He wants you and me to know how wonderful salvation is. Have you accepted this salvation? Do you know Christ as your very own? If not, you can know Him today. "Believe on the Lord Jesus Christ, and thou shalt be saved," says the Word of God. In fact, right now you can accept

Him. Wouldn't you like to bow your head, and pray this prayer to ask God to make it real in your life?

> *"Heavenly Father, I know that I'm a sinner, and that Jesus died for my sins on the cross. And I want now to take Him as my personal Savior. Please come and live within my heart, and bring the assurance of salvation. I pray in Jesus' dear Name, Amen."*

If you have meaningfully said that prayer, the events of the Tribulation which the Bible describes, and which we have discussed, will pose no great threat to you. You will be watching them from the battlements of heaven, until you return with Jesus Christ and with the rest of us to deal deserving defeat to the devil.

▼   ▼   ▼

CHAPTER 14

Antichrist, Armageddon, and the Second Coming of Christ

John Walvoord

Christianity by its very nature is a faith based on the historic past, the present work of God in the world, and a predicted glorious future. The history of the world as recorded in Scripture makes clear that God is working in our world to carry out His eternal purposes. Central in this is the work of salvation through Jesus Christ, who in history died on the cross for our sins and rose again. The result of this is that people today, as they put their trust in Christ, experience a supernatural new birth and an experience of walking in fellowship with God. The Bible also, however, is a book about the future, and about one-fourth of the Bible was prophetic when it was written. It is obvious that God intended that we should know something about the future. Though prophecy leaves many questions unanswered, it is also clear that God has given us all the facts we need to prepare for the future that the Bible predicts will ultimately take place.

Unfortunately, a great deal of confusion exists in the interpretation of prophecy. Most of this is occasioned by the fact that people hesitate to accept prophecy as a literal prediction of future events.

If a prophecy which is written in plain language is not interpreted literally, it opens the door to dozens of views as people guess as to what it might possibly mean. The history of prophetic fulfillment, however, is that God fulfills prophecy literally and about half of the 1000 prophecies of the Bible have already been literally fulfilled. This gives us reason to believe that the predictions which have not yet been fulfilled will have a literal fulfillment rather than some other interpretation.

Of major importance in prediction is the fact that Christ is coming again just as literally as He came the first time. All the major orthodox doctrinal statements of Protestantism, Roman Catholicism, and Greek Orthodoxy contain a statement to the effect that Jesus Christ is coming again to judge the world. This is a literal prediction and was considered to be so in church history. Confusion has arisen, however, because having accepted this as literal, many try to interpret in a non-literal sense the prophecies of events preceding Christ's return, as well as the events that follow. If interpreted literally, however, the prophecies of Scripture yield a consistent and intelligent picture of what God is doing in the world and things will ultimately work out for His glory.

Central in predictions of the future is the second coming of Christ and the events that will precede it. The most important character of preceding events is often called the Antichrist, or the future world ruler who will dominate the world before Christ comes again. He will be "anti" in the sense of *against* Christ and *instead of* Christ.

Armageddon is an English translation of the mount of Megiddo, a geographic location in northern Israel which will be the center of the final great world war. Antichrist, Armageddon, and the Second Coming of Christ are central to the predictions which will bring the great climax of the world when Christ returns. According to Scripture, the events preceding the Second Coming are catastrophic and world-shaking and form a dramatic prelude to the return of Jesus Christ. If the return of Christ is near, it is entirely possible that our present generation of people will experience what the Bible predicts for the end time.

In approaching these tremendous themes, it is important to have in mind the chronological development of major events as they occur in the end time, beginning with what is called the rapture of the Church.

First the Rapture

The next major event in the prophetic sequence is the rapture of the Church. The term "rapture" refers to the catching up of the church and its removal from earth and arrival in heaven, a major event of the future described graphically in 1 Thessalonians 4:13-18. Though many confuse the issue by trying to link the rapture to the Second Coming of Christ, actually this is an entirely different event as the details of the prophecy make clear. The rapture occurs some years before, and the period between the rapture and the Second Coming is one of the most dramatic prophetic periods in the entire history of the world.

If every true believer is suddenly and instantaneously taken out of the world, it obviously will have an important impact on the world because many Christians are in prominent places and their sudden disappearance will call for an explanation. Many will follow a powerful delusion and believe some explanation of the rapture other than the departure of believers in Christ. However, many others will come to terms with the Lord and recognize that the rapture is a tremendous event.

Romans 11:25 specifically mentions how Israel's eyes will be opened. According to this verse, "I do not want you to be ignorant of this mystery, brothers, so that you may not be conceited: Israel has experienced a hardening in part until the full number of the Gentiles have come in." In other words, in the present age it is difficult for a Jew to understand that Christ is the Messiah, but when the rapture occurs, this blindness will be lifted. While many will persist in unbelief, no doubt a great number will be saved. Because Israel has representatives in almost every country and every language, once they are saved they will become the missionaries to the world with the truth of Christ's salvation much as they were in the first century after Pentecost.

The rapture will, however, mark the end of our present day of grace in which the Church, consisting largely of Gentiles, has flourished, and will begin the time of the day of the Lord when God deals directly with human sin and divine judgment. Instead of dealing with the church combining Israel and Gentiles, God will deal in a special way with both Gentiles and Israel as separate people with somewhat different destinies.

The Day of the Lord

According to 1 Thessalonians 5:1,2, when the rapture occurs it begins a new period of time called "the day of the Lord." This is a familiar term in the Old Testament and applies to any period of time during which God dealt in direct judgment of Israel. This is described, for instance, in Isaiah 13:1-22 and is characterized as "a cruel day, with wrath and fierce anger" (Isaiah 13:9). The book of Joel almost entirely addresses this subject; it speaks of many days of the Lord as, for instance, in chapter 1, when the invasion of locusts causes starvation. Many descriptions of the day of the Lord go beyond what occurred in the Old Testament, for instance, Joel 2:30–3:3 with the verses that follow describe this terrible time of judgment which is still in the future. The day of the Lord beginning at the rapture will continue even through the thousand-year reign of Christ when there still will be direct judgment of open sin against God, fulfilling the prediction that Christ will rule with an "iron scepter." There will be a display of "the fury of the wrath of God Almighty" (Revelation 19:15). The major events of the judgment of God, however, may not be immediately fulfilled after the rapture but will gradually increase as the period between the rapture and the Second Coming is fulfilled.

Revival of the Roman Empire

The book of Daniel provides a broad prediction of how God is going to deal with the Gentile world, beginning with Babylon in the time of Daniel about 600 B.C. and continuing through the empires that followed, that of Medo-Persia, Greece, and Rome. The predictions of Babylon, Medo-Persia, and Greece have all been literally fulfilled and are now part of the historic past. The Roman empire, however, which was in power at the time of the first coming of Christ, is still a continuing part of God's purpose. It continued for many centuries after Christ and then eventually disappeared, but, according to Scriptures, will be revived in the end times.

Daniel 7 pictures the four empires as ferocious beasts, with Babylon depicted as a lion, Medo-Persia as a bear, and Greece as a leopard. The fourth empire is described in different terminology in Daniel 7 as follows:

> After that, in my vision at night I looked, and there
> before me was a fourth beast—terrifying and frightening
> and very powerful. It had large iron teeth; it crushed and
> devoured its victims and trampled underfoot whatever
> was left. It was different from all the former beasts, and it
> had ten horns (Daniel 7:7).

The Roman empire literally fulfilled the picture of a beast with
great iron teeth, crushing and devouring everything before it. Its
well-disciplined soldiers went into countries that were unprepared
to fight. The soldiers then conquered the country, carried off the
able-bodied men as slaves, left a detachment of soldiers to collect
taxes, and moved on to the next country. As the greatest empire of
the past, it was ruthless in its destruction of whatever opposed it.
Most of Daniel 7:7 has already been fulfilled.

The final statement in verse 7, however, states, "it had ten
horns." Nothing in history corresponds to this, and Bible expositors
have been struggling for centuries to explain this prophecy that has
not been fulfilled.

But Daniel 7:24 reveals that "The ten horns are ten kings who
will come from this kingdom." How can this be explained in view of
the fact that the Roman empire today is non-existent? In order to
understand this period, one has to recognize that the Old Testament described the events leading up to the first coming of Christ,
but then many Scriptures skip from the first coming to the Second
Coming and omit reference to what we call the present age of grace.

This is brought out in Christ's message in Nazareth, recorded in
Luke 4:17-21,

> The scroll of the prophet Isaiah was handed to him.
> Unrolling it, he found the place where it is written: "The
> Spirit of the Lord is on me, because he has anointed me
> to preach the good news to the poor. He has sent me to
> proclaim freedom for the prisoners and recovery of sight
> for the blind, to release the oppressed, to proclaim the
> year of the Lord's favor." Then he rolled up the scroll,
> gave it back to the attendant and sat down. The eyes of
> everyone in the synagogue were fastened on him, and he
> began by saying to them, "Today this scripture is fulfilled
> in your hearing."

This is a significant illustration of the absolute accuracy of Scripture. Christ here is quoting from Isaiah 61:1-2, which predicts His coming to the world and ministry to those in need. He quotes Isaiah 61:2, including the expression, "to proclaim the year of the Lord's favor." He does not quote the last part of the verse, "and the day of vengeance of our God." The point is that His first coming proclaimed the Lord's favor but the last part of the verse deals with His Second Coming and judgment on the world. Here, as in many other cases, the present age is not in view. While Old Testament Scriptures deal with the time of judgment preceding the Second Coming, they do not anticipate that the Roman empire will go out of existence for many centuries, only to be revived in the end time in the form of these ten kingdoms.

Scripture does not indicate exactly when this will happen, but as soon as the rapture occurs, the ten kingdoms are in the background and apparently the formation of the ten-kings power bloc will come together either just before or just after the rapture. The fact that the European Union is friendly today, geopolitically speaking—that is, the major players are not at odds with each other—provides fertile soil for producing a united Europe, which would fulfill, at least in part, this prophecy.

What is happening in Europe is especially prophetically signifi-cant. For centuries the major countries of Europe, particularly Great Britain, France, and Germany have been engaged in war. Usually when one war ends, regardless of who wins, the countries immediately begin to prepare for the next war. This has been going on for several hundred years. Suddenly, after World War II, this pro-cess stopped because all these countries now have the atomic bomb and the capacity to completely destroy the other countries. Accord-ingly, engaging in warfare would not help any of the countries involved—even if they won—because they would suffer terrible losses in the process. Facing this realistically, the countries of Europe decided to form an economic union and they established the Common Market. Having established friendly relationships with each other on an economical basis, many have for years predicted the coming together of a United States of Europe. Steps in that direction—including implementing a common currency—have already taken place. Accordingly, the situation described at the rapture of ten nations banded together is something that could occur at anytime and is strategic evidence that the rapture of the church could be near.

The Rise of the Antichrist

When false teachers taught the Thessalonian believers that they were already in the day of the Lord, Paul had to correct this. He argued in 2 Thessalonians 2 that they were not in the day of the Lord period after the rapture because the man of lawlessness had not appeared. 2 Thessalonians 2:1-3 states:

> Concerning the coming of our Lord Jesus Christ and our being gathered to him, we ask you, brothers, not to become easily unsettled or alarmed by some prophecy, report or letter supposed to have come from us, saying that the day of the Lord has already come. Don't let anyone deceive you in any way, for that day will not come until the rebellion occurs and the man of lawlessness is revealed, the man doomed to destruction.

His work is further described in 2 Thessalonians 2:4: "He will oppose and will exalt himself over everything that is called God or is worshiped, so that he sets himself up in God's temple, proclaiming himself to be God."

The "man of lawlessness" is another reference to the one who is also called the Antichrist. The word "antichrist" is mentioned four times in the Scriptures (1 John 2:18,22; 4:3; 2 John 7). As used by John, it applies to anyone who is opposed to Christ and is a false leader. The term has been used to describe the end-time ruler because his activities are so obviously anti-Christ, and he is Satan's substitute for Jesus Christ as King of Kings, Lord of Lords, and God. However, the book of Revelation and other passages of Scripture outside of the Johannine epistles never used the term.

The Antichrist appears on the scene as the conqueror of the ten-nation revival of the Roman empire. According to Daniel 7:8, a little horn comes up among the ten horns and uproots three of them, which signifies that he has conquered three of the ten countries. From there on, although Scriptures do not explain the reasons, he is regarded as the ruler of all ten nations. In other words, he takes over as the dictator of the revived Roman empire. From this position he rises to power gradually until finally he becomes the world ruler of scriptural prophecy.

2 Thessalonians 2:1-4 offers remarkable evidence that the rapture of the church occurs before the end-time prophecy. Paul is demonstrating that they are not in the day of the Lord as false teachers have taught them, because the man of lawlessness has not appeared. When will the man of lawlessness appear?

His full revelation comes in the middle of this last seven years of end-time prophecy when he claims to be God. But he will be revealed earlier than that, when he makes the covenant of Daniel 9:27 for seven years leading up to the second coming of Christ. In order to have this position of power, he has to be the one who conquers the Roman empire and becomes the head of the ten countries. This must occur, therefore, more than seven years before the Second Coming. If he has to appear before the day of the Lord can begin, it should be obvious that the day of the Lord will begin more than seven years before the Second Coming. This automatically disposes of counter-opinions which put the rapture at the Second Coming or during the Great Tribulation or at the beginning of the Great Tribulation or the beginning of the seven years, for the man of lawlessness will be revealed more than seven years before the Second Coming. Accordingly, the rise of the Roman empire will become a very important factor in determining how soon the rapture of the church may take place.

One of the great passages of prophecy in the Old Testament is found in Daniel 9:24-27, which predicts that there will be seven times seventy years of Israel's prophetic future. While it is very complicated and various theories have arisen about it, if it has to be fulfilled literally, the last seven years are still future. The first 69 sevens, or 483 years, were fulfilled just before the crucifixion of Christ when the Messiah was cut off. But the last seven years has never been fulfilled, and it will become an important element of the chronology of the end times.

In Daniel's revelation of the seventy sevens, or 490 years of Israel's prophetic future, a ruler will come on the scene during the last seven years that lead up to the Second Coming of Christ. He is described in Daniel 9:26 as "the ruler who will come." The same verse refers to the people of the ruler who destroyed the city in 70 A.D. But the ruler is a future ruler who at the end time does not destroy the city but does take control. According to verse 27 he will confirm a covenant with many for one seven. These are the last seven years of Israel's future. The covenant that the ruler imposes on Israel is a covenant of peace attempting to solve the problem of Israel in relation to the world around her.

The first half of the seven years is marked off as a special time. There is some debate among scholars as to what events take place, but a probable solution is that it will introduce a temporary time of peace for Israel during which Israel can relax from its present military preparedness and rely upon this ruler to defend them. However, this will be interrupted, according to Ezekiel 38 and 39, by an invasion from the north of six countries. All of these countries are named except the country from the far north, which is probably one or more of the states formerly in the Soviet Union. Because they are largely Moslems, they would love to attack Israel, and this is in prospect for this period. As Ezekiel 38 and 39 make clear, however, God intervenes and by a series of catastrophes wipes out the invaders.

The attack is an attempt to weaken the power of the ruler of the ten nations because he is Israel's protector. But when the invaders are defeated, their bodies scattered throughout the land, it tends to enhance the power of the ruler of the ten nations and makes it possible for him to extend his power over the whole world in the middle of the last seven years. This is anticipated in Daniel 9:27: "In the middle of the 'seven' he will put an end to sacrifice and offering." Apparently he will take over as ruler over the entire world. Revelation 13:5 confirms that his rule will extend for 42 months and will climax with the second coming of Christ.

This period of three and a half years which is the climax of the preceding events to the Second Coming is described in Scripture as the Great Tribulation. Daniel 12:1 describes it as "a time of distress such as has not happened from the beginning of nations until then." It is predicted that resurrections will follow of both the righteous and wicked. Daniel, like many Old Testament prophets, does not describe the period between the two comings of Christ. Actually, according to Revelation 20:11-15, the wicked will not be resurrected until after the millennial kingdom.

When Christ answered His disciples concerning the end times, He described the same period in Matthew 24:21, "For then there will be great distress unequal from the beginning of the world until now—and never to be equaled again." This is a specific period of time beginning three and a half years before the Second Advent and concluding with the second coming of Christ. The common tendency to blur this with the natural troubles which have beset the human race from the beginning is not justified by the description which the Scriptures give marking this period as a special time of limited duration.

The period of this end time is pictured in Revelation 6:1–19:10. Many expositors think this extends over the entire seven-year period, but others find that it is primarily fulfilled in the Great Tribulation of the last three-and-a-half years. The details given in the book of Revelation concerning the Great Tribulation are unfolded first in the seven-sealed manuscript which describes terrible judgments on the world, including the destruction of one-fourth of the world's population (Revelation 6:7,8). This is followed by another series of seven called trumpets. As these are sounded, devastating judgments will descend over the world, a period described in Revelation 9:14 as "the great tribulation." In the sixth trumpet, a third of the world and its population will be destroyed (Revelation 9:15). This is followed by a series of seven bowls of judgments which will be poured out on the world. In Revelation 16, these are devastating judgments on the entire world. The final one will be an earthquake and the graphic portrayal describes the total destruction of much of the world and its population. Revelation 16:18-21 records this devastating situation that will destroy all the nations of the world and most of the people who are surviving to that point:

> Then there came flashes of lightning, rumblings, peals of thunder and a severe earthquake. No earthquake like it has ever occurred since man has been on earth, so tremendous was the quake. The great city split into three parts, and the cities of the nations collapsed. God remembered Babylon the Great and gave her the cup filled with the wine of the fury of his wrath. Every island fled away and the mountains could not be found. From the sky huge hailstones of about a hundred pounds each fell upon men. And they cursed God on account of the plague of hail, because the plague was so terrible.

Armageddon, in connection with the final judgments of Revelation 16, is mentioned in verse 16, "Then they gathered the kings together to the place that in Hebrew is called Armageddon." Armageddon is the English equivalent of the mount of Megiddo, a geographic location in northern Israel located not too far from the

Mediterranean Sea. It is not a very high mountain, perhaps 800 feet in elevation. To the east of this, however, is the broad valley that extends through some 14 miles and extends to several other valleys, which is described in Revelation 16:16 as the central marshaling place for the final great war that will be underway in the months just before the Second Coming.

Actually, if all the Scriptures concerning end time events are put together, the war will extend all the way up and down the nation Israel for some 200 miles from the Mediterranean Sea all the way to the Euphrates River and millions of men will be engaged in mortal conflict. On the very day of the Lord's return, there will be house-to-house fighting in Jerusalem.

According to Zechariah 14:1-4, the nations will be fighting for power:

> A day of the Lord is coming when your plunder will be divided among you. I will gather all the nations to Jerusalem to fight against it; the city will be captured, the houses ransacked, and the women raped. Half of the city will go into exile, but the rest of the people will not be taken from the city. Then the Lord will go out and fight against those nations, as he fights in the day of battle. On that day, his feet will stand on the Mount of Olives, east of Jerusalem, and the Mount of Olives will be split in two from east to west, forming a great valley, with half of the mountain moving north and half moving south.

When the nations see the glory in the heavens which will be the sign of the Second Coming, they will forget their differences and unite to fight the army from heaven. This is why Satan will have arranged for them to be there. The war will be interrupted and brought to an abrupt end by the Second Coming of Christ.

The Second Coming of Christ

As the Scriptures have abundantly demonstrated, catastrophic judgments will lead up to the second coming of Christ before this event happens. The coming of Christ brings to a dramatic close these events as described in Revelation 19:11-16:

> I saw heaven standing open and there before me was a white horse, whose rider is called Faithful and True.

With justice he judges and makes war. His eyes are like blazing fire, and on his head are many crowns. He has a name written on him that no one knows but he himself. He is dressed in a robe dipped in blood, and his name is the Word of God. The armies of heaven were following him, riding on white horses and dressed in fine linen, white and clean. Out of his mouth comes a sharp sword with which to strike down the nations. "He will rule them with an iron scepter." He treads the winepress of the fury of the wrath of God Almighty. On his robe and on his thigh he has this name written: KING OF KINGS AND LORD OF LORDS.

When the heavens break open with the glory of Christ and He begins His descent to the world to take over, it is clear that this will be a time of judgment on the world. Earlier in chapter 19, the wedding feast is mentioned, referring to the fellowship of Christ and the church in heaven. The Scriptures record that there will be a terrible feast at this time, the slaughter of the great armies gathered there in the Holy Land, which will be destroyed by Christ. In the process, the world ruler called the beast and the false prophet who has supported him will be captured, and they will be cast alive into the fiery lake of burning sulfur (Revelation 19:20), the final place of judgment for the demon world and for the unsaved.

According to Matthew 25:41, the lake of fire was prepared for the devil and his angels but it also will be the place of final judgment for those who follow Satan instead of believing in Christ. Scriptures distinguish between the *lake of fire* and *sheol* in the Old Testament and *hades* in the New Testament; these terms are used sometimes to describe the grave itself and other times the state of people after the grave. *Sheol* and *hades* are viewed, however, as temporary. In the final resurrection of the wicked, recorded in Revelation 20:11-15, *hades* will be emptied and those in hades at that time who are unsaved will be cast into the lake of fire, their permanent place of judgment. As far as the Scriptures reveal, the beast and the false prophet will be the first to be cast alive into the lake of fire. It is most significant, however, that at the end of the thousand years when the devil is also cast into the lake of fire, the beast and the false prophet will still be there and "They will be tormented day and night for ever and ever" (Revelation 20:10). The beast and the false prophet will not be destroyed by the lake of fire;

they are predicted to receive everlasting punishment along with that of the devil.

The Second Coming itself will dramatically demonstrate the power of Christ. The heavens will be ablaze with the glory of God compared to lightning shining from east to west as described in Matthew 24:27. The heavens will be filled with the glory of Christ as He returns to earth accompanied by all the saints and angels who are in heaven. The church will be included in that dramatic procession, having been raptured earlier and taken to heaven before the tribulation. Now they will return to be with Christ forever.

It will be the most dramatic moment in the entire history of the world as Christ manifests His true authority which was hidden when He first came, but which will now be displayed to the entire world. As mentioned previously, according to Zechariah 14, He will return to the Mount of Olives from which He ascended, and when He does, it will be split in two from east to west, forming a great valley down to the Jordan River (Zechariah 14:4). Apparently the whole topography of the Holy Land will be changed and Jerusalem will be elevated, as indicated in Zechariah 14:10, and other changes will take place in the Holy Land. The judgment, which will begin with the casting of the world ruler and the false prophet into the lake of fire, will continue as all the armies that are gathered against Christ will be easily put to death along with their beasts (Revelation 19:17-21). Other judgments will follow, including the judgment and binding of Satan (Revelation 20:1-3).

Matthew 25:31-46 predicts the judgment of the nations of the Gentiles still living in the world. The sheep and the goats represent the saved and the lost and the separation will take place several days after the Second Coming. This should support the concept that there will be no rapture or resurrection on the day of the Second Coming itself. The resurrection of those who died during the Tribulation period who are mentioned in Revelation 20:4-6 also occurs after the Second Coming. The sheep-goat separation of Matthew 25 comes after the Second Coming, and if there had been a rapture, obviously the separation would have already taken place.

Clearly mentioned six times in Revelation 20, a millennial kingdom follows in which Christ will reign on earth and bring justice and righteousness to bear upon the world situation. The climax will come at the end of the millennium with the new heaven, new earth and New Jerusalem, and the beginning of eternity.

It would be impossible for any writer of fiction to describe a scene of greater significance or more sweeping events affecting the entire world than the period after the rapture of the Church. While the present world may seem to be one in which God is not dealing with sin and correcting the evil that does exist, it is clearly portrayed that in God's time and in God's way, every sinner will be brought into judgment. The only way of escape from the righteous judgment of God will be the grace of God provided in salvation through Jesus Christ. If there ever was a generation that should be considering the claims of Christ and the desperate need of every soul to be saved and forgiven by faith in Christ, it is the generation that is now living that may soon be plunged into these end-time series of events after the rapture takes place.

▼   ▼   ▼

Peace, Be Still

William T. James

Planet earth was near cataclysm. The atomic structure of all creation strained to explode while the One for whom and by whom all things were created descended the Mount of Olives riding on the donkey.

Apparently, all that kept the building blocks of the universe from flying apart were the hosannas of praise shouted by the people who spread the palm fronds before Jesus.

The indignant Pharisees, seeing and hearing the worshipful adulation, implored Jesus to tell them to stop their praising. The Lord knew their jealous, sin-blackened hearts—that they, in their unbelief, considered the praise blasphemy. As He always did, Jesus spoke truth that cut away all superfluous side issues.

> I tell you the truth that, if these should hold their peace,
> the stones would immediately cry out (Luke 19:40).

The King of kings moved toward the holiest of all places on earth to present himself as Israel's Messiah and King. In a short time, those people would reject Him and demand that He be put to death by the cruelest method of execution known in that day. When the praises turned to cursings and the Lamb of God was slain in the once and for all sacrificial act that provides redemption for lost mankind, the skies darkened to midnight black at midday. The earth convulsed mightily and split apart. Corpses came out of their graves and walked the streets of Jerusalem. Nature itself must have screamed in agony when the Son of God and God the Father separated because of humanity's sin, which Christ became in that awful moment the Trinity was split.

Before Jesus voluntarily gave up His spirit to death, He said, *"Father, forgive them; for they know not what they do"* (Luke 23:34). Could Jesus have been asking the Father to restrain the geophysical elements from taking vengeance on that generation of rebellious earth dwellers?

All of creation no doubt spasmed with the pain the Father, Son, and Holy Spirit experienced. Legions of angels leaned forward, ready for battle if the Son of God had called. But Jesus' words reflected only compliance with the will of His Father in heaven: *"It is finished"* (John 19:30). And the upheaving geophysical universe settled when the veil in the Holy of Holies ripped from top to bottom.

Neopaganism and Its Consequences

Practically every indicator within the scope of human affairs points to restlessness, turmoil, and to wars and rumors of wars. Jesus' words as recorded in Matthew 24:5-8 could easily be applied to our times. The Lord said in that account, "For many shall come in my name, saying, I am Christ; and shall deceive many. And ye shall hear of wars and rumors of wars; see that ye be not troubled; for all these things must come to pass, but the end is not yet. For nation shall rise against nation, and kingdom against kingdom; and there shall be famines, and pestilences, and earthquakes, in various places. All these are the beginning of sorrows."

Although He was referring specifically to the Tribulation period, that seven-year period of apocalypse which will conclude with His second advent at the time of Armageddon, He also said in Luke 21:28 that "when these things begin to come to pass" we are to "look up, and lift up [our] heads; for [our] redemption draweth near." Jesus said that these indicators would be "the beginning of sorrows" or birth pangs.

The Lord warned that these symptoms of the end time will increase in frequency and intensity as the time of His return approaches like the labor contractions a woman suffers when the birth of her child nears. His words seemed to emphasize that man's rebelliousness and wickedness will again be at levels like in the days of Noah and the days of Lot (Luke 17: 26-30). Mankind's incorrigible rebelliousness will bring God's wrath.

Certainly, this generation of earth dwellers cries out for *peace*. Most conspicuous in this regard is the global outcry for a cessation of hostilities between Israel and its Palestinian neighbors. The hue and cry for peace, however, can be heard from every quarter on earth. From nations in conflict with each other, from ethnic groups warring one against another, from communities experiencing ever-increasing violence, from families in turmoil, from individuals who murder and maim each other, every hour of every day, they cry *peace, peace*! when there is no peace (Jeremiah 6:14, 8:11).

This generation seeks to calm the rage, but does so through anything and everything but the one and only source of true peace, Jesus Christ. The poorest among our number seek comfort, solace, and sustenance from governmental bureaucracies. The middle class seeks to keep noses above the flood of taxes those bureaucracies issue forth. Yet at the same time, the middle class gropes for temporal pleasures, entertainment, and material goods that might provide moments of peace that never seem to come. The wealthy and elite grasp for satisfaction they perceive as attainable through the pursuit of money, power, and self-aggrandizement. Idolatry of every sort rules throughout every strata of every culture and society today. God is pushed farther and farther from the thoughts of men who seek only to praise their gods of this age.

Fires of discontent are the result of man's refusal to give God the praise and worship He alone deserves. That fire will soon produce seven years of hell on earth. As Jesus warned the Pharisees, "the very stones will cry out."

The Stones Begin to Shout!

When the 22-pound Mars rover named Sojourner began its work shortly after landing on that planet July 4, 1997, scientists began proclaiming almost with one voice that the geological pattern was telling the story of a catastrophic planetary flood. Many of these same scientists could discern and exclaim loudly that a planetary flood had occurred millions of years ago on the planet Mars 119 million miles distant. They cannot, however, bring themselves to admit that the catastrophic global flood reported in God's Word ever occurred on earth. They deny the flood of Noah's day even though the geological record attests to the truth of the biblical account and is readily observable all around them on their own planet.

The stones cry out from 119 million miles away, making manifest the foolishness of those who profess themselves to be wise. The so-called *scientific community* can claim with absolute authority that microbial life once existed on Mars because of formations they think they see inside a meteor fragment they speculate came from Mars. They can say with certainty that man evolved out of primordial soup without producing a single link of proof that one specie has ever made the evolutionary leap to become another specie. Yet when millions upon millions of sealife fossils (seashells, etc.), are found on the highest peaks on earth, the so-called empirical method is thrown out the door. Rather than admit that these mountain ranges were once under water due to a great flood that covered the whole earth, they choose to believe and put forth the unsubstantiated claim that the mountains have been somehow rising for many millions of years from a starting point below sea level.

Human beings lie because their foolish hearts are darkened. God's marvelously made creation cries out the truth where mankind fails to do so. The apostle Paul, writing under inspiration of God's Holy Spirit, spoke to the heart of man's disbelief and its consequences.

> For the wrath of God is revealed from heaven against all ungodliness and unrighteousness of men, who hold the truth in unrighteousness, Because that which may be known of God is manifest in them; for God hath shown it unto them. For the invisible things of him from the creation of the world are clearly seen, being understood by the things that are made, even His eternal power and Godhead, so that they are without excuse; Because, when they knew God, they glorified him not as God, neither were thankful, but became vain in their imaginations, and their foolish heart was darkened. Professing themselves to be wise, they became fools, And changed the glory of the uncorruptible God into an image made like to corruptible man, and to birds, and four-footed beasts, and creeping things. Wherefore, God also gave

them up to uncleanness through the lusts of their own hearts, to dishonor their own bodies between themselves, Who exchanged the truth of God for a lie, and worshiped and served the creature more than the Creator, who is blessed forever. Amen (Romans 1:18-25).

Our generation voraciously devours the evolutionary dogma with the same gusto the ancients hungered for their self-fashioned beastly gods. Idolaters of today differ from ancient idolaters only in that neopagans worship gods that are a bit more interactive. They excitedly praise Hollywood entertainers and shout their adoration to sports stars and sports teams from pews at the temple-like stadiums and arenas and through television altars in their homes. They fashion their objects of worship into shiny automobiles, pleasure boats, and other usable forms. Like the pagans of old, they give their hearts, time, and money to their idols which they name after birds, four-footed beasts, and creeping things.

Evolution has become the foundational undergirdings upon which humanistic agendas are built. God has been kicked out of our classrooms and our courtrooms. He has been replaced by relativism, which makes the individual a god unto himself.

Evolution says that all began in chaos but is getting better and better as the human animal progresses toward becoming the ultimate man. But in actuality, evolution *creates* chaos because it puts forward "values clarification" that says everyone has a right to know and do what is right in his own eyes. The ultimately evolved man will be the incorrigibly wicked and rebellious people of the apocalypse. The Antichrist will personify the lies wrapped up in the false faith so-called scientific minds of today term *evolution*.

Total chaos, the opposite of true peace, is unregenerate mankind's destiny. America's decline since the 1960's Supreme Court decisions to legalize abortion and outlaw God in classrooms and courtrooms and many other public places proves that chaos results from a godless, humanistic system.

Perilous Times in America

Often, in discussions involving the state of the world, it is said that societies such as those in Communist China, Cambodia, Laos, Vietnam, or the various brutal regimes in Africa have no regard for human life. Such accusations imply that America and western

Europe are the truly civilized societies and cultures of planet Earth. However, with more than one million children legally murdered while still in their mothers' wombs every year in the United States, the assertion that America honors life more than do the barbarous nations of Asia or Africa is hypocrisy. The hypocrisy is magnified many times over when we consider that this nation has had God's grace shed upon it in ways no other nation, with the possible exception of Israel, has ever experienced.

Darkness has not come upon America because of wicked regimes suppressing gospel truth. Darkness is engulfing us because we, as a people, are turning our backs on God. We are deliberately and methodically turning off God's light so that we can do our self-willed, sinful deeds under cover of darkness.

American money has inscribed on it *In God We Trust*. Today, it would be more accurate to say that our slogan is *"In money we trust."*

With the Dow Jones stock market figure over the 8000 mark as of the time of this writing, we live under the euphoric bubble of economic prosperity that causes national irrationality. While leaders at the highest levels of the United States government are examined in congressional hearings for alleged influence peddling to communist China and other avowed enemies, polls show that same leadership enjoys high approval ratings among Americans.

National news media, unlike during the Watergate hearings three decades ago, push information about the influence peddling to the back pages and middle of broadcasts when indeed they cover them at all.

The troubling statement *"character doesn't matter"* seems to sum up the majority of opinion in America so long as the economy continues to give us the good times we want as an entertainment, recreation, and pleasure-seeking people.

America's governmental leadership is not the source of America's problem. Rather, America's leadership is a manifest symptom of the sin-darkened hearts of a growing majority of our citizens.

God's Word speaks bluntly to a people who reject Him and choose instead to do what is right in their own eyes.

> The Lord knoweth how to deliver the godly out of temptations, and to reserve the unjust unto the day of judgment to be punished; But chiefly them that walk after the flesh

in the lust of uncleanness, and despise government. Presumptuous are they; self-willed, they are not afraid to speak evil of dignities.... But these, as natural brute beasts, made to be taken and destroyed, speak evil of the things that they understand not, and shall utterly perish in their own corruption, And shall receive the reward of unrighteousness, as they that count it pleasure to revel in the daytime. Spots they are and blemishes, reveling with their own deceivings.... Having eyes full of adultery and that cannot cease from sin; beguiling unstable souls; an heart they have exercised with covetous practices; cursed children, Who have forsaken the right way, and are gone astray.... These are wells without water, clouds that are carried with a tempest, to whom the mist of darkness is reserved forever.... For it had been better for them not to have known the way of righteousness than, after they have known it, to turn from the holy commandment delivered unto them...(2 Peter 2:9-21).

America's founding fathers determined to set this nation upon a foundation of God-given principles. Yet one federal judge can command that those godly principles, the Ten Commandments, be removed from a schoolhouse or courtroom wall. The Supreme Court of the land can declare God's Word null and void and His Son, Jesus Christ, a nondesirable entity by declaring Christianity too narrow and bigoted to be presented within America's educational process alongside pagan deities and pagan forms of worship which, in many cases, have governmental approval. The results of such foolhardiness are inevitable.

This disregard for God's Truth is disregard for life. Such disregard is, in some sense, worse than atrocities committed by those we consider barbarians in regions that have not been so blessed by God as ours. Jesus Christ is the way, the truth, and the life (John 14:6). To reject and blaspheme the only begotten Son of God is to display the ultimate disregard for life. Rejecting Jesus Christ, the Prince of Peace, brings the opposite of peace—chaos and war.

War in the Home

Humanism, the system embodying man's determination to construct the world in his own image totally apart from God's authority, is making an indelible imprint upon American family life. Homes are ripped apart by selfish actions that cast aside the notion of personal responsibility.

A generation has arisen from the chaos of evolution-based education. *Man is but the highest evolved form of animal life*, the hellish doctrine goes, *and, like the lower animals, has needs that supersede any obligation to some nebulous concept of morality.*

Hollywood portrays the supposedly liberated man or woman as a sexual creature not unlike a dog in the street who can simply mate on the spur of the moment, then separate after having satisfied their primal urges.

There are no consequences, only self-satisfaction and contentment until the next primal urge wells within.

Sexual innuendo and outright reference are every-night fare on sit-coms and regular TV programming. *It's just good fun*, the defenders offer when critics speak out. There is no real harm, they proclaim. Yet many who create the sexually oriented programs are among those who cry the loudest in the fight against sexual harassment in the military, in business, and in society. This sort of convoluted reasoning—that it is okay to program the minds of men with scenes of sexual debauchery in the name of "fun" entertainment but it is not okay for these same programmed men to put their fantasies into action by assaulting women in the workplace—God's Word calls *reprobate* thinking.

Growing numbers of men are following the *"if it feels good, do it"* tenets taught by humanism and vividly portrayed by Hollywood. Divorce rates continue to climb, the majority of them due to men leaving wives and children to pursue relationships that require of them little or no responsibility. This is not to say that women are not culpable as well. Statistics show a growing number of women deserting husbands and children for the same self-centered reasons.

Why get married? is another attitude that pervades American culture today. Single mothers who have never been married constitute a rising tide of irresponsible behavior that portends great trouble in the near future. Gangs of youth without fathers to nurture and discipline them cling to each other and rage against a society that neither understands nor seems to care except when crimes committed by the gang members on occasion directly touch our lives.

Abortion proponents give unwanted children (such as those who end up in gangs and who might predictably produce future gang members) as good reasons for ending pregnancies. Such children, if allowed to be born, they say, will only suffer the abuse of America's gang culture or worse. The truth is, however, that abortion imprints upon the minds of our children the idea that human life is a commodity like any other commodity and can be discarded without a second thought. Man, not God, it is implied, has authority over life and death. The message clearly has gotten through to the young gang members who slaughter each other each night across America.

War in the Streets

Americans have for decades heard of civil conflicts in Third-World countries where people face bodily injury and even death because of bloody fighting in the streets of their neighborhoods. Such murderous rampages continue to inflict millions of casualties. Wars resulting from civil unrest are perhaps more horrendous in nature than those in which uniformed armies oppose each other on battlefields. Helpless women and children who carry no weapons most often fall victim to roving marauders in these civilian versions of war.

Jesus' prophecy that there will be wars until His return certainly has been proven accurate.

Rumors of war, the second part of Jesus' prediction about deadly fighting that will mark human history as His return nears, rumble ominous warnings from America's inner cities. Although fighting in the streets of this nation has so far been confined to youth gangs sporadically shooting it out in our larger cities, troubling reports of increased drug dealings and other criminal activities in suburban and even rural areas should serve as a wake-up call. *Rumors* of wars threaten to turn into *actual* wars if *peace* is not forthcoming.

So-called *"gangbangers"*—inner city youth gang members—sometimes now receive something akin to diplomatic recognition by city officials and other leaders who desperately wish to negotiate an end to gang crime and gang war. Although such overtures to these juvenile thugs are well-intentioned, they serve to give gang leaders and the gangs themselves increased prestige, power, and authority, thus making the gang life more attractive to youngsters. Rarely is peace made and never is peace maintained through these "summit" negotiations.

The apostle Paul wrote in 2 Timothy 3 that in the last days, perilous times will come. He wrote in that account that many people will be *fierce* in those closing moments of human history. Death dealing carried on by the gangs and the drug dealers who rove our streets late at night and make thousands of new gang members through death threats and thousands of new customers through addictions indeed prove we live in a time when a growing number among us are of fierce demeanor. How long can it continue at the present rate of increasing ferocity until every street in America becomes a battle zone like those streets in so many Third-World countries?

The Seas and the Waves are Roaring

Jesus foretold:

> "There shall be signs in the sun, and in the moon, and in the stars; and upon the earth distress of nations, with perplexity; the sea and the waves roaring" (Luke 21:25).

The Lord alludes to man's intense interest in and preoccupation with things taking place in space. It seems hardly necessary to ask whether that prophetic reference fits this generation. All eyes turned heavenward when Sputnik first traversed the space above earth. Then Uri Gagarin's trip into space sent the U.S. Congress, the news media, and many worried citizens into orbit and America was pronounced woefully behind in the *space race*. U.S. scientists were given carte blanche to pursue the Soviets. Then came Alan Shepard, John Glenn, and all the rest. America's space program reached its zenith when Neil Armstrong dropped onto the moon's surface and issued the now-famous proclamation, "That's one small step for a man, one giant leap for mankind."

Telescopes in space have recorded spectacular stellar events, for example, comet fragments slamming into the planet Jupiter with stupendous impact. The space shuttle program routinely draws our attention to the fact that man's future points toward the stars. We witnessed the awful, yet awesome spectacle of the Challenger exploding, then falling ten miles to the ocean's surface, plumes of death streaming behind it.

Man's progress toward reaching into the heavens hardly skipped a beat, however, and now the great enemies of the Cold War, Russia and the United States, are supposedly allies in the quest for reaching those stars with cosmonauts and astronauts sharing the Mir space station and shuttle rides on a regular basis. Great plans are in the works for manned missions to Mars and beyond.

Jesus' prophecy has already been fulfilled and He was foretelling events scheduled to be most pronounced during the seven-year Tribulation period.

The next part of the Lord's prophecy, *"and upon the earth, distress of nations with perplexity"* could be used as a bold headline on the front page of every major newspaper in the world on any given day to encapsulate the present state of world affairs. No nation on earth is without distress. Leaders are perplexed as to how to remedy the overwhelming distress.

The United Nations, supposedly instituted to deal with such problems, is proven ineffective time and time again. The nations continue to cry peace, peace, when there is no peace.

U.N. leadership vies for power and influence within that confused body. More often than not, the most horrendous distress among nations goes unnoticed because the oppressed are overlooked by the heady, high-minded diplomatic elite who seek first and foremost to secure funding for their bureaucratic power bases.

The southern part of Sudan in North Africa, for example, is perhaps the greatest point of human stress on the planet. According to Kevin Turner, a missionary with the Voice of the Martyrs organization, millions of Christians have been murdered in that region and continue to suffer such horrific deaths as crucifixion and being buried alive. He reports that children are routinely taken from Christian parents and are sold into slavery and prostitution. Turner said he recently gave slave traders $1,000 for 15 children, stating that although it distressed him to in any way encourage slave trading, his higher duty was to see to it that the little ones were redeemed.

He then reported in a trembling voice and with a breaking heart that some slave traffickers are now engaging in the hellish business of harvesting the organs of the children they take from Christian parents.[1]

Is it any wonder that God's wrath is building while the seas and waves of human depravity crash upon this world? How terrible the judgments described throughout the book of Revelation will be upon the generation who turns a blind eye and a deaf ear to such atrocious inhumanity.

Jesus himself described the plight of the generation of apocalypse: "Men's hearts failing them for fear, and for looking after those things which are coming on the earth; for the powers of heaven shall be shaken " (Luke 21:26).

Peace, Be Still

Waves were breaking over the little vessel that rolled in the violent sea of Galilee. The terrified men did all they could to keep the boat from being swamped, probably shifting their bodies to offset the buffeting from one side and then the other. The storm got worse and all appeared to be lost. Despite their best efforts, they had lost control of their circumstances. Finally, they turned to the One who, astonishingly, was sound asleep in one corner of the boat.

Jesus of Nazareth awoke and calmly surveyed the heaving, tumultuous sea which threatened to destroy the tiny craft. (Read Mark 4:35-41.) You and I stand today within a sea even more violent than that stormy sea nearly 2000 years ago. It will get worse. Much worse. As a matter of fact, it will become so violent, God's Word says that if Christ Himself did not return, all life on earth would end. Man would destroy himself.

Half of earth's population will die during the seven-year Tribulation period. Many will be killed through man's own murderous efforts when God removes His restraining hands for a time. Billions will die as a direct result of God's wrath during the last three and a half years of the apocalypse. Great armies will march and roll and fly into the Valley of Jezreel. More than 200 million men will come from the east while millions upon millions more invade from west, north, and south of Jerusalem. All of unregenerate humanity will, through sin-engendered insanity, determine to battle to the final breath of the last man standing. Blood will literally flow and pool for many miles at depths up to three or four feet, according to God's prophetic Word.

When the rage intensifies to a level God can no longer tolerate, the dark, sulfurous clouds blanketing earth's atmosphere because of the terrible carnage of that dark hour, the very fabric of space itself, will scroll apart. A blinding laser-like path from heaven to earth will thrust forth. Heaven's armies will descend, led by the King of kings and Lord of lords.

While the sea of humanity on the planet's surface viciously roars in an attempt to prevent the heavenly intervention, those warring forces will turn from battling with each other to curse God and all His righteousness. Then Jesus Christ, mounted upon a stunningly white steed, will speak words sharper than a two-edged sword.

I am convinced they will be the same words Jesus of Nazareth spoke to that raging sea of Galilee nearly two millennia ago. They are the same words He speaks today to everyone who turns to Him, acknowledging that there is nothing and no one but Christ who can save them. He speaks those words to all who accept Him and trust Him to save them from their sins and to make them born-again children of God.

Just as His words instantaneously calmed that violent sea, thus saving the men in the little boat, Jesus' words will instantly end the warfare and rebellion at Armageddon. Christ's words to your troubled heart likewise will bring tranquillity and joy to your soul. You will never be the same when He speaks those life-changing words.

"*Peace, be still*" (Mark 4:39).

Revelation's thunder rumbles in the distance. Before the coming storm is full-blown, Christ will come for those who trust Him and Him alone for salvation. It will happen in a moment, in the twinkling of an eye.

Even so, come Lord Jesus.

▼   ▼   ▼

BIOGRAPHIES OF
CONTRIBUTING AUTHORS

William T. James

William T. James ("Terry") is an interested observer of historical and contemporary human affairs, attempting to analyze conduct, issues, and events in light of the Bible. He is frequently interviewed in national broadcasts.

James has authored, compiled, and edited five previous books: *Storming Toward Armageddon: Essays in Apocalypse; The Triumphant Return of Christ: Essays in Apocalypse II; Earth's Final Days: Essays in Apocalypse III; Raging Into Apocalypse: Essays in Apocalypse IV;* and *Foreshocks of Antichrist.* Each book presents a series of insightful essays by well-known prophecy scholars, writers, and broadcasters.

As a former public relations director for several companies, James has written and edited all forms of business communications, both in print and electronic media. Prior to that he worked as creative director for advertising agencies and did political and corporate speech writing as well as formulated position papers on various issues for clients he served. In addition to writing, he worked closely with clients and broadcast media in putting together and conducting press conferences and other forums.

▼   ▼   ▼

Dave Hunt

Dave Hunt is an internationally known author, researcher, and lecturer who is widely acclaimed for bringing relevance to the Bible in today's fast-changing world. A gifted writer, Hunt is the author of more than 25 books that span a wide literary range, including prophecy, social issues, biographies, devotionals, novels, a children's book, and an original screenplay. His books have sold over three million copies and have been translated into more than 40 languages.

Four of Hunt's books have been number-one Christian bestsellers: *The God Makers; Peace, Prosperity, and the Coming Holocaust; The Seduction of Christianity;* and *Beyond Seduction.* Hunt is also the author of *In Defense of the Faith, Global Peace and the Rise of Antichrist, How Close Are We?, A*

Woman Rides the Beast, *A Cup of Trembling*, and his most recent release, *Occult Invasion*.

Recognized as an authority on many topics such as modern and ancient religions, prophecy, cults, and the occult, Hunt speaks to tens of thousands of people worldwide each year. Hunt and his wife, Ruth, have four grown children and eleven grandchildren. They live in the Pacific Northwest.

▼   ▼   ▼

Bill Perkins

 Bill Perkins is executive director of Compass International, Inc., a nonprofit Christ-armoring ministry based in Coeur d'Alene, Idaho. Compass is best known for organizing the unique "Steeling the Mind of America" conference held each year in Vail, Colorado. The conference material covers a wide range of topics including biblical prophecy, apologetics, finances, evangelism, politics, and social issues. Past speakers include Josh McDowell, Frank Peretti, Alan Keyes, Chuck Missler, David Barton, Hal Lindsey, Henry Morris, Alan Sears, John Ankerberg, and Tom Cloud.

Perkins and his wife, Susie, have been married for 22 years and they have two homeschooled daughters, Jamie, 12, and Taylor, 6.

For information about Compass or *Steeling the Mind of America* conferences, or to be placed on the Compass mailing list, call or write:

Compass International, Inc.
460 Canfield, Suite 1000
Coeur d'Alene, ID 83815
(208) 762-7777

▼   ▼   ▼

Daymond R. Duck

Daymond R. Duck is a bi-vocational pastor who serves as minister to three small United Methodist congregations and also works for the U.S. Postal Service.

He entered the ministry in 1979 and completed the five-year Course-of-Study Program for United Methodist Pastors at Emory University in 1983.

Duck is the author of two books: *On the Brink: Easy-to-Understand End-Time Bible Prophecy* and *Revelation: God's Word for the Biblically Inept.* He has written several articles for a religious newspaper and has been interviewed on numerous Christian radio programs around the country, including The Southwest Radio Church. He has also spoken at prophecy conferences and is often asked to preach revival services.

Duck is a 1962 graduate of the University of Tennessee with a B.S. degree in agricultural engineering. He and his wife, Rachel, have three grown children: Sammy, Karen, and Jeff.

▼　▼　▼

Terry L. Cook

Terry L. Cook is a fundamentalist Christian researcher and retired Los Angeles Deputy Sheriff, as well as a former State of California fraud investigator/Deputy Real Estate Commissioner. He holds A.A., A.S., B.A., and B.S. degrees. He also holds California State teaching credentials in a variety of subjects and has completed some postgraduate study in theology. He is a California-licensed real estate broker and an FAA-licensed airline transport jet pilot (commercial) and flight instructor.

For the past six years, Cook, an ordained minister of the gospel, has been investigating current events as they relate to the fulfillment of "last days" or "end-time" Bible prophecies, with an emphasis on biometric identification technology, including smart cards and biochip transponder implants. He speaks regularly in large churches and other lecture forums, including appearances and interviews on radio and television.

In addition to his speaking ministry, Cook has produced several videos and books on the subject and is currently making available a package of information on implantable biochip technology and how it relates to the New World Order.

To contact Cook about his speaking ministry, write:

Second Coming Ministries
61535 S. Highway 97, Unit 9, Suite 288
Bend, OR 97702

▼   ▼   ▼

J. Randall Price

Dr. J. Randall Price is a pastor, author, and scholar whose latest published books include: *Ready to Rebuild*, *The Desecration and Restoration of the Temple as an Eschatological Motif in the Bible*, *In Search of Temple Treasures*, *Secrets of the Dead Sea Scrolls*, *The Stones Cry Out*, and *The Jerusalem Prophecy*.

A pastor for 21 years, Dr. Price has served in three different congregations in the state of Texas. He did graduate study in archaeology at the Hebrew University of Jerusalem, participated in field excavation at Tel Yin'am (Galilee), and was assistant director at Qumran, the site of the Dead Sea Scrolls. In addition, he is a certified tour guide to the State of Israel, having conducted 33 tours to the Bible lands of Israel, Jordan, Egypt, Italy, Greece, and Turkey. As the traveling speaker for World of the Bible Ministries, Inc., he conducts prophetic conferences in churches and with Christian organizations around the world.

Dr. Price received his Master of Theology degree (Th.M.) in Old Testament and Semitic Languages from Dallas Theological Seminary and his Doctor of Philosophy degree (Ph.D.) in Middle Eastern Studies and Archaeology from the University of Texas at Austin. He is an adjunct Professor of Theology at the International School of Theology and serves as President of World of the Bible Ministries, Inc. He also serves on the Advisory Boards of the Pre-Trib Research Center in Washington, D.C. and the Messianic Times (the world's largest Jewish-Christian newspaper) in Philadelphia, Pennsylvania.

Dr. Price has been extensively involved in video productions and he has made numerous appearances on network and national television programs. He is also a regular radio guest, having appeared on most of the nationally-aired programs including: USA Radio Network's Point of View (Marlon Maddoux), the Christian Broadcasting Network, the Southern Baptist Radio and Television Commission, How Can I Live? (Kay Arthur, Precepts Ministries), Southwest Radio Church's Watchman on the Wall broadcast, and Moody Broadcasting Network.

▼ ▼ ▼

Zola Levitt

 Zola Levitt is a Jewish believer educated in the synagogues and brought to the Messiah in 1971. He is best known as the host of the weekly national television program Zola Levitt Presents, and was formerly the host of two top-rated radio talk shows: The Heart of the Matter in Dallas, and the nationally syndicated Zola Levitt Live. Zola is also a widely published author with over 40 books in several languages, and has composed over 150 spiritual songs. His two musicals, *Beloved Thief* and *Mine Eyes Have Seen,* have been televised nationally.

A specialist in biblical sites, he conducts regular tours to Israel, Jordan, Greece, and Turkey. He holds music degrees from Duquesne University and Indiana University, and an honorary Th.D. from Faith Bible College.

Zola Levitt Ministries, Inc., a teaching and evangelistic association, is guided by the standard of Romans 1:16, "To the Jew first and also to the Gentile." Like the apostle Paul, the ministry works through the Gentiles to reach the Jews, and informs Gentile viewers and listeners of those principles of the faith which will be most helpful to them in understanding and witnessing to their Jewish friends.

▼ ▼ ▼

Noah Hutchings

Noah W. Hutchings received Jesus Christ as Savior and Lord in April 1951, and joined The Southwest Radio Church. The ministry currently produces a program heard daily over a network of 100 radio stations in English, and a daily program, Profecias Biblicas, aired in Spanish over stations in Mexico, Central America, South America, and the Caribbean.

Hutchings has written more than 100 books and booklets covering Bible commentary as well as prophetic topics. Some of his book titles include *Petra in History and Prophecy*, *Rapture and Resurrection*, *Why So Many Churches*, and *The Revived Roman Empire*.

Hutchings has traveled extensively in mission efforts, including 30 times to the Middle East, five times on Bible distribution tours to Russia, and five times to China, where he has been arrested twice on endeavors to get Bibles and Christian educational materials to the underground churches. He has also been personally active in mission work in Central America. Currently, a salvation booklet by Hutchings has been printed in Hong Kong in the Chinese language to be smuggled into China for mass distribution.

A member of the board of deacons of the Council Road Baptist Church of Oklahoma City, Hutchings is also a member of the board of the University of Biblical Studies in Oklahoma City. He lives there in Oklahoma City with his wife, Kim, and they have three grown daughters.

▼ ▼ ▼

Chuck Missler

An expert on Russia, Israel, Europe, and the Middle East, Chuck Missler gives intriguing behind-the-scenes insights to his audiences. He has spent more than 30 years in the corporate world as CEO of four public corporations contracting with the U.S. Department of Defense and has an extensive network of overseas contacts. With affiliates and associates in nine countries, Missler is a major contributor to several international intelligence newsletters. He has also negotiated joint ventures in Russia, Israel, Malaysia, Japan, Algeria, and Europe. In addition, Missler is an authority on advanced weapons and strategic resources and has participated in projects with SAMCOM-USSR, DSL, JCS, USACADA, DOJ, CCIA, and SDI. A member of the International Press Association, he is an honors graduate from the U.S. Naval Academy.

For 20 years Chuck Missler taught a Bible study in Southern California that grew to more than 2000 attendees. In 1992 he moved to Coeur d'Alene, Idaho, where he founded Koinonia House to distribute his books, lectures, and tapes. His dynamic style, conservative values, and adherence to biblical principles have made him a highly acclaimed speaker and critic.

His newsletter, Personal UPDATE, a 32-page Christian prophecy and intelligence newsletter, has grown to reach more than 50,000 monthly subscribers. He also has more than eight million tapes in circulation worldwide.

If you wish to receive a 12-month complimentary subscription to Personal UPDATE, contact:

Koinonia House
P.O. Box D
Coeur d'Alene, ID 83816-0347
1-800-546-8731

▼ ▼ ▼

Tim LaHaye

Dr. Tim LaHaye is a noted author, minister, counselor, television commentator, and nationally recognized speaker on family life and Bible prophecy. He is the Founder and President of Family Life Seminars and the founder of The PreTrib Research Center. He is also the father of four children and grandfather of nine. Snow skiing, water skiing, motorcycling, golfing, family vacations, and jogging are among his leisure activities.

Dr. LaHaye is a graduate of Bob Jones University, and holds an M.A. and Doctor of Ministry degree from Western Conservative Theological Seminary.

For 25 years he pastored one of the nation's outstanding churches in San Diego, California, which grew to three locations. It was during that time he founded two accredited Christian high schools, a Christian school system of ten schools, and Christian Heritage College.

Dr. LaHaye has written 39 books on a wide range of subjects such as *family life, temperaments, sexual adjustment, Bible prophecy, the will of God, Jesus Christ,* and *secular humanism.* The books in his current fiction series written with Jerry Jenkins, *Left Behind, Tribulation Force,* and *Nicolae,* are the number one bestsellers among Christian fiction books. These prophetic novels are based on Bible prophecy as portrayed by fictitious characters who live through the tribulation as new believers in Christ.

There are over ten million copies of LaHaye books in print, some of which have been translated into 32 foreign languages. His writings are best noted for their easy-to-understand and scripturally based application of biblical principles that assist in facing and handling the challenges of life.

Presently he speaks at many of the major Bible Prophecy Conferences in the United States and Canada, where his seven current prophecy books are very popular.

▼　▼　▼

Chris Corbett

Christopher Corbett is managing editor and senior writer for International Christian Media, which produces the nationwide Point of View Radio Talk Show. A graduate of the University of Chicago with a degree in political science, he is coauthor, with Marlin Maddoux, of *A Christian Agenda* and *Answers to the Gay Deception,* as well as the author of numerous articles and booklets on Christian worldview topics. He lives near Dallas, Texas, with his wife and two children.

▼　▼　▼

Thomas D. Ice

Thomas Ice is executive director of The Pre-Trib Research Center in Washington, D.C., which he founded in 1994 with Dr. Tim LaHaye to research, teach, and defend the pretribulational rapture and related Bible prophecy doctrines. Ice has co-authored over a dozen books on Bible prophecy, written dozens of articles, and is a frequent conference speaker.

He pastored for 15 years, and is currently pastor/teacher of Trinity Bible Church in Fredericksburg, VA. He has a Th.M. from Dallas Theological Seminary and a Ph.D. from Tyndale Theological Seminary, and lives with his wife, Janice, and their three boys in Fredericksburg.

▼ ▼ ▼

Dave Breese

Dave Breese is an internationally known author, lecturer, radio broadcaster, and Christian minister. He ministers in church and area-wide evangelistic crusades, leadership conferences, student gatherings, and related preaching missions.

Dr. Breese is President of Christian Destiny Inc. of Hillsboro, Kansas, a national organization committed to the advancement of Christianity through evangelistic crusades, literature distribution, university gatherings, and the use of radio and television.

Breese is active in ministry to college and university students, speaking to them from a background of theology and philosophy. He graduated from Judson College and Northern Seminary and has taught philosophy, apologetics, and church history. He is frequently involved in lectures, debates, and rap sessions on university campuses.

Breese travels more than 100,000 miles a year and has spoken to crowds across North America, Europe, Asia, the Caribbean, and Latin America. His lectures and debates at universities in the United States and overseas center on the confrontation of Christianity and modern thought.

Breese is also the author of a number of books, including *Discover Your Destiny, His Infernal Majesty, Know the Marks of Cults, Living for Eternity,* and *Seven Men Who Rule from the Grave.* His books, booklets, and magazine articles have enjoyed worldwide readership. He also publishes *Destiny News-letter,* a widely distributed periodical presenting the Christian view of current events, and *The Collegiate Newsletter,* a monthly publication dedicated to reaching college students with biblical truth and stimulating interest in the prophetic Word.

▼   ▼   ▼

John Walvoord

John Walvoord, theologian, pastor, and author, is described in the *Twentieth Century Dictionary of Christian Biography* as one of the most influential dispensational theologians of the twentieth century. Walvoord, who has been prominent in prophetic conferences advocating a pretribulational rapture, a literal thousand-year millennium, and distinction between Israel and the church, has written 30 books, including *The Rapture Question* (1957), *The Millennial Kingdom* (1959), and *The Prophecy Knowledge Handbook* (1990), as well as commentaries on Daniel (1971), Philippians (1971), and the Thessalonian epistles (1976). With R.B. Zuck, he edited the two-volume *Bible Knowledge Commentary* (1983, 1985).

Born in Sheboygan, Wisconsin, Walvoord graduated from Wheaton College, Texas Christian University, and Dallas Theological Seminary, where he later earned his Th.D. and joined the faculty (1936–1986). He became President in 1953 and Chancellor upon retirement in 1986. He pastored Rosen Heights Presbyterian Church in Fort Worth from 1934 to 1950 and edited *Bibliotheca Sacra,* the seminary's theological journal, from 1952 to 1985.

▼   ▼   ▼

Notes

Introduction—*Earth's Stormy Horizon*

1. *CNN News,* report by Walter Rogers, Jerusalem, June 9, 1997.
2. Richard D. Fisher, "Unilateral Armament," *National Review* 6-2-97: 61.
3. Ibid, p. 45
4. CNN News, May 23, 1997.

Chapter 1—*Flashes of Falling Away*

1. *Christianity Today,* January 6, 1997: pp. 20-30.
2. Kenneth E. Hagin, *Having Faith in Your Faith* (Rhema, 1980) pp. 3-4.
3. "The Viewpoint in the Science of Mind Concerning Traditional Beliefs" (Science of Mind Publications; Ernest Holmes, The Science of Mind (textbook) p. 30; cited in *Science of Mind,* September 1983, p. 47.
4. *Science of Mind,* March 1978, "Victim or Master," pp. 3-4.
5. Charles Braden, *Spirits in Rebellion* (Southern Methodist University Press, 1966) p. 390.
6. James Reid, *Ernest Holmes: The First Religious Scientist* (Los Angeles: Science of Mind Publications) p. 14.
7. Norman Vincent Peale, "What Does It Take To Be a Christian?" *Plus: The Magazine of Positive Thinking* April 1986: p. 3.
8. Ibid., May 1986, p. 23.
9. G.A. Pritchard, *Willow Creek Seeker Services* (Baker Books, 1996) p. 273.
10. *Plus,* April 1986, p. 3.
11. Richard Foster, *Celebration of Discipline* (Harper & Row, 1978) p. 26.
12. Calvin Miller, *The Table of Inwardness* (InterVarsity Press, 1984) p. 93.
13. Karen Burton Mains, *Lonely No More* (Word Publishing, 1993) inside back jacket.
14. Ibid., p. 122-24.
15. Erich Fromm, *Man for Himself: An Inquiry into the Psychology of Ethics* (Bantam Books, 1963) p. 59.
16. Promise Keepers Newsletter, Winter 1993.
17. William Law, Ed. Dave Hunt, *The Power of the Spirit* (Christian Literature Crusade, 1971) p. 141.
18. Peter Wagner, *Confronting the Powers* (Regal Books, 1996) p. 16.
19. Ibid., pp. 15-37, etc.
20. Session 12, White Alpha Course.
21. Plass, What Luther Says, Vol. 1, p. 36.
22. Muston, *History of the Waldenses,* vol. i, p. 31, cited in R.W. Thompson, *The Papacy and the Civil Power,* (New York, 1876), p. 489; see also E.H. Broadbent, *The Pilgrim Church* (London, 1931) pp. 100-01.
23. Henry H. Halley, *Pocket Bible Handbook* (Chicago, 1944) pp. 608-13.
24. Evangelicals & Catholics Together: The Christian Mission in the Third Millennium, p. 4.
25. *McCall's,* January 1978.
26. *Gastonia Gazette,* November 22, 1967.
27. Rev. J.J. Schroeder, O.P., *The Canons and Decrees of the Council of Trent* (Tan Books, 1978) pp. 52, 149.
28. David W. Cloud, *Flirting With Rome* (Way of Life Literature, Oak Harbor, WA 98277) p. 26.
29. De Semlyen, *All Roads,* p. 178.
30. *Cleveland Plain Dealer,* March 27, 1994, p. 4-B, "Catholics, Protestants work for Graham crusade."
31. Phil Donohue Show, October 11, 1979.
32. *Christianity Today,* September 6, 1985, editorial titled, "A Man Under Orders."
33. Cloud, *Flirting,* pp. 28-30.
34. *Vancouver Sun,* October 5, 1984.
35. *The Portland Catholic Sentinel,* September 25, 1992.
36. *Charismatic News Notes,* published by the Diocese of Rockville Centre, 129 Broadway, Hicksville, NY 11801, May 1990, "Billy Graham Crusade Scheduled for Nassau Coliseum: Assistance Sought from Catholics," p. 1.
37. David W. Cloud, *O Timothy,* Volume 10, Issue 9, 1993, p. 15; Cloud, *Flirting with Rome,* op. cit., Vol. 1, p.41
38. *Pittsburgh Sun-Telegraph,* September 6, 1952.
39. Paul Crouch, *Praise the Lord,* October 1996, p. 1.
40. Cited in John F. MacArthur, Jr. *Charismatic Chaos* (Zondervan, 1992) p. 148.

41. John Goodwin, "Testing the Fruit," Tape 2, Discernment Ministries, P.O. Box 129, Lapeer, MI 48446-0129.
42. *Charisma*, August 1993, p. 78.
43. *Christian News*, May 12, 1997, p. 11.
44. *Deseret News*, February 9, 1980, Church Section, p. 11.
45. *Kentucky Monitor*.
46. "The Plus Factor," published excerpts from a Peale talk on Schuller's "Hour of Power," copyrighted 1985 by Robert Schuller, p. 3.
47. ABC News, Nightline, March 4, 1997, from a transcript of the program, available from Federal Document Clearing House, Inc., p. 2.
48. James Brady, "In Step With Robert Schuller," *Parade Magazine,* April 20, 1997, p. 18.
49. *USA Today*, March 23, 1989.
50. Robert Schuller, *The Power of the Inner Eye,* p. 7.
51. *Charisma*, June 1944.

52. John Marks Templeton, *The Humble Approach* (The Continuum Publishing Company, New Revised Edition, 1995) pp. 37-38.
53. John Marks Templeton, *Discovering the Laws of Life* (The Continuum Publishing Company, 1994), inside front of jacket.
54. Templeton, *The Humble Approach*, p. 137.
55. Templeton, *Discovering*, op. cit., jacket
56. Ibid., pp. 6, 7, 208.
57. *Possibilities,* Summer 1986, pp. 8-12.
58. John Marks Templeton, *The Humble Approach* (Continuum, New Revised Edition, 1995), pp. 48, 53.
59. Ibid., p. 58.
60. Ibid., pp. 135-39.
61. Ibid., p. 60.
62. Ibid., p. 52.
63. "Acceptance Speech by Dr. William R. Bright Receiving the 1996 Templeton Prize for Progress in Religion," delivered in Rome, Italy at The Church of St. Maria in Trastevere, May 9, 1996, p. 1.

Chapter 3—*Harbingers of Humanism's Hurricane*

1. Joan M. Veon, *Briefing Book: UN Conferences and Goals and How They Will Affect the Family, the Church, and Society,* The Women's Group, Inc., Olney, MD, p. 24.
2. Kjos, Berit, *Midnight Call Magazine*, July 1997, pp. 26-30.
3. Ibid., pp. 116-119.
4. Katson, Trisha, Global Bureaucrats Are Expected to Seize Control at Istanbul Conference, *The Spotlight Newspaper,* May 20, 1996, pp.12-13.

5. Joan M. Veon, *The World Food Summit,* p. 2.
6. Katson, Trisha, Global Bureaucrats Are Expected to Seize Control at Istanbul Conference, *The Spotlight Newspaper,* May 20, 1996, p. 12.
7. Rothbard, David, Environmentalists Putting Earth Above People, "Point of View" Radio Talk Show, 5-19-97, Taped Message.
8. Ibid.

Chapter 4—*Today's Technology Churns Toward the Mark of the Beast*

1. Donald G. Small, Hughes Identification Devices, Excerpted from the Video *Mark of the New World Order.*
2. *The Orange County Register,* March 7, 1993.
3. AVID.
4. The *McAlvany Intelligence Advisor,* August 1994.
5. The Arizona *Republic*, June 20, 1989.
6. *Los Angeles Times*, August 17, 1994
7. *Personal Identification News,* (Sept./Oct. 1994).

8. *Current News Analysis & Research Service,* January 20, 1994.
9. MIA, August 1994.
10. *Mark of the Beast*, p. 113.
11. *AIDN,* December 1994.
12. *AIDN,* December 1994.
13. *The Los Angeles Times,* June 12, 1995).
14. *Roll Call,* May 22, 1995.
15. *NARC Officer,* Sept./Oct. 1995.
16. *Webster's New Collegiate Dictionary.*
17. *The Associated Press,* February 6, 1996.
18. *The Los Angeles Times,* April 4, 1996.
19. The *Phoenix Letter,* March 1996.

Chapter 5—*False Peace: The Pseudo-Storm Shelter*

1. See Sidney Zion, "The Palestinian Problem: It's All in a Name," *New York Magazine* (March 13, 1978), pp. 42-45.

2. Quoted in the article "Is Jordan Palestine, or Not?" *Dispatch from Jerusalem* (Fall 1993).

3. Yasser Arafat speaking to Orina Fallacei and quoted in *The New Republic*, *The Jerusalem Post*, International Edition (Friday, September 11, 1992).

4. However, Arabs in Palestine, most of whom came from Egypt, Syria, and Jordan, shunned the name "Palestinian Arabs." So the British were careful to refer to the Jews only as "Palestinian Jews," while referring to the Arabs as simply "Arabs."

5. Sidney Zion, "The Palestinian Problem: It's All in a Name," *New York* Magazine (March 13, 1978), p. 45.

6. See Feisal al-Husseini, *The Land, its People and History*, a PLO-version of Arab history as reported in the article "The Gospel According to Husseini," *The Jerusalem Post*, International Edition (December 12, 1992).

7. For a presentation of these facts and documentation see Ramon Bennet, *When Day and Night Cease* (Jerusalem: Arm of Salvation, 1993), pp. 193-202, and quotations throughout George Grant's *The Blood of the Moon* (Tennessee: Wolgemuth & Hyatt, 1991).

8. Gershon Salomon, *The Voice of the Temple Mount* (Summer 1995), p. 2.

9. The basis for this New Covenant is the atoning death of the Messiah, and thus becomes the shared reality for Gentiles as well as Jews who in the present dispensation of the Church have been included under its spiritual provisions through faith in Jesus (see Hebrews 8:6-13). Its provisions concerning the Land and outreach to the nations will be realized by the whole Nation of Israel (as promised by Jeremiah in this chapter), not simply a remnant left by grace (Romans 11:5), when it is fulfilled after the Second Advent of Christ.

10. Grant Livingstone, "Israel's Integrity and the SLA," *The Jerusalem Post International Edition.*

11. Remarks of Prime Minister Benjamin Netanyahu at the National Unity Coalition for Israel, Washington D.C., December 7, 1996.

12. Benjamin Netanyahu in a question/answer session following a scheduled speech on Israeli economic cooperation and prospects for foreign investment to the Foreign Correspondent's Club of Japan, Tokyo, Tuesday, August 26, 1997.

13. Shmuel Katz, author of the biography of Ze'ev Jabotinsky, *The Jerusalem Post International Edition*, August, 1996.

14. As cited by Dean Fischer, "This Is a Step Toward a Palestinian State," *Time Magazine* (September 27, 1993), p. 32.

15. This was so interpreted because the Vatican had previously stood with Arab sympathies against Israel because of its replacement theology that dictated a non-Jewish control of the Holy Land. However, Pope John Paul II's recent call for the faithful of the Roman Catholic Church to "combat anti-Semitism wherever it is found" was considered as direct opposition to basic Muslim purpose. Compare *U.S. News & World Report* (January 10, 1994), p. 9.

16. Associated Press article, "Weapons Still Pouring Into the Middle East," *Houston Chronicle*, August 12, 1993.

17. James Hackett, "Moslem Bomb: Not If, But When," *The Jerusalem Post International Edition*, May 23, 1992.

18. Dan Izenberg, "Eitan: Uranium Sites Revealed to Egypt," *The Jerusalem Post International Edition*, November, 1994.

19. William Rusher, "No Peace in Store for Israel," *San Antonio Express-News*, September 21, 1993, p. 11-A.

20. For recent arguments for a pre-tribulational invasion compare Zola Levitt and Tom McCall, *The Coming Russian Invasion of Israel* (Revised edition). Moody Press, 1992, and Hal Lindsey and Chuck Missler, *The Magog Factor* (Hal Lindsey Ministries, 1992), and "Magog Updates" in *Personal Update: A Newsletter of Koinonia House* (POB D, Coeur d'Alene, ID 83816-0347). A good survey of this position is also provided by Arnold Fructenbaum, *The Footprints of the Messiah* (Ariel Press, 1978), pp. 69-83.

21. *Ibid*, pp. 51-52.

22. *The Voice of the Temple Mount* (Autumn 1995), pp. 2, 7.

23. Austin Bay (researcher and writer on military and intelligence issues), as cited in his article "Violent Fringe Threatening Mideast," *San Antonio Express-News*, March 3, 1994, p. 4-B.

Chapter 7—New Europe's Eye of the Tornado

1. *The Christian Jew Hour (Messianic Perspectives),* "The Antichrist Among Us Now," San Antonio, TX (audiotape).
2. John Marks, "Arrivederci, Lira, Au Revoir, Franc," *U.S. News & World Report,* December 16, 1996; p. 49.
3. Ibid.
4. Daniel Singer, "The Real Eurobattle: The Move to a Common Currency Masks A Struggle Over the Social Shape of Europe," *The Nation,* December 23, 1996; p. 20.
5. Ibid.
6. Ibid.
7. Ibid.
8. Charles Trueheart, *The Washington Post,* "Juppe to Quit, Says France Needs New Prime Minister," *Arkansas Democrat-Gazette,* May 27, 1997, sec. A: 1, 5.
9. Singer.
10. Ibid.
11. Richard Medley, "Keeping Monetary Union on Track: Time for Another 'Kohl Shock,'" *Foreign Affairs,* November/December 1996; p. 21.

12. Ibid, pp. 21-22.
13. Ibid, p. 22.
14. Ibid, pp. 24-25.
15. Ibid, p. 25.
16. Ibid, p. 26.
17. Facts and figures in this section were taken from *Foreign Affairs,* July-August, 1997; p. 83ff.
18. Ibid.
19. Daymond R. Duck, *On the Brink* (Lancaster, Pennsylvania: Starburst Publishers, 1995); pp. 95-97.
20. Fred Coleman and Tim Zimmerman, "Chips off the Old Bloc: Russia Bows to NATO's Inevitable Expansion," *U.S. News & World Report,* May 26, 1997; p. 33.
21. Dr. Dave Breese, "Europe: The Rocky Road to Unity," *Future Times,* Spring, 1993; p. 5.
22. Ibid, pp. 5-7.
23. Duck, p. 106.
24. Ibid, p. 107.
25. Ibid.

Chapter 9—The Russia, Muslim, Magog Whirlwind

1. As calculated by the CIA. This is about 70% of Britain's GDP.
2. Ezekiel 38:19,20.
3. Ezekiel 39:9, 10. The shelf life of production Soviet warheads is seven years.
4. Ezekiel 39:12-14.
5. Ezekiel 39:15.
6. Genesis 10:2; 1 Chronicles 1:5
7. G. Husing, "Gugu," *Orientalistische Literaturzeitung* 18, 1915, pp. 299-302; J. L. Myres, "Gog and the Danger from the North in Ezekiel," *Quarterly Statement, Palestine Exploration Fund, 1932,* pp. 213-19; J. G. Alders, *Gog en Magog in Ezekiel,* J. H. Kok, Kamapen, 1951; M. C. Astour, "Ezekiel's Prophecy of Gog and the Cutherean Legend of Naram-Sin," *Journal of Biblical Literature,* 95.4, 1976, pp. 567-79.
8. Keil, C.F., and Delitzsch, F., *Biblical Commentary on the Prophecies of Ezekiel,* T. and T. Clark, Edinburgh, 1891, vol. 2, p. 157; Gesenius, Wilhelm, *A Hebrew and English Lexicon of the Old Testament,* Crocker and Brewster, Boston, 1872, pp. 534, 626, 955, 1121; Scofield, C.I., ed., *The Scofield Reference Bible,* Oxford University, 1917, p. 883; *The New Scofield Reference Bible,* English, E.S., 1967, p. 881.

9. F. W. Gingrich and Frederich Danker, *A Greek-English Lexicon of the New Testament and other Early Christian Literature,* University of Chicago Press, Chicago and London, 1957.
10. Josephus, *Antiquities,* 1.123; Jerome, *Commentary on Ezekiel* 38:2.
11. F. H. Colson, G.H. Whitaker, and Ralph Marcus, *Philo,* Loeb Classical Library, London, 1929–1953.
12. K. W. Nitzsch (1872); A. H. Sayce (1883); H. Delbruck (1887); A.T. Olmstead (1916); Ph. E. Legrand, "De la 'malignite d'Herodote," *Mélanges Gustav Glotz,* Presses Universitaires de France, Paris, 1932, vol. 2, pp. 535-47; J. A. S. Evans, "Father of History or Father of Lies?" *Classical Journal* 64, 1968, pp. 11-17; F. Wilke, "Das Skythenproblem im Jeremiabuch," in *Alttestamentliche Studien für R. Kittle,* J. C. Hinrichs, Leipzig, 1913, pp. 222-254.
13. W. Spiegelberg, *The Credibility of Herodotus's Account of Egypt in the Light of the Egyptian Monuments,* Blackwell, Oxford, 1927; O. E. Ravn, *Herodotus's Description of Babylon,* A. Busck, Copenhagen, 1942.
14. Herodotus, 4.64, 65, 70-75.

15. Kesses HaSofer, *Bereishis–Genesis,* A New Translation with a Commentary Anthologised from Talmudic, Midrashic and Rabbinic Sources, Mesorah Publications, Lt.

16. In Belarus, the Russians make up 13% of the 10.3 million population; Russians form 29% of the population of Estonia and 34% of the population of Latvia.

17. Much of this article was excerpted from information provided to members of the Inner Circle of Intelligence International Ltd., The Stoneyhill Centre, Brimpsfield, Gloucester, GL4 8LF, UK.

18. Ezekiel 38:5.

19. Ezekiel 38:4.

20. Dan McKinnon, *Bullseye Iraq*, Berkley Books, New York, 1987.

21. Ezekiel 38:13.

22. "Gog" is the leader of the people of Magog in Ezekiel 38. (Amos 7:1, in the Septuagint, implies that he is a demon king.)

23. The Heritage Foundation reported in January of 1994 that the army's budget is underfunded by over $1 billion, and the maintenance levels are the lowest in a decade.

Chapter 10—*America's Perilous Times Have Come*

1. Katina Johnstone, "A Neglected Child, a Gun, Death...," *San Diego Union*, December 21, 1993.

2. Joyce Price, "Crime at the Hands of Children," *The Washington Times*, December 29, 1993, A7.

3. Charles W. Colson, "Kids and Crime: Who's Responsible," *Citizen,* December 20, 1993, p. 10-11.

4. Charles W. Colson, *Against the Night: Living in the New Dark Ages* (Ann Arbor, Michigan: Servant Books, 1989), p. 44.

5. "Lake County Scuffle in the Culture War," *The Washington Times*, May 18, 1994.

6. David Barton, *America: To Pray or Not to Pray?* (Aledo, Texas: WallBuilder Press, 1991), p. 44.

7. Zbigniew Brzezinski, *Out of Control: Global Turmoil on the Eve of the Twenty-First Century* (New York: Charles Scribner's Sons, 1993), pp. 4-5.

8. Ibid., p. 10.

9. Stanley K. Henshaw, "Induced Abortion: A World Review, 1990," *Family Planning Perspectives* 22, no. 2, (March/April 1990): p. 76.

10. *Congressional Record*, 1993, 4322.

11. Francis A. Schaeffer, *How Should We Then Live: The Rise and Decline of Western Thought and Culture* (Old Tappan, N.J.: Revell, 1976), p. 227.

12. Joseph Sobran, "The Autocracy of Rights," *The Washington Times*, December 9, 1993.

13. Thomas Sowell, "History All on the Side of Jefferson," *The Washington Times*, April 29, 1993.

14. William Buckley Jr., "Public Service and the Lure of Power," *The Washington Times*, February 1, 1993.

15. Joe Mathews, "Beavis, Butt-Head & Budding Nihilists: Will Western Civilization Survive?" *The Washington Post*, March 1, 1994.

16. Barton, p. 109.

17. From an unabridged, printed sermon by D. James Kennedy, "Church and State," used by permission.

18. Barton, p. 9.

19. Karen S. Peterson, "Poll: 59 Percent Call Religion Important," *USA Today*, April 13, 1994.

20. Remarks by Vice President Quayle to the Commonwealth Club of California (San Francisco, California), May 19, 1992.

21. Michael Medved, *Hollywood vs. America: Popular Culture and the War on Traditional Values* (New York: HarperCollins Publishers, Inc., 1992), p. 48.

22. Joyce Price, "Crime at the Hands of Children," *The Washington Times*, December 29, 1993.

23. Ibid.

24. Dr. Ken Magid and Carole A. McKelvey, *High Risk: Children without a Conscience* (New York: Bantam Books, 1988), pp. 110, 119.

25. William M. Welch, "Age-Old Debate on Morality Takes New Life," *USA Today*, December 15, 1993.

26. Bryce Christensen, "America's 'Retreat from Marriage,'" *The Family in America* 2, no. 2 (February 1988): p. 8.

27. George Barna, *The Frog in the Kettle: What Christians Need to Know About Life in the Year 2000* (Ventura, California: Regal Books, 1990), pp. 112-13.

Chapter 11—*Energy, Ecology, Economy: A Foreboding Forecast*

1. Michael Sanera and Jane S. Shaw, "The ABCs of Environmental Myths," *Wall Street Journal*, September 4, 1996.
2. Caller to *Point of View* Radio Talk Show, May 22, 1997.
3. "Global Warming Treaty Costs for the U.S.," Brief Analysis 213 by the National Center for Policy Analysis, Dallas, Texas, September 6, 1996, summarizing the findings.
4. Ibid.
5. Michael S. Coffman, *Saviors of the Earth? The Politics and Religion of the Environmental Movement* (Chicago: Northfield Publishing, 1994) p. 30.
6. Sanera and Shaw, "The ABCs..." The forest figures come from Coffman, p. 37.
7. Carl F. Horowitz, "Enviro-Indoctrination in School? Curricula Focus on Political Views, Not Science," *Investor's Business Daily*, November 4, 1996, p. 1.
8. Ibid.
9. Ibid.
10. Michael Sanera and Jane S. Shaw, *Facts Not Fear* (Washington, D.C.: Regnery, 1996), p. 31, citing *Outside* magazine, 1994.
11. Horowitz.
12. Samera and Shaw, *Facts*, p. 31-32.
13. Horowitz.
14. Ronald Bailey, "Who Is Maurice Strong?", *National Review*, September 1, 1997, p. 32.
15. From personal correspondence, cited by Coffman, p. 145.
16. Mark Tooley, "Gore's God," *Crisis*, October 1992, p. 22.
17. Albert Gore, *Earth in the Balance* (New York: Houghton Mifflin, 1992), p. 260.
18. Ibid.
19. Ibid.
20. Tooley, op. cit. p. 23.
21. Ibid.
22. Coffman, op. cit. p. 197.
23. Larry Abraham and William Hoar, *The Clinton Clique* (Dunwoody, Georgia: Soundview Publications, 1993) p. 35.
24. Steven J. Milloy and Michael Gough, *Wall Street Journal* Editorial Page, January 7, 1997.
25. Ibid. Cost estimates come from Mario Lewis, Vice President for Policy at the competitive Enterprise Institute, a conservative think tank sympathetic to business.
26. Transcript of commentary by William Lind on National Empowerment Television, June 30, 1997.
27. Bailey, op. cit.
28. Michael McCoy, "Trekking to the Summit," *Earth Summit in Focus 2* (1991), UNCED, 2; as quoted by Dixie Lee Ray, *Environment Overkill*, p. 4; cited by Coffman, p. 197.
29. Daniel Wood, "The Wizard of Baca Grande," *West*, May 1990, p. 47.
30. David Felix, "The Tobin Tax Proposal," *Futures*, March 1995.
31. See *Our Global Neighborhood* published by the Commission on Global Governance (1995), "Financing an Effective United Nations" by the Ford Foundation, and Paul Kennedy and Bruce Russett, "Reforming the United Nations," *Foreign Affairs*, September/October, 1995, pp. 68-71.
32. Grigg, "Shaping...", p. 6.
33. Congressional Record, 1/22/96, regarding Senate Bill 1519.
34. Coffman, p. 201, quoting Rockefeller's Trilateral Commission book *Beyond Interdependence: The Meshing of the World's Economy and the Earth's Ecology*.
35. Ibid., p. 200, quoting press release issued by Rocard at Earth Summit.
36. Cable News Network report, *Our Planetary Police*, aired 3/7/93.

Chapter 12—*The Shout Heard Around the World: Overview of the Rapture*

1. William E. Bell, "A Critical Evaluation of the Pretribulation Rapture Doctrine in Christian Eschatology" (Ph.D. diss., New York University, 1967), pp. 26-27.
2. Larry V. Crutchfield, s.v. "Irenaeus" in Mal Couch, editor, *Dictionary of Premillennial Theology* (Grand Rapids: Kregel Publications, 1996).
3. Larry V. Crutchfield, "The Blessed Hope and the Tribulation in the Apostolic Fathers" in *When The Trumpet Sounds*, Thomas Ice & Timothy Demy, editors, (Eugene, Oregon: Harvest House Publishers, 1995), pp. 88-101.
4. *The Shepherd of Hermas* 1.4.2.
5. Crutchfield, *Trumpet*, p. 103.
6. Crutchfield, s.v. "Irenaeus" in *Dictionary of Premillennial Theology*.
7. Frank Marotta, personal e-mail to Thomas Ice, July 1, 1997. Quotation from *Apocalypse of Elijah*, 5:4.
8. Marotta, ibid.

9. A. Cleveland Coxe, American Editor, *The Ante-Nicene Fathers*, X Vols (Grand Rapids: Eerdmans, 1985), Vol. VII, p. 360, f.n. 17, 18.

10. Wilber B. Wallis, "Reflections on the History of Premillennial Thought," in *Interpretation & History: Essays in honour of Allan A. MacRae*, edited by R. Laird Harris, Swee-Hwa Quek, and J. Robert Vannoy (Singapore: Christian Life Publishers, 1986), p. 228.

11. C. P. Caspari, ed. *Briefe, Abhandlungen und Predigten aus den zwei letzten Jahrhunderten des kirchlichen Altertums und dem Anfang des Mittelaters*, Christiania, 1890.

12. Paul J. Alexander, *The Byzantine Apocalyptic Tradition*, edited with an introduction by Dorothy Abrahamse. Berkeley: University of California Press, 1985.

13. Timothy J. Demy and Thomas D. Ice, "The Rapture and an Early Medieval Citation," *Bibliotheca Sacra*, 152 (July-September 1995), pp. 306-17.

14. Caspari, 211.4. A copy of the Latin text, with English translation of the sermon can be obtained by writing The Pre-Trib Research Center.

15. Paul Boyer, *When Time Shall Be No More: Prophecy Belief in Modern American Culture* (Cambridge, MA: Belknap Press, 1992), p. 75.

16. Paul N. Benware, *Understanding End Times Prophecy: A Comprehensive Approach* (Chicago: Moody Press, 1995), pp. 197-98.

17. Frank Marotta, *Morgan Edwards: An Eighteenth Century Pretribulationist* (Morganville, N.J.: Present Truth Publishers, 1995), p. 12.

18. Morgan Edwards, *Two Academical Exercises on Subjects Bearing the following titles; Millennium, Last-Novelties*. (Philadelphia: Dobson and Lang, 1788). I was able to get a photocopy of the book at the Library of Congress in Washington, D. C.

19. John L. Bray, *The Origin of the Pre-Tribulation Rapture Teaching* (Lakeland, Florida: John L. Bray Ministry, 1982).

20. Dave MacPherson, *The Unbelievable Pre-Trib Origin* (Kansas City: Heart of America Bible Society, 1973). *The Late Great Pre-Trib Rapture* (Kansas City: Heart of America Bible Society, 1974). *The Great Rapture Hoax* (Fletcher, N.C.: New Puritan Library, 1983). *Rapture?* (Fletcher, N.C.: New Puritan Library, 1987). *The Rapture Plot* (Simpsonville, SC: Millennium III Publishers, 1995).

21. John F. Walvoord, *The Blessed Hope and the Tribulation*, (Grand Rapids: Zondervan, 1976), p. 47.

22. The following books are some of those which have the full text of Macdonald's utterance: MacPherson's *Cover-Up*, and *Hoax*. R. A. Huebner, *The Truth of the Pre-Tribulation Rapture Recovered* (Millington, N.J.: Present Truth Publishers, 1976), pp. 67-69. Hal Lindsey, *The Rapture: Truth Or Consequences* (New York: Bantam Books, 1983), pp. 169-72. William R. Kimball, *The Rapture: A Question of Timing* (Grand Rapids: Baker Book House, 1985), pp. 44-47.

23. Thomas D. Ice, "Why the Doctrine of the Pretribulational Rapture Did Not Begin with Margaret Macdonald," *Bibliotheca Sacra* 147 (1990), pp. 158, 161.

24. Columba Graham Flegg, *'Gathered Under Apostles' A Study of the Catholic Apostolic Church* (Oxford: Clarendon Press, 1992), p. 436.

25. R. A. Huebner, *Precious Truths Revived and Defended Through J. N. Darby*, Vol. 1 (Morganville, N. J.: Present Truth Publishers, 1991).

26. Ibid., p. 17.
27. Ibid., p. 19.
28. Ibid., p. 18.
29. Ibid., p. 23.
30. Ibid., p. 24.

31. Max S. Weremchuk, *John Nelson Darby: A Biography* (Neptune, N. J.: Loizeaux Brothers, 1992).

32. Ibid., p. 242.

33. J. N. Darby, "Reflections upon the Prophetic Inquiry and the Views Advanced in It" *The Collected Writings of J. N. Darby*, Vol. 2 (Winschoten, Netherlands: H. L. Heijkoop, reprint 1971), pp. 1-31.

34. Ibid., pp. 16-18, 25, 30.

35. F. F. Bruce, Review of *The Unbelievable Pre-Trib Origin* in *The Evangelical Quarterly*, (Vol. XLVII, No. 1; January–March, 1975), p. 58.

36. Walvoord, p. 47.

37. Kurt Aland, *A History of Christianity*, Vol. 1 (Philadelphia: Fortress Press, 1985), p. 87.

38. Aland, Ibid., p. 92.

Conclusion—*Peace, Be Still*

1. Point of View radio broadcast, Friday, July 10, 1997, KAAY-1090, Little Rock.

The William T. James monthly briefing paper that presents analysis of current issues and events in the words of the world's best-known writers, speakers, and broadcasters

issues and events
from prophetic perspectives

For a free issue of "i.e." simply fill in, then clip the coupon below and send to:

James Informarketing
P.O. Box 1108
Benton, AR 72018-1108

Please include with the coupon a self-addressed, business-sized envelope stamped with first-class postage.

Please send me a free issue of "i.e." I have enclosed, along with this coupon, a business-sized envelope stamped with first-class postage.

Name _____

Address _____
            (Street)

_____
(City)   (State)   (Zip)

Thank You for Your Order!

If you are pleased with your order and would like to purchase additional products, here is an order form for your convenience. See next page for descriptions.

NAME: _____

ADDRESS: _____

CITY, STATE, Zip: _____

PHONE: _____

Quantity	Publications	Check here to have your book signed by William T. James
	Book 1: Storming Toward Armageddon	
	Book 2: Triumphant Return of Christ	
	Book 3: Earth's Final Days	
	Book 4: Raging Into Apocalypse	
	Book 5: Foreshocks of Antichrist	
	i.e. newsletter: 1 year (8 issues) $16.50	

Low Book Prices

1 book — $14.95
2 books — $29.95
3 books — $42.00
4 books — $48.00
5 books — $63.00

Total Amount Enclosed:

$ _____

Please make your check payable to:

James Informarketing
P.O. Box 1108
Benton, AR
72018-1108

Storming Toward Armageddon: Essays in Apocalypse
335 pages
Texe Marrs, Tim LaHaye, Dave Breese, David A. Lewis, Robert Lindsted, and others

Triumphant Return of Christ: Essays in Apocalypse II
399 pages
Dave Breese, J.R. Church, John Wesley White, Phil Arms, Joseph Carr, and others

Earth's Final Days: Essays in Apocalypse III
367 pages
Don McAlvany, Dave Breese, Chuck Missler, Phil Arms, J.R. Church, D.A. Miller, David Webber, and others

Raging into Apocalypse: Essays in Apocalypse IV
312 pages
Grant Jeffrey, John Walvoord, Dave Breese, Chuck Missler, Henry Morris, and others

Foreshocks of Antichrist
418 pages
Dave Breese, Grant Jeffrey, Zola Levitt, Chuck Missler, John Walvoord, and others

i.e. — issues and events from prophetic perspectives
335 pages
Newsletter presenting what foremost Bible and prophecy experts have to say about issues and events of our day

The Collegiate Letter
A Dave Breese Ministry

Help spark a college student's interest in prophecy and love for God's Holy Word. You can sponsor Dave Breese's Collegiate Letter, which will be mailed monthly to the young person of your choice, or to anyone.

A one-year subscription for only $20 includes free books, position papers, and many extras that will inform, fascinate, and inspire.

The Collegiate Letter is produced by

Christian Destiny
P.O. Box C
Hillsboro, KS 67063

Complete this form and mail it to us, or call 1-800-777-8806.

NAME _____

ADDRESS _____

CITY _____ STATE _____ ZIP _____

I wish to sponsor:

NAME _____

ADDRESS _____

CITY _____ STATE _____ ZIP _____

Other Good Harvest House Reading

Foreshocks of Antichrist

William T. James, ed. Twelve internationally known prophecy experts share their visions of God's prophetic plan and the vital role Christians will play in it. Discover the significance of the Internet, the inevitability of a one-world government, and the eventual rejection of a "Creator God" by those who embrace globalism.

Prophecy Watch

Thomas Ice and Timothy Demy. Ice and Demy, creators of the Pocket Prophecy series, now offer a comprehensive, easy-to-understand overview of prophecy that takes readers from the present day through the final battle of Armageddon. Compiled from the popular individual books, this one-volume reference uncovers the meaning of current events and sheds light on future happenings, including the signs of the end times, the rapture, the tribulation, and the millennium.

Understanding the Last Days

Tim LaHaye. This informative book will help you come to your own conclusions about Bible prophecy and current world events while giving you a solid basis for testing popular prophecy teachings. In this long-trusted sourcebook, LaHaye provides solid guidelines for studying Scriptures in their own context; uses charts and illustrations to simplify prophecy concepts; and answers questions about the rapture, the believer's resurrection, the second coming, the antichrist, the millennial kingdom, and many other significant end-time issues and events.

Approaching Armageddon

Ed Hindson. Is there more than one judgment? Who is the antichrist? What signs should we watch for as we speed toward end times? *Approaching Armageddon* sheds light on God's answers found in the book of Revelation, illuminates the urgency of accepting Jesus Christ, and prepares believers with a "big-picture" of the times to come.